Additional praise for *Homegirls*

"Mendoza-Denton provides an extraordinary fusion of ethnographic insight and sociolinguistic analysis. I know of no better demonstration of how linguistic and cultural variables are entwined in social interaction."

William Labov, University of Pennsylvania

"A landmark work in sociocultural linguistics! The breadth and depth are spectacular and the humanistic presentation makes the description captivatingly accessible to both a professional and a public audience."

Walt Wolfram, North Carolina State University

"*Homegirls* provides a stunning and innovative linguistic, anthropolitical ethnography of how gang-affiliated Latina girls talk, dress, and interact. It is certain to become a classic in the fields of sociolinguistics and linguistic anthropology."

Marjorie Goodwin, UCLA

New Directions in Ethnography is a series of contemporary, original works. Each title has been selected and developed to meet the needs of readers seeking finely grained ethnographies that treat key areas of anthropological study. What sets these books apart from other ethnographies is their form and style. They have been written with care to allow both specialists and nonspecialists to delve into theoretically sophisticated work. This objective is achieved by structuring each book so that one portion of the text is ethnographic narrative while another portion unpacks the theoretical arguments and offers some basic intellectual genealogy for the theories underpinning the work.

Each volume in *New Directions in Ethnography* aims to immerse readers in fundamental anthropological ideas, as well as to illuminate and engage more advanced concepts. Inasmuch, these volumes are designed to serve not only as scholarly texts, but also as teaching tools and as vibrant, innovative ethnographies that showcase some of the best that contemporary anthropology has to offer.

Published volumes

1. *Turf Wars: Discourse, Diversity, and the Politics of Place*
Gabriella Gahlia Modan

2. *Homegirls: Language and Cultural Practice among Latina Youth Gangs*
Norma Mendoza-Denton

Forthcoming

Allah Made Us: Sexual Outlaws in an Islamic African City
Rudolf Gaudio

HOMEGIRLS

Language and Cultural Practice among Latina Youth Gangs

Norma Mendoza-Denton

Blackwell
Publishing

BLACKWELL PUBLISHING
350 Main Street, Malden, MA 02148-5020, USA
9600 Garsington Road, Oxford OX4 2DQ, UK
550 Swanston Street, Carlton, Victoria 3053, Australia

The right of Norma Mendoza-Denton to be identified as the author of
this work has been asserted in accordance with the UK Copyright,
Designs, and Patents Act 1988.

First published 2008 by Blackwell Publishing Ltd

10   2014

Library of Congress Cataloging-in-Publication Data

Mendoza-Denton, Norma.
   Homegirls : language and cultural practice among Latina youth gangs / Norma
Mendoza-Denton.
      p. cm. − (New directions in ethnography)
   Includes bibliographical references and index.
   ISBN 978-0-631-23489-0 (hardcover : alk. paper) − ISBN 978-0-631-23490-6
(pbk. : alk. paper)
      1. Youth–Language.   2. Latin Americans–Languages.   3. Teenage girls–Language.
      4. Sociolinguistics.   5. Language and culture.   I. Title.

P120.Y68M46 2008
401′.41−dc22

                                                                                          2007016800

A catalogue record for this title is available from the British Library.

Set in 11.5/13.5pt Bembo
by Graphicraft Limited, Hong Kong
Printed and bound in Singapore
by Markono Print Media Pte Ltd

The publisher's policy is to use permanent paper from mills that operate a sustainable
forestry policy, and which has been manufactured from pulp processed using acid-free
and elementary chlorine-free practices. Furthermore, the publisher ensures that the text
paper and cover board used have met acceptable environmental accreditation standards.

For further information on
Blackwell Publishing, visit our website at
www.blackwellpublishing.com

To Ona, who willed it.

To Grizzly, who lived it.

CONTENTS

FIGURES

TABLES

ACKNOWLEDGMENTS

I am first of all grateful to the former students at Sor Juana High School who allowed me to take part in their lives for several years, to tape record them, to copy their drawings, and to take notes and video even when we went to beauty salons and amusement parks. I am also grateful to the SJHS teachers and the principal who were all so supportive of this research. Many thanks to Guadalupe Valdés for generously facilitating an introduction to the school.

The original fieldwork for this project was my PhD dissertation, the idea for which was conceived in a flash and so funded in its entirety by my parents, Norma Denton Navarrete de Mendoza and Rodolfo Mendoza-Ortiz. They provided steadfast love and support, driving instruction for the right side of the road, and a car without which running after school-kids would have been difficult indeed. Rodolfo Mendoza-Denton and Ozlem Ayduk, my brother and sister-in-law, have been my academic role models, my support system, as well as sounding boards for many ideas on race, stigma, stereotyping, and rejection sensitivity. Teo Mendoza-Ayduk and his trilingual jokes preserved my sanity in the home stretch of writing.

Once fieldwork was completed, the write-up of the dissertation was funded by The Spencer Foundation, by an internship with Institute for Research on Learning, a dissertation grant from the Stanford Institute for Research on Women and Gender, and by the Linguistics Department at Stanford University. Further work has been done with support in the form of generous faculty leaves, grants, and other research support from the Spanish Department at The Ohio State University and the Anthropology Department at the University of Arizona. In 2002 I held a residency at the Rockefeller Study and Research Center in Bellagio,

Italy, which allowed me to write and present my work to a wide community of scholars, poets, writers, and artists. This book bears the indelible imprint of their encouragement to reach out to a wider audience through different kinds of writing.

Jane Huber was my indefatigable editor at the start of this series with Blackwell, and reviewed many of the chapter drafts with the keen eye and loving pen of an old-fashioned literary editor. I've also had the superb pleasure of working with the Anthropology editor Rosalie Robertson and with Deirdre Ilkson who have both been incredibly encouraging and helpful. Three anonymous reviewers pored over the entire manuscript and provided many excellent suggestions. I must gratefully acknowledge J. Baker, Ashley Stinnett, and Terry Woronov, all of whom played crucial roles at various stages with helpful comments, editing, and friendship that helped me see this project to completion. I would also like to express my deepest gratitude to Bambi Schieffelin, Perry Gilmore, Candy Goodwin, Jane Hill, Susan Philips, John Rickford, and most especially to my dissertation supervisor Penny Eckert for their mentorship, support, and guidance through the years. I am fortunate to have them as mentors and friends.

I have benefited profoundly from the advice and companionship of colleagues, friends, mentors, and students. From them I've had encouragement, enlightening conversations, incredible amounts of coffee, and comments over multiple written drafts over the course of many years. My heartfelt gratitude goes to: Don Anderson, Diana Archangeli, Jennifer Arnold, Mariella Bacigalupo, Rusty Barrett, Robert Bayley, Mary Beckman, Laada Bilaniuk, Michael Bonine, Don Brenneis, Shirley Brice Heath, Charles Briggs, Mary Bucholtz, Ron Butters, Jesse Callahan, Phillip Carter, Gianna Celli, Ralph Cintron, Colleen Cotter, Eric Cummins, Manuel Díaz-Campos, Wolfgang Diecke, Teun vanDijk, Alessandro Duranti, Joshua Fishman, Paul Foulkes, Susan Gal, Salvador García, Shelley Goldman, Mary Good, Chuck Goodwin, Lars Hinrichs, Rebecca Haidt, Kira Hall, Mike Hammond, Pete Haney, Diego Herrera, Paul Hodkinson, Kacy Hollenback, Judith Irvine, Miyako Inoue, Melissa Iwai, Rob Jones, Keith Johnson, Brian Joseph, Elizabeth Keating, Ghada Khattab, Emily Kidder, Don Kulick, William Labov, Robin Lakoff, Robert Lawson, Alaina Lemon, Bob Levine, José Limón, Charlotte Linde, Adrienne Lo, Jonathan Loftin, Natasha Mack, Bruce Mannheim, Elizabeth May, Sally McConnell-Ginet, Ray McDermott, Cecile McKee, James McMichael, Jacqui Messing, Miriam Meyerhoff, Mourad Mjahed, Robert Moore, Terrell Morgan, Salikoko Mufwene,

Ben Munson, Vivek Narayanan, Nancy Niedzielski, Dorothy Noyes, Brendan O'Connor, Claire Park, Tad Park, Thea Park, Janet Pierrehumbert, Robin Queen, Tanya Rhodes (and Jenai and Xóchitl), William Rietze, Jen Roth-Gordon, Dana Rosenstein, Ivan Sag, Otto Santa Ana, Natalie Schilling-Estes, Hinrich Schütze, Scott Schwenter, Joel Sherzer, Amy Shuman, Michael Silverstein, Julie Solomon, Griselda Suárez, Marcelo Suárez-Orozco, Chuck Tatum, Nicole Taylor, Maisa Taha, Silvio Torres-Saillant, Elizabeth Traugott, Adam Ussishkin, Tom Veatch, Sudhir Venkatesh, Jess Weinberg, Etienne Wenger, Don Winford, Andrew Wedel, Ruth Wodak, Walt Wolfram, Kit Woolard, Landon Yamaoka, and Ana Celia Zentella. All mistakes and inaccuracies remain my own.

Student and faculty audiences at University of Michigan, University of Chicago, University of California-Los Angeles, University of California-Berkeley, University of Texas-Austin, University of Texas-San Antonio, Harvard University, New York University, New Mexico State University, The Ohio State University, Duke University, Brown University, Grinnell College, University of Arizona, University College Dublin, Università di Firenze/Verona, and Universität Freiburg have also helped to shape this work with their questions and keen insights. Over the years the interns in my laboratory and the students in my sociolinguistics, face-to-face interaction, and history of anthropological theory classes have inspired me to craft accessible explanations that address issues both within and outside of the academy. I hope this work lives up to the inspiration they have provided.

Some associations leave a lasting personal and professional impact. My longtime partners in anthropological mischief and writing have been Galey Modan and Rudi Gaudio. It is through them that many of these ideas found their first expression. While I was at Ohio State, I was fortunate to be part of an intellectual environment where friendship and collaboration overlapped, and brain sparks flew in all directions. Jen Hay, Stef Jannedy, Bettina Migge, Elizabeth Strand, and Anthony Allen have been influential for me since that time. I conclude with many, many thanks to Aomar Boum for helping me to herd the wandering sheep of my thoughts.

ACKNOWLEDGMENT OF SOURCES

- Thanks to Diana Archangeli for permission to reproduce the MRI pictures in chapter 8.
- Penny Eckert kindly allowed me to reproduce the Northern California shift vowel chart in chapter 8.
- Lyrics to the song "Smile Now Cry Later" are by generous courtesy of Glad Music Publishers and Pappy Daily Music.
- Photo of Carmen Miranda provided by CMG Worldwide. http://www.carmenmiranda.net/
- Portions of the chapter 1 are an expanded and modified version of my article "Fighting Words" which I have been permitted to quote by U of AZ Press.
- Portions of chapter 6 are significantly expanded from a chapter in *Youth Cultures*, a 2007 collection edited by Paul Hodkinson and Wolfgang Diecke. Thanks to Routledge and Francis.
- Thanks to Routledge and Francis for allowing me to rework my article "Muy Macha" in Ethnos.
- Thanks also to the homegirls for letting me take their pictures.

All efforts have been made to trace copyright holders. Should any copyrighted works inadvertently appear without permission, please contact the author.

INTRODUCTION

The social bond is linguistic, but it is not woven with a single thread . . . nobody speaks all those languages, they have no universal metalanguage . . . we are all stuck in the positivism of this or that discipline of learning, the learned scholars have turned into scientists, the diminished tasks of research have become compartmentalized and no-one can master them all.

Jean-Francois Lyotard[1]

One of the things that occurs to me as I introduce the book that you are about to read is that I cannot be certain of the publics that this text will encounter. I have written *Homegirls*, a linguistic ethnography of a subcultural group of Latina girls involved in gangs in the mid-1990s, in the hope that it will be accessible to a wide variety of readers. Crafting an introduction that attempts to pull the book together and assumes a unified audience or forces a unique reading seems both self-defeating and formulaic . . . but do introductions ever "force" a reading? Or do they simply discourage alternative readings?

Is it glue or solvent when I try to address many different publics in one place?

Thus I write a series of short letters to different readers that I imagine may encounter this book, and follow these letters with a description of the chapters so that you may find your way. You may be one of those readers I have addressed; you may intersect or fall outside of the categories I have imagined. In any event it is my hope that you will read this book all the way through. Especially toward the end of the book, some sections are fairly technical, making use of specialized terms and arguments drawn from diverse and sometimes disparate fields: youth subculture studies, linguistics, criminology, and cultural and linguistic anthropology. I have attempted to clarify terms and craft these arguments in a way that I hope will make the whole work accessible to people outside of those fields.

I believe that the process of writing and the process of reading are dialogic. We stand in dialog with each other, you as you read this introduction and I as I await your reaction. I *am* out there waiting, expecting your reply, and expecting to engage you in dialog. I would like to hear from you, and you can always find me either through the ether of the internet or through this publisher. Here is my letter; please write back.

To the Undergraduate University Student

One of the main aims of this book is to convey to you the intricacy and interconnectedness of linguistic and cultural practices, and to introduce you to one way of viewing cultural description. We might define *ethnography* as a process where a researcher "closely observes, records, and participates in the life of" a group of people, and then "writes an account emphasizing descriptive detail."[2] An ethnography is always to some extent a case study, and as such, it can trace out causal links and explain situated behavior: I spent about two years eating breakfast and lunch with Latina and Latino youth at Sor Juana High School, going to many hours of classes, tutorial sessions, and sports practices. I hung around on weekends, for parties, conducted interviews and did volunteer work. I listened as young people explained why they did what they did. This type of long-term involvement is what makes an ethnography unique: because of the depth it can provide, we can understand the many different factors at play in a particular situation; at the same time it is limited because it is a study of a single situation. What I describe for the high school I observed could be similar to what you have seen in your own high school, but your school may have had different groups, different demographic characteristics, different gender processes. The generalization still holds: people in institutions (such as a high school) will use perceived axes of difference to manufacture sign systems that naturalize those differences: your social group might be reflected in music; your class in dress or language, or in the expectations of others; ethnicity in makeup: these signs may interchange places or be projected at the same time. The processes I describe at Sor Juana High School were a local arrangement, specific to the time and place I describe. They have probably changed beyond recognition. It's your turn to become more aware of sign systems in your own environment, knowing all the while that they are both arbitrary and historically grounded; complex, subtly patterned and interrelated. Good luck.

To the Professional Linguist

In linguistics we have traditionally delimited the scope of our field as involving only language, and this definition can be quite restrictive, occasionally referring only to the abstract structures we have isolated, and often turning away when it's time to look past the structural level and to introduce cultural interpretation. Here you will find accounts of structural phenomena in sociophonetics and discourse in the later chapters, as well as a summary of this book's situatedness within sociolinguistics. In order to get to that material and to derive the greatest benefit from these accounts, I will try to persuade you that we must look at language by looking beyond language, we must look holistically at the life-world of the people with whom we work and investigate the richness of practices that are inextricably tied to language, weaving with it one continuous tapestry. You will find that makeup, clothing, musical taste, and consumption are all related to linguistic and literacy practices described in the coming pages. Additionally, macro-social processes of nationalism, race-thinking, and what I've termed hemispheric localism also go hand in hand with language use and language ideologies in the emergence of the Norte and Sur gangs. These communities of practice are voluntary affiliation groups that I've shown to have reflexes that reverberate in linguistic structure. Starting at the phonetic level, the variation employed to signal these identities is embedded in discourse markers that connect low-level variation to broader interactional frameworks. Understanding the dynamics of sociolinguistic identities, and communities of practice, as well as what these can teach us about broader variation in language remains one of my goals.

To the Professional Anthropologist

About twenty years ago, Mary Louise Pratt famously griped of anthropologists and our ethnographies, "How, one asks constantly, could such interesting people doing such interesting things produce such dull books?"[3] Although Pratt's exasperation roughly coincided with and acted as harbinger of the experimental moment as described by George Marcus and Michael Fischer,[4] with reflexive ethnographic writing and humanistic anthropological writing gaining ascendancy, this moment has not yet . . . quite . . . reached linguistic anthropology. The reasons for this are varied, but partly arise from a privileging of empiricism (the fetishization of the transcript) and from the historical relationship of linguistic anthropology to linguistics. Linguistic anthropology and sociolinguistics are oriented toward external data more than to the subjective or interpretive experience of the ethnographer, though there is both a long-standing tradition of taking into account the role of the researcher[5] and of critiquing the ethnographer's role in data gathering.[6]

Occasionally discussions of ethnography offer simultaneous positive and negative definitions, stating for example that ethnography is *the* hermeneutic method par excellence and that it is variously taken to be incompatible with science[7] or anathema to quantification,[8] or that ethnography is "warm" while science writing is "cool."[9] Here I attempt to do more than simply combine or sequentially present "qualitative" and "quantitative" methodologies. I show that ethnographic understandings are enriched, supported, (and sometimes problematized) when we examine subtle linguistic patterns that can be mined quantitatively. In a similar vein, quantitative conclusions lose some of their stability when written through an ethnographic tradition that questions not only the place of the researcher,[10] but also the properties of one's subjectivity as a filter for knowledge production. All the while, I show that combining phenomenologically oriented members' categories with categories devised by the researcher might yet yield some fruitful insights.

To the Middle and High School Teacher

High school teachers were extremely kind to me in the execution of this project: they allowed me access to the school and their classrooms, and I was able to see up close the many nurturing and caring relationships between the students and their teachers. You will notice that I caution teachers in chapter 3 about the representations of their minority and language-learner students in materials handed out by law enforcement, materials that are required reading in many school districts around the country. I implore you to read these materials with a critical eye, considering that "moral panics" around immigration,[11] youth, and gangs[12] in the media and at the community level are cyclical, and not always related to what may be going on in the school or the community. The research for this book was conducted in the mid-1990s, at a time when the panic around gangs was quite high. The level of panic subsided during the early 2000s and appears to be on the upswing again.

Here in Tucson, Arizona, we have recently had an increase in the allocation of funding to law enforcement for the as yet nonexistent increase in gangs (more on this in chapter 3), and also a local scandal about a middle school that held separate meetings for Euro-American and Latino parents, and considered adopting uniforms – presumably as gang deterrents – for the Latino students only.[13] The issues outlined in this book affect schools not only in California, but across the country as school districts develop closer ties with law enforcement that often rely on systematic stereotyping of students based on language, ethnicity, and immigration background.

In chapter 1 I draw an extended case study of a girl who disidentifies with English instruction for social reasons. At first glance it may seem like this kind of behavior should be automatically condemned, but my aim is to elucidate the intricate factors that go into her development of such a stance. I want to show you the basis for her decision-making, and to consider that you might do the same thing if faced with her choices. I hope that this section will serve to make teachers aware of the complex factors that enter into children's public performances, and that these factors might lead them to mask competencies. Sometimes youth are involved in social dynamics that will lead them to decisions that go against the grain of school expectations, like not reading aloud in class or refusing to change for PE. It is up to teachers to work closely and mediate between students, administration, and parents who may have yet another set of expectations. My admiration and gratitude go to you who are in the position to influence young people and to act as role models and mentors outside the immediate family.

To the General Reader

I have worried about this book making the right impression on you. You may be picking up this book because you are concerned with gang activity in your neighborhood or in your city, or because you want to understand a slice of the increasingly complex world of youth in the United States. You may be concerned about the social impacts of immigration, the life-world of girls in schools, or you may be interested in language and culture more generally. I hope I've written a book that can answer some of your questions. I want to say a couple of words about the content and some of the transcripts you will find in this book. One of the challenges for me in writing this book has been not to fall unquestioningly into reproducing stereotypes of gangs and gang members, so I have steered away from the usual law-enforcement topics of illicit activity and violence and attempted to focus on young people's own explanations, their accounts of the world around them, and their words as they were collected and recorded by me. All participants were recorded with full consent procedures, and yet for reasons of privacy I have changed all their names, as well as the name of the school and all the place-names. Sometimes in the collection of recorded speech participants or researchers may say things that a reader may not approve of, ranging from language-mixing between Spanish and English (some people disapprove of this, linguists want to describe it), to swearing or telling bawdy jokes, to using sentence fragments or lots of "pause-fillers" and repetition. In the linguistic tradition, we transcribe people's words without any editing for "propriety" on the researcher's part. We would consider that kind of editing equivalent to censorship of our informants, of ourselves. Because young people's speech is already negatively stereotyped, some of it may "sound" to you upon reading the transcripts as though I am representing them as inarticulate by including every last pause, um, ah, repetition and breath. These are linguistic conventions that allow us to probe further into people's discourse. All of us pause, repeat, tease, tell jokes, switch between styles or languages if we have several. The crucial point in presenting these transcripts is to try to understand the sense that participants make of their own lives. I invite you to consider young people's words. Listening to them has been the greatest privilege of my career.

To the Homegirls Depicted in this Book

Q-vo. Ten years have passed and you are all grown up now. It's amazing. Some of you are moms, many of you have been to college, you work (often more than one job), and are raising young families. Some of you are self-made businesswomen, and meet not only your own financial responsibilities but those of extended family members. You still write poetry, dance on Saturdays, have picnics at the park, play basketball, and listen to Oldies and Banda.

I didn't tell you this at the time, but you have defied the expectations of researchers, some of whom predicted that any kind of gang involvement for girls would likely lead to troubled lives.[14] In every single one of your cases they were wrong. But then, who are they to tell you what you can and can't do? You've always been very independent. I'm not surprised.

★★★

Just writing these open letters has given me a bit of stylistic whiplash (and provided fellow linguists with more data!). There is no way to hold all the audiences in one voice. They've dissolved and slipped out the sides of my fingers.

Structure of the Book

Chapter 1 provides a slice-of-life description of the social and linguistic setting of Sor Juana High School, and discusses many of the subtle nuances of social categories among Latina and Latino youth in that context. I describe some of the routines in the daily ebb and flow of school life, and end the chapter with a reflection on the choice of self-presentation of one of the girls as a non-speaker of English. In chapter 2, I discuss aspects of ethnographic reflexivity, and analyze some of the issues that I faced as a Latina immigrant doing this research – different in many ways from the young Latina/o participants, but very similar in others. I detail my fractured introduction to a practice called *clowning*, a type of over-the-top mock insult routine, and follow another example of misapprehended clowning, where possible offense was taken by a passerby.

Chapter 3 discusses the literature on gangs, and the rise of the Norte and Sur gangs as found in accounts from the government, the police (as filtered down to the teachers at Sor Juana High School), gang researchers, and members of the community. Chapter 4 turns to the discourses of young people who are involved in the Norte/Sur dynamic, and it is through their words and explanations that we begin to see a picture of the Norte/Sur conflict that goes beyond that provided in police accounts, which focus on the territorialization of California. In young people's accounts, Norte/Sur becomes a locally interpretable conflict that allows stance-taking on some of the issues that others in the community are not addressing: issues of immigration, language, authenticity, race and racism, and class. In addition, an emergent aspect of these discourses of gang-talk is hemispheric localism, whereby young people interpret these local and regional conflicts and actively use them to reason about the wider world and power relations within it.

Gender and performativity are the focus of chapter 5, looking through the lens of girls' practices around makeup and bodily presentation. What sort of gendered interpretations arise in talk about makeup, about normative femininity and relations with boys? Chapter 6 similarly goes beyond the strict scope of spoken language and describes material cultural practices such as the circulation of networks of poetry, photographs, and drawings, connecting these practices to the clowning routines established in chapter 2.

Chapters 7, 8, and 9 comprise the sociolinguistic variation section of the book, where the focus becomes the linguistic patterns found in the recordings of the girls when they were interviewed during the course of fieldwork. Chapter 7 situates this research within the broader field of sociolinguistics, taking stock of its traditions as well some of the current trends. Chapter 8 examines the variation of a particular English phoneme – the vowel /I/, found in the word "bit" – and how this variation patterns according to the details of the communities of practice of the girls. Chapter 9 examines this variation further by looking at the patterning of the words in which much of the /I/ variation is embedded. I claim that the girls' innovative usage of these words extends processes present in the history of English while simultaneously creating an in-group code that is designed explicitly for the recipient. The concluding chapter draws together some of the threads in the study.

★★★

My brother read this introduction when I first wrote it and remarked: "your stated goal is to write a book for everyone, but the [opening] quote is totally antithetical to that." Hmmm. That's true. I've chosen to leave the quote in because it captures both my difficulties (what with the death of grand narratives) and the fractured nature of you as my audience, of audiences in general. Some readers will find Lyotard's words deeply resonant, while others won't identify with them. I hope some may be just a bit intrigued and try to pursue the source further. The whole book is like that: open to individual interpretation, open to creating ruptures, hoping to catch you off guard and entice you to read on in an area that you've thought outside the scope of what you do.

Notes

1 Lyotard (1984: 40–1)
2 This definition is pieced together from parts of the one found in Marcus and Fischer (1986: 18), except that I've made two important changes: no longer is an anthropologist the only type of researcher carrying out ethnography, and no longer are ethnographies unproblematically considered to be accounts of other cultures. See for instance Bakalaki (1997).
3 Pratt (1986: 33)
4 Marcus and Fischer (1986)
5 Labov (1972b), on the observer's paradox.
6 Briggs (1986)
7 See Aunger (1995) and Roscoe (1995) for discussions of debates on "ethnography vs. science."
8 Kamil, Langer, and Shanahan (1985)
9 Bishop (1992)
10 Marcus and Fischer (1986)
11 Jorge Bustamante (1994) has documented how during periods of economic recession, the American public holds a negative view of migrants and immigration, while during periods of economic expansion the public holds a more favorable view.
12 McCorkle and Miethe (2002)
13 Arizona Department of Education (2007)
14 Moore (1994), Moore and Hagedorn (2001)

CHAPTER 1

LA MIGRA

"M-I-I-G-R-A-A-A-A-a-a-a!" A fast-decaying echo followed the scream. It was the kind of echo where you can hear the sound waves buzzing in your ear.

Feet scurried all around; creeping under bushes, jumping over rocks, then frozen in mid-step behind cocked-open dumpsters. Hoping that the Border Patrol agent would pass them by, the immigrants held their breath, shoulders tense and armpits hollowed. The agent brushed aside weeds and grasses with her foot, counting backward quietly to herself. Leaves rustled, and a soft in-breath drew her eyes through a thicket and met them in a sustained gaze. Sergio knew it was over. He looked down and emerged defeated without a word. One by one the immigrants were found until only one remained. Time was running out. A bell's vibrato finally clamored.

"OK, fine, I give up!" huffed Laura, the designated border patrol agent. Yadzmin, the smallest of the "immigrants," only thirteen, had slipped between a candy machine and the wall. She came out yelling "I WO-ON! I get to be the Border Patrol tomorrow! *Lero-lero, candi-lero!* And YOU all have to be the immigrants and I'm going to get all of you! Nyah-nyah, nyah-nyah!" A twist of her hip marked victory and the end of recess as she skipped toward PE class.

Children's games often go unnoticed. I knew that as I watched them play that day. Only later do we reflect on them as diagnosis and prophecy: *ring-around-the-rosie* acted out the plague that killed more than a third of medieval Europe.[1] This time a playful cops-and-robbers chase, which the children called *"migra-tag,"* sprang alongside the referendum polls in California that year. Proposition 187, also known as "Save Our State" or SOS, had been introduced by then-Governor

Pete Wilson in the summer of 1995, and rumors swirled around the immigrant communities for months. Although everyone talked about what the impact of the proposition might be, somehow we under-estimated it, thinking that it was a fringe conservative movement. We thought it would never pass. Proposition 187 sought (and eventually passed and resulted in) the denial of social services to undocumented immigrants; public education and Medicaid were the main targets of the proposition. Other less expensive social benefits were also casu-ally included, like an afterthought: well-baby (prenatal and postnatal) care, emergency room visits, and school lunches. Proposition 187 passed in November of 1995, approximately one year after the begin-ning of this project. Any undocumented immigrants that were caught using social services could be summarily deported. That included a large proportion of the Latina and Latino students at Sor Juana High School (SJHS).

On the way to gym class Yadzmin found Lucia, Tanya, and Cristina, *las niñas Fresas* (lit. "strawberry girls": a Mexican Spanish slang term for a young person from the urban, middle-class, predominantly European-descent elite), and stopped to talk to them. They were get-ting ready for dance class, stretching on the wooden dance floor in their black leotards and tights. Mr Jones the dance teacher walked by on his way to the lockers. When he saw the girls he sang ridiculously, "Chi-qui-ta Ba-na-na." The girls looked up with quizzical expressions and parroted back, "Chiquita Ba-NA-na!"

"¿Qué onda? *(What's with him?)*" Lucia wanted to know.

"¿Quién sabe? *(Who knows?)* I have no idea why he always says that to us," said Tanya.

There was no way that the recently-arrived immigrant girls could ever have heard the commercial jingle that now looped in the back of my head. The ditty was introduced in 1945, when United Fruit Company unloaded its last military cargo and sent its fleet of ships to the Caribbean to harvest bananas. *Chiquita Banana* was a mass-marketing campaign aimed at entertaining war-weary Americans and familiariz-ing them with a new fruit from the Caribbean. Who would have thought bananas would become ubiquitous? At its peak, the song was played over 350 times a day on the radio, and Miss Chiquita, the ripe banana made flesh, was such a celebrity that UFC changed its name to Chiquita Brands. Around the same time, Carmen Miranda became not only the archetypal Latin sexpot but the highest-paid woman in the US at the time, linking Latinas, bananas, and big business.

Figure 1.1 Carmen Miranda: The South American Way.

. . . Hell-o A-mi-gos!
I'm Chiquita Banana and I've come to say
Bananas have to ripen in a certain way
When they are fleck'd with brown and have a golden hue
Bananas taste the best and are the best for you!
[. . .]
But, bananas like the climate of the very, very tropical equator
So you should never put bananas in the refrigerator!

Music © 1945 Shawnee Press Inc.

There were other variations of the song, with the main character shown in commercials first as an animated banana, emerging like a Botticelli Venus from the peel, and eventually personified by a long line of Latina women (and one Italian-American) with Miranda-esque ripe fruit head-dresses and Brazilian-Bahiana outfits.[2] The South American bombshell swept the country!

I'm Chiquita Banana and I've come to say
To a fellow's heart the stomach is the way
It's an ancient formula you must admit,
And we'll put it to the test with a banana split!
There's some ice cream in the freezer
That was purchased yesterday,
These bananas that I'm holding
are so flecked and ripe and golden . . .
"Oh I think I see a beauty,"
"She's a honey,"
"How'd we miss her?!"
"And her banana splits are something
that makes me want to kiss her."

"Norma, what does that mean, when he says Chiquita Banana?" the girls insisted. "I don't know," I lied. I was hoping that the angry flush spreading forward from my ears would not give me away.

At the time, I thought I knew. But to tell the truth, now I'm not quite sure why Mr Jones said that. Maybe it was just a fleeting moment captured on tape. A female schoolteacher from Texas who heard my recording of the incident claimed the moment was too small, too fleeting to make a big deal. Another friend, a Spanish immigrant to England, had a gut reaction: totally offensive. It reminded him of when he was a kid and the English children taunted him, yelling "Spanish Onion!" when he walked by. He could never figure it out, and for years he kept asking himself, *onions: WHY onions?* Twenty minutes after recounting this he came back and told me that he thought the Chiquita Banana comment was ambiguous. Maybe the teacher had no other way to relate. He didn't speak Spanish, after all. Maybe he understood Chiquita to be a diminutive, endearing somehow. There was just no way to know. Which is just as well because I didn't say anything at the time.

The Meaning of Dancing: Banda and Rock En Español as Class Codes

A few weeks after this incident Lucía and Tanya invited me to a Fresa party, held on a Saturday afternoon in a spacious rented party room at the Fox and Hound apartments. It was Tanya's fourteenth birthday, and half the teenage boys were sullenly playing cards and munching on pretzels, while the rest were nuzzling their girlfriends into the corners of the party room, done up in shades of forest green and maroon. I had brought some chocolate-chip cookies that my boyfriend Rob had baked – Jose and Domingo, the basketball-obsessed twins from Guadalajara, said "¡Esos Gringos! *(Those Americans!)*" and laughed: I think they were amused at the thought that my American boyfriend not only lived with me – in subtle ways I found out they disapproved of this – but even took orders to bake cookies. Tanya's mom had made a big chocolate cake. The girls at the party brought fruit salad and other small snack foods, and sodas. There was no alcohol, and at some point we played musical chairs. Pretty sedate really for my idea of a teenage party, and nothing like the blowout Alice in Wonderland drug-themed parties the wealthy Sor Juana High School jocks flippantly described and ranked in the school newspaper.

Tanya had dressed up as the *rockera* she aspired to be, with her curly brown hair down to the middle of her back; jeans, a white t-shirt, a belt with little silver spikes, and a black jeans vest. She was DJ on a boombox someone had brought (yes, back in the 1990s there were still boomboxes), and she was playing Rock en Español, but accepting requests for techno and a little bit of house music. Rancheras (Mexican country music), banda (polkas), and especially cumbias with their tropical rhythms were totally out of the question. In a later interview, Tanya explained:

TANYA: No es por insultar a nadie ¿no? bueno porque se sientan mal o algo así pero, o sea, yo la verdad, Banda solamente una vez escuché en una película [risa]. Y era una película de un pueblito, ¿ves? O sea, uno que es de ciudad, pus, no va allá en algo de, de un pueblito, no? No sé si te has dado cuenta que los únicos que bailan Banda son los de los barrios. Ahí de, de donde yo vivía, pus no se acostumbraba eso ¿ves? A mí me gusta Rock en Español, así Tecno, y no sé, o sea, tú sabes no, como que un estilo más americano aunque sea en español.

TANYA: *I don't mean for this to insult anyone OK? Like to make anyone feel bad, but the truth is that Banda, I only heard it once before, and it was in a movie [laughter]. And it was a movie about a little town. I mean, when you are from the city, you just aren't going to go for things from a little town. I don't know whether you've noticed that the only ones who dance Banda are the ones from the barrios. Where I lived, we were just not used to that. I like Rock en Español, Techno, you know, a style that is more American although it is in Spanish.*

Despite Tanya's insistence that Banda songs not be played at the party, I knew Güera liked Banda. Güera was from the high plains of Michoacán, a rural area of central-west Mexico where young people were not swept up in Americanized rock music. I listened to Banda when riding in Güera's car; she'd brake to the rhythm of it while I watched the pavement go by at my feet where the passenger side floorboard should have been. And she could dance Banda too, her long hair sweeping the floor as she hung backward, supported by her partner's arm in athletic dips. I had seen Güera dancing once with Junior, back when they were boyfriend and girlfriend and still spoke to each other.

I think Güera and Junior broke up partly because of the Piporro divide. Güera was a Piporra, a girl from the countryside whose family back in Mexico worked on a ranch. Tanya, a middle-class Fresa from the big city of Puebla, clearly looked down on anything from the Mexican countryside merely because it was rural and un-modern. Junior was not a Fresa, he was from a working-class background, but like Tanya he was from an urban area and similarly derided Piporros. In addition, Junior had gone and joined the Sureño gang, which claimed allegiance to the much more abstract "South," leaving very little room for the exploration of other communities. I think the low-grade annoyance of Piporro put-downs eventually got on Güera's nerves, straining relations with both Junior and Tanya.

Some time after the Güera/Junior breakup, I interviewed Junior and he expanded on Tanya's association of Banda music with rurality, linking it directly to the Piporros.

JUNIOR: Banda es música de Piporro. Me gustará bailarla pero por orgullo no la escucho.
Banda is the music of Piporros. I might like to dance it but out of pride I don't listen to it.

NORMA: ¿Por orgullo de qué?
Pride of what?

JUNIOR: De que no seas Piporro.
Of not being a Piporro.

NORMA: ¿Qué quiere decir Piporro?
What does that mean, Piporro?

JUNIOR: Un Piporro es una persona de rancho, bajado del monte, que oye tamborazos. ¡Un indio! ¡Que se dedica a crecer vacas, chivos!
A Piporro is a person who is from a ranch, who's come down from

the hills, who listens to big-drum music (Banda). An indio! Who raises cows and goats for a living!

"Güera" means blonde in Spanish, and this was unusual for a Piporra; as Junior mentioned, prototypical Piporros are thought to be of indigenous extraction. Güera was unusual in another way: she spoke totally fluent English from being a circular migrant, though she was still somehow placed in English as a Second Language (ESL) classes. When I first met her, I thought she might be from Russia, another common point of origin for young people in the ESL classes. She had wavy, very long white-blond hair, with sprayed-stiff "clam shell" bangs. For the party at the Fox and Hound apartments she had replaced her blue bandanna ponytail holder with a black satin ribbon, and the ponytail sprouted as usual from the top of her head. She wore a black satin shirt tucked into green jeans with black high-top sneakers. No blue today, no gang colors. I guessed she was trying to fit in with the Fresas. Tanya the would-be Rockera Fresa could be very disapproving of Güera's clothes, of her music, and especially of her boyfriends. She had hated Junior.

What Would You Do If Your Boyfriend Was Into Gangs?

At the party Güera told me that her new boyfriend Alejandro was in jail. She spoke to me in Mexican Rural Spanish code-mixed with English.

"Why is he in jail?" I asked her.

"He got in a fight with this guy, but that's not why he is in jail; the cops thought he was trying to steal something but he was only trying to get in a fight with some fool that insulted him." She caught her breath. "No fue su culpa. *(So it wasn't his fault.)* Anyway he's in jail, he's been there two months and has three to go but he sent me a Valentine's Day card. Look."

Güera produced an envelope that had a reluctant bit of white space left on it, just enough to write her address. The rest of the envelope was given to an elaborate drawing, where a man with a hairnet and a tear tattooed on his cheek kissed the disembodied hand of a woman, chivalrously, Cinderella-style. He seemed to be floating in the kiss, eyes closed, and on the corner of his wrist there was another little tattoo. The three triangular dots meant he was a Sureño. Inside there was a

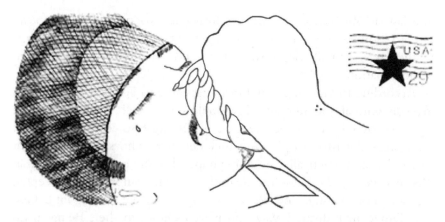

Figure 1.2 Valentine's Day Envelope from Alejandro to Güera.

card with a poem, Las flores son bellas pero frágiles, y así son las mujeres: bellas, frágiles, y necesitan alguien quien las cuide *(Flowers are beautiful but they're fragile, and that is how women are: beautiful, fragile, and needing someone to take care of them)*. This seemed pretty ironic to me since Alejandro was in jail and not in a great position to take care of anyone.

After showing me the envelope Güera wanted to know, "Do you like Norteños?" I hesitated and wondered who this might get back to, but she didn't wait to hear my answer. I think she wanted to get things off her chest. "I really hate Norteños because they broke the windows of my father's car. It was the only car he had. They wanted it and he wouldn't give it to them, so instead of taking it they just ruined it. Ever since then, I've hated Norteños," she said. And after a pause, "What would you do if your boyfriend was – into gangs, you know, what would you do?"

It was hard to imagine new-age, vegetarian Rob in any kind of gang, though he had been in an Ashram in India.

"Just imagine that he was in a gang, do you think he could change? Just hypothetically?"

"Ay, Güera. I don't know. It's important to be loyal, but you can't get sucked into a remolino *(vortex)*, you have to be your own person and watch out for yourself."

"Do you think I can change Alejandro? Tanya says that if he really loved me he could change for me. He would stay out of gangs, totally leave the Sureños if I told him to."

I wanted to tell her that I thought you can't really change people but we got interrupted. Just then, Karina walked by and having heard the last of our exchange, said no, forget it. No cambian *(They don't change)*. Someone else who was overhearing said anyone could change if they really tried. Tanya walked by and rolled her brown eyes in condemnation.

According to Güera, when Tanya first came to Fog City she too was friendly with all the Sureños. How could she not be? When she arrived from Mexico Tanya shared the same beginning ESL classes with them; they were the first people who included her, who said hello to her every day, and practically the only people that she could understand at first because of their resolute Spanish use. The Sureño boys accepted her as a "border sister," invited her to hang out by the parking lot behind the Target on Industrial Way, and played Oldies for her. Being in no position to refuse friendship, Tanya went along, listening to *Angel Baby* and other American songs from the 1960s that she thought were incredibly old-fashioned. But Tanya didn't really like the Sureños; she could tell by their accents and their mannerisms that they had been poor in Mexico, even if now her Mom had to work alongside their parents. Most of the Sureños were from the depopulated regions of the Mexican central-western states,[3] whose melancholy names were now borne by mom-and-pop restaurants in their new California neighborhoods: *La Jaliscience. La Michoacana. La Oaxaqueña.*[4]

Lock-Down Piporras and Cosmopolitan Fresas

Tanya looked around for some other social options outside the ESL classes. She joined the *Ballet Folklórico*, the Mexican folkloric dance group where Ms Carla, a bilingual Mexican-American teacher, was more interested in nurturing a small group of what Robert Smith[5] has perceptively called "lock-down girls." As the most recent of immigrants from rural Mexico, Piporras were the girls that other Latinas in the school sometimes complimented, sometimes taunted as being "traditional Mexican girls."

Tanya, a Fresa urbanite who had already been to raves with her cousins in Mexico, was a lot wilder than your average Piporra, and didn't get along with Ms Carla. Tanya found the Piporra group and its constant supervision too constraining, and when she finally met the other Fresas, she abruptly stopped speaking to all the Sureños in her class, and buried her nose in her books just to get out of there as quickly as possible. Soon enough Tanya was promoted out of the beginning ESL class and that is when her Fresa career really took off.

Güera, on the other hand, was still friends with all the Piporras who had been her network before she started hanging around with Junior. At Sor Juana High School, it was the locked-down Piporras who were considered "at risk," the target population of specialized school programs like Migrant Education,[6] a federally-funded program that provided academic assistance to youth whose parents' farm work resulted in long periods of school absences.

Piporras' daily routine consisted of going straight from home to school, staying after school for their extracurricular activities and supervised studying, and coming right back home to do housework and watch over their siblings, usually while both parents worked. Vested with the role of keepers of tradition, they were often asked and sometimes just expected to participate in activities which reproduced versions of Mexican traditions or activities that were emblematic of some version of Mexican femininity with silent abnegation thrown in. Thus it was often Piporras (and their mothers) who volunteered or were volunteered to cook Mexican food for school events that involved Latinos, or volunteered to sew innumerable tiny sequins onto dance dresses for the group. Being held to these rigorous gender standards meant that the Piporras were scheduled, protected, and secluded. Piporras' virginity seemed to be guaranteed by force of isolation. They were the ones who actually got scolded when they skipped school, while the Jocks and Fresas skipped constantly and no one ever said anything, though their absences got reflected in their grades. The scandal when a lock-down girl actually got pregnant! It was like nobody could figure out how it happened.

One subset of the Piporras usually ate together and retrieved their lunch from the cafeteria to consume it in one of the ESL classrooms, inhabiting a private, quasi-domestic sphere within the public school system. They were also to a certain degree excluded from the public sphere of school life, rendered almost invisible: their participation in extracurricular organized sports, for instance, was far lower than that of Latina girls in other groups. The principal of the school, who generously allowed me to do this study in the first place, said he would be happy if my study could help him understand just two questions: Why do Latina girls skip sports classes? And why won't they change for gym class?

Immigrant and culturally distinct communities offer cases where the expectations of the school, of the parents, and of society may not only fail to converge but in effect may create contradictory demands. Thus the Piporras' refusal to swim during their menstrual periods, while accurately aligned with parental authority and expectations, went deeply against the grain of what is commonly required of an American high-schooler, creating no end of conflict between parents and the school. The girls' negotiation and balancing of parental, cultural, and school expectations was especially complex, since contradictions sprang up in almost every arena – not only with respect to sports, but also with respect to how much and how late a girl may stay at school or fraternize with boys, and certainly with respect to how much girls should be taught about sex. And parents' standards were not the only buoys that Piporras tried to navigate. Linguistic expectations from teachers and classmates that dogged Piporras included the presumption of lesser English and greater Spanish proficiency. Because the Piporra designation subsumes ethnicity and class as well as gender, it allows us a window into the operation of these categories if we compare Piporras with other girls in the school.

It has been observed that immigrants' school success and eventual socioeconomic and class position in the new country are linked to pre-migration class position as well as their home countries' race-, class-, and gender-based oppression characteristics.[7] The SJHS Fresas are an instantiation of this generalization. In contrast to the Piporras, the more "Westernized" Fresa groups of recent immigrant girls, coming from Euro-Mexican families and higher socioeconomic status backgrounds in the big metropolises of Mexico, were regularly assumed by teachers to speak less Spanish than the Piporras (despite the fact that as bearers of the "standard" language they were often consulted by everyone for spelling and grammar). With more social freedoms and fewer responsibilities for the defense of traditional Mexican womanhood, the formerly-higher-SES (socioeconomic status) Fresa girls like Tanya were regularly promoted out of ESL classes. Subsequently, through exposure to mainstream curricula and the accompanying negative attitudes toward Spanish preservation, the middle-class Fresas also experienced greater language shift, little by little favoring English over Spanish and eventually fulfilling the assumption of greater English-speaking ability that others had of them from the beginning. Piporras, on the other hand, tended to maintain Spanish while they acquired English. Phenotypic Indianness and lower socioeconomic status functioned as the ratification of Piporras' authenticity as Mexican, and placed them under chronic stereotype threat, with interlocutors expecting their phenotype to correlate to Spanish use. Fresas' backgrounds matched Euro-American and school expectations much more closely than those of Piporras: in everything from their more consistent early schooling, prior familiarity with computers and with standard language varieties, willingness to change into exercise clothes for PE, even up to their parents' greater involvement with the parent–teacher groups, expectations of school "functioning" were stacked on behalf of the Fresas.

Once the stigma of Piporra-hood, potential Indianness, and ESL status had been lifted, Tanya began to mill about with the other Fresas in a small courtyard, near the cafeteria and far away from the ESL offices that had nurtured her when she first arrived. Mixing in a wider circle, she met young people from other Latin American cities . . . Guadalajara; Puebla; Lima, Perú; Bogotá, Colombia; and even one girl from Spain and one from Brazil. This kind of international flavor gave the Fresa group a self-styled cosmopolitan flair. At SJHS, all these urbanite Fresas came from higher socioeconomic backgrounds in their home countries than the Piporras: whereas most of the Piporras' parents were farmers or agricultural laborers in Mexico, the Fresas' parents often had solidly middle-class, white-collar jobs (school principal, architect, systems analyst). Notwithstanding the fact that most recent immigrants essentially start at the bottom, Fresas drew on their elite backgrounds in their home countries to reproduce class privilege in a new environment. Jose and Domingo, the Fresa twins from Guadalajara, told me how much they hated being identified with the poor indigenous Mexicans, with Piporros, with Indians. Fresas had been middle class in Mexico! They protested that it wasn't fair! They resented Americans' assumptions that "just because we came from Mexico we don't know anything," like rock music or basketball or computers. Jose started dating a Japanese student, and Domingo a girl from India. Perhaps they could avoid the stigma of being Mexican if they could imagine themselves as international, transcending race and state boundaries altogether.

Fresas' attitudes toward Piporras/os reproduced urban/rural and white/indigenous/black divisions prevalent in postcolonial Latin America, and those attitudes in turn were reproduced within the Norteño/Sureño gangs which will be discussed in greater depth in later chapters. Interestingly, Fresas not only mocked Piporros for being from "small towns" in Mexico (see Tanya's quote above), but also for being from the Latino ethnic neighborhoods ("los barrios") in the US – even though the Fresas themselves lived in the same "barrios." The only difference was that the upwardly mobile aspirations of the Fresas didn't allow them to see themselves as staying in the barrio.

When I interviewed Ernesto, a dark and thoughtful boy with a round face who came over from Mexico completely on his own and worked after school as a construction worker, he was outspoken:

"According to the guys from the capital, everybody else is an Indian. When somebody asks you where you're from, you need to think three times about what you're going to say."

Junior reminded him, "Do you remember that kid, El Chanclas?"

"Eyyy. *(Yes)*"

"El Chanclas was from Michoacán. According to the Fresas from the capital, people from Michoacán, from Durango, from other states are Indians. Not according to me! So in order to answer they have to think about it. They'll say, oh, I am from DF [*Distrito Federal*, as Mexico City is known in Mexico]; they are embarrassed of who they are, and of how they talk. And then you ask, where in the DF are you from? They'll avoid the question and say, oh, just around, around there."

Ernesto retorted, "I am not embarrassed. But we were poor. Over there, no tenía ni en qué caer muerto. *(I didn't even have anything to fall dead on.)*"

"Really?"

"**I** didn't. **Chanclas** didn't. So here we've changed, but not so much. To tell you the truth, I felt better in Mexico. I could speak my mind, I could say anything I wanted without having to think twice. And the school was better. Here they just make us do basic math that I already knew. Just because I don't know English."

Although 20 percent of Sor Juana High School's 1,200-plus student population was Latina and Latino, only a very slight majority of that group was native English speaking, the rest being Spanish-dominant recent immigrants. Here the distinction between citizen and non-citizen was not quite useful. Some of the Spanish-dominant, culturally Mexican recent immigrants were in fact US citizens, having been born in the US and schooled in Mexico, or perhaps shuttled back and forth in circular migration loops. That was the case with Güera. She had been born in LA but her parents thought it was not a great place to grow up. Too many gangs. So they shipped Güera off by herself at the age of four to her grandma's in western rural Mexico where there was plenty of fresh air for the kids but few jobs for the adults. When Güera came back to California after grandma died, she was ten, hardly knew her parents, and was not exactly inclined to listen to them either. She missed her grandma and everything about Mexico, and decided one day that she was totally, forever, exclusively Mexican. Graffiti on her notebook read proudly ¡*Puro México!*[8] even though she had American papers.

On the other hand, some of the Latinos who were "mainstreamed" in the school would have nothing to do with Spanish speakers, and hid a Mexican passport like a dirty secret. Sometimes they didn't even have Mexican or Salvadoran or Guatemalan documents to hide. As children they had been smuggled out so early, and had been without home-country documents for so long, that the only stable paperwork they had was in the name that was slapped on them by primary school administrators when they showed up to register the first day. This way Catalina became Kathy, Heriberto became Herb, Arnulfo became Arnie, and Xóchitl became Ann. Rita joked that she was no longer from Michoacán but from Michigan; that it was not too hard to get used to your new name since everyone except your parents used it. What was hard, she said, was remembering who you used to be.

Sor Juana High School

Nestled in the comfortable suburbs of the San Francisco Bay Area, in one of the counties with the largest Hispanic populations in the State of California (Santa Clara ranked eighth largest with 403,000 Hispanics, approximately 24 percent of the population of the county, according to the 2000 US Census), Sor Juana High School had changed drastically over thirty years of yearbook-recorded school history. Formerly, this high school and others in the surrounding area were almost exclusively Euro-American. In the mid-1990s Silicon Valley boasted high growth fueled by the tech manufacturing, blue chip finance, and recreation industries, where plentiful jobs attracted new immigrants from all over the world, but primarily from Latin America, East Asia, and Southeast Asia. These demographic changes contributed to an astonishingly diverse school environment, with students from African-American, Pacific Islander, Asian, Asian-American, and Latina/o backgrounds constituting a clear majority of the school population.

Sor Juana High School then was neither entirely suburban nor entirely urban. For the many well-to-do Euro-American youth attending Sor Juana, their experience of the school environment was decidedly suburban. They lived in the surrounding foothills – Foxbury

Hills – an upper and upper-middle-class neighborhood that ranks among the ten wealthiest communities in the United States. The students who lived in Foxbury Hills usually drove to school in their own or their parents' cars, and on any morning the parking lot of SJHS reflected the parental income bracket – BMWs, Volvos, Lexuses and Range Rovers routinely clogged the small streets around the school. The adolescent progeny of the Bay Area's wealthiest residents can attend public schools like Sor Juana High School because the tax base of the district is extremely strong, supporting an enhanced school environment that included sophisticated computer equipment, equestrian sports, and even sailing. A 1995 issue of the school newspaper, *The Sor Juana Times*, featured an article full of tips for students on stock investments, with portfolio management advice quoted directly from dot-com boomer siblings. The school was academically strong, achieving in 1994 the distinction of producing several top-scoring students on the nationwide Scholastic Aptitude Test, a feat rivaled by only a few other schools across the country.[9]

But not every student at SJHS drove or was chauffeured down from Foxbury Hills. Most of the Latino students, in fact, came on foot or by public transport from nearby Fog City. Their experience of the campus and of school life was completely different from that of students living in the affluent hills. Fog City is bisected by Industrial Way, one of the main urban highways in the area. Fog City students walked to and from school across the six-lane thoroughfare, navigating their way through the traffic and parking lots of the large discount stores, restaurants, service stations, and mini-malls that crowded the entire length of Industrial Way.

Unlike descriptions of Latino neighborhoods as located in "landscapes of neglect" in urban centers such as Los Angeles,[10] Fog City failed to live up to media images of the "inner city" with boarded-up store-fronts and dilapidated streets and buildings; it was rather a semi-urban community of workers for the service industries aimed at the suburbs: hotels, restaurants, fast-food chains, and janitorial services were the sources of employment for most Fog City students and parents, echoing Pierrette Hondagneu-Sotelo's[11] portrayal of immigrants as "cleaning and caring in the shadows of affluence." On a few occasions, fellow anthropologists visiting me from outside the area remarked, "*This* is a gang-infested neighborhood? But it looks so normal!"

Much as Fog City students experienced the environment surrounding the school differently from their Foxbury Hills peers, there was a similar disparity within the grounds of the school. From the very beginning until the end of the school day, most Fog City students did not come into prolonged contact with Foxbury Hills students. It would be a mistake to say that the school was segregated; the majority of teachers and the school administration as a matter of policy continually tried to promote an atmosphere of cultural tolerance and racial harmony within the school. As far back as 1985, however, the *Sor Juana Times* reported growing racial tensions on the campus. It is easy to see how these tensions might have evolved and been perpetuated if one takes a close look at the campus and the activities taking place within it on a day-to-day basis.

Same School, Separate Lives

Although Fog City and Foxbury Hills students populated the same campus during the day and only went home to separate neighborhoods after school, they might as well have been in separate worlds for all the contact they had with one another. Because of the way that classes, meals, and even sports were structured, many Fog City students had only sporadic and fleeting contact with anyone from Foxbury Hills. A striking example of this dynamic was the lunchtime meal.

Lunch at Sor Juana High School was the largest stretch of unstructured time that students spent on campus, their only collective leisure time from the institutional obligations of school, giving them the freedom to enter and generate their own symbolic worlds of play and friendship. Thus it is during lunch that social divisions were most noticeable, as students were left to constitute social groups with little apparent structuring on the part of the school.[12] It was during this daily forty-minute interval that many of the events that were salient in the minds of the students took place: lunch was the hour that Erika and Angie, who had known each other since the first grade, chose to publicly declare the end of their friendship; it was the hour that indignant members of opposing gangs scheduled a fight (and campus security arrived too late, when the bell had rung and all were running to class); this was also the hour that word of the mid-morning murder on a clear spring day in 1995 of Tejano music singer Selena spread, and Latina students carefully placed their lunch food around a Selena CD to create a makeshift Catholic altar near the back wall of the cafeteria. After-lunch classes always provided a continuing backdrop for lunchtime social events, as notes written during the lunch hour were delivered to their addressees by classmates.

At SJHS, the school unwittingly structured the use of space during lunch through the Free and Reduced Price Meals Program (FRPM). FRPM was a federal program available to students whose family income was at or below certain levels ($27,380 per annum for a family of four during the 1994–5 school year). Students found to be eligible for FRPM could obtain free or reduced-price breakfasts and lunches on a daily basis from the school. For families struggling to make ends meet, FRPM was an important benefit. But because FRPM benefits were only available through the school cafeteria and not through the many franchise food stands that dotted the campus quad during lunch, a *de facto* division emerged: students who could afford to buy the better-tasting food from the franchise-owned stands did so, while students whose parents qualified for the FRPM program ate in the cafeteria. In this way, a state-verified class division was instituted and re-enacted every day at breakfast and lunch on the campus of SJHS. Fog City students, especially the impoverished recent-immigrant Asian and Latino students, as well as lower-income African-American students, ate in the cafeteria. They sat mostly in single-sex groups, facing each other at long white Formica tables with attached orange plastic stools. Each table in the cafeteria bore a common-knowledge reservation for the group that customarily occupied it. This is how different groups knew where to go, day after day, to find their friends or to drop off their backpacks before going through the crowded lunch line. An atmosphere of *relajo*[13] reigned: a suspension of seriousness that purposefully subverted the still-sitting, strapped-down classroom ethos. Students wandered the narrow hallways created by the Formica tables, poking and nudging each other, sharing and forcing condiments on each other's food, and calling out over all heads in Spanish, Vietnamese, Tagalog, and English to interlocutors across the large, echoing room. Aside from *relajiento*[14] students, the cafeteria was patrolled on foot and with walkie-talkies by the dreaded hall monitors, whose job it was to ensure that order prevailed in the food queues and that rowdy students were sent to the assistant principal. Occasionally the assistant principal herself marched into the cafeteria in an attempt to impose order, and commanded students to stand quietly, single file, issuing stern orders accompanied by vague threats: "By the time I count to THREE, you all *better* be in one single line. ONE . . . TWO . . ."

Outside the cafeteria, the mostly Euro-American (and some established African- and Asian-American) residents of Foxbury Hills milled
about the inner quad. It couldn't really be said that many of them ate,
since a good number of the girls, continually watchful of their bodies
and fearful of weight gain, rarely ate, at least in public.[15] The boys sat
in dyads and triads on the steps of the fountain or on long aluminum
benches and consumed food from the franchise stands, while most of
the girls stood and socialized. Very few people brought lunch from home.
Perhaps once a month, when there was some delicacy available only
in the cafeteria, Foxbury Hills students would hurry through the lunch
line and saunter back out to the quad with their treats.

It was in the central quad area that many of the school-sponsored
lunchtime activities took place: small-scale rock concerts by one of
Foxbury Hills' many homegrown student grunge bands, or pep rallies,
or springtime fairs with booths selling cake and cheerleaders' kisses.
Latina/o voluntary attendance at these school-wide events was low, except for activities that were geared specifically toward them. On the day
that Banda music was featured, blaring *chun-ta-ta* from loudspeakers in
the quad during lunch, an interesting reversal took place: Fog-City
Latina/o students took over the quad with space-intensive Banda dancing, and Foxbury Hills students matter-of-factly filed into the cafeteria and sat at the long tables, waiting out the unsuccessful attempt by
the administration to mix up the social groups. As far as most students
were concerned, it amounted to little more than a temporary disequi-
librium in the ecology of school space.

Each subgroup within the complex social system of the high
school adopted a space that it considered its own. In the beginning
of the school year, old groups tentatively reclaimed the previous
years' spaces, and new groups simultaneously began to form and
"hang out" in territories they might later call their own. The geographic boundaries that emerged on the campus of the school were
powerful and consistent, demarcating socioeconomic, ethnic, and linguistic borders.[16] These boundaries served as isoglosses that divided
students in every detail, from the seemingly inconsequential such as
clothing and hairstyles to distinctions that would certainly endure over
the course of students' lives: courses taken, grade point averages, and
public perceptions: the "goody-goody" Piporras could be found in
the back room, the "troublemaker" Norteñas wearing red, swearing
and joking in the public theater of the parking lot in front of the
school.

Each of the different social groups in the high school carved out a space for itself in the landscape provided by these facilities. One crowd of mostly Euro-American, uniformly Foxbury Hills teens who might consider themselves "popular"[17] could be found hanging out on the very front central space right in the middle of the south corridor. The punks and the smokers relaxed whenever possible on the periphery of the school, behind the gymnasia, sneaking cigarettes near the baseball diamond or by the open spaces on the playing fields. Sometimes they cut class on the lawn of the soccer field, lying and staring at the sky until early afternoon when the soccer balls came out.

The different groups of Latinas/os in the school adopted certain different portions of the school campus as their "hangouts." During the time of my fieldwork, there were six main areas of the school where different groups of Latina/o students met, socialized and carried out joint activities, simultaneously creating and reinforcing their communities. Each of these groups had a unique "personality" and an overall orientation toward the mainstream goings-on of the high school, toward other ethnic groups at the school, toward other groups of Latinas/os, toward authority and toward language. Language among this diverse group was also widely varied, with some young people speaking Standard California Euro-American English, many speaking various forms of Chicano English, and others eschewing English altogether in favor of Mexican Rural Spanish, Standard (Urban) Mexican Spanish, and various dialects of Central American Spanish.

Linguistic identity as indexed by the dialects of the schoolyard is one of the key components of the construction of social and academic relationships at Sor Juana High School. In order to understand the complex relationship among language, academic placement, and social group formation at Sor Juana High School, we will locate Latina/o students' linguistic and educational situation within the larger picture of linguistic diversity at Sor Juana High School.

Latinas/os were cited by school sources (like the yearbook, the principal, and the *Sor Juana Times*) as one of the main component groups of the high school, comprising 20 percent of the high school population. This seemingly monolithic "Latina" group consisted of Chicanas, Mexicans, and recent immigrants from other Latin American countries, many of them Salvadorans. Within these groups, there were cross-cutting allegiances of varying strengths, as students divide themselves along national, ethnic, class, and Chicana/Mexican lines. In presenting the groups as described by students and observed by myself, I want to stress, along the lines proposed by Edmund Leach,[18] that the social categories I describe are not bounded sets, but rather parts of a single coherent system that is always fluid, always changing, precariously equi-librated, and constantly innovating on itself. Group boundaries were neither solid nor stable, and people moved in and out of groups with relative ease, depending on whether or not they spoke the group's language and shared the group's practices. In the case of the two groups we have just discussed, the Piporras and the Fresas, the language barrier was small (the Fresas spoke various urban dialects of Standard Latin American Spanish, the Piporras usually Rural Mexican Spanish), but the intra-cultural divide was large enough to prevent much interaction. On the other hand, once the acquisition of English had progressed far enough, Fresas usually moved into the Latina Jock group. This means that almost by definition, the Fresas consisted of recent-immigrant, (for-merly) middle-class Spanish speakers who had not yet acquired enough English to move into one of the predominantly English-usage groups. The Latina Jocks then were essentially the assimilated, English-language version of the Fresas, and indeed the similarity of the group was borne out by the many cross-group friendship lines that existed, as well as by the fact that when there were big school assemblies the Latina Jocks and the Fresas sat together on the bleachers.

Jocks, Latinas, and Popularity

Although participation in school-sponsored sports was not a necessary condition for Jock-category membership,[19] athletic activities usually went hand-in-hand with a constellation of traits that signaled the Jocks' over-all cooperation with the school as an institution, and by extension, their cooperation with the larger society in which the institution is embedded. In Penny Eckert's study, which dealt with an ethnically homogenous Euro-American high school, school-related activities were considered by rebellious students (*Burnouts*, to use the term common among the adolescents in Eckert's book) to be in collusion with the larger world of parental authority. School in general, and the specific activities asso-ciated with it, were resented and resisted by Burnouts for their role *in loco parentis*. In Eckert's study, school authority and parental authority, though not exactly overlapping, were largely aligned, especially in regard to the Jocks. But what would happen in a case where the school and the parents had different expectations and demands, such that in fulfilling one set of expectations a young person violated the norms of the other?

In this sense a Latina Jock girl (as well as a mainstream Euro-American Jock girl), who typically participated in sports, attended school-sponsored functions late at night, and devoted her weekends to extracurricular school-related affairs (i.e., the yearbook club) aligning her with mainstream Euro-American values, already incurred the disapproval of recent-immigrant parents of Piporras, who inculcated and sometimes just imposed more traditional gendered expectations. In this sense it could be said that Latina Jock girls, athletic, "popular," and acceptable to teachers, already stood on the other side of a wall, having acquired or shifted into cultural patterns that ran counter to a large part of what a "good girl" in the home culture might be. And despite the fact that a Latina Jock's parents may themselves have been second-, third-, or fourth-generation Americans aligned with mainstream Euro-American values, the large population of recent immigrants with a world-view rooted in rural Latin America still held Jock girls in some degree of contempt for having assimilated. Faced with little validation from their ethnic/cultural peers, it was no surprise that Latina Jocks turned to institutional sources of approval.

One essential aspect of a Latina Jock's identity was some degree of school spirit, be it in the form of running for elected office within the school government, of practicing organized sports, or taking part in clubs or activities such as cheerleading. Because by and large school-oriented activities were populated and organized by Euro-American Jocks, this meant that the greater part of the social networks of a Latina Jock consisted of Euro-Americans. Girls who identified themselves as Latina Jocks in this study claimed to know no Spanish (though some understood it passively), were usually Standard Euro-American English speakers, and knew some Latina girls from their neighborhood contexts, but were reluctant to name other Latinas as their friends.

The ideologically driven Latina gang girls called the Jocks "coconuts" (a common insult referring to being brown on the outside and white on the inside), and accused Jocks to their faces of being "whitewashed", or of "selling out" to the mainstream. These criticisms were noticed but ignored by the Jocks, whose activity in essentially separate social systems gave them little reason to care about these social evaluations.

A popular Latina Jock cheerleader named Jill did not particularly approve of or want to be accepted by the other groups of Latinas:

JILL: I see a lot of Latina girls, they just hang out with their own little group in a certain spot. I think it looks totally stupid 'cause
they're like trying to accomplish something but they're not, you
know? Like they're trying to – "look at me, you know . . . I'm
like above all of you guys." I don't know, that's the way I see it.
And I think it's just stupid. I don't think I'd like to [hang around
with them] anyways . . . just because . . . I don't know. Different
ideas I guess.

In this excerpt Jill criticized the ethnically-uniform groups of Latinas
for "hang[ing] out in their own little group," and acknowledged her
own discomfort at being scrutinized under their disapproving eye. Jill's
own social sphere mostly centered around the cheerleading squad, the
football team, and "crazy Foxbury Hills parties," the parents-gone-out-
of-town blowouts thrown by wealthy kids and weekly reviewed and
rated in a *Sor Juana Times* column. Although Jill's parents were of limited means (her mother earned money by taking care of other people's
children in her home in a modest neighborhood in Fog City), this did
not deter Jill from aspiring to move out of her neighborhood and to
New York City with her wealthy Foxbury Hills girlfriends when she
graduated from high school. And she did.

When I asked her about the extent of her friendship networks with
other Latinas, Jill said that although she used to talk to some of the
Latinas in her elementary school, they "just grew apart." We will see
more of what Jill means in chapter 8, when we examine the speech
patterns of a cross-section of English-speaking Latina girls and find that,
on the whole, Latina Jocks differ the most in speech patterns from other
Latina girls, to the extent that they can hardly be considered part of
the same continuum of variation.

Ethnic Diversity, Linguistic Diversity, and Educational Possibility

Sor Juana High School was a microcosm of the demographic situation
that increasingly faces schools across the country,[20] where rising immigrant populations have created diversity that challenges teachers,
exceeds school capacities, and provides students with opportunities for
learning about difference. Sor Juana High School, with a total student

body of 1,162 students, was 32 percent European-American, 22 percent Asian/Asian-American, 20 percent Latina/o, 14 percent African-American, 7 percent Pacific Islander, and 5 percent Other. It boasted student populations numerous enough to sustain cultural activities such as Mexican, Filipino, and Vietnamese classical dance troupes, and African-American Steppers.

The diversity of the student body, though usually depicted idealistically as a sort of mini-United Nations, also brought its share of challenges, especially when it came to instruction for students who arrived speaking languages other than English. In a few cases, immigrant students were absorbed into the educational system if their country of origin had English as its sole official language. But for other immigrant students the school undertook a complex procedure to classify them and assess their linguistic needs.

The 1995 California Education Code (Article 313) required schools to determine the language(s) spoken at home by each student. Upon each student's arrival, parents were sent the Home Language Survey, an instrument designed by the State of California Department of Education to determine the home language background of the student. The survey consisted of the following questions:

1 Which language did your son or daughter learn when he or she first began to talk?
2 What language does your son or daughter most frequently use at home?
3 What language do you use most frequently to speak to your son or daughter?
4 Name the language most often spoken by adults at home.[21]

Based upon parental answers to these questions, students were categorized and assigned a code corresponding to the home language. If all of the answers reflected an English-only household, the student was assigned a code of "English," but if *any* of the answers reflected the use of languages other than English, the student was assigned a code that identified the language used in the home. Thus, minimal use of another language by members of the household but not necessarily by the student could serve to classify a student as having a non-English language background.

According to this criterion, only 60 percent of Sor Juana students had English as their sole home language. These were considered to be the "mainstream" students, those who were following the high school core curriculum and had the opportunity to take college preparatory courses without other prerequisites. The "mainstream" student population included most Euro-American students, most African-American students, and certain Asian-American students whose families had been in the US long enough to have shifted home language away from the original heritage languages. The remaining 40 percent (467/1,162) of Sor Juana students had a language other than English as their home language.

Each student who was determined according to the above criteria to speak a language other than English in the home was assigned to one of two categories: Limited English Proficient (LEP) or Fluent English Proficient (FEP). The first category, with its unfortunate acronym of "LEP" (which led some kids to call each other "lep'rs"), has since been renamed "English learner" in more recent versions of the legal code, but the classificatory and remedial spirit remains the same. I will use LEP here for historical accuracy and consistency with the documents I examined.

Of the students who were found to have a language other than English as their home language, 61 percent (283/467) were classified as Limited English Proficient, while 40 percent were judged to be Fluent English Proficient. In effect, this means that fully one-quarter of the entire student body (24 percent (283/1,162)) was considered to have Limited English Proficiency. But how did the school determine which students were Limited English Proficient and which were Fluent English Proficient?

When I interviewed the program director of the school's English as a Second Language (ESL) program, she stated that in order to be reclassified as Fluent English Proficient, a student "has to score above the 36th percentile on a standardized reading test, pass a [state-administered] competency exam, have passing grades, and be *functioning* (my emphasis) in school." If any of these four criteria were not met, the student could not be reclassified as Fluent English Proficient.

The lockstep use of standardized testing, a legacy of the school reform movement of the 1980s, was especially treacherous for immigrant and minority children who were evaluated according to Standard English proficiency.[22] Inflexible grade placement, where grade promotion (and especially level promotion in the case of ESL students) was tied to designated cut-off scores on standardized achievement tests, could be especially discouraging for students who were orally fluent but whose written proficiency was not at the level required by the exams.

In addition to facing the hurdles of standardized testing and retainment, LEP proficient students additionally had to prove that they were "functioning." Even after having achieved FEP status, a student was still under observation by the school. A failed class (even a non–academic class like Woodshop, or Physical Education) or complaints from a teacher that a student was not functioning ("disruptive in class," as noted on report cards) could be enough to prevent a student from achieving FEP status. Thus, one important criterion to advance to the next level of "proficiency" was in some cases nonlinguistic. In the course of fieldwork, I encountered many *orally* fluent Chicano English speakers who continue to be classified as LEP because of "disruptive" behavior or low test scores.

Even by the school's own measuring standards there were many students who achieved a high degree of oral language fluency who nevertheless could not be reclassified as FEP. One additional exam that the school administered to LEP students was an individual Oral Proficiency Examination. The Oral Proficiency Examination was scored on a scale from 1 (lowest) to 5 (highest proficiency). According to this scale, 51 percent (92/181) of Latina/o Limited English Proficient students obtained the highest possible score on the oral fluency test. This examination, however, did not play a part in determining a student's Limited/Fluent status, but was used in assessing whether the student was eligible to be "mainstreamed" in some classes that were deemed to require mostly oral/listening skills as opposed to literacy (like Arts and Crafts, or Health).

So here a paradox emerges: even though fully half of the Latina/o LEP students had the highest possible scores in oral proficiency examinations, it was still the case that the great majority of these students were not succeeding in school, had high dropout rates, and were placed in low-level classes because of low grades, overall test scores, or behavioral issues.

The technical criteria by which an institution such as a school system assessed fluency would not be of such importance if LEP and FEP status were mere formalities, or served only internal recordkeeping functions. In fact, these acronyms played a large role in determining and predicting a student's educational opportunities. When classified as LEP, a student could not follow the school's regular course program for college preparation, but instead had to continue taking English as a Second Language courses. Although ESL courses counted toward fulfilling a student's high school graduation requirements, only the most advanced

ESL courses counted toward fulfilling the basic four-year college entrance requirements. College preparatory curricula to enter higher education in the University of California (UC) system or the California State University (CSU) system were standardized across the state, and a student's initial placement within the high school ESL system could easily determine whether or not they would be able to fulfill UC/CSU requirements by the time they were graduating seniors.

The Sor Juana High School 1993–4 course guide listed a total of twenty ESL courses spread over a number of areas, including ESL History, ESL Mathematics, ESL sciences, and even ESL typing. But only four of the twenty ESL courses (Advanced English, U.S. History, Civics, and Algebra I) counted toward UC/CSU requirements. This meant that for the vast majority of ESL students, the only way to have the opportunity of attending a UC or a CSU was to be placed in Advanced ESL as incoming freshmen (ninth-graders), so that they might be able to complete the four-year English course requirement for college entrance.

For the 1993–4 school year, the vast majority of incoming ESL students at SJHS were recommended by middle school officials for placement in beginning or intermediate sections of ESL. In fact, only five of thirty entering Latina/o LEP freshmen were placed in Advanced ESL that year.

The systematic outcome of this structured-level program was that the vast majority of orally fluent Latino students never moved out of the LEP designation, and as a result were ineligible to attend four-year institutions. Even when they did graduate from high school and attended a community college, the remedial ESL courses that they needed to take in order to qualify for enrollment in regular college classes would set them back at least one full year. The opportunity cost of that time was simply too high for poor families who relied on their children for increasing financial contributions to the household.[23]

During the time of my fieldwork, Latina/o students repeatedly came up against two practical effects that stemmed directly from the system of classification described above: erroneous placement and stereotyping. Armando had immigrated from Mexico when he was five years old. At fifteen, he was a fluent Chicano English speaker and had been promoted through ten grade levels without ever being reclassified from Limited to Fluent English Proficient. "He is just too rowdy," said the teachers. "I am bored in class," said Armando. "*What is this? This is a dog. This is a cat.* Give me a break! I'd rather get kicked out of class." What seemed especially ironic about Armando's case is that he did not speak Spanish at home with his family, but displayed a common pattern reflective of ongoing language shift: his parents spoke in Spanish to him and his siblings, and they all answered exclusively in English.

Alexandra was another student whose mother had fought a bitter battle with teachers as the girl was about to enter high school. Although she was a stellar student in middle school, her test scores were too low to have her reclassified as FEP. After two months of fighting and showing teachers Alexandra's personal diary in English (much to her dismay), the family finally gave up and secretly enrolled Alexandra in the public high school in the next district. They succeeded in getting her an FEP designation in her new school, and she went on to follow a regular college prep curriculum.

A final example of institutional barriers to student success comes in the form of a student article in the *Sor Juana Times*, the high school weekly newspaper. In the spring of 1994, Laurie Bexley, a half-Mexican, half-Euro-American student wrote an article entitled "Even Unintentional Racism Hurts."[24] In this article, Laurie chronicles the experiences of her mother at SJHS teacher–parent conferences. She writes:

> When I first came to Sor Juana, I wasn't doing well in Biology, and when my mom went to [teacher–parent conference] night, she talked to my teacher about it. My mother has a very thick accent, and it is clear to almost everyone that she comes from Latin America. When she asked my teacher what was wrong, he replied by telling her that students at Sor Juana come from very different schools, and that my junior high probably didn't prepare me as well as others for this course.
>
> When my mom went on to say that I went to [a prestigious school in Foxbury Hills] and had a 4.0 in the past, he was stupefied.
>
> "Oh, oh, oh. Laurie is your daughter, I'm so sorry I thought you were someone else's mother," my teacher replied.
>
> It was pitiful. My teacher had made an obviously racist assumption that because my mother was Hispanic I went to an inferior junior high, and that was the reason for my problems in Biology.
>
> It doesn't stop there, though. I've seen it time and time again, and it all gets swept under the rug by the administration who likes to focus their efforts on the prestigious, rich, white kids at Sor Juana.

All of the above student experiences reflected to some degree the way that academics were structured for Latinas/os at SJHS. Laurie Bexley's piece specifically pointed to the common stereotypes conflating neighborhood residence, ethnicity and school performance.

Interpreting Fluency: Researcher Effects and Ethnographic Uncertainty

As I mentioned above, Güera was a very fluent English speaker who had moved back and forth between Mexico and the US. She was the official translator for the recently arrived Spanish monolinguals in her beginning ESL II class. Her class schedule included Bilingual World Studies with Junior; mandatory mainstream Health classes; a Special-Education math course that had only African-American and Latino students in it; and Cosmetology as her elective. Because she spent her very early childhood in the US, and because some of her relatives spoke English, Güera's phonology was near-native. What struck me about her, and the reason I became interested in following her progress, was that she had poor reading and writing skills despite her excellent speaking skills and listening comprehension. At the time of the interview, Güera was in danger of failing Beginning ESL II. From our interview:

NORMA: Aha. Y este.. a tí que te gusta más hablar, inglés o español?
            Yeah. So . . . what do you prefer to speak, Spanish or English?
GÜERA: Español.
            Spanish.
NORMA: Español, porqué?
            Spanish, why?
GÜERA: No sé. Me gusta más español.
            I don't know. I like Spanish better.
NORMA: Lo que se me hace interesante . . . es que, pues tú teniendo ya tanto tiempo aquí, acostumbrada al idioma de acá, ¿no? que te juntas mucho con Mexicanos, y que hablas mucho español.
            What I think is interesting is that you, having been so long here, and being used to the language here, you hang out mostly with Mexicans, and speak a lot of Spanish . . .
GÜERA: Yo pienso que aunque hablara mucho inglés yo, hablaría siempre español . . . algunos dicen, no, que nomás 'ta aprendiendo inglés, y ya no, habla español, porque de muchas, [toca la mesa] aquí, nomás aprenden el inglés y ya no quieren hablar español, y eso, a mi me cae gordo!
            I think that even if I spoke a lot of English, I would only speak Spanish. There are a lot [of girls] here, [taps the table], that as soon as they learn English, they don't want to speak Spanish anymore, and that, I really hate!

NORMA: Mhmm.
           Mhmm.
GÜERA: Y tu les hablas español y ellas te.. te contestan en inglés, eso
           me cae gordo a mí.
           And you speak in Spanish to them, and they . . . answer you in
           English, I really hate that.

In this excerpt exploring Güera's language attitudes, she declares a
preference for Spanish. I remark to her that her insistence on Spanish
is remarkable in this context, since she speaks English so well and is
very much accustomed to life in the United States. My question is implicitly one of membership as well. Since her English was so good, if she
wanted to socialize with other speakers as well, why wouldn't she?
Certainly she had everything that could enable her to join other
groups if she wished. Her answer was very revealing. She *denies* being
able to speak a lot of English, and states that *even if she did*, she would
still choose to speak Spanish. I have previously analyzed the foregoing
interview excerpt as follows:

> This crucial sentence shows not only her rhetorical position with
> respect to the language question, but also her self-perception which, despite
> her near-native phonology, does not allow her to construct herself as an
> English speaker. Güera looks down on people who refuse to speak Spanish
> after having learned English (an indirect reference to Norteñas), imply-
> ing that they shun much more than a linguistic code by opting for English.
> She even disapproves of inter-speaker codeswitching, one of the linguistic
> devices most often used by Norteñas.[25]

Looking back at this interview, I realize that there is a presupposi-
tion in my question that Güera might be reacting to as well: it sounds
as though I am implying that it is somehow odd for a fluent English
speaker to hang around only with Mexicans and to speak exclusively
in Spanish.

My original interpretation stressed linguistic disidentification[26] in an
effort to account for the paradox of Güera's native-like fluency and her
poor reading and writing grades. What if in addition to these factors
there was also an added element of opposition to notions introduced
by the ethnographer? It is possible that her note of caution against language loss and identity denial was not only rhetorical, but also meant
specifically for me, and that it is only now, with several years' hindsight, that I am able to interpret her admonition. As I started doing

the interviews, I struggled with self-presentation, with the meaning that everything from my appearance to the life choices I'd made might have for students contemplating their own choices.

Güera knew I spoke both languages, and that I was dating Rob – un gringo güero *(a Euro-American)* – from California. After we'd gotten to know each other well, and were on joking/teasing terms with each other, she and some of her other Sureña girlfriends didn't bat an eye as they informed me: "I'd much rather be with a Mexican than with an American." They had met Rob, thought he was nice (it was especially good that he spoke Spanish), but it was also clear that they didn't really approve. All along the girls tried (unsuccessfully) to set me up with eligible older Mexican guys, just as they tried to mold me by teaching me about makeup, about cooking, about ways to dress and dance. Special allowances were made for me because I hadn't in fact grown up either in Mexico or in the US, so the girls suspended judgment and tried to inculcate in me what they thought I'd missed.

Güera teased me all the time, about not being so good at Banda-dancing, about my skirts (Dickies pants or at least jeans would be better), about the American boyfriend. In hindsight, I now see that she might have been positioning herself relative to me and my choices in answering my interview questions. This is of course what people do in the course of everyday conversation. Why should linguistic anthropologists think that we are merely tape decks, faithfully recording statements about language and then neutrally reproducing and analyzing the ideological statements of people we have interviewed? This is not just another instance of figuring out that the presence of the researcher crucially affects the nature of the data gathered, and figuring out ways to lessen that effect, as William Labov[27] advocated thirty-five years ago in naming the observer's paradox (discussed in greater detail in chapter 7). This awareness of researcher positionality from within the sociolinguistic literature ought to have made us linguists more open to the interpretive turn within anthropology, and yet in both sociolinguistics and linguistic anthropology there is truly a dearth of self-reflexive work. There are of course some exceptions,[28] but by and large linguistic anthropology operates unaffected by questions of reflexivity and of the nature of our data.

Over the course of two years of participant observation and friendship with Güera, I *was* able to observe repetition of a pattern in many different interactions (with teachers, with other students, and with her relatives) bolstering my perception that Güera strategically constructed herself as a non-speaker of English. It is because of this repeated confirmation of the initial observation that I continue to believe that Güera is an example of the effect that language ideologies can have on learning motivation and consequently on educational outcomes. I believe that her socially precipitated disidentification with English negatively affected her motivation to refine her reading and writing skills in English at an important post-primary learning period, and since the school's support for Spanish language instruction was extremely limited (from the school's perspective, the main goal for all non-native speakers was to learn English as quickly as possible), this disidentification might have affected her literacy skills in Spanish as well.

With the hindsight of ten years, I can also now begin to address how and why my presence affected some youth more than others, and how my status as a barely older youth at the time, neither from the US nor from Mexico, shaped some of my interviews. Within the interviewees' words were lessons meant for me.

Notes

1 Horrox (1994)
2 Chiquita Brands (2006)
3 See Bustamante (1994) for detailed statistical breakdowns of sending-state data collected from migrants in crossing.
4 The Mexican states of Jalisco, Michoacán, and Oaxaca provide the roots for these nostalgic names.
5 Smith (2005)
6 For Migrant Education please see the US Department of Education website: http://www.ed.gov/programs/mep/index/html
7 Gibson (1988), Gibson (1997), Perlmann (1988)
8 *Puro México* means "Pure Mexican" or "100% Mexican."
9 School principal, p.c.
10 Davis (1990), Valle and Torres (2000), Hyams (2003)
11 Hondagneu-Sotelo (2001)
12 Gibson (1988), Eckert (1989), Orenstein (1994), Taylor (2006)
13 Marcia Farr defines relajo as "joking talk that, like fiesta or carnival, turns the social order 'upside down' and thus provides a space for social critique" (Farr 2003: 160).
14 Relajiento is a person who jokes around, see note 13 above.
15 See also Orenstein (1994), Taylor (2006).
16 Willis (1977), Eckert (1989), Foley (1990), Eckert (2000)
17 The equivalent of the "Jocks" in Eckert (1989) and Eckert (2000).

18 Leach (1954)
19 As Eckert (1989) points out.
20 Portes and Rumbaut (1996), Suarez-Orozco and Suarez-Orozco (2002)
21 California Department of Education (1995)
22 Smitherman-Donaldson (1986), Valdés (1994), Ogbu (1999)
23 Matute-Bianchi (1986), National Coalition of Advocates for Students (1988: 28), Gibson and Ogbu (1991), Matute-Bianchi (1991)
24 Bexley (1994)
25 Mendoza-Denton (1999)
26 For other accounts of linguistic disidentification and resistance in literacy and learning see Gilmore (1985) and Valdés (2001).
27 Labov (1972b)
28 Briggs (1986), Rickford and McNair-Knox (1994), Cukor-Avila and Bailey (2001), Gaudio (2001), Jacobs-Huey (2006), Modan (2006), Wertheim (2006), Modan and Mendoza-Denton (2005)

CHAPTER 2

BEGINNING FIELDWORK

I had vague ideas about community projects that I hoped would emerge from the research participants themselves. When I reflected later, these notions seemed arrogant, as if I thought I knew the hopes and aspirations of this Latino community. I realized I had to question all my assumptions about this southern Latino community, such as defining as problems certain aspects of their lives that to them, were not problematic at all.

Sofia Villenas[1]

Stereotype Threat

When colleagues at conferences hear about my research, they often ask me what part of LA I'm from, as if that will help them place me. Every time I hear this question I marvel at the presuppositions on which it rests, and my mind goes wild calculating backwards to the origin of the query. I read between the lines and attribute to my colleagues a train of thought that whizzes noisily in my head: "Chicano gangs are in LA, Norma's work is on Chicana gangs, she looks Chicana, modern anthropologists sometimes work with their 'own' groups, so she must be a Chicana from LA. Possibly a former gang member . . ." and then I find myself in dialog with this cascading anxiety: "Well, I *have* broad shoulders, a muscular build, and a scar meandering across my lip from a childhood accident that could promote the last interpretation. And now that I've been taught, I could hold my own in a fight. I can see how you could think that." Could it be that my colleagues then take a step back and think, "No, it couldn't be. One mustn't stereotype. But wait. Maybe if I just ask what *neighborhood* in LA she's from, maybe that will help me figure it out? Maybe if she's from East LA, she *is* an auto-ethnographer." No sooner have I whipped myself into suspicions of my colleagues than I think, it's me, it's my interpretation of the situation. *I'm* just paranoid and under stereotype threat,[2] imagining that strangers asking if I'm from LA means I have been cast as a gang member, when *it is actually me that is fearful of a stigmatized identity*.

Another time I was told in a sweet, supportive tone by a senior colleague at a national education conference how brave I was, and how hard it must have been for me to make something of myself, coming from the LA barrio. This comment was more overt. I'm not always just paranoid. When I replied that I was not from California but from Mexico, that didn't seem to clear it up. Next question: "What part of Texas?" I could conceivably stretch to understand this mix-up, since I have *trompe-l'oreille*[3] phonology, haven't lived in Mexico since I was eleven, and much of my schooling since then has in fact been in English. Visual ethnicity cues plus native-like English continually trump my claims to foreignness (despite my Mexican passport). On this occasion I finally had to clarify, "No, no, I really am from Mexico, Mexico the *country*." As opposed to what? The ethnicity?

It's not just me. The instances vary in their overtness, but in both cases assumptions are being made.

A Reader's Manual

It is a responsibility of anthropologists to explain ourselves, who we are and where we come from, often with what read like embarrassing or distracting results,[4] drawing accusations that we seek attention for ourselves unnecessarily, when the "real" subjects of the study are the people among whom we worked.[5] And yet there is not only a responsibility but an obligation, given the history of anthropology: deep ethnocentrism; involvement in colonial administration; anthropometry (historically applied to the sorting of gangsters and criminals, and to providing the foundation for scientific racism);[6] and participation in the practice of display of human beings, starting with Columbus bringing an Arawak Indian before the court of Queen Isabella,[7] continuing with anthropologists who have displayed people in freak shows and museums, in "native villages" at the Chicago World's Fair, all the way down to recent exhibits of the remains of Saatje Baartman, the "Hottentot Venus."[8] We have indeed a sordid story behind us. For these reasons it is essential to clearly set out as much as possible anthropologists' backgrounds, our assumptions, our overt and hidden agendas (which are sometimes not clear even for us), and our epistemologies in order not to repeat some of our past mistakes. Who are you, who am I, to represent someone else? What is the representational distance between a freak show, a museum display, and a book?

Talking about where you come from as an anthropologist gives the reader a chance to question you. And yet I am mortified to do it. I have often thought that my mortification is because I didn't grow up in a family where public self-disclosure is liberally practiced, or I tell myself that I am actually a bit shy by nature. Or possibly there is a gendered dimension, where I am embarrassed by drawing attention to myself in performance.[9] I quickly have to discard the latter in my case, since in my creative writing I electively mortify myself constantly.

Additionally it stands to be noted that no matter how much I try to make clear who I am and to clarify my status as a not quite near-native anthropologist, there are still questions about the nature of knowledge that self-disclosure leaves unresolved. As far back as St Augustine,[10] Montaigne,[11] Leibniz,[12] and Hegel,[13] European philosophers and social historians (who, for right or wrong, are the intellectual lineage of modern anthropology), have grappled with the inherently perspectival framing of philosophical and political standpoints, and the (im)possibility of objectivity. Chicana/o writers[14] and postcolonial and subaltern theoreticians[15] have updated this concern by stressing the conditions of production of knowledge and history, and by addressing the way in which concealed and hidden knowledges are renegotiated, altered, and managed both by the "human subjects" (as per the government designation) with whom we work and by (native) anthropologists in the retelling.[16] As you read this, you deserve to know that I was not a neutral instrument in this project. What I present as a text was filtered through my sensibility, my interpretation as well as my equivocation. Even what I noticed and considered as "data points" were selected in my perception according to the sum of my prior experiences and my take of the situations encountered. For this reason I want you to know who I am, as much as can be gleaned through this indirect medium, and "nouveau-solipsistic"[17] as it may sound. It will affect how you read this work.

Heading into the *Copacabana*

I am from Mexico. Both my mother and I were born in the northern mining town of Cananea, Sonora, the birthplace of the first Mexican strikes against American copper companies which led to the Mexican revolution; I take pride in coming from a long line of unionizing workers and revolutionary troublemakers. My father's side of the family is more from the center of the Republic. I lived with my parents and with my younger brother principally in Mexico City all the way through primary school, which classifies me as an almost legitimate *chilanga* (native of Mexico City, insufferable from the point of view of inhabitants of the periphery). My family has both experienced and been propelled by the tremendous social upheavals that have accompanied Mexican history and politics in the last century. Rural-to-urban migration was a formative experience for my paternal grandparents and for my mother and her sisters. Shifts in gender roles have been ongoing since at least my great-grandparents' generation, and within my nuclear family a dramatic increase in education has resulted in whiplash class mobility. My maternal grandfather (Denton) was a copper miner in Sonora, near the border with the United States, my grandmother a baker, a tailor, a farmer, and cook; my paternal grandfather from Guanajuato (Mendoza) was a small merchant in the dendritic economy[18] of Mexico City. My father became first an accountant, then a financial auditor, and finally spent the bulk of his career working for the United Nations, which resulted in four major international relocations starting when I was eleven. My mother raised my brother and me with scrupulous gender equality and first-language maintenance while we were stationed away from our country, first in the US, then in the Ivory Coast, and finally in Thailand. I went to college in Thailand, China, and the United States.

Although fellow anthropologists could imagine I might be from LA, gang members themselves *never* made that assumption. Despite the fact that I could speak fluent Chilanga-Spanish and fluent English it was clear to them that I was definitely not a Chicano English speaker, not from California, and not recently from Mexico. The rest could tolerate uncertainty.

When I started as a graduate student in the Linguistics Department at Stanford University, my original project was to work on emergent West African Creoles. I wanted to go to the Ivory Coast, where my family had lived from 1981 to 1987, to study the incipient creolization of popular African French. In preparation for my fieldwork there, I had started to take classes in the School of Education, where I met Guadalupe Valdés, a sociolinguist who told me about the local gangs that she was encountering in the course of fieldwork for what would become her 2001 book, _Learning and Not Learning English_. She told me that she had heard about gangs in one of the interviews that she recorded with a girl I will call Lydia, a recent-immigrant Mexican fourteen-year-old whom she had been following in her transition from middle school through high school. The gangs were called the "Norteños" and the "Sureños"; the Northerners and the Southerners.

One morning as I was getting ready to go to my classes, I thought about what Valdés had said about the gangs. If they focused on regional differences, and the regional difference had particular traits, maybe these designations were used as part of a repertoire that might signal transnational orientation, as in Susan Gal's study of gender and language shift from Austrian to German,[19] or John Gumperz's studies of India in the 1950s and 1960s,[20] or Niloofar Haeri's study of diglossic Cairo.[21] Maybe these Northern and Southern Mexican Spanish accents would function as acts of identity,[22] or might correlate with attitudes schoolchildren held toward the institution, or each other.[23] I imagined that Northern Mexican immigrant children would be able to distinguish through the use of dialect features their Central and Southern Mexican counterparts and form cohorts, maybe even gangs. I was wrong about the initial shape of the assumption – I had thought that the split referred to regional affiliation in Mexico, but instead Sur and Norte referred to an oppositional dynamic pitting recent immigrants against those of long-term resident status. Despite this difference, my initial suspicion of fine-grained dialect differentiation proved right, and the linguistic findings that I present in chapters 7, 8, and 9 of this book present some new contributions to what we know in linguistics and anthropology about the way in which speakers use social microstructures in deciding what linguistic and semiotic resources to fashion into social meaning in their everyday communities. The larger work – the entire book – is an attempt to take the reader through various stages of ethnographic discovery from my perspective: I start with the broad topography of the social landscape of Latinos at the school; move through the process of discovering the distinctions and contradictions in the usage of the terms Norte and Sur, and the application of these distinctions to wider hemispheric processes of localism and political stance-taking by Sor Juana High School youth. Taking the distinctions that young people made in their social groups as cues, I explore material cultural aspects of Norte and Sur and move on to increasingly fine levels of linguistic analysis toward the end of the book.

The particular gendered/classed/ethnicized standpoint that I represent shaped and affected my interactions, what kind of data I was able (and unable) to gather, as well as my interpretation of the larger picture that was forged by me through the process of ethnography. I consider myself to have forged it because even though the "linguistic data" were external (other people's conversations, their reactions to this project, discussions about it in the context of my questions), the interpretation of all of these events remains subjective. In many cases, the most I can do is recount in detail for you what happened from my perspective, and leave it up to you to decide how it can be interpreted.

The *Chiquita Banana* segment at the beginning of the book is a good example of my hesitation to impose an authoritative interpretation. I needn't have told you about my doubts over its meaning. I could easily offer an interpretation by just recounting the incident from my perspective. I was present when the incident happened. I recorded it on audio-tape. I transcribed it and double-checked it for errors. And yet what followed was a Rashomon-like experience of not being sure how the interaction could have been perceived, asking others what they thought happened, and getting a different answer from teachers, students, and scholars with different positionalities, leaving me to wonder whether my own experience as a narrator for this work is reliable at all. And later, much later, I remembered an event from my own past that has now colored my view of why I spent so long trying to understand the Chiquita Banana incident, why it turned over constantly in the back of my mind, refusing to go away. It is not just a research question: whether the incident in fact depicted a gendered, racialized stereotype that the girls had to live with, even though the girls themselves were not fully familiar with it at the time. I also remembered something else, and the puzzling part is that this took years to surface: I myself was the target of a similar taunt when I first started as a new immigrant in the seventh grade at a public school in Westport, Connecticut. At the time, some of my classmates took a Barry Manilow song called "Copacabana,"[24] and invented some lyrics that were supposed to be about me: *"Her name was Norma, she was a showgirl . . ."* They sang the song when they saw me, and although I didn't quite understand this when it was going on (my English was not strong enough to get the double entendres), it still angers and saddens me today. I somehow blocked the Copacabana song from my consciousness even after transcribing and analyzing Chiquita Banana; the fact that it took years for me to realize that this was a factor in making me puzzle over that episode is significant indeed. It wasn't until I was researching the background for Carmen Miranda and discovered that she actually starred in a movie called *Copacabana* that the connection between those long-ago taunts and the girls' experience came to my conscious awareness. I am not recounting this to create a rhetorical parallel of oppression, for I realize full well the privileged standpoint from which I speak; I am a child of voluntary rather than economically-driven migration.[25] The point here: No ethnographer is a blank notepad just as no linguist is a tape recorder. The perceptual filters that we bring to fieldwork situations are powerful indeed, and not always conscious. You will read in the following chapters an account that is my interpretation of years of fieldwork and research with a group of young people who allowed me into their lives, and I will invite you to draw your own conclusions. I have been and will be providing guideposts to show you where my ethnographic interpretation might be guided by factors such as my background, my social class, and my own subjective and affective reactions to people around me and to events at the time.

Replicability and Subjectivity

Because ethnography, as the prime methodology of cultural anthropology, is essentially an experiential and to some degree subjective method, I am not claiming that every researcher will be able to replicate the results attested here. The conversations you will find are epiphenomenal; they are the emergent products of the ethnographic method, the real-time interactional decisions and the circumstances and backgrounds of the interlocutors, including me. There is one limited exception: for the sociophonetic results in particular, I do claim some degree of replicability, provided the same data set is used (the tapes of my interactions with those speakers), and comparable measurement and statistical techniques. Interestingly enough, this qualifies as "doing science" by classical diagnostics. Despite my introductory words highlighting subjectivity and critiquing the claims of objectivity in anthropological science, I am Janus-faced: I submit the results to scrutiny by fellow phoneticians, who understand themselves to be scientists, and I do expect replicability at a more abstract level, such as, for example, finding that social microstructures govern sociolinguistic patterning, or that frequency and saliency effects of discourse markers allow them to serve agentive functions.

The claims I will be presenting and supporting are laid out in subsequent chapters. But for now, let's focus on the gang dynamic in the schools as a potential sociolinguistic topic.

Confronted by My Own Stereotypes

In the fall of 1993 I had approached Guadalupe Valdés, who immediately offered to introduce me to Lydia, the Sureña whom she had interviewed at the high school where she had just started doing fieldwork. Valdés suggested offhand that I might encounter "linguistic resistance" to English language learning, an idea that she followed up in her own work[26] and that provided the first linguistic puzzle around which to orient my research. Not long afterward, I accompanied her to the high school. I looked up to her tremendously and wanted to take my cue from her at the fieldsite. Well-respected and professional, she walked into the high school in a business suit and all doors opened to her – she had cultivated a long relationship with both the schoolchildren and the staff. She asked to speak to Lydia, a short girl with curly blond hair teased and matted stiff with hairspray. My own stereotypes were challenged as soon as I saw her – I was expecting a dark-haired, dark-skinned girl (like a younger version of myself) and momentarily couldn't believe that this petulant cherub was part of a Mexican gang. Valdés and I invited her for ice cream, and she was more than happy to get out of class. Apparently Lydia also had an older sister, Larissa. Lydia talked slowly and disaffectedly, her languid voice remarkably low for her age. She was wearing a deep blue sweatshirt and jeans, rather ordinary-looking to me at the time. When we returned to the main English as a Second Language office Valdés mentioned my wanting to do some work with young people in the school, to which the administrative staff was very open: both Lydia and Larissa needed tutoring and had near-failing grades. "When can you start?"

The next time I went to the school by myself and tried to emulate Valdés in dress and demeanor to present myself as a respectable, professional academic. When I got there I was introduced to some of the teachers. One of them was Miss Melanie, a young Chicana probably not much older than I was. Mrs Gilmore was possibly 45, and was an old hand at ESL teaching. They invited me to have lunch with them in the teachers' lounge. I quickly found that the only advantage to the teacher's lounge was that coffee was actually served there (at the time no coffee was served to the high school students, surely an anachronism now where students have espresso carts roaming all around the campuses). I was twenty-three years old when I undertook this project.

Once I began tutoring at the high school regularly, I started what eventually became my fieldwork by volunteering as a math, English, and science homework tutor in the Activity Center at Sor Juana High School, a popular stopping point for students during free class periods. The Activity Center was both home base and lounge, an extended living room where some people read and did homework while others ate, listened to music, talked, or painted their fingernails. I'd decided that to get to know the students I would need to spend my downtime in the cafeteria and the hallways, not eating with the teachers in a private lunchroom. My first student cafeteria lunch I was invited to sit at a table with some girls whom I would later realize were peripheral Sureñas: cherubic-looking Lydia and her friends Ona and Cristina, all recent-immigrant Spanish speakers who were in their first year of high school. They were all in beginning ESL with Güera, the girl with the jailed boyfriend from chapter 1.

Lydia jostled bystanders in the cafeteria line, giving dirty looks to another girl, which I came to understand was called *mad-dogging*. Around her neck a painstakingly hand-woven Catholic cross made from blue thread suggested penitence by crochet. Behind Lydia was Ona, a moppet with long hair coated in hairgel, going all the way down to her waist in waves. Every piece of clothing on her body was blue or purple and at least five sizes too big, so that the ends of her sleeves hung slack, almost to her knees. Despite her black lipstick and gangland duds, she was really quite shy, and her oversize clothes spilling onto the ground caused her to be shaped like a button mushroom rising from the floor. Cristina, the third of these girls, was small for her age and had smooth black hair with bangs that were cut straight across. In one of the pictures I have she looks tristful, tiny, childlike in a white sweatshirt with dancing teddy bears on it. The first time I met her she indignantly maintained that she was not a Sureña, but definitely a Norteña. Lydia and Ona paid no attention to her protest and shook their heads as she itemized her evidence: 1) she had been born in LA, 2) she liked

Figure 2.1 Segregated tables at Sor Juana High School during lunch.

Oldies music, and 3) she didn't like recent immigrants. She also claimed to feel more American than Mexican. Despite the fact that she had just arrived from Mexico, had no Norteña friends, and by virtue of her Spanish dominance her networks were limited to ESL students, Cristina used *birthright* to lay claim to the Norteña label. I owe to her articulate protests my first inkling that the Norteña/Sureña gang dynamic was not strictly based on geography, or nationality, or where you had grown up. You could "feel" more American than Mexican and *that* could be allegiance, grounds for faith and constant loyalty.

Are You a Cop?

For several months before I developed a better understanding of what the labels Norte and Sur meant to participants, I heard students talking obliquely about them, and even then quite seldom, in resolute tones and anxious glances over protectively curved shoulders. Before deciding to research this topic in earnest, I felt wary about asking, paranoid of being taken for a "narc" – a narcotics agent – or a cop, sensing touchiness enough not to pursue any of it unless others broached the topic. At some point I even began to doubt that the dynamic Valdés had identified was widespread at all, since after Cristina moved away to Oregon with the farm crop rotations my clearest contact disappeared. My interest in gangs as a topic diminished, I continued to pursue my creolization topic, and continued tutoring for another few months, all the while getting to know the students better, and following their ups and downs at lunch.

One day I went into the bathroom, and spotted some graffiti in a stall:

PURO SUR MEXICO 100%

Putaaas

(whores)

I held my breath as I read it. The dynamic I had doubted was right there, conversing back and forth for all to see. I registered an overwhelming sense of my own illiteracy: whatever the signs were, *I just couldn't read them.* Signs were all around me but I didn't know how to interpret them. I read and re-read the graffiti, the bold strokes of initial assertion, the vehemence in the act of obliteration. Looking back, I see I was strangely oblivious. The signs were there all along. Perhaps that was part of their design, to be everywhere, unnoticeable.

It was then that I decided to pursue this project.

A Semiotic Crisis

The consequent awareness that everything I did was a sign, deciphered in spite of any resistance or desire on my part, was overwhelming. My jacket that tried to seem professional was a beacon, fired to all eyes, and I completely unaware of what they read! Early on I reasoned that the groups had different colors, and stayed away from the most obvious ones: red and blue, burgundy and navy. Gradually green was added to my schema (Filipino or Samoan gang) and purple (taken sometimes as a variant of blue) and brown (Brown Pride Locos). The only colors "left" as far as I could tell were orange and yellow (ugh) and black. I felt suitably noncommittal with black and wore little else for about four years. Ten years later I still have bright red and blue avoidance. I wanted to project neutrality, a kind of unmarkedness, at the same time realizing the futility of that effort. My own signification eluded my grasp. I had no idea who I was to these girls.

My background of growing up partly in Mexico, being fluent in both Spanish and English, and simultaneously not having really grown up in the US but in other countries (Ivory Coast, Thailand) made me an insider/outsider to the Latino community in California. The designations of "halfie anthropologist" and "native ethnographer" don't even begin to capture my position. Lila Abu-Lughod uses the term "halfie" as a broad gloss for "a person whose national or cultural identity is mixed by virtue of migration, overseas education, or parentage."[27] Dorinne Kondo[28] productively uses the concept as well to analyze how her research in Tokyo was constrained by ways in which she, a US-born and raised ethnographer, could act around her own relatives in Japan. But what do you call it when the population one is working with are already themselves "halfies," already bicultural and transnational along a continuum, and the ethnographer is interpellated into some of these identities? I must be a halfie of halfies, an ethnographic quatroon or octoon.[29]

For starters, although I am often ascribed many different kinds of identities, as you can see in the beginning of this chapter, I am not straightforwardly part of the community of people of Latino extraction who grew up in the United States. I was in public junior high school in Connecticut for one year until my father had a job transfer, and then lived in other countries where I encountered neither Mexicans nor Chicanos/Latinos my age. While living in the Ivory Coast my brother and I would joke that we were the only Mexican teenagers in all of West Africa until we found out about a pair of Mexican siblings our age who had moved to Senegal. I missed all of the Chicano accoutrements of growing up in the United States, missed a probable Fresa upbringing in Mexico, and missed also the experiential basis that provides a common ground for US Latinos of my generation. I can code-switch a mean streak, but I'd never heard Oldies before and it wasn't until college, living in Bangkok, that I figured out who Cesar Chávez[30] was.

At another level, my experience was very much a parallel to that of the girls. My growing up in Mexico was arrested at precisely the same age as many of these girls and young women had emigrated. In them I could see traces of myself, rewound. At this age they were experiencing many of their firsts: first job, first live basketball game, first unsupervised date, first institutional trouble, first kiss! For me, as for them, all of these things had taken place away from my home country. I identified with the newness of all these experiences, and with the bewildering parental conflicts that seemed to come out of nowhere. Talking to the girls I found that sleepovers, for instance, were just as wrong for their parents in California as for mine in the Ivory Coast.

You Could Be Our Mascot!

After many months of breakfasts, tutoring and lunch at the high school, I began to become friends with the different groups, and slowly the barriers started to yield. I eventually received invitations, *exhortations* even, to join the gangs. Some girls desperately wanted to find a place for me, and appointed emissaries to let me know that it didn't hurt that much, to be beaten up, that it was only a few minutes, only three or four, and that they would teach me to fight so that I could get something out of it too. Another time I was offered the role of an honorary member (a "mascot," as it was so tactfully put) who didn't have to be "down" for fights but who could still claim. I never accepted even the watered-down version of the gang status. Becoming part of one gang would automatically mean I couldn't talk to anyone else. But it did cross my mind. Months of befriending people who are constantly on the lookout can certainly fray one's nerves, so that girls' offers of protection were tempting indeed. But I am getting ahead of myself here. The first thing that happened was that I slowly started to dress differently.

I have an early picture of myself at the high school looking a bit pale, wearing no makeup and with a flat pageboy. I am standing next to Ona and Lydia during lunch; they are in bright blue and purple, I am in a black jacket and a long skirt, trying not to look like a high school student and as much as possible like my own professors.

When I started socializing more frequently with people outside of the tutorial atmosphere of the Activity Center, the way that I dressed changed gradually. At first it started because I was going to gym class, and participating in occasional games of volleyball or basketball, so I

Figure 2.2 Emergency makeup application on Norma.

had to keep some gym clothes around. The rest of the time, little side-long glances were flashed in my direction, tactful suggestions were made about relaxing and wearing jeans (instead of long skirts), shopping expeditions were organized, and party invitations always accompanied by exhortations to get ready and dress up together. Sometimes, if we were driving somewhere, the girls would make me pull over on the side of the road and apply makeup so that I could be "presentable." And so gradually people began to treat me differently, and some senior scholars, much to my surprise, complained from just a little eyeliner that I was "going native."

During part of the time that I was doing fieldwork, I lived in one of the large cities in the Bay Area, and commuted to the more suburban location of the girls' school. One Saturday some Norteña girls and I had been invited to a party and resolved to get dressed to the nines. The girls and I spent the afternoon at a Norteña's house, getting ready. While we were there they insisted on selecting some of their own clothes for me to wear, a black pair of Dickies work pants and a white t-shirt. As soon as they were selected, I threw them on and said, "Do I look good?" One of the girls, Thelma, took a quick glance and replied, "Yeah; iron your pants and iron your shirt." "Are you sure?" I hesitated because when I was a teenager I *never* ironed my clothes, at a time when the height of fashion in my prep school was to look grungily rumpled. I honestly couldn't believe teenagers would spend time ironing. Thelma elaborated:

> THELMA: You gotta take pride to do your clothes
> you know **I** have to iron,
> when I go out I have to iron my shit for half an hour
> or forty-five minutes, you know,
> my pants, you know
> they gotta be
> cre::ased
> you know they gotta-
> NORMA: Even the t-shirts?
> THELMA: The t-shirts you know,
> they gotta go with the line right here you know,
> [. . .]
> yeah, cause when they-
> when they see you
> your line right here
> and your creases going down
> your line you know
> then goes down to your tennies,
> and everyone goes
> who:a,
> you know
> and then there's competition for who could iron their
> Dickies better you know?

I relented and was taught the proper way to iron pants (everything was symbolic, and since they were Norteñas, a four-pleat crease was required on the front panel of their Dickies pants), and was also instructed on the proper way to starch and iron creases into the white t-shirt I was going to wear. Makeup application was painstakingly executed, Mary Jane flats from Chinatown finished the outfit, and we were good to go. On the way to the party we stopped at the Safeway supermarket in my neighborhood to pick up some food and drinks, and I got to experience the difference this outfit made. With my hair all feathered out, full makeup and perfectly constructed outfit, none of the tellers recognized me. Old ladies held their purses tight as we walked by them in the chips aisle; mothers pulled their kids close to them and avoided eye contact as they shuffled quickly past. This was *my* Safeway, the one

I went to once a week, and the other shoppers were afraid of me! I was still reeling from this realization when I also noticed that a different set of people were now acknowledging us: the normally serious young Latino workers (whom I now noticed had freshly laundered, carefully creased pants with their Safeway-issue shirts), now cracked small smiles and said, "Hey," recognizing distinction, semiotic care and its distance from necessity.

One guy started talking to Thelma and asked her if she liked Oldies, and pretty soon they were trading the names of their favorite songs. After more small talk, and talk about what schools they attended, the boy said, "So . . . what do you claim?" "Varrio Norte Fog City," said Thelma proudly, "And you?" "Varrio Norte Muirtown Locos," smiled the young guy. Just then a Euro-American security guard walked past and glared at me specifically. I was dying for him to ask me for my ID card.

Experiencing the reversal in the reactions that were elicited by my manipulated appearance, the frightened eyes of formerly friendly strangers, and the knowing, inclusive recognition of previously neutral others marked an important shift in my awareness of Norte and Sur. No longer were these gang affiliations abstract categories into which young people sorted themselves, they now implied embodied stances indexing what Sidney Mintz has called "webs of signification, that we as individuals spin [and which are] exceedingly small and fine [. . .] and for the most part reside within other webs of immense scale, surpassing single lives in time and space."[31]

What Do You Claim? A First Sketch of Norte and Sur

As in many other schools across the nation,[32] street gangs came to play a part in the social networks of all ethnic groups at Sor Juana High School. However, the definition of a "gang" by the police, by school administrators, and by members themselves is ever more inclusive. The term "gang member" sweeps in its wake everything from the hardcore incarcerated to the "wannabe's," groups of young people who participate in the symbolic display of gang culture (e.g., by writing gang slogans or graffiti on their school notebooks, or by wearing baggy clothes) but have little to do with any committed aspects of gang affiliation.

Although the Norte and Sur gangs respectively trace their history to the Nuestra Familia and Mexican Mafia gangs that developed in Southern California prisons as far back as 1958,[33] the connection between prison gangs and street youth gangs is tenuous, and in this particular geographic area the youth street gangs have evolved far from the original Northern/Southern California split that originally characterized the prison gangs. Norte and Sur today have come to stand as placeholders for an agglomeration of meanings, which I will broadly gloss as Chicana/o and Mexican for the present discussion. An extended development of these localistic concepts will be found in chapters 3 and 4.

In the setting of SJHS the concept of a gang as a small, closed group does not apply. Although *official* gang membership is restricted to a small group, inducted through a ritual process, many more youth participate in the oppositional dynamics of gang identity than are actual members of the gangs. Often the official members are indistinguishable from the unofficial wannabe's. The best analogy I can think of is that of rival soccer teams. On the one hand there are the actual players who are officially on the team, who have had to pass some sort of qualifying test to be on that team, are called out for games, and participate in the team decision-making process. On the other hand are the sports fans, sometimes passionately committed to the cause and who wear the team colors, team insignia, and occasionally participate in team-oriented activities. An outsider would never know the difference between a player and a fan if they were both wearing sports jerseys. Often what school officials and the police see as "gang fights" would be more aptly described as "fan fights."

Unlike previously described gangs, which are organized around concepts of territory[34] and capital flows,[35] the Norteñas and Sureñas (and their wannabe's) at SJHS were organized around ideology. Many discussions of ideology highlight the role of the state and institutional apparatuses in the creation and dissemination of top-down hegemonic norms,[36] so it is in a sense a bit ironic that the gangs – entities that are described by the ruling national classes of both Mexico and the US as operating against the interests of the state – invoke state-oriented discourses in their rationalizations.[37] Operating almost completely outside the boundaries of the Mexican nation-state (but not outside the pull of history and memory),[38] the young Norte and Sur gang members stand in conflict over issues of hemispheric localism, authenticity, race and phenotype, class, and the question of whether linguistic competence or allegiance determines group membership. These questions are at the heart of the conflict between Norte and Sur. As Jean and

Table 2.1 Indexical markers: endpoints on the continua of Norteña and Sureña identity

Name	*Norteñas*	*Sureñas*
Color	*Red, Burgundy*	*Blue, Navy*
Language	*English*	*Spanish*
Numbers	*XIV, 14, 4*	*XIII, 13, 3*
Music	*Motown Oldies*	*Banda Music*
Hairdo	*Feathered hair*	*Vertical ponytail*
Makeup	*Deep red lipstick*	*Brown lipstick*
Place	*Northern Hemisphere*	*Southern Hemisphere*

John Comaroff remind us, ". . . the ideologies of the subordinate may give expression to [the] discordant but hitherto voiceless experience of contradictions that a prevailing hegemony can no longer conceal."[39] Although the United States and Mexico may wish that gangs would go away, and denounce their existence in congressional hearings, it is youth gangs that are actively negotiating the contradictions of migration, language, globalization, and citizenship in the border regions between the "Global North" and the "Global South."

At risk of oversimplification I have laid out in Table 2.1 some common symbolic markers that Norteñas and Sureñas adopted to signal their identity. I'd like to emphasize that these were the generalizations I observed in the field, so they might be specific to the one high school and the particular moment of time in which the work was carried out.

It's important to note that the categories that are reified as separate endpoints on this table were on a continuum, so that it would be completely erroneous to state, for example, that Sureñas only spoke Spanish (in fact, chapters 8 and 9 provide an extended discussion of the linguistic patterns of native English-speaking Sureñas). Nonetheless, this tabular representation allows for the discussion of the broad contours of the conflict and some of the endpoints of stylistic play. Each gang adopted a symbolic color that members made their uniform, often wearing variations of that color in at least one article of clothing every day, and occasionally wearing entire outfits composed of the color. Issues around makeup as a symbolic display of gender and ethno-nationalist stance are discussed specifically in chapter 5.

The conflict between Norte and Sur was ideological and had place-indexical and nationalistic bases, so that the "North" became broadly symbolic of Chicanas, of the US, and of the Global North, and the "South" of Mexicans, of Mexico, and by extension of the Global South. Broadly allegorical and ideologically recursive,[40] concepts of "North" and "South" participated in entire webs of signification, tying language, race, class, ethnic nationalism, and a dynamic that I have called hemispheric localism which will be discussed in the following chapters.

As we saw from the discussion of Banda music in chapter 1, Sureñas placed great symbolic importance in keeping up with the latest popular culture developments in Mexico. Thus, they were great aficionadas of Banda music, a fast-paced type of polka which was the height of the *avant-garde* in Mexican rural areas. Not for them the urban, Western-oriented, creolized form of Mexican Rock music known as RNE – Rock en Español. Rock en Español was in their view associated with the wealthy Fresas of the Mexican megalopolises – reminiscent precisely of the type of color- and class-based oppression that many of them had fled in the first place.

Norteñas, for their part, had adopted as part of their symbolic capital a specific type of American music that they called "Oldies." Oldies were mostly drawn from the late 1950s and early 1960s recordings of mostly African-American artists and a few Latinos under the Motown label. Some of the songs included in this time period are "Angel Baby,"[41] "Duke of Earl,"[42] and "Lowrider,"[43] as well as many of the Doo-wop hits by artists such as The Platters, The Penguins, The Marvelettes, and The Lovelites, to name a few. The marked popularity among very young people of these older songs is an interesting phenomenon in itself: the songs demarcate the broader community of Chicanos. Oldies, though sung primarily by African-Americans, were Chicano music *par excellence*, closely identified with the main time period of the struggle of the Farm Worker Movement.[44] It was the music that Norteñas' mothers and grandmothers had listened to – thus the songs were gravid with meaning for Norteñas since they were active reminders of the continuity of Chicana history. This is not to say that these young people didn't listen to contemporary music – R&B and hip-hop were especially favored, and a group of Latina girls who called themselves "the Disco Girls" dedicated themselves wholeheartedly to following those developments (more on them and their language variation in chapters 8 and 9).

Norte and Sur organized themselves around concepts and displays of cultural identity. Newly arriving students were, by virtue of their Chicana or Mexican background, recruited by one or the other of the gangs, or merely asked where they stood in relation to the social structure by wannabe's and neutral observers. Gang members made use of the diverse cultural resources around them to construct oppositional identities. Norteñas and Sureñas each were associated with a color (red and blue, and various shades thereof, respectively); a number (14 and 13, often seen as XIII and XIV in graffiti, and originally referring to the alphabetical ordinality of the letters "M" (Mexican Mafia) and "N" (Nuestra Familia); a language (English and Spanish); and different ways of dressing, wearing makeup and hair, and, according to some students, even different ways of walking. In this setting, everything from the color of one's lipstick to the brand of one's sneakers became a symbolic act.

Along with outward markers of allegiance came attitudes that the group members held toward each other. Norteñas saw Sureñas as poor, unsophisticated newcomers who, according to one Norteña, "remind me of all the things I'm embarrassed of." Sureñas, on the other hand, saw Norteñas as overly Americanized, and hopelessly losing sight of what it might mean to be authentic, even to the degree that they no longer spoke good Spanish. In fights (and in passing, to provoke fights), the gangs drew on the racist discursive practices of their respective countries of orientation: Norteñas called Sureñas "wetbacks," "scraps," and told them to "go back to Mexico."

In many cases girls who considered themselves Sureñas overwhelmingly disidentified with English, since they viewed it as symbolic of Americanization, assimilation, and loss of Mexican-ness. As I've outlined in the case study of Güera in chapter 1, many of the Sureñas were native Chicana English speakers, but within their peer group they were dominant Spanish users. Rapid-fire Spanish (incomprehensible to language-shifted Norteñas) along with coded Spanish literacies and language games thus became symbolic of "Mexican pride." Sureñas' attitude ran directly counter to larger social expectations that immigrants would learn English, and was especially in conflict with school ESL programs which most of them attended.

Norteñas, on the other hand, identified with a Chicana-centered ideology that stressed their bilingualism and bicultural identity. Since the majority of them were born in the United States or had immigrated as young children, they were for the most part native English speakers. The dialect of English that they spoke, though, was Chicano English, markedly different from Standard English in phonology (pronunciation) and lexicon (vocabulary). These differences, which might sound to mainstream Euro-American interlocutors like a "Spanish accent," are in fact new patterns of an emerging ethnic dialect.[45] As we will see in chapter 9, the patterning of Chicano English phonology and discourse as used by core Norteñas and Sureñas closely follows historical trends in Old English, and parallels developments in many other dialects of English around the world. But usage is not the same as ideology, and that is one of the rich complexities of this sociolinguistic situation. While core Norteñas and Sureñas were quite nearly parallel in their linguistic behavior (as we will see in chapters 8 and 9), one would never know it from their proffered ideological stances toward language.

Young people I spoke to repeatedly pointed out the connection between language use and group identity. For instance, while talking on the phone to a Norteña, whom I will call Sad Eyes, she asked me if I had noticed that a newly arrived girl named Cristina was looking more like a *chola* (gang-identified girl) every day. Yes, I replied. Indeed, Cristina had been wearing darker lipstick and baggier pants as the school year progressed. "She wants to be jumped into Norte," reported Sad Eyes. "Oh yeah," I say, "How do you know that?" She matter-of-factly replied: "Her eyeliner's all the way out,[46] and the other day I sat around and talked to her and she was talking to me in English the whole time, you know." "Is that a sign, that she's talking to you in English?" "Hell, yeah," retorted Sad Eyes, "She just got here, too."

Norteñas and Sureñas continuously created alliances that established and reinforced their individual and group social identity. Both groups had distinctive creative pastimes, linguistic codes, and routine hangouts. And yet describing them in this typological and binary fashion makes the groups (and the girls) sound static and rather sterile. I'd like to introduce you to T-Rex, a girl who was a formidable presence in the high school, and who is one of the "key informants" for this entire book. She will resurface in most of the remaining chapters where I cite her words and follow her actions; eventually her speech joins that of other girls to illustrate the micro-patterning of sociolinguistic variation. It is to her articulation of a broad picture of Norte and Sur (and to her generosity) that I owe many of the understandings developed in this work.

Meeting an Icon: T-Rex (AKA: Trinidad, Trini) of the Norteñas

All around school people talked of T-Rex as the most "bad-ass" of the Norteñas. When Güera talked of her it was in a nervous bragadoccio that made me think she was bragging about something that wasn't exactly the truth. "Everyone thinks Trinidad is so tough. But she's afraid of me, ¿ves? *(you see?)*"

But with T-Rex an award-winning athlete who was lionized for ruthless fighting, I wasn't so sure I believed Güera. What I really wanted to do was interview T-Rex.

For a few days I asked the kids that came through the Activity Center whether they were friends with T-Rex or knew her. I was hoping for an introduction, since neither my personality nor the fact that she was a known gang member made it possible to have a casual, out of the blue encounter, or a cheery, American-style self-introductory handshake. Everyone I asked knew of her, or had heard rumors about her, or told me of fights that they had witnessed, but no one claimed to be close enough to her (or maybe not close enough to me) to introduce me. Finally one of the Piporros, Carlos, said he was good friends with her from pickup games of basketball in the neighborhood. Carlos was a Spanish-language dominant (ESL) student from rural Mexico, dark-skinned and with a close haircut and a Zacatecas accent. He wore blue almost every day, and hung around the Activity Center. He was shy and had a handsome face, and smiled protectively when talking about T-Rex in a way that hinted at a crush. I was surprised; most people had told me that Norteños wouldn't socialize with Piporros, and regarded them as a recruiting pool for Sureños, removed only by initiation. I eventually found that part of T-Rex's arsenal was the ability to cast a spell on allies and enemies, therapists and cops alike.

Carlos took me over to the principal's administrative office, where T-Rex was working that day. She greeted me sweetly. She had eyes the color of a fawn and was wearing a plain black T-shirt and red Nike sneakers with khaki Dickies pants, with a clean-scrubbed face that looked younger than her eighteen years, and long reddish hair with blond highlights. I asked if I could interview her and she agreed cheerfully to meet me Friday afternoon after school. She never turned up.

The following Wednesday I was sitting talking to students after finishing up tutoring and was about to leave. I headed out one door of the Activity Center, but then saw T-Rex coming in the other door, going straight to the head teacher with a question. I thought, maybe I'll just stay here for a minute. I decided to wait for her and pretend that I was coincidentally going out the same door as her and "bump" into her at the door.

She immediately recognized me and said, "Oh I'm sorry about Friday. I wound up skipping school." At least she had remembered me, she was thinking about Friday.

"Don't worry about it, it's OK."

Suddenly she surprised me by opening up, "I've been having a really bad day. I skipped class, and I'm mad at my boyfriend." She paused and asked me if I still wanted to do the interview, because she felt like talking to someone today.

"Can you stay, can you stay for my practice? And we can go somewhere, go eat something afterwards?"

"Yeah, sure," I said.

T-Rex was captain of the varsity basketball team, tall and powerful and with sharp aim for the basket, a record scorer for the school. The team was on a winning streak. She whipped up and down the court, all business, choreographing passes and shots from the floor. She had applied eyeliner between leaving her job in the principal's office and entering the basketball court. When I first saw it, the eyeliner looked to me a bit like Elizabeth Taylor in Cleopatra, but with a basketball uniform and high tops.

I shot some baskets with her after practice and then we took off in my car. The first thing she asked me was, "Do you write books or something?"

"Yeah, I have to do a big research project," I said nervously. I had been trying to get this interview for a while now, and was worried that I might botch it. "I am interested in Latinos and their groups in the school. You know, there's almost no research on Latino high-school groups, on how they get along, what groups are even there. We know a lot about language and teenagers in high schools, and almost nothing about groups of Latinos." After considering this for a moment, she agreed that it was important, and pointed out that only someone from the outside could do it, someone who was not from the neighborhood and wasn't down for any particular group. We talked a little bit about career aspirations. I wanted to teach and to write. She hadn't decided yet, but was leaning toward working as a parole officer. She was one of many kids who told me that they wanted to work in the criminal justice system. Somehow it was the flip-side of imaginable careers: to be in gangs or to be a cop. The thing that struck me the most is that she said, "I don't wanna be behind the counter at a Taco Bell. I want to be important. I want to have an office. Get phone calls." Getting phone calls meant you were important enough to be addressed at a distance, not across the counter of a service interaction.

As we drove down Industrial Way I suggested that we get some coffee at a bookstore café that I frequented. She had never been there, and started teasing me, "Coffee?? What the fuck? Coffee is for white girls!"

"What are you talking about? Coffee is originally from Mexico," I said.

"You're acting like a white girl!"

"Shut u-up!" I protested, suspecting that she might be right.

But she was in full clowning mode: "Oooooh, let's go drink coffee," she cooed affectedly, imitating a Generic White Girl. "Come on, Tiffany," she said, vivifying her imitation with reference to one of the varsity tennis players. She cracked herself up. "Coffee is what white girls drink."

"Well, don't your mom and your grandma drink coffee? They're Mexicans!"

"OK, never mind. You're right. Coffee is for white girls and for old people."

As we pulled into the underground parking lot of the bookstore cafe, T-Rex started telling me more about her background. She'd had a rough early childhood, growing up in Mexico with her grandmother, and then was sexually abused by an older male relative when she finally got to California. "THAT," she said, "is when T-Rex started to come out." In her mind, she had gone from a sweet seven-year-old named Trinidad in her pueblito *(small town)* in Jalisco, to become T-Rex, a nickname she chose because, as she said, Trini can be all cuddly and sweet, but if you make her mad T-Rex will come out and kill you.

I sat in the car with her in the darkness of the parking lot, and was heartbroken for that little girl in Mexico. I found T-Rex's immediate frankness both moving and confusing. She spoke of physical violence and past suicide attempts, of forgiveness and of incredible sadness and difficulty in her efforts to keep her family together despite its problems. A veteran of years of therapy, she had a well-developed sense of self and the psychoanalytic vocabulary with which to explain it. She seemed incredibly old. All I could do was listen. When we finally got hungry we went upstairs to the café, and T-Rex ordered a "Mexican flan," the only food listed on the menu that she thought she might like. I had a cappuccino and collected another round of teasing from her. As soon as we sat down, T-Rex acted nervous and edgy, raising her chin defensively as she looked around. She thought people, starting with the cashier, were mad-dogging (staring at) us and giving us attitude. And maybe they were. I just didn't really notice.

She insisted that we leave and go to Taco Bell, and when we were finally sitting down there she said to me. "You realize I could be jumped, at any time?"

"Yeah."

"You're not scared to be with me?"

"No."

"OK, well, you know, I just need to tell you, and you gotta promise me, that if anybody jumps me you're not gonna try to defend me. Promise that you're going to get in your car – walk away, and get in your car, and leave. Cause I'm gonna be O.K."

I looked down and didn't know what to say.

She continued, "Cause you – first punch you throw, you're involved. You don't wanna be involved in anything like that. So promise me. Es mi pedo. *(It's my business.)*"

She was testing me.

"Fine."

I continued, "T-Rex, you realize that I have to talk to the Sureñas too, I'm really in with them because I'm tutoring for ESL."

"Well yeah, but," she objected, "I get jealous about my friends some-times, I think. If I see you with Sureñas, I'm gonna be like – I'm gonna be mad. I might not be able to handle it . . . No, I mean, I know it's your work, as long as it's really special with me."

An Introduction to Clowning

Some time after I got clowned on (without even realizing it) for drink-ing coffee, T-Rex and I settled into occasional socializing. As with other girls, I interviewed her at home, on outings with her friends, and in public places, where she always looked around to make sure there were no Sureñas in sight. When there were, they would glare at each other and whisper to their friends, mostly without tangible outcomes. One day I wanted to take her for an activity somewhere else, since I was a little stressed from all the increased vigilance. I had arranged for us to attend a free women's film festival at UC Santa Cruz on a weeknight in February. T-Rex had been working at Target (where the parking lot was the neighborhood hangout) since Thanksgiving. She had made "friends with hella bitches," all of them older Norteñas, I was told over the phone, and she wanted to invite some of them to the movies with us. T-Rex had quickly risen to floor manager because of her people skills: she could motivate even the most deadbeat of employees, and despite her bad reputation (or perhaps because of it) she had a soft touch in asserting her managerial authority. She was sweet and girly-voiced in her commands, and didn't need to repeat herself. Things got done, full stop. Her street reputation preceded her, giving her the luxury of being saccharin and threatening at the same time. Additionally, she flitted attentively around customers and talked them into making durable goods purchases: refrigerators, lawnmowers, and washing machines were her favorites because the high profit margins boosted her bonuses. Apparently Target liked her too, they just kept promoting her.

The film festival was going to take place at 6 p.m. on the Santa Cruz campus, so we needed to leave plenty of time to drive down, park, and find the theater. I pulled up to Target and immediately spotted the girls: T-Rex the tallest, with her long mane of reddish-blond hair, and the other girls looking like smaller apprentices, five-foot one-inch T-Rexes in training wheels. T-Rex called shotgun and they piled in, filling up my Toyota Camry, which was decidedly not a chola-worthy car but on the plus side for them was at least burgundy. We cruised down the neighborhood and while I searched for the exit to the freeway they "threw" gang signs out the windows and yelled at passers-by, blowing kisses at teenage boys and making faces at the cops. I have no idea why we didn't get stopped. I was already rehearsing in my head what I would tell the officer.

Once on the freeway, the girls started telling bawdy jokes. I didn't know Paola and Mayté very well, but I did know Adriana, whose hands looked to me like a little girl's: short and chubby, with dimples where the knuckles were supposed to be. She was Mexican from her dad's side and Puerto Rican from her mom's, and shuttled between the East Coast and the West. Biculturally Latina, it seemed her policy to date only African-American boys. I think she was hoping to avoid anything that reminded her of her estranged dad.

All the girls had graduated from nearby high schools, and had been completely mainstreamed (no ESL, since they were all native speakers of English), and although they didn't know each other before starting at Target they quickly became partners in mischief. The whole way down to Santa Cruz they told bawdy jokes, razzing and clowning on each other.

Below is a transcription of the clowning-session in the car where T-Rex, Adriana and I are discussing Adriana's new boyfriend Habib:

T-Rex: You're a nasty bitch [bæč] Adriana.
Adriana: Let me just call him and then –
T-Rex: He didn't even call you back, he don't care.
           BITCH [biyač]
           Didn't I tell you? I said, I said, you **got** his number.
           I gave you fuckin' credit for getting his number
           All guys, you fuckin' beep[47] 'em once and that's it.
           You know how they fuckin' trip,
           Like, I got this bitch in check, you know?
           Fuckin' if you keep beeping them that means you're like,
           like you're on their nuts.
           You just beep them once and if they don't call back you say
           fuck it
           and don't ever fuckin' call them again.
Adriana: But he **didn't** call.
T-Rex: He **should** be fuckin' calling right away if he really cared,
           if he really cared about this bitch right here, but Habib just
           called her ass to say, Happy Valentine's Day, I wanna have
           sex.
Norma: Did he really say that to you?
Adriana: Nooo.
T-Rex: Yes he did!
           He said that she got too many pimples.
Adriana: He hasn't even seen me.
Norma: Look at me, **I** have so many pimples, and I am fuckin' twenty-
           four years old.
T-Rex: You know why? Because you bitches are horny bitches that's
           what you are.
           Do you two bitches see my face, and do I have any
           pimples?
           My boyfriend got the biggest dick
           just by seeing the motherfucker my pimples go tssshhhh
           they go out OK?
           my face comes clear OK?
           see, I got the special touch.
Norma: Right, they see him once and they go tsshhh, let's get out
           of here.
T-Rex: Whhhaaat? Bitch, don't try clowning me Norma, I'll fuck
           your shit up!

Affectionate banter, just beyond the line of unacceptable, was one possibility in girls' interactions with each other. Even my efforts to mitigate T-Rex's too-true report of Adriana's pimples were met with counter-banter about the similar state of my own face. Within the space of a single interaction, my understanding of the terms of it, and of clowning, was completely transformed. At the beginning of the interaction, I'm treading lightly, participating but concerned that T-Rex is clowning on Adriana, concerned that her feelings might get hurt. When I started this ethnography I was always worried about people's feelings. What I didn't quite get, despite an intellectual understanding of linguists' accounts of verbal art and speech play (where clowning is also called "ritual insults" or "playing the dozens"),[48] was that these ritual insults did not constitute an event where feelings would really be displayed, but rather display a skill of saying something outrageous, only to be topped by the next over-the-top move: a language game. I had tried to spare Adriana's feelings at the expense of interpellating myself into the discourse (where of course I got clowned on in passing, just for coming into that interactional space). First drawn in after the pimple remark, I clown back at T-Rex, contesting aggrandized claims that she has made about herself and doing it in clowning mode. Though not a particularly skillful clown, it's a clown nonetheless, and she recognizes it as such. When she play-threatens for a moment, "I'll fuck your shit up!," no one thinks for a minute, even in passing, that this might be an actual threat. By the end, all the participants have come closer to an understanding of what's at stake in the interaction, and a redefinition of terms: we could clown on each other. This was a pivotal moment in terms of my involvement in the girls' discourse.

The weather worsened as we drove down the swerving redwood-forested highway to Santa Cruz, and by the time we reached the campus it was almost completely dark from storm clouds. The girls were dressed in full gang regalia. Paola had a teardrop tattoo that made her look like she was wincing, plus she had the heart-shaped bordeaux lips, tiny tube top and baggy pants of a bad-ass Betty Boop. Mayté had her eyeliner all the way out and a hairsprayed helmet of hair that she didn't want to get wet, so she pulled Paola's black and red nylon 49ers jacket over her head. I lent my black dinner jacket to Paola and it hovered comically around her. We started wandering around without a map of the campus, and I approached a passing student to get directions. A preppy-looking undergrad politely offered to walk us to the theater. As soon as he did this and started making small talk with me, the girls fell several steps back. Before I knew it, they were giggling busily, whispering and calling out "OOoooOOOoooo." It took me a moment to realize that they were teasing/clowning on me, and that they thought I might be flirting with the guy. As he kept talking, I looked down and tried to conceal my urge to laugh. The girls started imitating the way we walked, holding hands and making kissing noises, mwah-mwah-mwah loudly with each other, and I think it was Adriana who yelled "Órale, homegirl!" Collegiate eyebrows were raised all around us. When we finally reached the theater and the stranger and I shook hands amid claps and squeals, he played to his audience and asked for my number. Ecstatic, the girls could hardly contain themselves and began evaluating every aspect of the stranger.

The movies were already playing, and we bumped our way into some seats in the back. What I had hoped would be a fun and cheap outing for the girls turned out to be only twenty minutes of short independent films, one of them an interracial Mexican/White lesbian romance. Afterward, the film-makers sat in a panel and took questions from the audience. Several starstruck UCSC students took the floor, and one after another asked interpretive questions about film technique, symbolism, and dénouement. Meanwhile the girls slumped in their seats, utterly bored and rolling their eyes. "Have you noticed we are like the ONLY Mexicans here?" said Mayté loudly. Suddenly T-Rex, who had been following the academic affair, had a question and flailed her arms until she was recognized. She stood straight up and in her most serious tone contributed to the discussion on nationalism and sexuality. "Hey, I just wanted to say that I'm Mexican and I don't think that her being Mexican and growing up strict has anything to do with being bisexual. She was just fucked up." The crowd was taken aback, not knowing whether to interpret the ambiguous remark as homophobic. "Well," the film-maker responded condescendingly from behind a black and white Mexican guayabera shirt, "the film's protagonist clearly made a concession in her sexuality for the sake of ethno-nationalism." T-Rex could tell that she wasn't getting a straightforward answer, and all her sensors screamed disrespect. "I'm going to get that bitch," she muttered when she sat down. "Trini, just chill out," I said. As soon as the presentation ended, I did my best to get the girls out of there before they had a chance to further consider how to jump the offending film rat. It's not a good idea to be rude to a group of rejection-sensitive gang girls.

"Let's go get something to eat," was my faux-cheerful suggestion. "I saw a Taco Bell on the way in." My deflection tactic worked. As we walked out of the theater into a dimly lit orange hallway we could see that it was both raining and sleeting outside on the wooded campus, with clumps of freezing rain collecting high on the redwood branches and dropping like eggs from above, splattering on the ground. We ran to the car, laughing as Adriana, Paola, and Mayté piled in one on top of the other in the back seat. They left the front empty for T-Rex. I sighed with relief – another narrow miss in the landscape of potential trouble – as I got behind the wheel. The girls, however, were just getting started.

As we drove down the hill leading out of campus, we saw a college student who was making his way down on foot. He must have gotten stuck in the sleet unexpectedly. As soon as we were within earshot, he whipped around and stuck his thumb out expectantly. "LOOK! A BABY-DOLL!" cried Adriana. And I thought: oh no, here we go. They started yelling: "He needs a ride! STOP, STOP, STOP," they all chanted. "But we don't have any room." "Oh, they'll just squeeze back there," said T-Rex from the front seat, and ordered everyone: "C'mon bitches, move your asses." We pulled over and as Pulpa sat on Adriana's lap the guy got in. They all squirmed until finally Pulpa was laying across everyone, with her head on the stunned-looking guy's lap. He was so grateful we had stopped that he just kept thanking us.

"Where you goin', babydoll?" said Mayté.

"Just to the bottom of the hill," said the guy. He was about twenty years old, tall and had a sopping wet muffin-cut of straight blond hair. Brown cords, boat shoes without socks and a heathered green sweater made him look a disheveled prep-school guy.

"Homeboy," T-Rex started, "This is my homegirl Paola, and that's my homegirl Mayté, my homegirl Adriana and my homegirl Norma. And I'm T-Rex." Her lilting Chicano English intonation left no doubt that she was the real thing. "Um. I- I- I'm Paul," he said uncomfortably. I could tell that he was a bit confused, not knowing quite what he had landed himself in. In a moment of extreme double consciousness, I could see us (me and the girls) as he might be seeing us: vaguely threatening strangers who weren't from around Santa Cruz. I could also see that the girls were innocently curious, doing nothing but joking and teasing him, exactly what they did anytime they met a "babydoll" (a cute guy). I wanted to reassure him, but was overcome with a laughing attack when T-Rex started a clowning session with, "Norma here likes college guys." She had decided to take the situation into clowning mode to loosen up the stranger. "Isn't that right Norma?" "Why you laughING?" She turned around, "Adriana, shut your legs!" T-Rex said, "It smells in here! Tell your *panocha* to shut up! Adriana here has a talkative pussy, it be talking back, it be clowning." By this time everyone in the back seat except Paul was in hysterics. Full clowning mode had taken over, and the next clown had to bring the house down. I had to focus on the driving because it was raining so hard, but I could see through the rearview mirror that the windows were steaming up from all the laughter, the bodies, and the talking in the back seat. "Hey Paul, do you have a girlfriend?," said Adriana. "Um, yeah," he answered hurriedly. "Is she good in bed? 'Cause I bet you never done it with a Mexican." Paul squirmed. "You go down on her?" "What?" he asked worriedly. "You like to go downtown?"

We had quickly reached the bottom of the hill and were entering Santa Cruz proper. "Oh, oh, you can drop me off right here!" said Paul. I pulled over to the side of the road and Paul hurriedly jumped out and scurried off into the rain. After he was swallowed by the darkness, Mayté humphed and whispered, "Well, he wasn't very polite." "Homeboy was uptiiiight!" "Nah-ah, he liked us!" chimed Paola.

After a short silence I said, "You guys scared him."

"We DID? You think WE SPOOKED HIM?"

I explained, "There's four of us and one of him. You shouldn't do stuff like that." The girls were genuinely surprised, and in the mirror I could see their faces, angelic once again, eyes flickering reflections of oncoming traffic lights. They looked at each other in disbelief. They were so disappointed and sad that Paul had left before getting to know them.

For weeks afterward I thought about this incident. I _felt_ as though I _had_ witnessed a momentous instance of cross-gender and cross-sub-cultural misrecognition, with the girls alternately seeming like playful pups stalking a terrified lizard, and then again like potty-mouths threatening an unsuspecting stranger who had never had female sexual joking jabbed in his direction. The speech mode was clearly clowning, but Paul had no idea what was going on, and may not have understood that it wasn't anything malicious (in contrast with the guy on campus who had walked us to the theater, and who had played along with the joke). And although I was more familiar with clowning, practicing it, reading linguistic accounts of it, I recognize it's still different and disorienting when it's directed at you. The interaction in the car happened so quickly that there was no time to say anything to Paul to reassure him. I was only left with trying to step back and practically scold the girls for the ritual insult routine of which I'd earlier been a part.

My guess is that Paul was thereafter suspicious of Latina girls. And who would blame him? He may have felt threatened. Maybe the incident motivated him to think that anyone with that kind of look or accent is unpredictable or scary. On the other hand, possibly the ribald nature of the jokes might have created or confirmed a stereotype in his mind of sexualized Latinas. Or perhaps he walked away from it, and was able to think of these girls as funny/outrageous. Or maybe he never thought about it again.

My analysis of these instances of clowning (the coffee clown, the zit clown, and Paul's clown) suggests that clowning, bragging, and braggadoccio, dependent as they are on shared frames between interlocutors ("a joke," or "a clown," or "language games where you ritually insult or verbally duel with progressively more outrageous and unbelievable claims"), are *precisely the kinds of speech routines that might lead to instances of misrecognition and stereotyping*. I recurrently witnessed braggadoccio taken seriously as "gang-related threats" by Sor Juana High School teachers. The different frames were impossible for me to reconcile that rainy day in Santa Cruz, and I felt a deep malaise both at Paul's reaction and at my scolding of the girls.

Notes

1   Villenas (1996: 715)
2   See Mendoza-Denton, R. (forthcoming) on stigma and Steele (2003) on stereotype threat.
3   Literally, "deceiving the ear."
4   A revealing example of how ethnographic confession can be received by colleagues is found in Nancy Scheper-Hughes' (1993) review of Ruth Behar's (1993) Translated Woman: Crossing the Border with Esperanza's Story. Scheper-Hughes states: "Ms. Behar is the mother confessor, a willing and nonjudgmental ear to the many slights and sins that Esperanza chooses to reveal . . . This obscurity is breached in the final chapter however, when the anthropologist steps forward to tell her own story of rage and redemption, attempting to link her biography with that of her subject . . . it is only through the redemption of a MacArthur fellowship that Ms. Behar can prove to herself and others that she, like Esperanza, is a force to be reckoned with. Beware the fury of a patronized woman!" (Scheper-Hughes 1993: A1)

5   As advanced by Mascia-Lees, Sharpe and Cohen (1989).
6   Gould (1996)
7   Fusco (1994)
8   Saatje Baartman was a Khoisan woman from South Africa who was born in 1789, then taken to England for "study" by European doctors fascinated with her sexual anatomy. She was displayed before medical and anthropological academics and was exhibited as a freak in fairs in England and France. Baartman died in 1815 at the age of twenty-six, and her dismembered remains were kept at the Musée de l'Homme in Paris until 2002. She is emblematic not only of European attitudes toward the sexuality of colonized female subjects, but also of the crimes perpetrated in the name of colonial anthropology and other "sciences." For an excellent documentary on Baartman's story and the return of her remains please see Maseko et al. (1998), Maseko and Smith (2003).
9   An argument made by Sawin (2002) for folklore and performance.
10 Augustine (1993)
11 Montaigne (1991)
12 Leibniz (1985)
13 Hegel (1996)
14 Moraga and Anzaldúa (1983), Anzaldúa (1987)
15 Spivak (1990), Alonso (1995), Boum (2006)
16 Kondo (1986), Lawless (1992), Jacobs-Huey (2006)
17 Patai (1994) coined this particular turn of phrase in an exasperated column in The Chronicle of Higher Education.
18 Dendritic economy describes the informal economy of decentralized migratory marketplaces that occurs mainly in colonial or postcolonial societies, with primarily vertical market chains (like branches of a tree), that limit sellers' price information. See Smith (1974).
19 Gal (1978)
20 Gumperz (1958), Gumperz (1971)
21 Haeri (1996)
22 Le Page and Tabouret-Keller (1985)
23 Eckert (1989), Foley (1990)
24 Manilow, Sussman, and Feldman (1978)
25 Gibson and Ogbu (1991), Portes and Rumbaut (1996), Gibson (1997)
26 Valdés (2001)
27 Abu Lughod (1991: 137)
28 Kondo (1986, 1990)
29 And so the castas reinscribe themselves in academia.
30 For a biography of César Chávez see Levy (1975)
31 Mintz (1985: 158)
32 Monti (1994), Bettie (2003)
33 Donovan (1993: 16)

34 Moore (1991)
35 Padilla (1992), Venkatesh and Levitt (2000)
36 Althusser (1971), Gramsci (1971), Williams (1977), Woolard and Schieffelin (1994), Philips (1998)
37 Louis Althusser's focus on ISAs – Ideological State Apparatuses (schools, churches, media, etc.) – as securing the reproduction of social formation (Althusser 1971) has found strong critiques, for instance Stuart Hall (1985) who writes that Althusser elides "the contradictory field of ideology, ideologies of resistance, of exclusion." (Hall 1985: 99).
38 Camarillo (1985)
39 Comaroff and Comaroff (1991: 25)
40 Gal and Irvine (2000)
41 Performed by Rosie and the Originals (1960).
42 Written and performed by Gene Chandler (1962).
43 Written and performed by War (1975).
44 Daniels (2002)
45 Santa Ana (1991), Fought (2003)
46 Having your eyeliner "all the way out" indicates a sweep of eyeliner that extends from the inner to the outer corner of the eye, all the way to the temple.
47 Beepers were popular in the 1990s as paging devices, prior to the ubiquity of cell phones.
48 Labov (1972a), Goodwin (1990), Morgan (1998)

CHAPTER 3

NORTE AND SUR: GOVERNMENT, SCHOOL, AND RESEARCH PERSPECTIVES

Stereotypes dominate the debate about gangs. The most popular stereotypes are those that emphasize the criminal tendencies of gangs and the social and personal pathology of gang members. This is no less true for academic criminology, because the leaders of the field have adopted the control ideology of criminal justice agencies.

Albert DiChiara and Russell Chabot[1]

Introduction

Research on gangs, especially on Latino gangs, has long espoused the conviction that gangs are a territorial phenomenon. Both in research and in the dominant public imaginary, "the barrio" has long been portrayed as very nearly synonymous with "gang turf." Like its semantic cousins "the ghetto" and "the projects," the barrio has been understood as primarily an urban spatial entity defined by poverty, danger, and social dysfunction among "ethnics," now Jewish, now Irish, now Italian, Black, or Latino, one succeeding the other,[2] depending on urban migration patterns. The barrio is imagined from the outside as an entity within the city where the centrifugal/centripetal processes of labor economics, having already cast off heavy industry to overseas locations and managerial workers to the suburbs, now engulf in poverty those that could not or would not be assimilated into "productive" citizenship. The barrio then becomes a kind of vortex, virtually inescapable for those who grew up there, ignored by authorities who refuse to invest in its infrastructure,[3] riddled with poverty, and salted with terrible schools leading to dead-end jobs that render its population multiply marginal and socially vulnerable:[4] an underclass. In the much-reviled but still present underclass framework, gang members are the stepchildren of the city, and gangs themselves are at best marginalized and malformed playgroups, at worst social tumbleweeds collecting adolescent and adult psychopaths. The flip-side of the barrio-danger portrayal, mostly present in the entertainment media, is that youth in street gangs symbolize the attraction of danger, of disorder, of rebellion, individualism, and nonconformity: a distinctively American longing for youth, for rebels, and for a cause.

This chapter is divided into two sections: A preamble notes the necessity of focusing on noncriminal aspects of gangs and challenges researchers to move away from traditional, criminality-oriented definitions pervasively presented by law enforcement agencies and scholars. The main body of this chapter is a selective synthesis of the published literature on gangs, specifically of concepts of localism and territoriality within the definition of the gang itself. These concepts are selectively drawn out of the gang literature in order to create the framework for understanding, in the next chapter, the complex and shifting ground in the concepts of Norte and Sur as they are employed by youth in discourse.

There are currently many and varied introductory texts on youth gangs in general,[5] including girls in gangs,[6] so I will refer the reader to those works for systematic reviews of the field. While in chapter 5 I directly address some of the claims in the literature on girl gangs, this chapter focuses on Latino gangs to provide the context for Norte and Sur. From the beginning then, as far as researchers are concerned, gangs have been about social control and deviance; about American migratory adaptation; about inner-city streets;[7] about the (multiply) "marginal man;"[8] about poverty and the "underclass;"[9] and about masculinity.[10] It is relatively recently that other aspects and locations of gangs have been studied: rural and suburban gangs,[11] non-violent gangs,[12] internationally structured gangs,[13] and female gangs[14] have started to come into focus. Comparisons with other groups not traditionally considered gangs have also emerged, as well as questions such as "Why aren't fraternities considered gangs?"[15] Political, civic, and pro-social activities of gangs have also just begun to be considered by Margarita Muñiz, Sudhir Venkatesh, Marie "Keta" Miranda, and David Brotherton and Luis Barrios,[16] as have other angles such as the historical dimensions of gangs.[17]

In the pages that follow, I define the concept of hemispheric localism and review the scant documentation on Norte and Sur, the gangs which are at the heart of this study and which are believed to have started in the prison system and then moved to the streets. In the process of moving out of the prison system they have become more akin to the "street political organizations" recently defined by David Brotherton and Luis Barrios:

> [A street political organization is] a group formed largely by youth and adults of a marginalized social class which aims to provide its members with a resistant identity, an opportunity to be individually and collectively empowered, a voice to speak back to the dominant culture, a refuge from the stresses and strains of barrio or ghetto life and a spiritual enclave within which its own sacred rituals can be generated and practiced.[18]

It is this conceptualization that I will take as an operational definition for the "gangs" in this study. Whereas American gangs of all ethnicities have been understood by public policy and theorized by scholars to be about physical territory or territorial control of capital flows, including the prison versions of Norte and Sur, the "street political organization" counterparts to these prison gangs in the Northern California Bay Area transcend these traditional definitions. Norte and Sur at the street level are groups who use concepts of territoriality to recognize power inequalities around them and who do battle over ideological positionings with respect to these conflicts. There is no suppletion in the discourse of young people: there is no abandonment of allegiance to the beloved "Varrio Norte" or "Varrio Sur," and its specific streets. What these youth have done is to take an already polysemous binary (Norte/Sur) and extend its meaning. Chapter 4 of this book documents the semantic shift of Norteño/Sureño from a primary denotation of territory to broader understandings by members as shown in discourse projected through concepts of language, race, class, and nation. This ideological projection, with its widening recursive repetitions,[19] functions as an interpretive framework that allows participants to invoke a global-hemispheric dimension. Members' concepts of the mission and purpose of the gang as a social organization respond to broader contextual pressures that include members' knowledge of Latino migration dynamics, their own gangs' internationalization, as well as their understandings of worldwide political relations. It is this ideological projection from young people's own condition, and their recognition of its embeddedness in and analogy to wider domains, that defines hemispheric localism and serves as a vehicle for the politicization of youth.

Preamble: A Focus on Gangs but Away from Crime

David Brotherton observes that although an interest in the criminal activities of gangs appears to be self-explanatory, a concern with anything else regarding them requires an explanation.[20] Why is it that scholars feel the need to *justify* exploring non-criminal aspects of gangs?

Albert DiChiara and Russell Chabot protest the focus on criminality, arguing that while such an emphasis might be useful for obtaining federal funding for research, it erases other aspects of gangs, especially the gang's grounding in the community, and "the gang's response to the social forces that negatively affect their community, sometimes in the form of positive activities and political activism, [. . . a] truly organic feature of the urban gang."[21] As we observed in chapter 2, definitions of gangs by the police and by teachers expand in widening circles, and throw a blanket of suspicion over minority youth who have very little to do with the criminally propelled concerns under the traditional definitions of gangs. At the same time, it is my contention that the Norteño/Sureño gang battles have emerged organically as on-the-ground responses to the preoccupations of everyday life for Latino youth in California – migration, class, citizenship, race, and language. It is precisely this definitional seepage in both directions (authorities are more willing than ever to label Latino kids; Norte and Sur are more than anyone else providing youth with a forum for political participation in the issues of the day) that results in the commonality, the *pedestrianization* of gang affiliation, and makes it imperative for researchers working with youth to shift their focus away from traditional, exclusively crime-oriented definitions of gangs.

State entities exercising de facto control over public ideologies routinely utilize and fund the research of scholars studying gangs. This is a mutually beneficial arrangement, judging by the citation boosts that academics receive in police and school documentation, and by their employment in the legal system and in government hearings as expert witnesses. Most central to what concerns of police are the dimensions of criminal activity among the gangs: quantitative documentation of the number of gangs, extent of violence, number of drug arrests, extent of underage sex and drinking, witness and victim intimidation, interstate commerce, extortion, racketeering, loan sharking, prostitution, etc.[22] These are the statistics that the police turn over to the government in their justification to fund police-work (the more dire and alarming the problem, the better the funding), and they are the same statistics that are routinely handled by the media and fuel ongoing "moral panics."[23] The overdramatization of the gang threat is acknowledged even by researchers who collaborate with the police;[24] a recent example from Tucson, Arizona is the doubling of the personnel and budget of the gang task force; in this case, funding was obtained based on the idea that the gang threat was increasing in *other* cities. A policeman interviewed on the nightly news said: "Tucson hasn't experienced an increase, but when it comes, we want to be ready!"[25] Pre-emptive strategies have a couple of different effects: on the one hand, in order to keep state and county-supported funding, police departments have to show results, busting youth and designating gangs based on whatever cohorting groups exist in the area (taggers, car clubs, etc.); on the other hand, increased police attention leads to competition for notoriety among youth who compete to break into top-ten "badass" lists.[26]

In order to better understand the criminal aspects of gangs, both researchers and the police engage in extensive mapping of gang territory;[27] in the decipherment of gang graffiti,[28] and even in its representation within police documents. An example of this is shown in Figure 3.1, from a stack of documents that was given to SJHS administrators in a gang prevention workshop conducted by the police. I've modified the handout to obscure the specifics of the police department and school district, but preserved the details of the drawings. If its purpose is utilitarian, we must ask ourselves: Why is street style so artfully copied? And what is the purpose of visually fixing young people in these illustrated police thesaurii?

Documents emanating from state-sponsored institutions are primarily aimed at controlling, tracking, and obliterating gangs; thus it may seem a quixotic enterprise to write a book about young people who claim to be in gangs and to believe that it does not contribute to the purpose of destroying them. One of the baseline decisions that I've made here is to avoid systematic documentation of police concerns – i.e., hard partying and status offenses such as running away that disproportionately impact girls.[29] It is sometimes difficult to divert the attention of (not so) well-meaning academics and journalists who operate from

Norteño 14	Original Pinoy	Crips	White Power
Bloods	Crips	Norteños	Sureños
Bloods	Crips	Sureño 13	Bloods

Figure 3.1 "Gang Signs:" Fog City Police Department handout to teachers.

their own stereotypes and really want to know: *Did they do drugs? What drugs? Did they have lots of sex? Is it true you have to have sex to get into a gang?* (The latter was dismissed as ludicrous in this and other studies interviewing girls directly.[30]) *Did they drink a lot? Did you participate?* (No. And this next one from a male mathematician:) *Can I hang out with you and some of those girls?* (Um. Hell no!) These are all the questions that I am *not* seeking to answer, though sometimes they are addressed in the interviews by participants who are well aware of the stereotypes surrounding gang youth.

It's not that I think that delinquent behaviors are irrelevant to my work on the nondelinquent aspects of gangs. Three factors temper any ethnographic impulse to exhaustively document: 1) as noted above, Latina and Latino youth already face profiling and increased suspicion at multiple levels, and there are few voices that balance the debate to refocus on what young people are saying, what their reasons and hopes are when they call themselves gang members; 2) a second concern is that I learned of the details of people's lives in a privileged fashion, with youth often begging me not to tell their teachers/parents/the cops, and I learned these details knowing that young people only signed off on consent forms because they honestly believed no consequence would come of it; and 3) research circulates publicly; it is altogether impossible to keep it out of the hands of the police, whose first step might well be chasing down identifiable gang members or scoping out identifiable locations. "We find 'em, we fix 'em, we fry 'em," was the motto of one police respondent to the National Gang Investigator Survey.[31] This book is my response in negotiating the trust that young people placed in me, and my attempt not to contribute to further pathologizing of youth or to the sexualization of young women of color. Am I participating in some sort of code of silence by not revealing their every last detail? Maybe. Am I avoiding young people's continued persecution by the police by spotlighting factors that have traditionally been of little interest to law enforcement? I hope so.

For the purposes of this chapter, and in order to provide necessary background to argue for the formation of new concepts of localism among the young Norteñas and Sureñas, I limit my examination to the documentation of existing dimensions of territoriality, specifically for US Latino gangs.

Localism and Territoriality in Gang Research

Localism in political science and sociology is understood as a valuation of the local (local organizations, local development, local space/time, and local commodities)[32] which stands in contradistinction to cosmopolitanism or globalism.[33] Localism can be conceived of attitudinally as a loyalty to one's local attachments, and behaviorally as a willingness to support and participate in the economic, social, and political affairs of one's locality.

Much research on gangs has understood them to be at the core about "defensive localism," where the loyalty aspect can take on a combative stance. Christopher Adamson explains:

> [Historically, t]he gang has performed important community functions which can be subsumed under the rubric of defensive localism. These functions include defense of territory, the policing of neighborhoods, the upholding of group honour, and the provision of economic, social, employment, welfare and recreational services.[34]

Defensive localism then is a gang's protective stance toward its capital, whether it be human, social/cultural, economic, or territorial. Such capital has traditionally been thought to be centered on the concepts of turf and neighborhood,[35] or on the protection of material exchanges taking place in a neighborhood, i.e., "drug turf,"[36] or prostitution rings.[37] Spatialized interpretations have their roots in the early sociological work on gangs within the human ecology paradigm which took as its main laboratory the city.[38] This paradigm tried to account for the lack of integration of underprivileged European immigrants and African-American internal migrants into American cities,[39] with one of the main emphases being the transmission of "Old World" ethnic gang traits to the "New World" gangs.[40] According to Fredrick Thrasher's 1927 study of 1,533 gangs in Chicago, "[Gangs] are one symptom of a type of disorganization that goes along with the breaking up of the immigrant's traditional social system without adequate assimilation to the new."[41]

These early localistic/territorial ideals in the literature have dictated "that gang members live in the territory they defend as their turf," so that according to Joan Moore, Diego Vigil and Robert García,[42] new theoretical explanations were needed in the 1980s just to account for "fictive residence," that is, membership in a neighborhood gang by a non-resident of the neighborhood.[43]

Malcolm Klein, in his book *The American Street Gang*, still considers territoriality as one of the "less controversial" definitional parameters to characterize gangs, though his definition of "street" admittedly goes beyond the merely territorial and is intriguingly meant to characterize the *practices* of gangs (hanging out on the streets of one's neighborhood more often than not without specific plans, just looking for excitement). In Klein's conceptualization, skinheads, white supremacists, bikers and lowriders are not really street gangs if they are "inside, working on their materials," or outside cruising purposefully on their rides.[44] Klein sees aimlessness, lack of employment opportunities, and an apolitical nature as a reason for gang youth being in the street in the first place, and predicts that this type of bored loitering is conducive to the gang halfheartedly indulging in "cafeteria-style crime – a little of this, a touch of that, two attempts at something else."[45] Research accounts that emphasize lack of "productivity," worrying about whether youth will be able or motivated to join the adult work world, raise some important issues regarding the influence of ambient adults in the lives of youth.

Youth Gangs and Their Adults, Yesterday and Today

Street gangs in the United States have been documented as far back as the founding days of the state,[46] observed in Philadelphia from the 1780s.[47] Fredrick Thrasher initially hypothesized that (white ethnic) gangs were a transitory, age-graded phenomenon that young people grew out of as they entered the world of work, and that (white) gangs would fight each other as their shifting residential patterns brought them into contact. A combination of intermarriage among the various white immigrant groups and defensive behavior against black migration contributed to the rise of interethnic white gangs which focused more on territorial defense and on attacking blacks than on attacking other whites on the basis of (Polish, Irish, Jewish) ethnicity.

There is an important difference between the traditional white gangs and contemporary minority gangs in terms of the pathways to adulthood: minority youth of today have few social parachutes to slow their fall if they should get in cafeteria-style trouble. Christopher Adamson documents and contrasts the history of European-American and African-American gangs, observing that white street gangs benefited from the patronage of adults, who would mobilize white youth not only for voting campaigns, but used them to forcibly maintain segregation by encouraging attacks on African-American migrants in the cities of the Eastern Seaboard and the Midwest.[48] Politically powerful adults in cities such as Chicago would sponsor gangs, contribute to their treasuries, and take members under their wing.[49] They might also lessen police crackdowns in exchange for some of the gang's profits.[50]

anomie

So embedded were the white youth gangs in Democratic machine politics and in power structures in Chicago that during the nineteenth and twentieth centuries a career in gangs could easily morph into one in politics: it did for Cook County Commissioner Frank Ragen (the founder of "Ragen's Colts" gang, whose motto was "hit me and you hit two thousand"),[51] as it did for longtime Chicago Mayor Richard J. Daley, at seventeen a member and at twenty-two president of the Irish-Catholic Hamburgs, a gang based out of the Hamburg Athletic Club which engaged in more brawls than sports. When he became mayor, Daley complained, "all the [police] ever wanted to do was hit you over the head . . ."[52,53]

Nonwhite gang members have never had developmental path into the structures of state power, even if they did exhibit an interest in politics. Political and civic action among African-American gangs include neighborhood protection services by the Black Sisters United in Chicago,[54] the Black Gangster Disciples' involvement in grass-roots organizing,[55] and the Vice-Lords' 1960s urban renewal programs.[56] David Brotherton and Luis Barrios[57] document the Almighty Latin King and Queen Nation (ALKQN)'s emerging political consciousness, their renunciation of violence and the role of religion. Less well documented are political activities of Chicano gangs, though John Donovan considers the Norteños to be a "stray branch of the Chicano movement."[58]

Chicano Gangs

Mexican-American youth gangs have radiated out of the epicenter of migration that is the Los Angeles/US–Mexico border region, and have certainly played a part in Los Angeles politics, most notably in the 1940s during the Zoot Suit Riots.[59] The most detailed studies of Mexican-American gangs in Southern California during the 1970s–80s were conducted by Diego Vigil and Joan Moore and their research teams. An anthropologist and a sociologist, they provided early models for conducting collaborative research with pintos *(Chicano prisoners)* and gang members,[60] models that have had a enduring impact and inspired the work of Irving Spergel, John Hagedorn, Marie "Keta" Miranda, David Brotherton and Luis Barrios.[61] Diego Vigil and Joan Moore concentrated on problems such as anomie, social reproduction, and the continuity of social order and disorder under societal strain theory.[62]

Mexican-American gangs provided Vigil and Moore with several counterexamples to Thrasher's classic[63] definition of gangs: 1) Mexican-American gangs were not a transitory phenomenon that youth left behind as they grew up. Many active members were in their thirties and forties, and there were generational continuities in gang membership that provided deep familial ties to barrios and to the politicized Chicano rights movements;[64] 2) Mexican-Americans were not becoming more assimilated, as Thrasher had predicated was the function of European ethnic gangs. Moore attributes this to visible phenotype differences and to racism and continuing residential segregation;[65] 3) Because of this residential segregation, lack of city investment in barrio infrastructure, continuing immigration and growing population density, there were structural barriers to employment opportunity that created general scarcity and overcrowding. Moore stresses that contemporary American gangs "are overwhelmingly Black and Hispanic youth. [. . .] when we talk about gangs we are talking about quasi-institutionalized structures within the poor minority communities."[66] In East LA, the targets for gang violence were often adjacent or newly arrived Mexican-American groups rather than groups of other ethnicities. Particularly significant for an understanding of Norte and Sur, these early studies help explain how gang dynamics were transformed from interethnic white rivalries in the nineteenth and early twentieth centuries to intraethnic rivalries today. These indications of conflict between long-established residents and newly arrived immigrants of the same ethnicity arise again and again with immigrant gangs (for instance, some accounts of the San Francisco Chinese gang Wah Ching attribute its formation to recent immigrants' formation of societies for protection against established Chinese-American residents).[67] Such conflicts presage the workings of the migratory-status divide between the Norte and Sur gangs, and help us understand how language, which in its variation serves to distinguish different immigrant generations, can become on the one hand a "gang identifier" for the police and on the other a source of and carrier for oppositional meanings within the gangs, as we will see in chapter 4.

Hemispheric Localism

The concept of *Hemispheric Localism*, coined here for the first time, should strike one as a bit of a paradox. If localism, especially defensive localism, is the valuation of the immediate community, and a group's propensity to defend it, then how can localism be hemispheric? I argue that hemispheric localism is a projection onto the hemispheric political stage of processes that began locally in the history of groups of Latinos in California, and that through processes of symbolic analogy and metonymy this meaning system becomes projected as a wider political analysis. Young people involved in Norte and Sur become political analysts (and actors), organizing their experience through the lens of their participation in these groups, synthesizing their understanding of the larger processes of race, language, capital structures, and global power relations, with increasingly larger ideological projections such that the "Global North" and the "Global South" become tangible and explainable. Young people, in other words, interpret, animate, take sides in, and make sense of global realities around them through the scope of Norte/Sur gang affiliations. These affiliations are positionalities both in the historical sense and in the perspectival sense: not only do gang groups display historical continuities in terms of group formation and political thought in the Mexican–US borderlands, but by "taking sides" as a Norteña/o or a Sureña/o, youth interpret and stancefully deal with the world around them. The young people we hear from in the next chapter had no problem deciding which new students had the potential to be a Norteño or Sureño, whether the newcomers were Salvadoran, Mexican, Indian, or Japanese. At each decision point, an organic/dynamic evaluation took place; I posit that these evaluations took the following factors into consideration:

1 language use;
2 language ideology;
3 perceived phenotype/race;
4 performative speech act (claiming);
5 country of origin;
6 perceived economic position;
7 social class prior to immigration; and
8 neighborhood residence.

These factors are not listed in order of importance, but they should give the reader an idea of the complexity of allegiances in what is traditionally understood as simply "neighborhood," or "turf" wars. The combination and differential weighting of these factors resulted for the young participants in broad ascriptions along the continuum of Norte and Sur. These evaluations structured relations of membership and even attributional understandings of world regions.

In order to explain in the next chapter how the complex combination of factors that I call hemispheric localism arises in the discourse of youth, I must first take us through the literature to explain the various kinds of localisms that different entities in the public sphere use to define Norte and Sur. Despite Sur having been the subject of a widespread moral panic in 2005,[68] there is not an extensive or even a modest literature on Norte and Sur Latino gangs, not even a single academic book aside from this one dedicated exclusively to the conflict. Nonetheless, the US government recently had hearings to evaluate the looming threat to national security that Norte and Sur might represent.

Norte and Sur: The Government, Police, Research, Community Perspectives

> *Mr. BURTON. You said there is no connection between al-Qaeda and any of these gangs, like MS-13. Can you tell us why you said that? There are a lot of people in this country that are concerned about the gangs in Central and South America working with terrorist groups that might want to do us ill.*
>
> *Hearing before the 109th US Congress, April 20, 2005*

In April of 2005, whipped partly by the fervor surrounding post 9–11 protection of the United States from foreign entities, the United States Congress held hearings on the Gang Deterrence and Community Protection Act of 2005 (HR1279), before the Subcommittee on Crime, Terrorism, and Homeland Security. Several gang experts were brought in, and this is part of the testimony that Congress heard:

> Gangs from California, particularly in the L.A. area, have a major influence on Mexican American and Central American gangs in this country and in Latin America. Hispanic gangs in California have separated into two rival factions, the Norteños, which are primarily found in the Northern California area, and Sureños, found to the South and predominantly in the urban areas surrounding L.A.
>
> A rivalry exists between these factions [...] most Hispanic gangs in California align themselves under the Norteños or the Sureños.

[. . .] Hispanic gangs aligned under the Norteños will generally add the number 14 after their gang number, those under the Sureños will generally add 13.[69]

A couple of months later, Congress held more hearings on gangs, this time to consider the Alien Gang Removal Act of 2005 (HR 2933), legislation that would allow for the immediate deportation of anyone who could be demonstrated to even associate with gang members. As part of the hearings, Congress heard the testimony of Michael Hathmon, staff counsel for the Federation for American Immigration Reform:

> When I was a young man in Southern California, the term 'Mexican street gang' more often meant a car club devoted to cruising rather than street racing. [. . .] This was a quintessentially American social phenomenon. A gang member may not have been college material, but a good auto body and upholstery worker didn't need a white-collar job to make a decent middle-class living. [. . .] The role of foreigners in the rise of criminal gangs is undeniable [. . .] this legislation responds to a dangerous vulnerability in public safety and can be feasibly integrated into our existing immigration regulatory scheme.

Although at the time of this writing in 2006, neither one of the 2005 congressional acts had passed (they seemed to have stalled at the hearing phase, pending other immigration reform), the proceedings in the first excerpt clearly portrayed the Norteño and Sureño gangs as not only territorially based *in* California, but as active exports *from* California in the first place. In the second excerpt gang members themselves are portrayed as having progressed historically from uneducated, benign nuisances who were nonetheless "quintessentially American" (so much so that one could wax nostalgically about how well they stayed in their place) to dangerous, subversive criminals whose ranks are fed by a continuous stream of immigration from outside America. The ominous refrain, "this is no longer West Side Story," is a recurrent one not only in government accounts of gangs but in police and media accounts as well.[70] Interestingly, this discursive move on the one hand attempts a break with romantic notions of gangs present in homegrown Americana; on the other hand it has the function of de-Americanizing Latino gang youth, rendering them discursively eligible for deportation, especially the Sureños as currently targeted through alien removal proposals affecting MS-13. By passing proposals that drastically lower the bar for gang identification (merely being seen in a photograph where others are throwing gang signs would render one a deportable gang member), scores of peripherally involved youth and others in the community are imbued with guilt by association.

As in other domains of discursive production of gangs, government hearings show that the Norte/Sur gangs are understood as both spatialized within California and simultaneously drawing upon elements coming from outside the body politic. By depicting young Sureños organized at the street level (defined to include minors as young as eleven, in HR 2933 above) as part of "dangerous" or even "terrorist" movements, government authorities run the risk of completely mischaracterizing the object of their intended description, so distorting them that they become monstrous and unrecognizable.

Compare the following statements on Norteños and Sureños, the first (a) by an educational ethnographer calmly describing the transnational cholo element in a high school near Sacramento, California; the other (b) by an expert witness (Paul Logli, president, National District Attorneys Association) who raises every level of alarm when called to testify at the congressional hearing for the Gang Deterrence and Community Protection Act of 2005, discussed above:

(a) "Chola/o refers to a Mexican-American street style that sometimes marks identification with gangs but *can merely mark racial/ethnic belonging* [emphasis mine . . .] there were two groupings of cholas/os which represented two gang affiliations: sureño (south) and norteño (north). The sureños tended to be immigrant students who primarily spoke Spanish, while the norteños tended to be second-generation Mexican-Americans whose primary language at school was English.[71]

(b) We know that we have come to look at stateless terrorists as our enemy and we're developing ways to stymie those attacks. And I would advance to you the theory that we are facing the same challenge and threats with the transnational gangs that are almost freely operating within our borders. In my jurisdiction, we have recently seen an increase of Hispanic or Latino gangs that are now engaging in the typical turf wars [. . .][72]

Are these two statements really talking about the same thing? Clearly we would want to distinguish Latino gangs as a form of "ethnic belonging" from claims of "stateless terrorism," but the criteria for gang identification for youth gangs and prison gangs are one and the same at the level of the government and the police.

The California Police Perspective on Youth

In my dealings with Sor Juana High School teachers and school counselors, I encountered copious evidence that materials distributed to teachers in the mid-1990s by law enforcement authorities all over California routinely tied language and immigration status specifically to the targeted identification of minority youth as gang members, and the portrayal of immigrant families as potential incubators of gangs and criminal activity. In a pamphlet entitled "GANGS: Keep them out of your community!" risk factors listed as contributing to gang-involvement include not only "low individual self-esteem," but also "coming from a Limited-English speaking home."[73]

In support of a report called "Gangs 2000," widely distributed to police departments, schools, and teacher associations in California, the California Department of Justice, Bureau of Investigation reports its distribution of a questionnaire to 105 criminal-justice agencies in California with gang units.[74] One of the questions asked of these criminal-justice agencies was: "What do you believe is the biggest contributor to the street gang problem in California?" Among the top answers: "Immigrants experiencing a new culture and language difficulties."[75] Additionally, in the same document, it is reported that an expert panel was convened composed of representatives from police and sheriff's departments, probation departments, the California Youth Authority, crime prevention units, and the school system. Panelists were asked to identify emerging events for the purpose of forecasting gang trends. The two events having the largest cross-impact in the expert panelists' perception of criminal street gangs in California were: "(1) the non-white population [of California] exceeding 50 percent; and (2) the immigration quota changes [referring to the Immigration Act of 1990 which raised the ceiling of the total number of immigrants per year]."[76] California officials and authorities in this government document explicitly point to the "non-white" population and to immigrants (and their cultural and linguistic characteristics) as being the most important factors in the presence of gangs. The fact that these documents are distributed as required reading to teachers all over the public school system, from the elementary grades all the way through high school – teachers are encouraged to act as informants and evidence-gatherers for the police[77] – means that immigrant and other minority youth face the high burden of being stereotyped as a potential gang member even before setting foot in the school. If Norte and Sur youth gangs are indeed street political organizations as I claim, or just mark "racial or ethnic belonging" as per Julie Beattie's understanding,[78] the teachers would never know, given the official documents that muscle their way to their desks. All that a teacher would know before meeting a child or youth is: if this child is Latina/o, if this child is an immigrant, and if their family speaks a language other than English, they might be in a gang. That's quite a way to start the school year.

Below is one more example, my reproduction of materials police used in 1996 to conduct a training session with teachers at Sor Juana High School:

YOUTH GANGS OPERATING IN FOG CITY:

A. VARRIO NORTE

Characteristics:
* Claim color Red
* Male Hispanics
* Roman Numeral XIV

B. SUREÑOS

Characteristics:
* Claim color Blue
* Male Hispanics
* Roman Numeral XIII
* Recent immigrants from Mexico

C. TUNAY NA PINOY (TNP)

Characteristics
* Male Filipino
* Claim color Blue in most areas
* Generally Drive Toyota, Datsun, or Honda Civic two door cars.

In these materials we see that recent-immigrant status *does* appear in the description of Sureños, but not language (though presumably Spanish dominance would be an entailment of recent immigrant status). In the Tunay Na Pinoy (Filipino) gang description, merely driving a two-door Toyota, Datsun, or Honda Civic becomes a possible gang identifier! Other documents identify hairnets, white t–shirts, Dickies pants, and other truly ubiquitous clothing items as "gang identifiers," but given the wide imitation and circulation of youth styles across different subcultures, these identifiers wind up serving as convenient handles for the police and pretexts for the uneven application of clothing standards to some youth and not others,[79] both on and off school premises. Many parents needlessly worry that their children might be endangered by wearing a specific color to school. I try to assuage parents' fears by telling them that if their children do not participate in the symbolic system of gang membership to begin with, then wearing a red jacket, for instance, will not put them in danger (although, as we can see above, this appears to be the diagnostic for gang membership that school administrators and the police apply). In order to be "mistaken" for a gang member by other members, their child would have to follow highly stylized rules of speech, hair, makeup, style of clothing, and even have a certain gait, in which case there wouldn't be much of a "mistake." Since the colors are only secondary characteristics, this is also why certain schools' policies of adopting school uniforms to combat gang membership make very little sense. Any element, even within the confines of a uniform, can be turned into a symbolic marker, and these will shift within the community of members faster than parents or the police can ever track them.

Carlos, the boy who had a crush on T-Rex, was once stopped by the police for a random search because he was wearing a white t-shirt and slicked-back hair under a hairnet. When they couldn't find anything on him except for his wallet attached to his belt loop with a chain, they busted him for carrying a weapon: the chain, they claimed, could be used to strangle someone. Carlos was let go with a warning, but he felt humiliated in front of his family, who relied on him for income. The reason he had attached his wallet to his body, he told me, was because he kept losing it on the bus.

Another glaring characteristic of the material presented above is that, in the mid–1990s, girls were mostly excluded from the descriptions. In the late 1990s, it was even difficult for many police departments to classify girls as potential gang members or to identify girl cliques because working definitions of possible gang members excluded girls as a matter of policy.[80] Nowadays this gap in the research has begun to be addressed,[81] highlighting some of the special issues facing girls involved in gang membership.

The Gang Research Perspective

The documentation of Norte and Sur at the street level is where research is the scarcest. In the many reviews of gang research, the Norte/Sur dynamic is barely mentioned, and usually subsumed under the older Nuestra Familia/Mexican Mafia (I abbreviate these as NF/MM, but they are also called "La Ene" and "La Eme") prison gangs, obscuring the pervasiveness and different orientation of the younger street component. Information is especially lacking on street-organized Sureños, while narratives of former convicts suggest that the Mexican Mafia explicitly envisioned its structure as similar to the Sicilian Mafia. Gus Frias in particular draws out the purported embodied similarities between La Eme and its Sicilian counterpart: "Their interpersonal skills manifest a restraint with gestures [and] a sparse use of words . . ."[82] This sparse use of words will become important as we examine mechanisms of memory in later chapters.

John Donovan's is one of the only accounts to discuss the history of the Norte/Sur rivalries, based on anonymous Norteño manifestos found within the California Youth Authority and in the prison system in 1985.[83] Donovan calls NF and MM "supergangs."[84] Donovan traces the tripartite influence of Nuestra Familia, the Chicano Rights movement, and the pinto *(prisoner)* self-help movement in the concretization of Norte. I would add as an important factor the role that correctional institute administrative decisions to separate inmates by north/south regional provenance within California had on the creation and strengthening of these regional superstructures.

Nuestra Familia got started circa 1967 in the California Youth Authority's correctional facility in Tracy, California,[85] where the Mexican Mafia had already formed by 1958.[86] Mexican Mafia members, who were mostly leaders of gangs already existing in the Maravilla barrios of LA, began to opportunistically target rural youth whom they derisively called "farmers" or "hicks."[87] The vulnerable youths banded together as a "defensive reaction" to form Nuestra Familia.[88] History is retained in the appellations: "farmer" today circulates not as an insult but as an in-group address term, an emblem of pride used by young Norteños explicitly linking themselves to the Chicano farm workers' movement.

What started as urban–rural animosity between inmates was puzzling to and mishandled by prison officials.[89] As the conflict worsened, and while facing a space shortage due to skyrocketing minority incarceration rates, correctional authorities made the fateful decision, purportedly for the safety of vulnerable inmates,[90] to institute a policy of separating convicts *by the region that they came from within California*. This geographic sorting for the sake of disciplinary hygiene and effective surveillance not only had the effect of recognizing and bolstering the emerging North/South territorial division, but effectively spread this spatial consciousness to the far corners of the California correctional system where, through continuous sorting by the system itself, the now-entrenched NF and MM were provided with a steady supply of new members. By 1978, Nuestra Familia, the Mexican Mafia, the Aryan Brotherhood and the Black Guerrilla Family were the largest and most influential gangs in California prisons, with La Eme being by far the oldest and largest.

Nuestra Familia, which has from its very beginning left behind documentation pointing to it as an extraordinarily literate and education-oriented gang,[91] took the bull by the horns to address the lack of education of its incoming inmates by instituting an educational structure within the prison system where better-educated inmates were assigned to tutor other *familianos*, teaching them literacy and numeracy, and assigning to them works such as Marx's *Das Kapital*.[92] A confiscated document of Nuestra Familia from San Joaquin Valley in the 1970s indicates that "Schooling is mandatory and will be done daily [. . .] with the exception of Sundays and Holidays. Tests will be given every Friday by the schooling department."[93] Political writings and strategies for consciousness-raising have also been documented.

By 1985, the Norte and Sur youth counterparts of NF and MM were no longer straightforwardly doing the bidding of the older inmates: "young Hispanics are thinking more in terms of their own ideas rather than aligning themselves with the older organizations," claimed a Federal Department of Justice report.[94] This is evident in the anonymous Norteño manifesto discussed by Donovan: "Nuestra Raza's future behind the walls [depends on the will] to adopt new and more meaningful and fulfilling ideals . . . [we shall] learn to function . . . as working, contributing individual[s], vital to the day to day success of the whole society . . . [Our goals are . . .] advancement towards equal justice . . . [and] aiding those of latin descent *and other minority groups.*"[95]

Donovan identifies as significant in the creation of the Norteños the politicization across the country of persons of Mexican descent that the

Chicano civil rights movement sparked. This politicization becomes essential, as we will see in the next chapter, for the development of hemispheric localism, which recognizes injustice in both transnational and domestic power structures. The Norteño manifesto excerpt above provides evidence of an emerging political consciousness, as well as the recognition of the similarity between the plight of Chicanos and the condition of other minority groups. Aztlán (the mythical homeland of Chicanos), Aztec symbols, and the iconography of the United Farm Workers movement continue to provide potent semiotic resources in both Norteño and Sureño art; the UFW eagle has specifically been adopted by Norteños and is present throughout Norteño websites on the internet. *Teen Angels* magazine, which publishes art, photos, and poetry by inmates in the correctional system, is replete with Aztec/Catholic religious and cholo iconography that has also now boomeranged out not only to the streets but to the malls as well. Available for purchase at the corner store and at such mass chains as Urban Outfitters in many urban areas are yesterday's gang icons. "Jesus is my homie," proclaims a t-shirt usually worn by Christian students and subversive hipsters, with a decidedly Chicano-art-inspired drawing on the front. Ironically, none of them ever get stopped by the police.

A Description from Within the Community

One of the most articulate, and in my view, accurate, descriptions of the Norteño–Sureño dynamic on the street level that I have seen comes not from the police, Congress, or academic research, but from a community writer for an online magazine called *De-Bug: The Online Magazine of the South Bay*. In mid-2005, contributor David Madrid published an article questioning the San Jose Police Department's crackdown on merchants selling gang clothing, arguing that targeting the ubiquitous symbols worn by gang and non-gang youth alike completely missed the mark and ignored the underlying social dynamic in the community. I believe the following extended excerpt from his article portrays a valuable perspective: that of local community activists who are not employed by the police but who work on outreach with youth:

> Contrary to the City's understanding, the escalating San Jose gang problem is not about colors, but rather is an ideological clash that meets on

the streets. The conflict is ultimately between U.S. born Chicanos vs. newly immigrated Mexicans. And since immigration will only be increasing in San Jose in the future, city policies towards solving the "gang issue" must address this root cause tension.

On the streets, the conflict is understood as being between the "North" (Chicanos wearing red) and the "South" (immigrants wearing blue). [. . .] Chicanos see themselves fighting to protect their neighborhoods from an invading immigrant force. In my neighborhood, I hear anger from Norteños who claim, "Our City is being infested." They feel compelled to "exterminate." Blue, immigrant Latinos, see their identity as being about the Mexican struggle, one facing discrimination in the U.S., even by Chicanos.

The North vs. South belief system affects all Latinos in these gang-dominated neighborhoods. Youth get labeled, whether or not they are affiliated. It's even common to hear non-gang members use the derogatory terms [. . .] to describe the rival gangs of their neighborhoods or social crowd. The ideology of Northern or Southern supremacy has become a common form of discrimination among Latinos here in San Jose.[96]

In the introduction to this chapter I mentioned that Norte and Sur were more like street organizations as proposed by David Brotherton. Although Norte and Sur in my estimation have not gone as far as to foreswear partying like the Almighty Latin King and Queen Nation as described by Brotherton and Barrios,[97] some of the evidence presented in this chapter points to increasing politicization and engagement by Norteños and Sureños with a broader vision of what their intentional communities might be about.

The following chapter relies heavily on exact transcriptions of my face-to-face interviews with young people claiming Norte and Sur. I analyze coexisting and conflicting discourses produced by different members when asked how Norte and Sur might be defined and distinguished. This analysis reveals not only that multiple semiotic referents are invoked when a member claims Norte or Sur, but also shows that young people categorize social phenomena around them and interpret them through the prism of the Norte/Sur opposition.

Notes

1   DiChiara and Chabot (2003: 77)
2   Thrasher (1927)
3   Moore (1991), Acuña (1996), Villa (2000)

4   Vigil (1988)
5   Cummings and Monti (1993), Yablonsky (1997), Huff (2002), Vigil (2002), Covey (2003), Short and Hughes (2006)
6   Burris-Kitchen (1997), Chesney-Lind and Hagedorn (1999)
7   Sánchez-Jankowski (1991)
8   Park (1928), Vigil (1988)
9   Vigil (1988), Auletta (1982)
10 Erlanger (1979), Vigil (1988), Yablonsky (1997), Mirandé (1998), Smith (2005)
11 Monti (1994)
12 Barrios (2003)
13 Hazlehurst and Hazlehurst (1998), Duffy and Gillig (2004)
14 Quicker (1983), Campbell (1984), Campbell (1987), Portillos (1999), Taylor (1993), Joe and Chesney-Lind (1995), Mendoza-Denton (1996), Joe-Laidler and Hunt (1997), Miller and Brunson (2000), Joe-Laidler and Hunt (2001), Hunt and Joe-Laidler (2001), Miller (2001), Hunt, Joe-Laidler and Evans (2002), Miranda (2003), Shalet et al. (2003), Hunt, Joe-Laidler and Mackenzie (2005)
15 Sanday (1990), Mendoza-Denton (1996)
16 Muniz (1993), Venkatesh (2000), Miranda (2003), Brotherton and Barrios (2004)
17 See for instance Rawlings (1999) on the "lawlessness of reckless youths" in 502 BC Rome. See also Hopwood (1999).
18 Brotherton and Barrios (2004: 23)
19 Irvine and Gal (2000)
20 Brotherton (2003)
21 DiChiara and Chabot (2003: 78)
22 Curry and Spergel (1988), Curry and Spergel (1992), Esbensen and Huizinga (1993), Chesney-Lind, Shelden and Joe (1996), Laidler and Hunt (1997), Fleisher (1998), Hunt, Joe-Laidler and Mackenzie (2000), Cepeda and Valdez (2003), Fleisher and Krienert (2004)
23 Cohen (1972), Lucas (1998), McCorkle and Miethe (2002)
24 Klein (1995)
25 KOLD News 13, Tucson Arizona (2006)
26 Vallaraigosa (2007), Winton and McGreevy (2007a), Winton and McGreevy (2007b)
27 Moore, Vigil and García (1983: 185), Donovan (1993), Klein (1995)
28 Hilliard (1983), Phillips (1999)
29 Chesney-Lind (1993)
30 Moore and Hagedorn (2001)
31 Klein (1995)
32 i.e., the local food movement
33 Gouldner (1957), Ritzer (2003)

34 Adamson (2000: 273)
35 See for instance, Klein (1968), Stumphauzer et al. (1977), Erlanger (1979), Moore, Vigil and García (1983).
36 Padilla (1992), Venkatesh (2000)
37 Klein (1995)
38 Thomas, Park and Miller (1921), Park (1952)
39 Venkatesh (2003)
40 Thomas and Znaniecki (1920)
41 Thrasher (1927: 217)
42 Moore, Vigil and García (1983:182)
43 But see Adams and Winter (1997) for a discourse-centered approach to graffiti.
44 Klein (1995: 23)
45 Klein (1995: 22)
46 Haskins (1974), Espinoza (1984)
47 Meranze (1966)
48 Adamson (2000)
49 Thrasher (1927), Cohen and Taylor (2000)
50 Adamson (2000)
51 Willrich (2003)
52 Cohen and Taylor (2000: 120)
53 As a peripheral participant living inside American college fraternities in two separate institutions more than twenty years apart – Johns Hopkins 1987 and MIT 2004 – I can attest to the indulgence with which delinquent behavior by fraternity brothers was treated by the sponsoring elders, many of whom were politically powerful figures who had belonged to the frat and served up current "frat brothers" their first jobs. The white gangs of the 1920s can be thought to have on the one hand turned into the racist skinheads of today, and on the other morphed into some of today's college fraternities, complete with secret, sometimes violent initiation rites, group-sponsored racism and sexism, delinquent behavior, and indulgent attitudes from adults around them.
54 Venkatesh (1998)
55 Hagedorn (2007)
56 Dawley (1973)
57 Brotherton and Barrios (2004)
58 Donovan (1992: 35)
59 Rioting started June 3, 1943 and lasted several days. See Leonard (2006).
60 Moore (1978), Moore and Vigil (1993)
61 Hagedorn (1988), Spergel (1990), Miranda (2003), Brotherton and Barrios (2004)
62 Merton (1938), Merton (1949), Moore and Vigil (1993)
63 Thrasher (1927)

64 See Moore (1978).
65 Moore (1991)
66 Moore (1991: 6)
67 Lee (1999)
68 Especially Marasalvatrucha 13, MS-13, the Salvadoran Sureños, discussed in 109th Congress, Hearing on Gangs and Crime in Latin America.
69 United States Government, 109th Congress, Hearing on HR 1279 (2005: 25)
70 Klein (2006)
71 Bettie (2003: 14)
72 United States Government, 109th Congress, Hearing on HR 2933 (2005: 18)
73 Northern California Gang Investigators Association: Undated, circulated ca. 1993 (1993: 3)
74 California Department of Justice (1995)
75 ibid. (57–58)
76 ibid. (63)
77 California Department of Justice (1995)
78 Bettie (2003)
79 As in the proposal made in 2006 in Tucson, Arizona by Naylor Middle School administration that only Latino children should wear uniforms. Arizona Department of Education (2007)
80 Curry, Ball, and Fox (1994), Curry (1998)
81 Mendoza-Denton (1996), Mendoza-Denton (1997), Brotherton and Salazar-Atias (2003), Miranda (2003), Nurge (2003), Chesney-Lind and Pasko (2004), among others.
82 Frias (1989: 69)
83 Donovan (1992)
84 Frias (1989) and Mendoza (2005), two *veterano* leaders of la Eme, similarly stress their status as supersets by calling them "gangs of gangs."
85 Khan (1978), Donovan (1992)
86 Frias (1989), Mendoza (2005)
87 Donovan (1992)
88 Khan (1978)
89 Donovan (1992: 32)
90 Khan (1978: 66)
91 Khan (1978: 37), Cummins p.c.
92 Cummins p.c.
93 Khan (1978: Appendix F)
94 Federal Department of Justice Report (1985: 92–4)
95 Anonymous B, ca. 1985, cited in Donovan (1992: 30–3), emphasis mine.
96 Madrid (2006: 1–2)
97 Brotherton and Barrios (2004)

CHAPTER 4

HEMISPHERIC LOCALISM: LANGUAGE, RACIALIZED NATIONALISM, AND THE POLITICIZATION OF YOUTH

> NORMA: *What does it mean to claim?*
> T-REX: *You claim your barrio*
> *You claim your hood,*
> *You claim your boyfriend*
> *You claim something that is yours.*
> *That is really valuable to you.*
> *(CGN side B: 8:00)*

One of the boys I met in the tutorial center was a real math and soc-cer wizard. He would drop by unannounced between pickup games and classes and help his friends with their math homework, since he was in the highest level of calculus that was offered at SJHS. He was a Sureño whose true name I never knew. His moniker was Junior, a name that implied that he had been someone's protégé within the struc-ture of the gang, or that he had started especially young, or maybe someone along the way thought he had a babyface. Everyone called him Junior, even the teachers. With his help the Sureños had been get-ting pretty good at math before I arrived on campus that fall. And although he liked math better than any other subject and did well in class, it was the only class he was taking that counted toward college entrance requirements. He was in English as a Second Language classes the rest of the day, in bilingual US history and bilingual World Studies, and his elective was auto mechanics. All of these counted as credits toward graduation but not toward college entrance requirements, so no matter how brilliantly he did in calculus, and he did, he would not go straight to college. My guess is that's why he wasn't signed up to take the

Advanced Placement Calculus test, the standardized instrument designed for giving advanced American high school students college credit.

When Junior saw that I was becoming a regular at Spanish-language math tutoring, he took a cautious interest in me and we became math buddies. We would sit together at one table and tutor whoever needed help, sometimes coming up with different ways of solving the same equations. He would teach me calculus vocabulary in Spanish (which I needed because I had left Mexico right after the sixth grade), and the latest ways to solve equations from Mexico City, contrasting them with how equations were solved in the US. Who knew that there were distinctive "math dialects" across countries? We would race to see who could come up with a solution first in their own dialect (mine a patchwork of US and Thai math methods), and when there were no delinquent equations to solve we'd play math or logic games.

Junior had been in the US only for a couple of years before I met him, arriving at sixteen from Mexico City (known by Mexicans as the DF, short for *Distrito Federal*), so he was a Chilango like me. People from other states in the republic sometimes badmouth Chilangos, make fun of the DF accent, our distinctive intonation, and say that we are snobs. Because Mexico is such a centralized country (more than one-fifth of Mexicans live in greater Mexico City), the DF is a symbol for the unequal relations between the core and the periphery of the Mexican state. At about 20 million (the third largest urb in the world),[1] the DF is both a terminus for in-migration and a site for all that is associated with overpopulation: pollution, chaos, and glaring inequalities. But being with a fellow Chilango gives you license to criticize: you make fun of the same places, you know the same streets and love the city for all its flaws. Junior was just five years younger than I was, so we even listened to much of the same music. I imagined that he and I were *both* really from DF, even though I hadn't actually lived there for the latter half of my life and doubted my own claim to membership. He was from a neighborhood not too far from where my parents were living, and this made me curious about him: he'd grown up in the same place as I would have, if I'd stayed. I wanted to know how he became a Sureño. At first we never talked about it, and just focused on the math.

One day in the tutorial center, in a lull between math games and trigonometry, I gathered the nerve to tell Junior about my research project. I was always anxious during that initial moment of disclosure, worried that students would think I'd had an ulterior motive for befriending or tutoring them all along, or that they would perceive me as aligned with the teachers or even with the police. I remember thinking that they might have encountered researchers before, academics who might have come and gone at a time when children, especially immigrant children with so few advocates, needed someone stable in their lives. The school was close to several public and private universities, and I worried more globally: maybe the Latino community had had enough of being experimental/ethnographic/linguistic subjects. A colleague, Silvio Torres-Saillant, once put it most succinctly to me when explaining his qualms about the anthropological enterprise and its relation to colonialism: "Don't put me under a microscope. Don't study in me what you wouldn't study in yourself."

Junior reassured me that I had a good project that was interesting to him. This felt like an odd reversal, him patiently reassuring me while he signed bilingual consent forms in triplicate, but I also appreciated it, especially coming from a participant. He was one of the few young people in this study who was a legal adult and could sign his own consent forms (minors had assent forms but legal consent came from their parents). We soon scheduled an interview outside of our shared study-hall mentoring duties, outside of the main stage of the school altogether, so that instead of sitting in the center courtyard where both Sureños and Norteños might walk by, we sat on the lawn behind the music building, briefly shielded from the noise of passers-by. At some point T-Rex managed to walk by anyway, mad-dogging Junior and making a point to come over and check out my interview with a member of the opposing gang. When she walked up, the tension was palpable. Junior looked away without acknowledging her, and she asked me if she could see me later in the day.

I was particularly interested in talking to Junior because T-Rex and other students talked behind his back; they'd say that he was a "purple traitor," a switcher who had once been a Norteño and had thus "mixed red into blue." This complicated matters for me because I wanted to broach the subject of his affiliation in the most neutral way possible, not making too many assumptions about his past networks. He was in ESL classes, but since I had spoken to him mostly in Spanish while tutoring, I didn't know how proficient his English might be. Interviewing him was a turning point in my research, and for this reason I will be focusing parts of this chapter closely on his interview, reproducing and analyzing his transcribed words.[2] I also incorporate the transcribed words of others as they stand in agreement, contradiction, and dialog with Junior. Before this interview several months into my research, my understanding of the way in which members gained entry into a gang was essentially static, simplistic, and over-determined. I more or less believed that youth who were already members scoped out potential inductees, offered them membership, and then "jumped" them in. I was missing a whole dimension of negotiation and contestation around membership that didn't reveal itself in the first layer of descriptions.

At first I was primarily going on participants' overt statements, their sense-making of how the categories worked. Ona, for instance, had told me that if you were just coming from Mexico then you had to be Sureña, "The ones from this country are Norteños," she explained to me. "The ones who are Mexican or Latin American, since they come from the South, they are the Sureños." All the people I had met up until then essentially followed the formula: a recent Mexican immigrant was eligible to become a Sureña/o; US-born of Mexican immigrant parents could be a Norteña/o. Because of this initial understanding, I was puzzled that recently arrived, Spanish-speaking Junior had started with the Norteños. I couldn't even imagine why or how he might have switched.

Dismantling Ideology (with Junior, Güera, and T-Rex as Guides)

As Mary Weismantel and Stephen Eisenman observe, after Jean-Paul Sartre's[3] work on anti-Semitism, a totalizing ideology "does not arise from the innocent perception of pre-existing difference, [. . .] but presupposes the 'facts' marshaled to support it."[4] Some of the presupposed "facts" that participants touched upon in our discussions of gang membership were language, ethnoracial categories, social class, education, neighborhood residence, and gender, all in the construction of a larger politicized ideology that I term *hemispheric localism*, the projection of neighborhood-based, spatialized discourses of "turf" onto broader domains that play out debates over race, immigration, modernity, and globalization. The vehicle for such a projection is in many instances language, and as such it is one of the resources that participants call upon in their descriptions of others and their affiliations. With a multiply indexical ability to locate its users, language becomes the loud-speaker through which emergent political consciousness can be broadcast: language will advertise one's acquaintances and their trajectories; one's national background (Salvadoran, Mexican, Guatemalan); length of residence; and social class before and after the moment of migration. Language would even advertise whether one was a circular migrant, fluently at ease in both languages, or if one had migrated as a child but hadn't but hadn't set foot in Mexico since. Small shadings in word choice and popular expressions revealed whether one only talked to grandparents on the phone or ran around with one's cousins during the summer. Young people used the shifting indexicalities of language[5] and other symbolic modes of expression to continually, dynamically forge the nature of what they considered to be "gangs."

In chapter 2 I have presented, though accompanied by a caveat, a clean tabular display lining up the designations "Norte" and "Sur" with language, hairstyles, music, and so on. Now we must proceed to inter-rogate this display, taking the voices of Junior, his ex-girlfriend Güera (interviewed separately), Sita her Sureña friend from India, and T-Rex the Norteña as our guides. Instead of presenting my findings as omni-scient-ethnographer-observer facts, tabulated to line up with the ideolo-gical categories of Norte and Sur, I aim to show 1) that the constitution of these ideological categories in discourse is fraught with contradic-tion, with different actors taking diverse stances on the constitution of definitional statements such as "barrio," or finding different meanings and motivations for membership; and 2) that practice often diverges from the ideologized presentation of structured differences. In this chapter, we will get at some of these contradictions through discourse analysis. In later chapters, we will examine the subtle gradations of affiliation through analysis of the sound system, and investigate how and whether the categories that participants and the ethnographer erect in their expla-nations line up with participants' own phonetic behavior.

Understandings of the terms Norte and Sur shift continually in time and place and might be inflected by one's status as a core or peripheral member, as someone operating on the inside or outside (of prison), as a researcher, as a cop, as a male or female gang member, as an aspir-ing member or someone who wants to get out. As we have seen in the previous chapter, all of these parties have stakes in defining Norte and Sur in the public sphere, and their representations have differential weights: the police, for instance, define gangs in ways that can permanently affect members (and non-members of the same purported age, language background, and ethnicity) in the justice system. School counselors, often in close contact with the police, selectively transmit some of these understandings to other teachers. Veteranos[6] on the inside define gangs in ways that portray some young street members as basically playing with legos. Researchers, depending on their stripe, are contributing to debates in their own disciplines, and a subset of these, such as Meda Chesney-Lind, Marie "Keta" Miranda, and myself,[7] are engaged in projects with underlying feminist epistemologies that try to bring to the forefront more of members' words and images, all while still bound by our limitations as academics. The media are given to moral panics, the latest of which is a meltdown about the number of current and former gang members serving tours of duty in the army in Iraq. The Chicago *Sun-Times* showed pictures of graffiti from the Almighty Latin King and Queen Nation all over army bases, on tanks, on mosque walls, accompanied by anxious commentary from Army superiors who were afraid they might be creating the ultimate killing machine: a committed Latino or black gang member with elite army training.[8] Gang members of course create their representations as well, and produce copious material culture, ranging from novels and autobiographies,[9] to graffiti,[10] to websites and lately self-published web videos.[11] Some of these representations are targeted for repression, elimination, preservation, publication, or dissemination by the other parties.

This book is itself a representation that tries to be veridic without leading any cops to any actual members, and updated enough, but not too up to date so that some absurd detail such as feathered hair may not wind up listed in gang training manuals as an identifier that can get a kid slapped with a felony. You've been warned. Some or all of this may be hopelessly out of date, the names are fake, some people and places are composites, and I've erased identifiers from my tapes. I avoided approaching youth through law enforcement officers at any level, or through anyone that had already branded a particular youth as delinquent. Save for my initial contact into the school through Guadalupe Valdés and her connection in the English as a Second Language office, all my contacts with youth were through other youth. No cops were harmed, approached, or even glared at in the research for this study; in fact, I was mostly terrified of getting chased (the young people could run faster) and deported (now *there* we would be together) right alongside my "subjects."

Exploding Localism: The Interview with Junior

The day of my interview with Junior was also the first time I ever saw the Homies, all lined up on Junior's dark blue t-shirt, looking a bit like Mexican Hello Kitty's©, except Hello Kitty says "Think happy thoughts and boys will buy you diamonds!" while the Homies t-shirts blare: "Homie Harrassment!" depicting police helicopters ("ghetto birds") flying menacingly with searchlights over the Homies. Later I learned that the Homies toys were part of what the police and teachers considered gang symbolism. In the following years the judgmental momentum would build further and the two-inch-tall figurines spit from gumball machines momentarily landed the big time: national headlines in the *Washington Post* and the *New York Times* upbraided them as bad role models. Possessing the monitos *(translation: 'figurines,' literally: 'little monkeys')* became prosecutable in certain jurisdictions.[12]

The first question I asked Junior, despite the potential Sureño symbolism of his blue t-shirt, was whether he still considered himself to be in a gang at all, a Sureño. I just wanted to make sure, in case I'd misinterpreted something along the way.

NORMA: Tú todavía o sea, te consideras como Sureño, ¿no?
Do you still consider yourself a Sureño?

JUNIOR: Bueno sí, pienso que [. . .] siempre lo seré . . . Yo he tratado de dejar, verdad así, pero no se puede, porque es algo que . . . algo que ves un Chicano y los desprecias. No por lo que es, sino por la forma que es, la forma que actúan, de que aquí no hablan español, de que a los *wetbacks* los desprecian, y sabiendo que sus padres o alguien pudo ser así ¿no? Aunque ellos no sean. Entonces, ellos, el modo de pensar de ellos hace que uno odie ves, como piensan, no quien sea, sino como piensan. Entonces si hay un Chicano que piense diferente, pues, chido ¿no? Pero la mayoría que se juntan con Norteños es porque piensan así: ah, que porque hablas español, eres **mojaro-mojado**, y quién sabe qué . . .

Yes, I do, well, I think [. . .] I will always be one . . . I have tried to leave it, but I just can't because it is something that . . . one just sees a Chicano and one looks down on them. Not because of what they are, but because of the way they act, that they don't want to speak Spanish, that they look down on "wetbacks", knowing that their parents or someone else could have come over that way. Even if they didn't. And if there is a Chicano that thinks *differently, well that's cool. But the majority that hang out with the Norteños think that way: because you speak Spanish, you are a **wetback**, and so on.*

Language and Belonging: Code Choice

Junior's concept of who might be a Sureño and who might be a Norteño appears here intricately tied to language. Not just the language that people use, but according to him, the language that people don't use, the language(s) they actively choose to use and the ideologies they hold about others' language use. Even proficiency holds an ideological dimension, as Junior elsewhere minimizes his own English proficiency by reducing it to strict functionalism, saying: "I may speak English but it doesn't make me less Mexican; I'm just doing it to make life easier!" And yet, according to the excerpt above, Mexicans/Sureños speak Spanish and Chicanos/Norteños don't. In the last line of this utterance (highlighted), Junior displays in his own production a feature of language contact that suggests that the language-components of Spanish and English are not as hermetically sealed as he has presented them.

In his first attempt to say the Spanish word for *"wetback,"* **mojado**, he utters instead the word **mojaro**, and immediately repairs it in his speech stream. It's not a mistake: self-repair is a completely normal part of the speech stream of any speaker. What is notable about this particular instance of self-repair is that the substitution of [r] for [d] is characteristic of a Spanish/English bilingual, since American English /d/ appearing intervocalically (between vowels) is pronounced with a flap that sounds exactly like Mexican Spanish /r/. It is thus a type of slip-of-the-tongue interference from English into Spanish at the level of the phonological (sound) system. Other researchers working with bilingual Spanish/English-speaking children have uncovered the same processes,[13] an indication of the fluidity of the phonological systems of bilinguals,[14] and especially of bilingual children.[15]

Junior's self-report in the interview setting is of proud Spanish purism and determined monolingualism, but evidence of his incipient bilingualism lies just below the surface: it is in the bilingual-rather-than-monolingual types of repairs that he makes, in his codeswitching between English and Spanish (as in the English utterance *"wetback"* in the excerpt above), as well as in switches in direct quotations of

English speakers: when English speakers appear in his narratives, they always do so speaking in English, and he appears answering them in English as well. In recounting the beginning of a fight with some Norteños, he narrated:

JUNIOR: Me empezaron a patear al carro, no que, *what's up?* que, *step out.*
Me bajo, abro la puerta, y le digo, *hey, what's your problem?"*
(They started to kick my car, they're all) "what's up;" (all) "step out".
(I get out, open the door and say,) hey, what's your problem?

This type of quotative code-switching is common in bilingual speakers generally.[16] By examining whether Junior's language practices align with what he proclaims to be his language use, we begin to notice small cracks in the edifice, and appreciate just how much work and ideological fortification it takes to maintain the categories of Spanish and English as separate and exclusive. In other words, although students (and teachers!) at this school repeatedly produce ideologies of North and South as being indexed by language, their language practices said otherwise. Not only Junior, but others as well invoked for me clean ideological distinctions that in the very next moment were repeatedly, messily, turned inside out by displays of complex competencies in the language they had disavowed. One additional point worth noting in Junior's excerpt above is that he ascribes to Norteños the view that speaking Spanish is equivalent to being a wetback. He does not contradict this view but rather considers it hurtful and hypocritical, *"knowing that their parents or someone else could have come over that way."* He continues to outline how Norteños distance themselves from their Mexican-ness:

JUNIOR: Los Norteños niegan a México. El inglés afecta mucho, porque muchos Chicanos..dicen "No, que no hablo español puro inglés . . ."
Norteños deny Mexico. English has a big role, because many Chicanos would say, "Oh no, I don't speak Spanish, only English."
NORMA: ¿Pero sí hablan?
But do they speak it?
JUNIOR: **Sí** hablan pero lo niegan.
*They **do** speak it but they deny it.*

In this excerpt Junior has upgraded the charges against the Norteños: beyond stating that they merely don't speak Spanish, which could be construed as arising from residential history and not necessarily their fault ("... we don't begrudge them that," in the excerpt on p. 122), he now portrays Norteños as actively cloaking their proficiency, surreptitiously understanding Spanish but refusing to speak it, the weighty consequence of which is to *deny the whole country of Mexico*. This righteous indignation over the denial of heritage lent a moralistic tone to Junior's pronouncements.

School counselor Mr Carnie expressed a very similar, though not particularly moralistic, version of this argument with the signs reversed, stating in his interview that the gang conflict arose because Norteños spoke English and Sureños refused to learn it. Mr Carnie was a young school counselor who was interested in gangs, had received training in gang identification from the police, and had worked with children in the detention school which was one step up from incarceration in juvenile hall.[17] Throughout the time of my fieldwork, he was one of the main sources of information for other teachers about what they considered to be the gang problem in their school, and transmitted his own percepts of language proficiency to other teachers in meetings that I attended.

Exactly how much English and Spanish the different groups of Latinos really spoke or understood would be impossible to assess, however, since there was no systematic attempt to find out how much Spanish anyone in the school knew (except for the Euro-American students in Spanish classes). The only English proficiency testing that was administered was the high-stakes ESL-placement testing described in chapter 1, and that did not capture the complicated spectrum of bilingual proficiency that youth brought to school.

Conflict Resolution

The perception generated from the routine claims by Norteños and Sureños not to speak the other language was thus "common knowledge" at the school, both among the students and the teachers, and the circulation of this knowledge and public posturing around these claims was one way the rigidity of gang affiliation based on language was (re)produced and (re)enforced. In one of a series of failed attempts at gang-resolution interventions, school officials organized a lunchtime meeting to talk through the differences between Norteños and Sureños at Sor Juana High School. The meeting was widely publicized and students were promised that they would not be profiled or punished for attending, and that there would be no police there. At the meeting, girls and boys clad in red and blue lined up on either side of the classroom, eyeing each other suspiciously. When it was time to begin and Tlaloc, the Sureño, started speaking in Spanish, a burly Norteño nicknamed Piqui yelled exasperatedly, "What are you saying!?" and demanded a translator. It was too much for the Sureños. Some screamed in Spanish that Piqui was just pretending not to understand, while others lobbed incendiary insults in Spanish to test his claim. After a fight nearly broke out, and teachers with frazzled nerves realized that they could not stop the meeting in the middle of recess with ten minutes left (plenty of time to go and start a fight outside), an activity was organized where students were asked to sit quietly at desks and write down on loose sheets of paper why they thought there was a problem. Tlaloc testily asked, "In Spanish or English?" and Counselor Carnie practically blurted out, but in the most soothing tone possible, that whatever people were comfortable with would be fine. Sighs of relief spread all around when the class bells rang. This incident illustrates but one instance of how the ideology of language lines was constantly re-created by both students and teachers.

T-Rex, the "down" (committed) Norteña first introduced in chapter 2, also identified language as one of the features that divided Norteños from Sureños:

> T-Rex: Sureños say that we're embarrassed to speak Spanish,
> that we um,
> we betrayed Mexico and we don't deserve
> to call ourselves Mexicans.
> They don't really like to learn about English,
> and they have a bad attitude about it.
> They say that they're gonna be truly Mexican until they die.
> And I think **that's** cool cause we have the same idea,
> but it's stupid because if they're in school they should
> progress, and get better at it because without learning English
> they ain't gonna get nowhere in this life.
>
> (Trini@Home B 29:12)

Although in this excerpt T-Rex has equated progress and a better future with learning English at school, she also acknowledges that Norteños and Sureños at some level have "the same idea," namely, "to be Mexican until they die." This acknowledgment is key to understanding why the categories of Norteño and Sureño are so fluid. If both groups are fundamentally about "the same idea," and if the only differences lie in subtle differences in implementation of practices that both groups share, then maybe it is in the redundant marking across many different levels of indexicality – language, clothing, music – that the tenuous distinction can be made.

My Faux-Pas: Wrong Phonology, Wrong Discourse!

The symbolic importance not only of language but of the very details of pronunciation as well as my own initial lack of awareness of the norms governing them were made most evident for me in an interview that I had with a so-called "hard-core" gang member, a recently released former inmate named Manuel. T-Rex was aware of my desire to talk to some of the older gang members to get their perspective, so she offered to arrange a meeting for me with one of the most important leaders that she knew in Nuestra Familia, the prison-based gang that the Norteños considered the institutional extension of Norte. Manuel was the father of one of T-Rex's friends, the diminutive Greñitas, a twelve-year-old Norteña with light brown hair who was not afraid of anyone, had a fighting reputation, and who only associated with much older people. She'd been through a lot, with her dad intermittently in prison. When I met her she said to me, "You gotta grow up. You can't be a sweet little kid all the time. You gotta grow so you can take care of yourself." Greñitas was the only example that I saw of multi-generational gang membership, and one of the few examples of a girl whose membership had been influenced by an older male relative, despite the widespread assumption in the gang literature[18] that female gang members are primarily inducted through men in their social/familial networks.

Manuel, Greñitas' dad, had just gotten out of prison and it was rumored that he would be running the Foxbury Norteños' meetings as soon as he got out. Upon his release, T-Rex set up a meeting for me with Manuel at a laundromat on the far side of Silicate Way, and escorted me to it. The laundromat was in a Latino neighborhood, between a

Mexican taquería[19] and a convenience store. Stacked with machines, the one-room station had folding tables but no chairs, and was lit by an incandescent bulb. When T-Rex and I arrived Manuel was doing laundry, and wearing a shirt that young people called a "wife-beater": a ribbed white undershirt without sleeves designed to show off the wearer's muscles. Manuel had evidently been working out: his torso and arms were huge, and covered with tattoos: monochrome visions of women, cars, hourglass clocks, and prison cells. Whole narratives wrapped around the shifting outlines of his biceps. Though his face looked tired, his body was so muscled-up that I couldn't even hazard a guess at his age.

As soon as we walked in, T-Rex affected her coolest and most distant persona: she had arranged the meeting but was not about to facilitate it. She greeted Manuel with a silent upward thrust of her chin ("looking in"), which he answered with an identical gesture. It was evident that he respected her.

Manuel turned, folding his laundry in my direction but without looking directly at me, and began speaking in English, slowly and softly. "What's your name?" I was transfixed under the glare of the bulb. "Norma [norma]," I answered automatically, with clear tense Spanish vowels and a brief trilled [r]. Manuel's head immediately jerked up, but he answered even more slowly than he had first spoken: "What's the matter? You don't speak English? Cause MY name is Manuel [mæːnyuɛːl]". He emphasized the Englishness of his pronunciation by lengthening the vowels that don't exist in Spanish.

I had unthinkingly, in the first syllable of my name, phonetically claimed a contested identity, and Manuel's reaction was to take my nervous diction as a direct challenge. He assumed that by uttering my name in Spanish I was staking a claim to a Mexico-based identity, and symbolically linked myself to Sur.

I decided to detract attention from my blunder by repeating his name the way that he said it (but without his sarcasm), and mentioning something about how nice it was to meet him. Even that sounded all wrong. Fishing for another topic in the silence that followed, I remembered his tattoos.

"So, um," I said, "Can I ask you about the meaning of your tats?"

The silence that followed was interminable. Manuel stood silently with a downcast face.

Suddenly T-Rex spoke. "Oh, we gotta GO, huh?" she said to me.

"Yeah." As she answered herself, I followed her outside.

On our way home she explained to me in parables the inappropriateness of my questions. She began: "Imagine that you are going to someone's house. It's their space, and you don't want to invite yourself over, right? Like that, the tattoos are stories, they are people's personal stories. Just like you gotta be invited to the house, you don't ask people about their personal stories. You have to be invited. You have to get to know them. Then they tell you."

Following the efforts of Charles Briggs in *Learning How to Ask*,[20] I believe it is crucial for sociolinguists and linguistic anthropologists to talk about the moments in one's fieldwork where misunderstandings produced important insights. The story of my faux-pas with Manuel brought me to several realizations, two that have implications for ethnographic practice and one for linguistic theory.

1   Even as a near-native anthropologist, there will always be areas, however small, where assumptions will not be shared. Two such areas came up in this encounter: the symbolic importance of pronunciation as an act of identity, and the privacy of personal narratives as conveyed by tattoos (which confusingly for me, were visible so I assumed them to be public).

2   These small areas of distance can become wide lacunae precisely because one is a near-native researcher, and is thus held to more stringent rules than might otherwise be the case.

3   In terms of linguistic theory, Manuel's immediate identification of me as a Sureña based on my phonology recalls the work of Thomas Purnell, William Idsardi, and John Baugh,[21] where listeners categorized a voice on the basis of a single word as sounding African-American, Chicano, or White. One could argue that something similar was happening, but at a much more fine-grained level, in my interaction with Manuel. On the basis of a single segment (the tap [ɾ] vs. trill [r]) he assigned me a category more complex than just "Chicano" or "White," and provided an interpretation within a specific, locally-relevant group.

We have seen how participants are exquisitely attuned not only to code choice but to the implementation of micro-variables in their assessment of linguistic "claiming." Returning to Junior's interview, we will see how recursivity functions in fleshing out details within the categories; such recursivity and redundant marking create connections across other modes of signification that allow the categories of "Norteño" and "Sureño" to move beyond the linguistic and onto other arenas such as race and class.

Recursive Categories

According to Susan Gal and Judith Irvine, "fractal recursivity" (which I will henceforth just call recursivity) is a process of a sign system whereby "an opposition salient at some level of relationship, [is projected] onto some other level."[22]

In the following excerpt, Junior suggests that the Mexican/Chicano distinction on which the Sureño/Norteño dynamic rests exhibits such recursivity within each category:

JUNIOR: Hay una clase de Norteños, y otro tipo de Norteños. Norteños Chicanos y Norteños Mexicanos. Hay mu::chos Norteños que son Mexicanos. ¡Y indios! ¡Traen aquí el nopal en la cabeza, en serio!
There is one kind of Norteños, and then there is another kind of Norteños. Chicano Norteños and Mexican Norteños. There are a lot of Norteños that are Mexican. And they are Indios! They practically have a prickly pear cactus [the plant depicted on the Mexican flag] growing out of their head!

NORMA: Hhhhh

JUNIOR: En serio, los ves, y son Norteños y, ¿por qué?, no sé, eso sí no sé, ¿verdad? A la mejor les gusta más el rojo, y no sé, entonces no sé o, algo, ¿verdad?
Seriously, you see them, and they are Norteños, but why? That I don't know. Maybe they like red, I don't know.

NORMA: Mhm.

JUNIOR: Pero. Los Norteños, los pochos, muchas veces le andan echando aquí a los Norteños Mexicanos. Hay unos problemas. Te digo porque yo tengo muchos problemas con los pochos, yo y mi primo, nos quieren picar ahí, los Norteños los pochos. ¿Porqué? Bueno, porque es Mexicano. Bueno, mi primo no hablaba ni inglés, entonces tenía como un mes de México y se puso a vestirse puro de rojo. Entonces.
But. Norteños, the Americanized ones, a lot of the time they go around picking fights with Mexican Norteños. And then there are problems. I'm telling you because I have a lot of problems with the Americanized ones, my cousin and I have problems. Why? Maybe

because he's Mexican. My cousin couldn't even speak English, and
he had only been here from Mexico for about a month, and he started
wearing all red. So. [This refers to the time when Junior and his
cousin were Norteños.]

NORMA: Pues sí.
          That's right.

JUNIOR: Entonces, lo que pasa es que hay eso, ves, y lo mismo hay
          con los su, las Sureñas, los Sureños hay pochos, y los Sureños
          Mexicanos, lo mismo.
          So that is what's happening, see, and the same thing is happening
          with the Sureñas and Sureños. There are Americanized Sureños and
          Mexican Sureños.

NORMA: Y hay Sureños . . . ?–]
          And are there Sureños . . . ? –]

JUNIOR: [**Hay** Sureños pochos!
          *[There sure **are** Pocho/Americanized Sureños.*

A terminological note here about my translation here: "Pocho" as Junior
uses it in this excerpt is a derogatory term used by Mexicans for an
Americanized Mexican, a slur which carries a particularly judgmental
connotation. As Guillermo Gómez-Peña puts it, Pochos are "instant
traitors, inauthentic and bastardized Mexicans [. . .] forgotten orphans
of the Mexican nation-state."[23]

Junior suggests that in fact one way of understanding the Norte/Sur
dynamic is as cross-cutting axes of identity, which I've represented in
linear fashion below, if one would organize it from more Mexican to
more Americanized:

Mexican Sureños > Americanized Sureños > Mexican Norteños >
Americanized Norteños

Although not present in the subcategories he has created, Junior raises
the topic of the Indio, saying that the Mexican Norteños are in fact *so*
Mexican that they are actually Indios and have "growing on their forehead" one of the strongest symbols of traditional, indigenous Mexico,
the prickly pear cactus.[24] This framing implicitly situates racially
defined Indios at the far left of the linear continuum, hinting that the
Norteño/Sureño categories involve more than nation, language, and
assimilation, but encompass race as well. By invoking the Indio as an
endpoint in the continuum, Junior implicitly invokes the flip-sides of
that coin as well: the mestizo and the white.

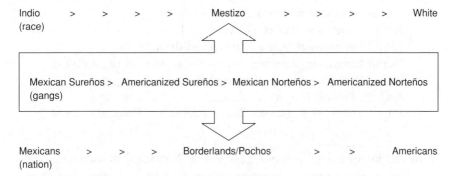

Figure 4.1 A simplified, linear representation of the complex relationships between race, gang, and nation.

Strikingly, although Norteños and Sureños have "the same idea, to be Mexican until we die," not all Mexicans are created equal. Any identification with Mexico's actual indigenous population is taken as an insult by these youth groups that fight to define Mexican-ness and authenticity. Figure 4.1 attempts to represent the complex dynamic that Junior has invoked. Because it is linear and two-dimensional, it necessarily fails to capture some of the complexities we have already talked about: Fresas, for instance, cannot be represented on this chart, since they are both "White" and "Mexican." It should also be noted that the entire gang continuum is depicted by Junior as fitting within the "Pocho" and "Mestizo" categories.

Nevertheless, with Junior's suggestion that the categories can be sliced into ever-smaller recursive bits, the opposition that started as rigid and fixed, with polarized endpoints that conceptualized space or language, has become became a recursive, racialized continuum in the retelling.

Indios and Mestizos: Continua of Racism and Phenotype in Latin America

> Me he enamorado de una chica banda,
> Me he enamorado de su negra piel [. . .]
> Pelos parados como un penacho,
> Bailes como ritos a Xipe-Totec,
> Su piel morena chichimeca,
> pero en el punk ella aún cree.

I've fallen in love with a banda-girl.
Fallen in love with her black skin [. . .]
[With] her mohawk like a feather head-dress
[With] her dancing like the rites to the goddess of ritual flaying
[With] her Chichimec [indigenous] dark skin,
And yet she still believes in punk.

Café Tacuba, "La Chica Banda," Album: Re. 1994

Why did Junior bring up Indios (indigenous Mexicans) in such a derogatory way in the previous excerpt? What does his statement say about the ways that racial consciousness defines gangs in this setting? In order to better understand these issues, and how they relate to the hemispheric mapping of the Norte and Sur gang categories that spreads out concentrically with Mexico as its center, we must first review the colonial history of racism toward indigenous people in Latin America and briefly contrast it with the US setting.

Young immigrants to the United States who are from Latin America bring with them a set of unique, historically grounded Latin American postcolonial concepts of race, and at the same time are exposed to and integrate US concepts of race into their worldview, whether they live in New York,[25] California,[26] Washington,[27] North Carolina,[28] or Rhode Island.[29] As we continue to examine how Latino youth understand race as a system of distinction that feeds into gang membership, understanding the historical background of their concepts of race is crucial. This takes us back to the fifteenth century, to New Spain, as the colonies were known, where Spanish colonizers were settling among the indigenous people throughout Mexico and the rest of Latin America.

De Las Castas a La Raza

In order to preserve the economic and political privilege that was acquired in the dispossession of the indigenous population, as early as the fifteenth century Spanish colonizers in Latin America created an elaborate legal kinship system of ranked castes to describe the various phenotype "mixtures" of the indigenous population, Indios; imported and enslaved Africans, Negros; and Europeans.[30] The representative of the "pure" race, the Spanish-born colonizer, was always at the top of the racial hierarchy, and was immediately followed by the Criollo, Spanish by blood but born in the colonies so already stigmatized.[31,32] In colonial Latin America, a mixture of Spanish and Indio was known as a *Mestizo* (from the Latin *mixtus*, mixed); of Spanish and African, *Mulato* (from the Latin *mulo*, mule); of Spanish and Mulato, *Moro* (from Latin *Maurus*, Moor); and so on in taxonomic elaboration. In Mexico at least twenty-five legal categories[33] operationalized inheritance laws and created social structure anew, making of any Spaniard, regardless of prior status, an aristocrat who could dress in silk, ride horses, travel and trade, and hold government or church posts,[34] while Indios, associated with agriculture and mining, paid tribute in wealth taken from the land, and Africans were bound in servitude.[35] The more Indio blood one had, the lower one's status, though there was a way to move up the caste hierarchy: by "whitening" or mixing with European, one's offspring could reverse the "contamination." Magali Carrera explains:

> Mestizo blood that continued to mix with Spanish blood was perceived to be purifiable. That is, the mestizo-Spaniard union produced a castizo, and castizo blood combined with Spanish blood became fully purified, with the offspring returning to the quality of the Spaniard. On the other hand, if mestizo blood mixed with African blood, Indian, or other casta blood, the result could only be further denigration.[36]

Within this system, it was "the common opinion of both Indian leaders and colonial officials that Africans [. . .] should only be encouraged to marry among themselves [. . .] Miscegenation represented so great a threat that the Viceroy of New Spain petitioned [. . .] a total prohibition against African-Indian marriages or a requirement that their children be considered slaves."[37] In Mexico, Blacks were at the absolute bottom of the racial hierarchy; in other Latin American countries, Indios were confined to the lowest strata.[38]

No sooner was this system established than the practice of passing arose – rejecting one's assigned category and assuming, typically, a higher caste in order to have access to the enhanced privileges. Passing anxiety was huge among the more elite castas, where all sorts of bodily signifiers became imbued with racial meanings, and refined colonial mestiza ladies meticulously cultivated the little mustaches on their upper lip to distance themselves from indigenes who were thought to be hairless.

From Peru to Brazil to Mexico, castas have been immortalized in art, in miniature paintings that reminded Spaniards of their travels – the earliest tourist tchotchkes; in elaborate drawings that bio-artistically catalogued all the castas and their accompanying flora and fauna; and in enormous murals that still today are displayed in the national centers of memory such as Mexico City's main square, the *Zócalo*. Serving the continental *mestizaje* myth with idyllic, domesticized images of our "original families," these racist caste systems and mythologies of miscegenation are deeply etched into the Latin American national imaginaries, for the very potent reason that they are still with us today, having resulted in centuries of differential capital and power accumulation that reflects racist beginnings despite the official political disavowal of the caste systems.

Twentieth-century Latin American political leaders such as Benito Juárez and José Vasconcelos in Mexico, and Jose Martí in Cuba, sought to overturn 1) the colonial holdovers of foreign control of material capital through expropriation, and 2) the internalized colonial holdovers of Criollo control of social and cultural capital by positing *mestizaje* as a transcendent, liberatory movement, a new Latin American consciousness predicated on the "cosmic race" of Mestizos,[39] a mixture that, according to the social-evolutionary ideas of the time, took the strongest from both bloodlines and resulted in a strengthened people.

Ana Maria Alonso points out the "disturbing Nietzchean undertone celebrating the mestizo Superman,"[40] and argues that despite mestizaje's rejection of nineteenth-century racism based on biological inferiority, and its celebration of an egalitarian and transformative potential, this myth of ethereal racial intermixing that creates a transcendent, universal, "cosmic" race – *La Raza* – nevertheless obscures power relations and relegates Indios to the status of national patrimony, firmly rooted in the land, in tradition, and in the past, with no stake at all in the future of the nation except as reminders of where history began.[41] All mestizos are equal, but some (the whiter ones) are more equal than others, and Indios are altogether outside of the race to nation and to modernity. According to Charles Hale, mestizaje "has been a remarkably effective ideological tool in the hands of elites in many parts of Latin America, a unifying myth put to the service of the state and nation building."[42] By the time of the 1990 census, only 8 percent of Mexicans identified as indigenous, partly because census officials equated reported use of an indigenous language with indigeneity.[43]

Scholars of Latin American colonialism have long argued that Latin American race-making involves a continuum (much as Junior has implied) that privileges economic, regional, and cultural passing and "whitening" rather than the rigid one-drop North American black/white binary.[44] Instead of policing purity by monitoring the legal boundaries of whiteness and blackness (where one could be "outed" by claims of hiding black blood somewhere in one's ancestral line), postcolonial Latin Americans take mixing for granted, and while supposedly celebrating it, focus instead on the cultural trappings that might make one more or less white, Black or Indio. It is in this way that language (typically more standard Spanish or Portuguese), social class, occupation, and urbanity become signifiers for both whiteness and modernity, co-defining them in lived practice rather than as abstract categories.

Throughout Latin America, even though everyone is supposedly mestizo, being labeled white passes for a kind of compliment. In Mexico, Güerita *(translation "blondie")* is used as an honorific address term by vendors in marketplaces, as a way of politely calling the attention of women you don't know, while the equivalent across the continent in Chile is "Lolita," which also implies youth and whiteness.[45] The quotidian nature of these evaluative terms amounts to their normalization, so that they become a neutral forms of address like "Miss," except that instead of flatteringly commenting on one's fictive marriageability and sexual innocence, racial honorifics such as Güerita focus more on the desirability of one's fictive race and class.

"They Say We Are a Bunch of Indios"

We can point to other ethnographies of Mexico and to popular cultural forms to establish continuities, almost eerily similar in phrasing, between attitudes toward Indios in Mexico, attitudes toward Indios at SJHS, and popular representations linking, for instance, Indios with banda music (such as the excerpt above from the popular band *Café Tacuba*, a favorite of the Fresas).

Jacqueline Messing[46] in her study of language revitalization in Tlaxcala, Mexico, addresses the deep politics of the label "Indio." She documents a discourse of denigration of Indian-ness throughout Mexico, even among self-identified indigenous groups that are trying to revitalize Mexicano, a language spoken in central Mexico. Efforts to revitalize Mexicano are hampered by the fact that English instruction, widely perceived as the vehicle of modernity, competes with Mexicano instruction at the secondary level. The internalization of the stigma of being labeled "Indio" is evident in Messing's account of children who "accuse classmates of being 'from Zacatlán,' a town that they say is 'full of Indians, speaking [Spanish] with accents, who are barefoot, and poor.' "[47]

Recall Ernesto, the kid who came over on his own from Michoacán and who said to me in his interview, as he described relations among recently arrived immigrants: "According to the guys from the capital, everybody else is an Indian. When somebody asks you where you're from, you need to think three times about what you're going to say." The word "Indio" carries with it, both for Ernesto and for the students in Messing's study, connotations of backwardness, of rurality, and of ignorance. In the excerpt below, Junior discursively distances himself from these associations.

> JUNIOR: (Los Norteños) están orgullosos de ser de este país, verdad, de ser Americanos, eso es lo que ser Nuestra Familia, puros Chicanos, puras personas que no conocen nada de México, que nunca han vivido en México. No se les culpa eso, se les culpa de que porqué piensan mal de nosotros. Porque dicen que somos unos indios, ¿verdad?
>
> *Norteños are really proud of being from this country, of being Americans, of being Nuestra Familia, exclusively Chicanos, people that don't know anything about Mexico and have never lived in Mexico. One does not begrudge them that, the problem is that they look down on us. Because they say that we are a bunch of indios, you know?*

One recurrent ideological contradiction in the excerpts from the youth at Sor Juana High School is that while rejecting Americanization and holding up Sureños as the defenders of all things Mexican, young immigrants still reject identification as "Indios" (and consequently Piporros, as we saw in chapter 1) as both hyper-Mexican and insufficiently modern. Junior resents that anyone might say that he is Indio, and employs the term in a discourse of denigration paralleling the uses in central rural Mexico discussed by Messing.[48]

Racial Contradictions

There was a further tension that recurred in the interviews, which I will show here by juxtaposing excerpts from Junior's interview with excerpts from an interview with his ex-girlfriend Güera. Skin color in the gradations of Mexican indigenous/European/African colonial mixing known in Spanish as mestizaje was used as a potent symbol, especially by Sureños, of who might be, or should be, truly Mexican and brown (Sureño) vs. more Americanized and lighter-skinned (Norteño).

In the excerpt below, Junior adds phenotype to the list of devices used to characterize Norteños:

NORMA: ¿Cómo se conoce un Norteño?
How can you tell a Norteño?

JUNIOR: Por la cara. Porque son güeros, la mayoría. Porque son Americanos. Sus padres son, un Americano, y un Mexicano, muchas veces.
By their face. Because most of them are blond [white], the majority of them are. Because they are Americans. Their parents are, one American, and one Mexican, much of the time.

Thus not only are Norteños understood to be English speakers by choice (and snubbing Spanish by choice), they are also identifiable as being ethnically mixed or perhaps altogether güeros. These initial explanatory systems, coupled with their more complex unraveling which Junior described as our conversation progressed, display the workings of language ideology as it is linked to racial ideology in the local definition of gangs. In the presentation of Norte and Sur as two separate gangs defined at least partially through language, then through race, this definition becomes fortified through recursivity involving several other domains.

From Junior's confident definitions above one might draw the conclusion that visual inspection (presumably of phenotype, that is to say skin color and facial features) is enough to tell between Norteños and Sureños. Sureños then are dark-skinned (but not quite Indios, as we see in the above quote), while Norteños might perhaps be more mixed. But even though it would appear that Junior is focused on light skin color as a marker of whiteness and American-ness, he was of course also aware of considerable variation among Mexican immigrants. His own ex-girlfriend was circular-migrant Güera whose blond hair potentially meant that she could be thought by outsiders to be less "Mexican." Sita, her friend from India, joked in her interview (with Güera present) that when she first saw Güera with her pale-blond hair she thought she was white. We all howled with laughter, as though it were the most farfetched joke.

Güera had a couple of reactions to her "phenotype-status," in different symbolic domains. One reaction, in the material culture realm, was to wear makeup and accessories that literally hid her whiteness (more on this in the next chapter), while another was to discursively insist on a general dislike for güeros as potential friends and dates and to express admiration for boys with dark skin. Below is an excerpt from our interview:

GÜERA: A mi me gustan, morenitos me gustan, porque los gringos . . . ¡ay, no, no me gustan!
I like, I like dark-skinned guys, because gringos, oh, no, I don't like them!

NORMA: ¿Porqué?
Why?

GÜERA: No sé, no me gustan.
I don't know, I don't like them.

NORMA: ¿No te gustan por gueros o por gringos?
You don't like them because they're blond or because they're gringos [Americans]?

GÜERA: No sé pero, creo que porque están muy güeros, y luego no me gusta como . . . su forma de ser de ellos. [. . .] casi los únicos que echan desmadre son los mexicanos, ¿no ves? Los mexicanos son divertidos.
I don't know, I think it's because they're very blond, and also I don't like their personalities [. . .] just about the only ones that raise a ruckus are the Mexicans you know? Mexicans are fun.

NORMA: Mhmm. Relajientos.
Mhmm. Relajo-makers.[49]

GÜERA: Ellos no, como, en las clases, yo, mira, ese tiempo que Health, en el sexto periodo, había casi gringos, y nada de desmadre, ahí bien callados, como topos.
They [gringos] don't, like in classes, remember when I had Health 6th period? There were just about all gringos there and there was no bedlam, they were all quiet, like moles.

GÜERA: No, una clase con un gringo, no, no me gustaría con ellos.
No, having a class with a gringo, no, I wouldn't like it with them.

In the interview, Güera expresses her attitudes toward gringos *(Americans)* and güeros *(blonds)*. Güera prefers the darker skin tone that is considered normative and symbolic by the Sureñas and Sureños that are her friends. She even makes disparaging remarks about people whose skin tone is similar to hers (it is also clear from other conversations I've had with her that she does not think of herself as ethnically or racially white). Güera also expresses a general dislike for the learning style and social interaction style of mainstream, white/American students. She later admitted to dropping out of her mainstream Health class *because* there were only Euro-American students there.

Class and Class Consciousness

In addition to skin color and language use, Junior spent some time outlining issues of class that were also important in the dynamic between Norte and Sur:

> JUNIOR: Un Mexicano siempre está . . . a las modas, es muy lento . . . los Norteños son.. como tienen más dinero que nosotros, y todo esto, mejores *cars*, mejores trabajos, por el inglés y todo eso, ellos am, tienen mejor ropa, a veces, mejor forma.. actitud no.
> *A Mexican immigrant is always . . . slow to take up fashions. Norteños have more money than we do, better cars, and better jobs, because of the English (that they speak) and all. And they have better clothes, and other things. But not a better attitude.*
> [. . .]
>
> NORMA: ¿Tú piensas que los Norteños son más ricos que los Sureños?
> *Do you think Norteños are better off than Sureños?*
>
> JUNIOR: Son más ricos, pero. Tienen mas fácil de agarrar las cosas. Muchos de ellos tienen padres que son Americanos, que tienen buenos trabajos. O primos que tienen carros. O ropa buena. Y sus primos quién sabe qué son, ¿verdad? Abogados. Un padre de un Sureño, trabajando en el campo. En las yardas. Trabajando duro, ¿ves? Pero por falta de educación. Ahora, nunca ves a un Norteño papá trabajando en el campo, ¿ves?
> *They are better off but . . . they have also had an easier time getting things. Many of them have parents who are Americans, who have good jobs. Or cousins who have cars. Or good clothes. And their cousins are, who knows what the might be? Lawyers. The father of a Sureño, he is working in the fields. In people's backyards. He works hard, you know? But it's all because of a lack of education. Now, you never see the father of a Norteño working in the fields.*
> (Junior 2: 28:50)

Junior's astute observations on class and capital accumulation were plainly confirmed in my sample of self- and other-identified gang members (the methodology for sample selection is described in detail in the linguistic chapters). By and large, the Norteñas' parents owned their own homes (T-Rex's parents had bought their home when T-Rex was fifteen and the parents were in their mid-thirties), while Sureñas' families lived in relatively crowded rental apartments on roads shooting off from Industrial Way. In contrast, T-Rex and her younger brother Teo each had their own room, while Güera shared a room with her two sisters and an occasional aunt. As for Junior's percept that Norteños had "better clothes," nowadays T-Rex is the first to admit that she was totally spoiled: as the Norteña trendsetter, she owned no fewer than fifteen pairs of expensive red sneakers! Dickies pants weren't cheap, and she was a stickler for exactly the right kind of Mexican pride t-shirt, not the mass-produced ones you might find at the mall, but the originals, hand-silk-screened, numbered and signed by the artist. While Güera and the other Sureñas (and even some of the Fresas) were expected to work while in high school to help with the family household expenditures, T-Rex and Angie (whom you'll meet in the next chapter) worked strictly for pocket money, and only entered the labor force once they started going to college.

Occupational characteristics of the young Norteños' and Sureños' parents were also accurately described by Junior. Despite the historic identification that we saw in the last chapter of Nuestra Familia and of Norteños with the United Farm Workers movement and the struggle for Chicano civil rights, the parents of this generation's Norteños were no longer working in the fields. Although the youth still called each other "farmers," and proudly drew UFW eagle-icons on their notebooks, their families had been in the United States long enough, saved enough, and achieved enough stability to move into the service economy and abandon seasonal agricultural labor. The unstable farm jobs that they had left behind were now, as Junior observed, being filled by recent immigrants from the countryside who were more likely to be the parents of Sureños. Furthermore, even when the Sureños' parents worked in the service economy, they were typically filling the lowest-paid rungs of it: for example, the divorced mom of one Sureña (Güera) worked a full shift at a McDonald's, while the dad of a Norteña (T-Rex) had two much-better-paying jobs, one as a chef at an Italian restaurant and the other at a French restaurant. T-Rex's dad was exhausted from the hours but earned three times as much, and this along with his wife's income from a hotel housekeeping job was enough to pay the mortgage of a three-bedroom, two-bath home in the Bay Area, one of the most expensive housing districts in the country.

Junior's analysis opened up for me new ways of understanding Norteños and Sureños and their relationship to class, especially of considering the possibility that across first- and one-and-a-half generation migrants there is enough job and residential mobility to create pervasive class conflict within closely spaced school immigrant populations. T-Rex's parents arrived when her Mom was pregnant with her, while many of the Sureñas' and Piporras' parents were more recent arrivals who were still moving with the crop rotations or had only recently established themselves in service jobs. Based on Junior's analysis, one of the predictions we might make is that as the migratory stream continues and those who are now farm-workers achieve residency and move into steadier service jobs with longer-term contracts, another class of workers will come and replace them, creating further recent/established immigrant conflicts and a whole class of "new Sureños" coming from the South.

How Junior Found Out That He Was (underlyingly) Sureño

I return to my original question, the one that motivated my pursuing an interview with Junior in the first place. Why had Junior switched? And why had he started out with the Norteños? Here is his answer:

NORMA: Entonces tú eras Norteño antes pero no hablabas inglés.
So, you used to be a Norteño before, but you didn't speak any English.

JUNIOR: No, y yo no, no sabía ni por qué era.
No [I didn't], and I didn't even know why I was [a Norteño].

NORMA: ¿Ni **porqué** eras Norte-?
*You didn't even **know** why you were a Norte-?*

JUNIOR: Yo, yo fui porque, ahí donde vivía, pu::ro Norteño había.
I, I was there because where I lived there were only Norteños.

NORMA: Ah, pus sí, qué onda.
Is that right?

JUNIOR: Y yo no sabía nada de Sureño. Y ellos "Sureño" y . . . pensaba que eran los gringos.
And I didn't know anything about Sureños. And they would say "Sureño," and I thought they were the gringos.

NORMA: Aha.

JUNIOR: Una vez me puse a pensar: Sur. Y México está al sur. Y le pregunté a mi cuate, "¿Porqué nos creemos Norte si somos del sur?" Dijo él: "Ah, eso, nunca preguntes eso." Y ese cuate después me dijo: "Ah, sabes qué, tienes razón", en casa de mi primo, mi primo nomás se quedó callado. Al cabo no sabía qué ondas. *One day I started thinking: Sur. Well, Mexico is to the south. And I asked my friend, "Why do we think we're Norte if we are from the south?" and he said, "Oh, that, you should never ask that question." And then that same guy later said, "Oh, you know what, you're right." And this was at my cousin's house and my cousin was just silent. He didn't know what was going on anyway.*

NORMA: Mhhmm.

JUNIOR: Me cambié para aquí para Fog City, y supe todo. Quiénes eran Sureños, quiénes son Norteños, quiénes son los Crips, los Bloods.

I moved over here to Fog City and then I found out everything. Who were the Sureños, who were the Norteños, who were the Crips and the Bloods.

In the answer to this question, we find Junior appealing to concepts of localism. As we have seen through transcripts from his interview, Junior and others have interpreted the categories of "Norte" and "Sur" to be about language, about race, about class and nation, almost everything except the localism (neighborhood or state-wide) that is the hallmark of the government, police, and research depictions of Norte and Sur. And yet in Junior's retelling, even as localism is invoked, it is transformed. Junior's response frames his own membership in the Norteños as accidental, stressing that he "didn't even know" why he was a Norteño, and that he only fell into it because of the neighborhood where he was temporarily living when he first arrived, which was populated by Norteños. And although neighborhood localism is clearly invoked in his explanation, it is in his reflexive account, in his retracing of his thought process, that we find the germinating seeds of hemispheric localism. By reinterpreting, in his recent-immigrant experience, the Norte/Sur spatial dynamic as being not about the gangs but about the relative location of Mexico and the US, the concepts of Norte and Sur become dislodged from their history within the California correctional system. Young immigrants like Junior who have little exposure to the origin stories emanating from the prison-bound founders of the Norteño and Sureño movements reinterpret the story of origin as being about the migratory dynamics between the US and Mexico. This is facilitated by the already circulating discourse of spatiality in talk about migration in Mexico.

The Imaginary of El Norte

Here I make the claim that young people are aware of and orient to historical discourses of migration from Mexico to the US, and that this serves as a foundation for awareness of hemispheric North/South relations among nation states, situating youth as social actors who "take sides" in their own epic stories of migration. Would you be moved by the place that you came from, proclaiming loyalty to your origins, or would you cast your lot with your destination, with "progress" (in the words of T-Rex)?

The general Mexican designation of "El Norte" to refer to the United States, especially when talking about migration, is one that migrant youth are socialized to from the earliest childhood. Ethnographic work by Gustavo López Castro[50] and Leticia Díaz[51] illustrates how migration to "El Norte" is conceptualized as something of a rite of passage by children as young as the fourth grade residing in Zamora, Michoacán, one of the regions with the highest out-migration rates in central-western Mexico. One of the children in Diaz' study proclaims, "When I get big, I'm going to go to El Norte!"[52] López Castro additionally cites a popular saying in the Michoacán region: "Cuando un muchacho prueba el Norte, se vuelve hombre." *(When a boy has a taste of El Norte, he becomes a man.")*[53]

López Castro's research is especially germane here, since many of the youth interviewed for his study as well as for this study came from Michoacán. He has collected narratives along with ethnographic data in the rural schools where underage deportees, some of whom were traveling alone, had been returned. I translate here from his 2005 study:

> Almost all the children [in Zamora, Michoacán] know and can recite the stories of other deported children, with luxurious detail, and even with embellishments added from their own imaginations. The important thing here is not the truthfulness of fact or similarity to the original story, but the role that the retelling has in the reaffirmation of values inculcated by the socialization to transnationalization; one of those roles is to serve as a an archetypal story. For instance, the children of Atacheo affirm that it is certainly possible to cross the line, but one shouldn't be like nine-year-old Juanito, who couldn't get across because he got nervous and said that the smuggler who accompanied him was his uncle and not his father; or like seven-year-old Lupita who started sobbing and screaming for her mother when they were stopped for a border check in San Clemente.[54]

Junior and his recent-immigrant friends certainly had their own tales of crossing, and now that they were on the other side, now that they had successfully crossed into El Norte, they were trying to determine exactly what that meant. I'd like to focus for a moment on Junior's account of his own reflexivity, when he reasons to himself that, after all, Mexico is in the south. He then asks his friend, "Why do we think we are Norte if we come from the south?" Not only does this question turn out to be unmentionable, "That you must never ask," says the enigmatic friend, implying that the quandary is both common and unknowable; it is such a paradox that it stumps both his cousin and their friend. They go away to think about it: does Norte refer to migration? To geography? Or is it just the name of the gang we're in? The friend returns with a verdict: "You know what, you're right." In the resolution and coda of this narrative, the puzzle is resolved by Junior moving to a Sureño neighborhood, and finding in this new geography the correct answers: who are the Norteños, the Sureños, the Crips, the Bloods.

Norte, as it turns out, refers to it all: it is the migratory process, the neighborhood Junior was first living in, and the physical location of Mexico relative to the United States. We have seen Norte and Sur recursively projected onto language, race, onto whole countries (the US and Mexico), and onto differentials of class and privilege. The last refraction of these signifiers that we will examine is the projection of Norte and Sur onto the hemispheric stage, a projection that I've called hemispheric localism.

Projecting North and South Onto the Hemispheric Stage

As I defined it in chapter 3, hemispheric localism is "a projection onto the hemispheric political-stage of symbols and processes that began locally in the history of groups of Latinos in California . . . Young people involved in Norte and Sur become political analysts (and actors), organizing their experience through the lens of their participation in these groups, synthesizing their understanding of the larger processes of race, language, capital structures, and global power relations, with increasingly larger projections such that the 'Global North' and the 'Global South' become tangible and explainable."

I believe that the evaluation of who belongs in which category is made organically and dynamically by the youth involved, with each actor exercising agency and weighing different factors in their determination of membership. Having given you the evidence, let me restate here factors I believe are considered in this evaluative process; their relative weighting surely depends on the eye of the beholder, and her dynamic assessment of the situation at hand:

1 language use
2 language ideology
3 perceived phenotype/race
4 performative speech act (claiming)
5 country of origin (Mexico/US/other),
6 perceived economic position (as signaled by clothes, cars, parents' occupation),
7 social class prior to immigration, and
8 neighborhood residence.

These factors may be combined to result in broad ascriptions along the continuum of Norte and Sur, attributions that stand quite apart from the status that results from formal processes of induction into the gangs.

But what of youth who are not from Mexico or the US? Below we will see that these same North/South evaluations structure possibilities of membership and even attributional understandings of world regions.

Sor Juana High School had a number of students from different countries, both immigrants and so-called "foreign students" who had entered through state-sponsored mechanisms such as educational exchange programs. Young gang members' interactions with these foreign students and other immigrants provide further illustrations of the workings of hemispheric localism.

Telescoping Out: Norte Becomes Hemispheric North

Takako, a relatively wealthy seventeen-year-old exchange student from a Tokyo inburb, went through several phases during her one-year stay at SJHS. When she arrived, she was a Japanese punk-girl, with colored spikes of hair, ripped-up fishnet stockings, and combat boots. Defiant and assertive, her anti-institutional attitude won her immediate points with anyone invested in challenging school authority in general, and worried her American host family. For a while she appeared to gravitate toward the SJHS Europhile punks, who were dripping in chains and utility fasteners that attached to nothing. Most inconveniently, because of her lack of English skills she shared almost no classes with them. The majority of her classes – prime prank real estate – were spent in the English as a Second Language classrooms, and gradually her friendship circles and style became oriented toward the Latina students. Her lack of Spanish skills quickly channeled her toward the Norteñas, who even in their looking-in seriousness found her tongue-wagging faces aimed at the teachers hilarious.

One day, either through sincere flattery or inspiration, she started wearing red, and soon afterward she could be seen in the furthest back lot, behind the playing fields, skipping classes and smoking cigarettes with the Norteñas. According to other Norteñas she was not considered a full member, though, and her higher socioeconomic profile was used by Norteños for securing food, booze, and for transportation since she had a car.

This was T-Rex's explanation:

T-REX: Norteños sometimes use, you know, girls who got money.
You know, just to let them kick back and party with them?
So they could buy everything, and tssshhhh-
That girl was rich.
So you know, they use to use HER.

But you know, she –
You know, we used to call her, like *China* ([čina] with Spanish phonology)
you know, Chinese, China?
's call her China
and she was cool, you know,
she used to smoke out.
But she didn't know who she was, inside of her, you know?
I have a picture of her.
Yeah, no, she didn't know who she was.
You know what I'm saying?
She started wearing her eyeliner and everything, you know?
But she didn't know who she was, you know?
If she knew, she wouldn't have hanged around with us.

She was just . . .
Nobody, you could say, you know?
And she-
You know she wanted it to find her personality in the gang

T-Rex acknowledges that while Takako was "cool," her Norteño association hinged precariously on a case of confusion, of her not knowing who she was "inside." While she could don the outward markers of membership (eyeliner, partying), her not knowing who she was made her a "nobody." From this excerpt it's not clear whether the term "who she was inside" is meant by T-Rex to invoke some kind of ethno-racial category (by which she couldn't really be Norteña if she was "China"), or whether it is meant as more of an inner attitude, an issue of poise or deportment where not "knowing who you were" was a critique of Takako's switch from the Europhile punks. The latter interpretation is supported in the last line, where T-Rex states that Takako wanted to "find her personality in the gang," strongly implying that if you knew and felt secure in who you really were you wouldn't switch around from group to group.

Although Takako was granted honorary membership in the Norteños, and that membership appeared to be connected to material advantages that she could offer them, there were also other cases of other non-Latinos gaining legitimate membership into Norteño networks. Most of those cases were of African-American or Euro-American youth, both of whom were considered to be already from the "North," and who had a stable but still peripheral claim.

One additional detail worth mentioning here is that core, jumped-in members of both gangs had de-facto exogamous dating practices. Many of the core members expressed the reluctance to get involved with members of their own gang; "Too messy, you don't know what's going to happen after that," explained T-Rex.

Many Norteñas dated African-American boys – T-Rex's boyfriend in high school, for instance, was Terrell, a tall, sweet-natured basketball player. These dating and friendship networks had a large role to play in the stylistic resources that were available to girls in the Norteña networks, and I believe they influenced everything from verbal art practices (like clowning) to the style of dancing. T-Rex, for instance, used to make fun of Sureños dancing to Oldies because she thought they danced them like rancheras or banda; "Sureños just came from Mexico and now they wanna dress like cholos!"

T-Rex and other Norteñas worried about anti-Black attitudes in their own extended families back in Mexico and in the wider Latino community. This racism was amply exemplified in some Fresas' and some Sureñas' attitudes toward African-Americans. Junior, for instance, called African-Americans mayates *(literally: 'black scarab beetle,' a strong slur in Spanish)*, a term that T-Rex found deeply offensive. Tanya, the *rockera* Fresa, talked about the "ideal man" in her interview, informing me that her fantasy date didn't have to be blond, but he definitely had to be white, preferably fair-skinned, and with lots of chest hair. None of the Sureñas at Sor Juana High School to whom I spoke had dated African-American boys, and they were largely critical of most relationships other than those involving Sureñas-Piporros, with one notable exception of a world region from which it was acceptable to date boys: Southeast Asia.

Sureñas repeatedly asserted that they did not date Asians, but the latter category only seemed to include Chinese and Japanese boys. A few relationships emerged between Vietnamese and Filipino boys and Sureña girls. These relationships were insistently predicated *not* to involve any Asians, and not coincidentally DID involve groups that were low-income immigrant arrivals, were known to have powerful gangs, and at the same time were out of the strict Norteño/Sureño dating practices.

Sita from Gujarat: Sur Becomes the Hemispheric South

Ideologies of which states belonged to the hemispheric South tended to separate students as well. Below I outline a relatively complex case of a girl from India, a country that was considered intermediate between the North and the South (sometimes classmates argued overtly about this in the ESL classes, pointing to the maps on the walls). Sita was a soft-spoken fifteen-year-old girl who had immigrated to Foxbury from a Gujarati-speaking area near Bombay, and had lived in Northern California since the age of five. Two different Latino neighborhoods, ethnically heterogeneous and with depressed rents (which incidentally have quadrupled in a ten-year span), provided points of entry for Sita's family.

Living in these low-income neighborhoods, Sita's family was relatively isolated from the other, more well-to-do Indian immigrants. Sita did not admit knowing any other people from India besides her cousins – and this despite a self-identified Indian/Indian-American population of 10 percent at Sor Juana High School. I conducted a group interview with Sita, Güera, and another eighteen-year-old girl. Sita was identified by Güera as someone who kicked it with the Sureños, and in the interview tapes one cannot fail but notice that her English phonology is a curious hybrid, with Chicano English intonation, Spanish words sprinkled in, and some Gujarati features.

Sita's explanation for her participation in Sur unfolded about one hour into the group interview:

NORMA: How come you're a Sureña?
SITA: Cause you know
I grew up with –
where a lot of Mexicans used to be
and that's the only color I knew about
and so I started hanging around with them
cause where I used to live
you know where they all hang out on Sureño Street?
I used to live there
On Washington Ave?
[. . .]
they still hang out over there
and I used to like,
talk to them
stuff like that you know?
So then I got used to THEM
so then they say, "oh I claim this and that,"
and then I said can I claim that? huh-huh
and they said ye[a:h]
NORMA: [Oh] so you had to ask?
Like if you could claim?
SITA: Yeah.
NORMA: Did you get jumped in?
SITA: No
nuh-uh
I just hanged around with them.
and at that time they used to claim me
but then after that
after two years I stopped claiming it
NORMA: How come?
SITA: Because like

When I came here Lola and them said that I was a liar.
They said I was lying and I didn't know anybody from the
Sureños.
so then I said forget it you guys
then if you wanna be like that then be like that
so then I stopped.
Even though when I came here
everyone came by the office
just looking at how I am and what I claim
sometimes I got into fights with them
they were calling me scrap and stuff
and then that got me pissed
and then I said "Fuck you, Norteños,"
like that,
and then they told the whole entire school that I claimed shit
and that I claimed Sur.

(Sita I/II/5:12)

Sita's affiliation with the Sureñas and Sureños relied partly on neighborhood localism, and the challenge she eventually suffered also hinged on it, since *once she moved away from that specific neighborhood* (to a more expensive neighborhood where her parents had bought a house), Sureñas challenged her affiliation. Sita was deeply offended by this: all her friends in her two previous neighborhoods had been Sureños, she was still good friends with Güera, and she told me that she had been trying to learn some Spanish. She did speak some Spanish with me, and her English was also under the influence of Chicano English. Sita's experience of living as an immigrant, living side-by-side with Sureños in the same neighborhoods, made her an "Honorary Mexican," according to Güera, and provides a contemporary parallel to the early twentieth-century history of California immigrants of Sikh and Mexican origin finding common ground in their migratory struggles.[55]

In Sita's example, social class (as signaled by place of residence) and the commonality of lived experience entered heavily into calculations of perceived hemispheric origin, and of whether or not she "belonged" in the Sureñas. The challenge to her membership did not come because she might be "passing" racially (Güera and other girls validated Sita's appearance by frequently admiring her dark skin and eyes, and saying how fantastic it was that in the blue clothes and the long eyeliner she looked "totally Mexican!"). Sita's challenge instead came because by moving to a different neighborhood she was interpreted as severing the localistic ties that provided the "proof" that she belonged. As for others in the community of Indian immigrants in the Bay Area, their parents were H1B (skilled worker) visa holders, living in relatively upscale suburbs.[56] The children of these higher-socioeconomic-status Indian immigrants, although occasionally also in the ESL classroom, were neither interested in joining nor considered for membership by the Sureños.

The Salvadoran Case: Why MS 13 Were Sureños

Ever since I had met the Sureños, it was clear that Salvadorans were incorporated into the Mexican-identified gang by virtue of their positioning both with respect to time-depth of immigration and to their place in the broader imaginary of global migratory circulation. Like the Sureños, they were primarily recently-arrived immigrants, and they were migrants from the global South to the global North. Had there been only one or two Salvadorans, they might have been absorbed into Sur 13 without distinction, but with greater numbers and the already-established presence of circular-migrating gangs from El Salvador,[57] they had acquired the critical mass to nurture a clique of their own: Mara Salvatrucha 13 (MS 13). The Mara Salvatrucha of Foxbury associated with the largely Mexican Sureños, wore blue, proclaimed their Spanish-language dominance, drew elaborate Old-English font signs reading MS 13 on their notebooks and the backs of their hands, and populated the beginning levels of classes for Limited English Proficient students at Sor Juana High School. Sitting in tutorial one day I chatted with Athena (a switcher who was a Sureña at the time) in English, and Marlin, one of the Salvadoran boys who had a crush on her, walked by and gently prodded us to speak Spanish, mockingly implying that our use of English was snobbish: "Ay, sí, las rucas 'muy, muy,' hablan mucho inglés. ¡ Hablen español!" (*Oh yeah, look at you, snobby girls speaking lots of English. Speak in Spanish!*)

Though the young people at Foxbury claimed no ties to El Salvador's organized supergang *La Mara*, they adopted the widely recognizable name of Mara Salvatrucha as their gang identifier, inheriting also its reputation for ruthlessness. To distinguish themselves from the Mexican Sureños, they grew out their sideburns (or rather attempted to, since some of the members were still in the early stages of puberty and found that their fine but scraggly sideburns could not be coaxed to fill in the correct shape). The sideburns were the distinctive feature that locally marked them as Salvadorans despite their otherwise vigilant observation of broader Sureño dress norms: blue clothing, Dickies pants, and the occasional hairnet. During a gym class interview with Ckristafer, a member of MS Sur, I learned that there were some non-Salvadorans who became MS 13 members. Ckristafer chuckled as he told me of a younger Mexican boy nicknamed Aquaman, a former Piporro who upon becoming a member of MS adopted a Salvadoran identity complete with Salvadoran Spanish speech patterns:

> CKRISTAFER: Comenzó a hablar así como nosotros. Así, igualito, nos copiaba. Ese vato, cuando le preguntaban que si de dónde era, decía que era de El Salvador, y como le habíamos contado, todo se lo sabía, y decía hasta de qué parte y de qué barrio.
> *He started speaking like us. Just like this, exactly the same, he would imitate us. That guy, if someone asked him where he was from, he would say he was from El Salvador, and because we had told him all about it, he knew everything, and would even say what part of it, and what neighborhood.*
> (Pandillas4/MS Sur/3.12.94/11:54)

Aquaman's efforts point to the importance of the dialectal distinctions between Salvadoran Spanish and Mexican Spanish in the construction of MS Sur personhood. It was not enough, in Aquaman's judgment, to be from the global South, or to speak Spanish. The specific features of Salvadoran Spanish had to be deployed to support his fantastic persona of a Mara Salvatrucha member. In other work I have shown that Salvadoran and Mexican children at this school are keenly aware of the differences between the varieties of Spanish spoken in different parts of Latin America, and used dialect imitation and national/ ethnoracial stereotypes to perform the linguistic work of both social affiliation and distinction.[58]

The Wedding Fight: MS 13 Becomes MS 14

Local incidents and intra-gang politics sometimes disrupted the affiliations that were in place, leading young people to establish new allegiances that went against their own prior practices. These moments of rupture were extremely revealing; one of the most extraordinary instances of the unraveling of the relationships that structured the logic of hemispheric localism happened in the summer between the first and second years of my fieldwork.

Shortly before the beginning of the school year, a Sureño wedding took place between a Mexican groom and a Salvadoran bride. The groom was a Sureño who had attended SJHS a few years back, and the bride was the older sister of one of the current Salvadoran MS Sur members. After the wedding ceremony there was a party, where Mexican Sureños and Mara Salvatrucha Sureños danced and socialized. Then, one of the Mexican guests reportedly got drunk and started a fight. According to Yasmeen, a Salvadoran-Brazilian guest at the party, a violent melee followed: "Some had belts, some had bottles . . . they started fighting right there in the salon and all the Salvadorans, all the guys were getting into it . . ." It was the height of humiliation: the wedding party was ruined, the bride cried bitterly, and after such a dramatic face threat, the Salvadoran Sureños decided to switch sides, from Sur to Norte.

At the beginning of the new school year, when all the parties found each other again on the campus of Sor Juana High School, Counselor Carnie witnessed a scene that he found extremely perplexing: during lunchtime from his office window he could see Robert, a sixteen-year-old Salvadoran, walking slowly and deliberately right up to a group of Sureños. Robert said nothing, looked at no one in particular but stared flatly ahead with a folded-up red bandanna perched on his shoulder. This defiant gesture Mr Carnie recognized immediately as some type of provocation; he ran outside yelling and used his walkie-talkie to call for teacher reinforcements. The boys quickly dispersed.

Shortly afterward (one assumes this got fully settled later off school grounds), the MS clique insisted on being called "Mara Salvatrucha XIV Norte." With this gesture, MS XIV Norte reconfigured the symbols of alignment between the groups: they physically relocated, moving their symbolic space from the old Sureño hangout near the English as a Second Language offices to the Norteño hangout space – closer to the front of the school and in full view of anyone who cared to notice. Additionally, the new alliance between Norte and MS resulted in some dramatic changes, not the least of which was in wardrobe: overnight, all the Salvadorans who had worn nothing but blue for the whole year that I had known them showed up to school in red outfits from head to toe. Red Nike Cortez sneakers with matching laces, burgundy sweatshirts, and red and black school notebooks appeared, while in the neighborhoods blue MS 13 graffiti were scratched out and replaced with fine fresh sprays of red MS 14 Norte. The sideburns the boys kept though, presumably out of a continuing need to distinguish themselves from the Chicano Norteños.

Additionally, in their new hangout space and seemingly out of nowhere the Salvadoran beginning ESL students demonstrated a previously cloaked linguistic competence in English. Students who had earlier insisted that Spanish be spoken to and around them turned out to have quite strong English verbal skills, with a high degree of fluency and no trouble at all communicating in the English-dominant settings of the Norteño hangouts. Barbeques, basketball games, and cruising on the weekends now all happened in English. Impressionistically, their newly revealed phonology sounded distinctively like African-American English, disclosing the source of their skills.

Athena and some of the Salvadorans' old Sureña friends did not like these new changes at all. Yasmeen, for instance, complained about the apparent contradiction in their prior stances: "It's like, 'barrio, barrio, barrio'. And what do they do for the barrio? Mess it up." Athena was more pointedly critical, repeatedly provoking Marlin:

ATHENA: I go, "come here, come here and beat my ass."
I go, "Then I'll really know you're a Norteño."
huh-huh.
They get mad but I don't care.
And then in class,
cause Marlin is in my class
and I'm all "Look Vicki at the map.
Where is El Salvador?
Is it on the North side or on the South side?
She goes, "It's on the South Side."
I go, "then why are they claiming North side when it's on the South side?"
I go, "Marlin, what's your problem?"
Marlin was such a good boy before,
and now he thinks he's ~bad~.
he thinks he's all
~ha:rd~
(.)
~co:re~
and stupid.[59]

This appeal to the actual hemispheric location of El Salvador highlights the terms of contestation of the Norteño/Sureño identity. Does hemispheric location trump local dynamics of affiliation? Athena thinks it should. Does everyday linguistic practice determine or at least indicate the direction of one's allegiance? Does a new speech act (such as tagging differently) supersede one's previous claim? Cuca, a recently inducted Norteña, mused in an interview with me:

CUCA: Now they, like, only speak English.
NORMA: Right.
CUCA: And it's like,
         One thing they don't understand is like,
         MS is supposed to go, like, with their color flag,
         for blue?
         And I don't see why all of a sudden they go with the Norteños,
         go for red now.
NORMA: Un hnn.
CUCA: It's like they should just stick with their color.
         And the way they tag now is different.
         The way they tag is Norte now.
         They **never** used to tag Norte, even when they were Sur.
         They just tagged MS.
         Now, since they went Norte and everything
         they tag "Norte MS" and all this.
         It's like the MS, and the Norteños,
         they just combined into one big family.

The multiplicity of interpretations of the actual colors can be seen in Cuca's explanation. An additional reason, according to her, for the Salvadorans staying as Sureños is because the Salvadoran flag is predominantly blue. This explanation, which basically appeals to the properties of the colors themselves and not to anything hemispheric or linguistic or political, cannot be discounted: it is present in many youth's explanations of why someone might switch (they stopped liking the color red, or they like blue better). The "color preference" explanation is sometimes the first line of explanation that people use, and just like explanations involving neighborhood localism, it is not displaced in young people's discourse, but recurs in conjunction with all the other factors.

Norteños and Sureños Against Larger Forces

Sometimes, there were extraordinary events that fostered unity between Norte and Sur. In the months leading up to the passage of Proposition 187,[60] Norte and Sur members demonstrated in the streets together, and attended information seminars peacefully together. The ones who could vote on both sides got organized and turned out to register together, and brought their relatives when possible. I watched the voting returns on a big-screen television at a pizza parlor with an uncharacteristically mixed group of Fresas, Norteñas, and a couple of Sureñas including Sita. All of us had people we loved and cared about who would be directly affected by the passage of the proposition. When the proposition passed, together we watched young people from all the different groups disappear from school, some of them permanently, fearing that they might be apprehended and deported on school grounds. After this traumatic episode, a sort of depressed peace took over. When a Norteña called a Sureña a wetback, T-Rex snapped: "Don't be stupid, that was your parents, that was your grandparents."

The Gorditos Incident

The most dramatic example of Norte/Sur pragmatic unity was recounted to me in a narrative by T-Rex, the story of a major fight that didn't happen because the police showed up. In the transcript below I mark with symbols from the International Phonetic Alphabet particularly noteworthy pronunciations that are part of T-Rex's style. We will discuss these stylistic dimensions of T-Rex's speech in later chapters; I mark them here to show how she uses them in the texture of this narrative, as discourse markers, particles that manage information and aid its flow and at the same time give a particular flavor to her speech:

> T-Rex:　It happened at Rillito Park.
> There was a lot of Sureños,
> a lot of Norteños,
> we had bats,
> we had everything [ɛvɾiɾiŋ];
> we were prepared to **kill** each other.

The cops came and everybody started running.
And the funny thing [ţiŋ],
that you're gonna laugh about,
was that um,
I was trying to get over a fence?
and um,
and fuckin',
me and a Sureño were both trying to jump the same fence,
cause we were both gorditos *(fatties)*,
so the cops was coming,
so he helped me up and I helped him up.
So we started cutting out.
So when it comes down to the cops
we both would cover up for each other.
[. . .]
The funny thing [ţiŋ] is,
cuando se quieren pelear con los negritos,
(when they want to fight with the Black kids,)
 también estamos ahí nosotros.
(We are right there too.)
Talk shit.

NORMA: Wow. That's tremendous.

T-REX: We're always fighting
but we're always together.
We could call ourselves wetbacks,
Mexicanos, mojados *(wetbacks)*, but nobody else could.
That's the thing [ţiŋ],
that's the whole thing [ţiŋ].

NORMA: Would you defend a Sureño if-

T-REX: -Hell, yeah, I will!
Una negrita me dijo,
(A Black girl said to me,)
"Yeah, that fuckin' wetback."
I got out of the fucking car and I said to her,
"Don't ever fucking call him a wetback in front of me,
I'm a wetback,
you got something to say, tell me. "
See, hay un dicho.
(There's a saying),
You can call me mojada *(wetback)* if you're Mexican
but if you're not don't fuck with it.
Don't fuck with me.
Only my raza *(people)* could call me mojada

cause they know how it feels to be a mojada.
That's the whole thing [t̪iŋ].

T–Rex&N@N's 4:29

Leaving a detailed discussion of the discourse markers for the linguistic section of the book, in this retelling of the fight story we find that the commonalities that T-Rex points out between Norteños and Sureños are pervasive, to the point where she claims to defend them and to stand up for them because only they understand the experience of migration. I must underline that this is an enormous statement coming from a girl who was considered the toughest, the most hard-core, and the de-facto leader of Norteñas for many miles around. She is on the one hand drawing attention to the arbitrary, socially constructed nature of the gangs, and on the other hand she is unwittingly foreshadowing the events of her own life. As hard-core as she was at the time that this ethnography took place, five years later T-Rex married a Sureño.

In a separate discussion, another admission of a yearning for unity came from Junior. Toward the end of his interview, which was the last time I ever saw him, Junior finished by reflecting on the destructive nature of the conflict:

En realidad no se trata de nosotros. Los que se benefician son los comerciantes. A ellos les conviene que haya eso. La Mafia, Nuestra Familia quieren que los Sureños y Norteños hagamos el trabajo. Pero entre ellos, abajo, hay conexiones.

This is not really about us. The ones that benefit are the dealers. It is to their advantage. La Mafia and Nuestra Familia want us the Sureños and Norteños to do the work. But between them, below the surface, are the connections.

[. . .]

Todo lo de afuera son chigaderas de la calle. Son chingaderas porque la verdad, ¿a qué llevan? Al Americano le conviene que uno se esté matando. ¿Porqué? Porque si estuviéramos juntos todos los Hispanos, no importa quién seamos, nos va mejor, más oportunidades para trabajar.

Everything on the outside [of prison] is just street shit. It's shit because honestly, what does it lead to? The American benefits if we continue killing each other. Why? Because, if all the Hispanics were together, no matter who we were, we would fare better, and have more work opportunities.

Pero así nos ven separados, peleando. Igual a los Crips y a los Bloods. Los güeros están bien unidos. ¿Cuándo ves una pandilla de rojo y de azul de güeros? No. Entonces, así es lo que pasa.

But this way they see us separate, fighting. Same for the Crips and the Bloods.
The Whites are totally united. Have you ever seen a red or blue gang that is
made up of whites? Never. So, that's how it is.

Junior 3: 8:50

Junior's and T-Rex's excerpts taken together point to the realization by Norteños and Sureños that there are deep commonalities in their experience that transcend their conflict over different ways of being "authentically Mexican." In T-Rex's case, she realizes that larger forces (such as the police) that threaten both Norte and Sur call for a united approach, while Junior's excerpt underlines the apathy of the prison gangs and their desire to manipulate their street counterparts without any loyalties to them. Junior's prescient statements of unity across the gang boundaries for the sake of social advancement re-create and reflect the original Chicano consciousness and critiques of racism that Nuestra Familia pintos *(prisoners)* articulated in the Norteño manifesto. These critiques became important again recently, during the 2006 protests for immigration reform, where Norteños and Sureños once again marched together in the streets for a common cause.

Notes

1   Brinkhoff (2006)
2   Though as Ochs (1979) and Bucholtz (2000) remind us, transcriptions always already reflect some theoretical viewpoint.
3   Sartre (1948)
4   Weismantel and Eisenman (1998: 122)
5   Silverstein (1976), Ochs (1981)
6   Older, long-time gang members who have already been through the prison system.
7   Chesney-Lind (1993), Chesney-Lind (1995), Miranda (2003), Mendoza-Denton (1996), Mendoza-Denton (1999)
8   Main (2006)
9   Mowry (1992), Rodriguez (1993), Shakur (1994), Mendoza (2005), Simpson (2005)
10   Phillips (1999)
11   pelon408 (2006)
12   De Los Santos (1999), Gowen (2002)
13   Goodwin, Goodwin and Yaeger-Dror (2002)
14   Flege (forthcoming)
15   Khattab (forthcoming), Mendoza-Denton (forthcoming)

16   Myers–Scotton (1995), Zentella (1998)
17   Juvenile hall, also known as "juvi," is a correction facility for minors.
18   Campbell (1984)
19   Taco/food stand
20   Briggs (1986)
21   Purnell, Idsardi and Baugh (1999)
22   Gal and Irvine (2000: 38)
23   Gómez-Peña (2006)
24   The prickly pear cactus is a plant indigenous to Mexico and depicted on the national flag. Mexican mythology has it that in their search for a new capital, Aztecs looked for a sign: that of the eagle with a serpent in its beak, perched atop a prickly pear cactus. When they saw this, Tenochtitlán the pre-Columbian capital was founded. Thus the prickly pear cactus is symbolic of indigenous Mexico.
25   Zentella (1998)
26   Valdés (1994)
27   Modan (2006)
28   Villenas (1996)
29   Bailey (2002)
30   Katzew (1996), Hendrickson (2004)
31   Alonso (2004)
32   Similar to *pieds noirs*, French colonists born in Algeria generations ago and still today stigmatized after repatriation back to France. Smith (2006)
33   García Saíz, (1989), Carrera (2003)
34   Klor de Alva (1996)
35   Katzew (2000), Hendrickson (2004)
36   Carrera (2003: 147)
37   Klor de Alva (1996: 60)
38   Wade (1997), Oboler and Dzidzienyo (2005)
39   Vasconcelos and Gamio (1926), Weismantel and Eisenman (1998), Alonso (2004)
40   Alonso (2004: 465)
41   Alonso (2004)
42   Hale (1996: 2)
43   Messing (2003), Flores Farfán (1999)
44   Bailey (2002), Wade (1997), Oboler and Dzidzienyo (2005), Domínguez (1997)
45   Bacigalupo, p.c.; no reference to Nabokov
46   Messing (2003)
47   Messing (2003: 40)
48   Messing (2003)
49   Please see chapter 1 note on relajo.
50   López Castro (2005)

51 Díaz (2000)
52 Díaz (2000)
53 López Castro (2005: 10)
54 López Castro (2005: 12) my translation.
55 LaBrack and Leonard (1984), Pinsky (1987), Lindel (1991)
56 Mankekar (2002), Shankar (2005)
57 Movimiento de Jóvenes Encuentristas (1999)
58 Mendoza-Denton (1995)
59 The transcription reflects a voice quality known as creaky voice, which is commonly heard as a raspy quality to the voice.
60 Please see chapter 1 for details on Prop 187.

CHAPTER 5

"MUY MACHA": GENDERED PERFORMANCES AND THE AVOIDANCE OF SOCIAL INJURY

The body is the inscribed surface of events.
Michel Foucault[1]

"Such a Pretty Girl!"

Early in the fall of 1995, the nationally syndicated American television talk show, *Geraldo*, featured a special show on makeovers. An otherwise pedestrian topic, commonplace on daytime television, had a twist this time: today Geraldo was going to show us makeovers of six girls who were involved in gangs. "Uncovering the hidden beauty within" was the subtitle of the show, a mantra repeated at the opening of every commercial break.

Geraldo Rivera (the former Jerry Rivers), the talk show host, introduced the gang girls in question, and the guest makeup artists who were to unlock the hidden, secret beauty of these young women. The hair and makeup artists were all prominent New York City salon stylists, and they were joined by a fashion consultant, who was to help in choosing new clothes. One by one, six girls between the ages of fifteen and twenty came out in their "regular" clothes: big white t-shirts; large, pleated khaki pants, called Dickies; Pendleton plaid wool jackets; and severe dark makeup. Linda, the second girl, was wearing a beanie, a black wool ski cap that covered her entire head and forehead, including her eyebrows. Many of the girls wore deep, dark eyeliner that extended the line of their eyes to their temples, and some of them wore black lipstick. Geraldo introduced them – all the girls but one were

African-American and/or Latina. Two of the girls were Nuyorican[2] twin sisters, accompanied to the show by their mom. The girls stood serious and proud before the cameras in sideways poses, one shoulder thrust forward, hands deep in their pockets, feet perpendicular to each other, and tilted-back heads that looked *down* at the cameras.

Fifteen minutes later, the girls had been transformed: they paraded out from the side wings in tiny wool sweaters, miniskirts, heathered tights, and high-heeled Mary Janes. At each girl's appearance, the audience would cheer and clap, and Geraldo and his makeup artists would discuss the transformation: "She really is *such* a pretty girl," gushed the coiffeuse, "all I did was give her [hair] some lift and bounce." Linda of the beanie came out in a mass of curls, looking a little confused. She was wearing a short black jumper with black tights and a fitted white shirt with huge dangling cuffs. Her jumper had no pockets, and she wrung her hands distractedly. "You look sooo . . . *feminine!*" remarked Geraldo, exhorting the audience to admire the difference between the "before" and "after" pictures. The audience ooohed approvingly, and Geraldo bounded up to Linda to ask her whether she would continue to dress like this. "Um, yeah," Linda said rather unenthusiastically. "Maybe."

Bad Girls and Drag Queens

This episode of the Geraldo show is based on the premise that there is something *aberrant, unfeminine,* and *rectifiable* about girls who are involved in gangs. What is it that is so unsettling to Geraldo and to the rest of the public, obsessed as we are with representations – including this book – of "bad girls"? And what laws of gender are the girls breaking, such that it is deemed necessary to give them correctional and rehabilitative therapies like makeovers and juvenile halls?

In discussing how notions of power, femininity, and ethnicity permeate the discourses of and around girls involved in gangs, I explore how the cholas of Foxbury perform and inscribe on their bodies a specific kind of femininity that not only confounds wider community notions of how girls should act, dress, and talk, but throws into question the very gendered category that girls are expected to inhabit.

In this chapter I elaborate on contemporary understandings of play as performance and gender as performance,[3] specifically calling drag queens to the rescue in understanding the politics and aesthetics of cholas, and what – if anything – it may be that these different systems of gendered symbolic display have in common.[4] I conclude the chapter by addressing the "female liberation hypothesis" in gang research through an analysis of girls' discourse of "being macha."

Critical theoretic approaches to drag have generated many questions about the status of the subject. Is there an a priori gendered subject *before* drag? Similarly, we may ask if there is an a priori girl-subject before the chola. Is it the case that underneath the hard exterior of the chola there is a little girl, waiting to be coaxed out? Certainly this is the assumption underlying the "Gang Girl Makeovers" segment of the Geraldo show. Its mission of "uncovering the hidden beauty within" assumes an underlying feminine gendered subject, and proposes that, if only the girls could see for themselves how pretty they might be "inside," if only they could realize some deep inner wish for femininity, then they could/would stop being gang members. The heteronormative project of turning them into feminine girls on the outside has still another aspiration: if the girls could realize their "pretty potential" on the outside, maybe the positive attention derived would make them want to stop being gang girls. A happy byproduct of this process might be the assimilation of gang girls into mainstream beauty norms to make us television viewers feel just a little bit safer, a little bit better about neutralizing their difference and their potential level of threat.

In her analysis of Jennie Livingston's *Paris is Burning*, a quasi-ethnographic film about African-American and Latina drag queens in New York City, Judith Butler poses the next logical question in the debate: Is *all* of gender drag? She explains:

> To claim that all gender is like drag, or is drag, is to suggest that "imitation" is at the heart of the heterosexual project and its gender binarisms, that drag is not a secondary imitation that presupposes a prior and original gender, but that hegemonic heterosexuality is itself a constant and repeated effort to imitate its own idealizations. That it must repeat this imitation, that it sets up pathologizing practices and normalizing sciences in order to produce and consecrate its own claim on originality and propriety, suggests that heterosexual performativity is beset by an anxiety that it can never fully overcome, that its effort to become its own idealizations can never be finally or fully achieved, and that it is consistently haunted by that domain of sexual possibility that must be excluded for heterosexualized gender to produce itself.[5]

Questioning the "naturalness" of gender and showing the ways in which it is socially constructed, and the attendant disciplinary and punitive methods that aid this construct, are two of the of the main thrusts of contemporary feminist theory. Here I incorporate anthropological and philosophical notions of cultural/gender performativity specifically to address performative styles that overtly use the "tools" of one kind of performativity to achieve another. Drag, for instance, uses the tools of feminine gender performance to achieve a radical destabilization of hegemonic masculine gender norms. It also indexes, like all social play and social dramas,[6] agonistic struggles and underlying tensions within society.

Destabilization of gender norms is by no means the only effect of drag performances, however. Drag has the potential for reinforcing and policing the boundaries of the heterosexual project, of naming what is feminine, and holding us to it, so that drag queens, as Butler puts it,[7] out-woman women. Contrapositively, cholas in California personify and to some extent dictate what good girls are not: they *are* the girls that Moms, and the police, have warned us about. And their gender transgressions are always apparent, with their penchant for beating up boys, forming exclusive female societies, and cultivating an appearance that refuses to conform to either Mexican or American notions of what little girls are made of: "My dad dice que me miro como lesbian *(says I look like a lesbian)*, my mom dice que qué guangajona *(complains that it's baggy)*," reports fourteen-year-old Maureen. "How much you wanna bet that I can go outside like this y no me dicen nada *(they won't say anything)*."

The threatening nature of these girlish transgressions was evident in police attitudes toward cholas. The 1993 *Gang Training Seminar Handbook* of the Northern California Gang Investigators Association attributed some rather mysterious powers to gang members:

> Typical gang members are intelligent but may lack formal education. They are "street smart," able to fend for themselves, and are accomplished in the art of manipulation.[8]

Cholas were also perceived as threatening by the teachers, who, in collusion with and under direction of the police, attempted in one school to install the ultimate Foucauldian panopticon[9] of see-through windows in the boys' restrooms. Cholas were also threatening to some of the

Euro-American kids in the school who criticized them – but never to their faces – for wearing sarapes *(a type of traditional Mexican long wool poncho)* to school. As Judy, a self-consciously trendy Euro-American girl once told me: "Those Mexicans in the blankets, those cholos, they think they're so tough, they think they're so hard." And yet, other groups clearly imitated chola style, especially the punks, boys *and* girls, who trafficked in *bricolage*,[10] and copied chola makeup techniques to the utter dismay of the "owners" of the style.[11]

The symbolic and unconventional use of makeup among the girls claiming Norte and Sur at Sor Juana High School literally painted gender and ethnicity on their bodies. In this display, the girls embodied the ideology of what it meant to be a chola, and wrote on their faces a semiotics that worked parallel to and in careful concert with other symbolic behaviors all focusing toward the same end: the articulation of a distinct style, different from their parents, who continually asked why their little girls must dress like this, when we have none of this in Mexico, it must be all of this bad American influence. A style distinct from the mainstream, which was convinced that they must be acting like this *because* they're Mexican, and a style distinct from that of other subaltern groups within the school, now in alliance and now in conflict with the various articulations of African-American and Asian-American identities, but always questioning and underlining the various tensions extant within the Mexican diaspora. Both signifier and signified, the cholas' bodies were inscribed with the traces of conflict: assimilation, ethnic pride, covert prestige, and the pride of survival were all etched on the surface of their skins, rewritten every morning in the mirror with the help of Maybelline, Wet n' Wild, and Cover Girl.

Additionally, there were in this particular neighborhood, at that particular moment in the mid-to-late-1990s, differences in the semiotics of personal appearance – Norteña and Sureña hair, eyeliner, and lipstick, were crucial to members' identification of each others' allegiance. Long, feathered hair was a local marker for Norteña membership: "Your hair has to be all feathered, with fixer [hairspray]." This is in contrast with a hairstyle that I have termed a "vertical ponytail," characteristic of Sureñas and consisting of straight long hair, with the portion above the ears gel-slicked close to the head and gathered into an orderly ponytail cascading from the top of the head. I often observed the smoothing and rearranging of ponytails, hair by hair, until they were perfect. In all cases, however, the hair had to be long. Another option for hairstyle was to wear a bandanna, known as a *paño*, over the head or forehead (this was also acceptable for boys who sometimes also wore hairnets). The paño was often a very sentimental object, since many of the girls saw it as symbolic of their membership in the group. Again, because of the ubiquity and easy commercial access to these objects, I would caution against interpreting any young person with a bandanna as a gang member. In this particular neighborhood at this particular time, wearing a paño low over the forehead was a skill, likened to the wearing of dark sunglasses. As T-Rex described it to me, "It looks bad,[12] this way you can look at people, and watch them as they walk by. Here, you can have my paño, so you can see yourself and you can see that you're cholita."

Different methods of applying eyeliner look completely different, and are easily visible at distances of several feet. Liquid eyeliner, for example, has a more defined, "sharper" outline than solid eyeliner, and solid eyeliner looks different if used alone vs. in conjunction with liquid. Try this at home. Eyeliner is an effective method of identification since it can be worn by itself and without any of the other symbolic markers such as clothes, making the girls easily distinguishable to each other but inscrutable (and indeed, frightening) to anyone else. Brown and red lipstick − different even to the naïve observer − also differentiated the girls from each other, with Sureñas wearing brown eyeliner as lipstick, and Norteñas wearing red or burgundy lipstick.

Despite all of these differences, there were many similarities in general style that members of both of these groups had, and common signaling devices that they recognized across boundaries. I will talk about some of the similarities in the following section.

The Lexicon of Makeup

I was originally intrigued to look into this topic because I found over and over in my data remarks about eyeliner. Whenever I would ask "How do you know who is a chola?", girls would mention eyeliner as one of the principal markers of identity. Xiomara, a Sureña, once pointed out to me all of her chola friends, and then gave me the following heuristic: "If you want to know who's a chola, just look for the eyeliner. Everybody could notice that that's a chola." T-Rex cautioned against spurious correlations: "One way you can tell a fake chola is 'cause they do their eyeliner wrong. All the way out to their pelo (hair). And it goes up."

The public nature of the eyeliner, and its commonly agreed-to meaning, with length of eyeliner signaling intention as well as willingness to fight, was evidenced in girls repeatedly interpreting long eyeliner as a provocation, as well as by remarks like the following, from a diminutive Norteña whom I will call Xóchitl: "When I wear my eyeliner, me siento más macha *(I feel more macha)*, I'm ready to fight."

I have mentioned that T-Rex was one of the top leaders of a neighborhood group of Norteñas, a large group that, despite what the police or city council might think, thought of themselves as "running" the neighborhood of Foxbury. When the need arose, up to seventy Norteñas were "down for" this neighborhood, and were commanded by T-Rex to defend territory, pursue unfriendly boy trespassers and, as they said, "take care of business." This particular neighborhood was for all intents and purposes a girl-dominated space. But what happened when they wanted to hang out together? T-Rex regarded feminine makeovers as a type of drag, a way of diverting and throwing off unwanted police attention:

T-REX: [Dressing feminine] That's a GOOD cover up, you know?
And that's how Norteñas do it,
they dress all fancy, and stuff,
with mini skirts and high heels?
They [the cops] don't know they're Norteñas you know?
'Cause you don't know what's under the . . . the clothes you know?

Precisely because we can't know what's under the clothes (Sureña? Norteña? Piporra? Researcher?) we are able to understand both chola-dressing and normative feminine-dressing as different types of gender drag. Elements of this interplay between the hidden and the revealed are also echoed in the larger context of young people's discussion of "Mexican masks" in chapter 6.

"Bedroom Cultures"

Angela McRobbie and Jenny Garber[13] observed that the focus in the British subcultural studies tradition on male adolescents and their public street cultures structured a gender gap in the literature by virtue of girls' confinement to domestic spheres (see fuller discussion of subculture studies literature in chapter 6). Their classic article on the articulation of girls' "bedroom cultures" focuses on the consumption of mass-mediated images and its role in the subjectivity of girls. In the Sor Juana High School context, gang girls were not a bedroom culture,[14] and neither did they consume mainstream media. Still the bedroom was their main site for the bulk of their artistic production surrounding makeup, since it was a morning ritual that took place generally before they left the house, and was their main site for experimentation, innovation and practice with different types of makeup. The school bathroom was another studio for the production of this ephemeral art form.

The interaction that is transcribed below took place one afternoon when T-Rex invited me over to her house. While in her bedroom we started discussing chola style, and she played Oldies for me ("Duke of Earl" was her favorite) and showed me the various physical aspects of chola style. She took turns painstakingly showing me how she applied her makeup, and then proceeded to put it on me, remarking admiringly on the change.[15] At one point she drew in my eyeliner, long and hard, and we had the following interaction:

T-REX: You would never be noticed like you were a fucking teacher.
         Doesn't it make you have power, doesn't it just..
NORMA: I don't even recognize myself.
T-REX: Think about all the shit.
         You're hard.
         Nobody could fuck with you,
         you got power.
         People look at you,
         but nobody fucks with you.
         So when you walk down the street,
         you got the special walk, *[begins to walk deliberately, swinging her upper body]*
         you walk like this,
         you walk all slow,
         just checking it out.
         I look like a dude, ¿que no?
                    (don't I?)
         I walk, and then I stop.
         I go like this *[tilts head back – this is called looking "in"]*
         I always look in, I always look in,

I never look down.
It's all about power.
You never fucking smile.
Fucking never smile.
We never wear earrings,
　just in case we get in a fight.
It's not our style to wear earrings, ¿me entiendes?
　　　　　　　　　　　　　　(you know?)

NORMA: Hhhnhhnhn. *[laughing]*
T-REX: Cause that's the weak spot.
NORMA: Uh-huh.
T-REX: Look, just look all tough, like this,
　OK, I'll throw a four, like this,
　and then you throw a one.
　Like that, looks ba:d.
　And if you're at a party,
　and you see a dude that you like,
　don't ever smile.
　Just walk up to him and kiss him.

In this excerpt, T-Rex articulates much of what is powerful about cholas' use of eyeliner. She highlights a power-based interpretation of her own makeup practices, where her inscrutability and threatening demeanor allow her to go wherever she wants and command the kind of attention and respect that is not usually given to little girls: "Everybody looks at you but nobody fucks with you."

Later, while writing up this chapter, I called up T-Rex to check on a couple of facts, and she told me the following:

Don't forget to tell them that eyeliner is really important.
　When I turn on the eyeliner, when I really put it on, you know long and shit, it makes me feel like another person, it makes me feel tough. Just wearing the eyeliner even without the clothes makes me feel brave.

In addition to explanations involving power and toughness, cholas also invoked ethnicity to rationalize other choices regarding makeup, so that when the discussion turned to lipstick and foundation, ethnicity-based explanations emerged. A basic rule of thumb was that, since being

Norteña and Sureña involved highlighting a (Mestiza) Mexican-based identity of some sort, dark skin was something that was valued.

Mosquita and Adriana, two Sureñas who were making themselves up in the locker room one day, gave me advice on what sort of foundation to wear: "Always wear brown 'cause that's the color of your skin. If you have eyeshadow, go for the second darker one next. You have to use darker cover-up. You can't wear cover-up lighter than you 'cause they tell you that you want to be white. You gotta do it darker than your skin, or the same color as your skin. I'm making yours darker 'cause you're morena *(dark skinned)*. Porque eres más *(because you are)* darker."

This apparent valuation of dark skin is fraught with conflict, since as we saw in chapter 4, both the Norteña and Sureña groups participated in Latin American race-thinking that devalued both Indian-ness and Blackness. In the example above with Mosquita and Adriana, wearing dark foundation was valued not as an aesthetic choice, or as an active claim to Indian-ness or Blackness, but as a way to block the inference that one wants to be white. It's quite a tightrope to achieve the right color skin so as to be not-white and not-Indian/Black at the same time.

This aesthetic of not-wanting-to-appear-white is so pervasive that it affected Latina girls who were fair-skinned (and there were a lot of them, since one of the key sending states in immigration, Michoacán, has a large population of French descent, especially in the rural areas). Güera the Sureña wore foundation that was about three shades darker than her face, as well as dark contact lenses to cover up her light-colored eyes. Sureñas sometimes also dyed their hair black; Norteñas might dye it reddish. Blue hair would be completely out of the question, however, since that style was clearly marked as "punk," or in other words, (mostly) white.[16]

Another reason that the girls cited for wearing very heavy foundation was that if it should happen that you got in a fight, then heavy foundation masked the bruises from teachers and parents. If you feather your hair right, I was told, and you wear heavy enough foundation, no one can tell that you were in a fight. Here the technology of femininity is used as an instrument to outwardly display stance, to reify ethnic ideals, as well as to mask behavior that can have negative repercussions from the girls' perspective.

As far as body image, the body ideal, like almost every other physical ideal, of the cholas was willfully and radically opposed to what was and is still valued within the normative Euro-American beauty ideals. Since the chola hierarchy was partly based on physical power, girls who were physically powerful, in the sense that they could beat up other cholas and cholos, were at the top of the hierarchy. All of the top leaders, the downest cholas, of the various groups that I met over the course of my fieldwork have been fairly zaftig girls. They were considered the most powerful, beautiful, and sexy, and would pride themselves on turning every single head in a room as they walked in. They were often quite athletic. T-Rex, for instance, was captain of the basketball team and Most Valuable Player two years in a row. These girls prided themselves on both substantial size and physical power. And they made merciless fun of Euro-American girls' preoccupation with weight and with food issues.[17]

In the spring of 1994, I went to a Norteña quinceañera or fifteenth birthday party, a kind of traditional Mexican debutante ball. Every plate, dish, dress, napkin, flower, and curtain in the whole place was red, and most of the guests were prominent Norteños. First came the religious ceremony, a Catholic mass (where the quinceañera walked down the aisle wearing a beautiful white dress and long eyeliner), and then there was a party, with lots of food. As the party got going, T-Rex and a Norteña friend of hers, Pati, and I were standing in line to take some food. Right ahead of us there was an Anglo Norteña, who was fretting about the food, and hesitant to take very much of it because she felt that it was embarrassing to eat in front of boys. T-Rex and Pati looked at each other in disbelief, and when we returned to our table they severely criticized the girl and intimated that she was not really a down Norteña because she had Anglo attitudes toward food.[18] A real Norteña, they said, would never be embarrassed to eat in front of anybody. "We feel proud of ourselves and our bodies," they snapped defensively, aware of the intrusion of the aesthetics of the other, "We look good like this. Norteñas don't diet."

Theorizing Cosmetics

One of the very interesting features of all of this discourse is that it fits uneasily within recent feminist writings on makeup and the body. Whereas most of the recent writings emphasize the totalizing power of advertising and normative cultural practices, there is little effort to examine the fragmented standpoints from which women operate. To be sure, much of the work being done is extremely valuable in exposing overall tendencies. We can hardly argue with Janet Bordo, who writes:

> The general tyranny of fashion – perpetual, elusive, and instructing the female body in a pedagogy of personal inadequacy and lack – is a powerful discipline for *all* women in this culture. But even as we are all normalized to the requirements of appropriate feminine insecurity and preoccupation with appearance, more specific requirements emerge in different cultural and historical contexts, and for different groups. When Bo Derek put her hair in corn rows, she was engaging in a normalizing feminine practice, But when Oprah Winfrey admitted on her show that all her life she had desperately longed to have hair that swings from side to side as she shakes her head, she revealed the power of racial and gender normalization, normalization not only to "femininity," but to the Caucasian beauty standards that still dominate on television, in movies, in popular magazines. Neither Oprah nor the . . . many women who ironed their hair in the 1960's have creatively or playfully invented themselves here.[19]

Bordo's discussion above assumes that "*all* women in this culture" orient to the same hegemonic ideals of beauty that are supplied through the various media for public consumption. This model does not say that all women are the same, but it places different women as similarly oriented to the mainstream: for instance, one can be Latina, African-American, or Asian-American, and still be attending to the dominant Euro-American hegemonic norms, creating what I will call the "Oprah effect" – when members of minority groups judge themselves by the aesthetic norms of the dominant group. The same assumption of a single orientation, a singly defined "eye" that women cast on each other, underlies the discussion by Judith Goldstein, who in her analysis of home makeup videos, writes:

> The transformation of the innocent gaze into one of critical judgment, which occurs upon entry to the world of beauty, is at once social and subjective; it is aimed at other women and at oneself. This combination of equalizing (standardizing) and effacing emphasizes that together women potentially constitute what I will call a "female aesthetic community" while it finesses what might otherwise divide or unite them. This community is democratic, and, in its erasure of difference, oddly utopian.[20]

Here I am not arguing against the powerful, generalized and pervasive nature of the disciplining practices that contemporary society reserves for women, but I do want to make clear that when the technology of femininity is used for unintended ends, there is a moment of rupture that can open up new possibilities within the system. The fact that the girls often refuse to use cosmetics for their intended purposes, both at the micro-level, where the preferred lipstick is actually brown eyeliner in many cases, and at the macro-level where foundation is used to signal ethnic pride and negotiate racialized standpoints no matter what one's skin tone, *this* is completely destabilizing to the way that we can understand the girls and how their symbolic cosmetic system works, and is the reason they are read as unfeminine and threatening. Other people know that there is something going on symbolically, but they don't know what. It is as though cholas are ungrammatical: they use the elements of a symbolic system that we are thoroughly familiar with, but refuse to conform to (white hegemonic) community notions of how these symbols ought to be used. What they are to "mean" is no longer recoverable from the surface.

This refusal of the hegemonic paradigm allows us to understand that these young women are completely differently situated and *not orienting* to much of the normative discourse. I would propose that the cholas (and many other subaltern groups with their own aesthetic norms) are not only outside of the "female aesthetic community" but want no part of it, actively rebuffing and contradicting it. In the whole two and a half years of my fieldwork, I did not see a single chola reading a mainstream (or any kind of) fashion magazine. For a brief and singular period, these girls were free from the "Oprah effect."

Despite this differential standpoint, using the tools of but standing outside mainstream feminine consumerist culture, many of the cholas that I interviewed shared Geraldo's assumptions. As they moved out of gang participation, they echoed the idea that dressing like a *chola* is unfeminine. Here is an excerpt from an interview with a fifteen-year-old girl who had been involved off and on with the Sureñas, and whom I will call Agata:

AGATA: Eighth and ninth grade I was in a gang,
and I was blue.
I moved, and I got out of it
and I grew up totally,
I started dressing up like a young lady,

and then I got,
I started wearing Dickies again, and fighting,
and doing dumb stuff . . .

Agata here distances herself from her *chola* behavior, since at the point where I am interviewing her she is trying to stay away from being a Sureña. For her, "dressing like a young lady," could be translated as "not dressing like a chola," as is the case with Raisa, who tried to distance herself from the Norteñas as she headed off for college, and complained about her chola friends: "They should stop wearing Dickies and start dressing like girls, you know, they have to grow out of it."

The fact is that, as the girls in my study passed from their teens to their twenties and ceased to identify as cholas, I increasingly found "coming of age" narratives, where girls spoke of gang participation as the transition to adulthood, and equated getting out of the gangs with growing older. As Rebecca, a 21-year-old ex-Norteña, said to me, "You can't be a teeny-bopper forever." Rebecca had gone on to college, and she and her former homegirls were still close although most of them now had new friends, or got married, or had kids. Rebecca didn't dress like a chola anymore, and I'd also noticed other changes about her – in college, she started worrying more about her appearance vis-à-vis mainstream norms (her college was populated mostly by Euro-American students), and she had gone on a diet. She also had begun to mainstream various aspects of her persona. Gone was the eyeliner, the Dickies, and even the Chicano English intonation.

Can we analogize between cholas and drag? Would it be correct to say that Rebecca stopped being in gang-girl drag and returned to Goldstein's female aesthetic community, dominated by normative notions of whiteness and femininity? Are girls destined to give up their alternative femininities as they grow up and leave the gangs? Or was there something more enduring that resulted from the temporary subjectivity in being a gang girl?

The Discourse of Being Macha: Prophylaxis from Social Injury?

The literature on gangs reviewed in chapters 3 and 4 traditionally paid little attention to girls. Frederic Thrasher's classic study,[21] for example, hypothesized that girls lacked the "ganging instinct." As this historical gap has begun to be addressed, contemporary research accounts of the eventual social outcomes for gang-involved girls have given rise to a fierce debate, summarized by David Curry[22] as the "social injury" hypothesis versus the "female liberation" hypothesis.

On the social injury side stand Joan Moore and John Hagedorn,[23] who hold that long-term consequences from gang involvement are much more devastating for girls than they are for boys. "Joining a gang and wearing its conspicuous clothes [. . .] labeled [girls] as unacceptable to the wider community. Many had joined the gang to escape abusive families, but gang membership actually constricted their futures."[24] According to the "social injury" hypothesis, gang membership leads to irreversible social stigmatization in neighborhoods that are already economically depressed, and to sexual stigmatization that results in the narrowing of non-gang marriage prospects. To escape almost certain futures of drug addiction and prison, Moore advocates marriage to "a reasonably square man with a reasonably stable job."[25] In an eerie parallel with the Geraldo segment in the beginning of the chapter, Moore and Hagedorn[26] have defined girls by virtue of their heteronormative appeal, and hinged their futures on their acceptability to potential marriage prospects. The researchers bemoan girls' conspicuous clothes and tie those aberrant, unfeminine, and rectifiable symbolic displays to their supposed inability to attract nice normative men. It almost makes one wish for a makeover.

On the "female liberation" side of the debate are Anne Campbell,[27] Mary Harris,[28] and Meda Chesney-Lind,[29] who have variously argued that girls in gangs are able to find female-dominated spaces that allow for alternative constructions of femininity and community that are not controlled by males. Other researchers provide supporting evidence; Sudhir Venkatesh documents parallel female gang economies,[30] and Keta Miranda's ethnographic work details girls' "talking back" in the public sphere, and constructing their subjectivities through their own video documentary work.[31]

The findings emerging thus far from my own work lean toward the so-called female liberation hypothesis, in that *none* of the girls that I've been able to keep in touch with have had, in the past ten years, "socially injurious" outcomes. The girls, now all out of gangs, have maintained long-term continued contact with each other, writing letters, calling and emailing when any of them went away for work or college, while those still in the neighborhood continue to invite each other to barbeques and babysit each other's children. What was it in their gendered discourses that may have served to protect them from social injury?

In order to explore how the discourse of "being macha" might be a protective factor from socially injurious outcomes I would like to draw attention to the words of girls themselves, to the orientations that they have in their everyday lives toward issues of gender and power. One of the key informants in this study (and an iconic leader in terms of language variation and other symbolic behavior), T-Rex, talked at length about being a macha gang girl and about her future. T-Rex was not the only girl who talked about herself this way (recall the words of Xóchitl earlier in the chapter, who talked about feeling "macha" with eyeliner). In T-Rex's account I found her sketching out a discourse that equated being macha with generational change and with her hopes for the future.

The discourse of "being macha" is one to which the Norteñas and Sureñas at Sor Juana High School introduced me. Prior to this field-work, I had never heard the term "macha" used with the positive valu-ation that T-Rex and Xóchitl describe. I had only heard "macha" in the pejorative compound *mari-macha* (Mexican Spanish derogatory slang for lesbian). But just because I'd never heard it in my short experi-ence growing up in Mexico doesn't mean that a multiplicity of mean-ings for machismo didn't already exist. Alfredo Mirandé[32] carried out interviews for a sociological investigation into how Mexican-born and US Latino men understand and use discourses of machismo. One of his findings is that many of the men, especially in the Mexican-born category, had positive valuations for the concept of being "macho." These associations included selflessness, being honorable, having high moral character, standing up for oneself, honoring one's family, and taking care of one's responsibilities. Similar results were found by Edwardo Portillos, Nancy Jurik, and Marjorie Zatz[33] in a study of the term "machismo" specifically among Latino gang members and their coun-selors in Phoenix, Arizona. Both gang members and counselors acknow-ledged sexism and oppression, and some suggested machismo was a way of coping with oppressive social conditions (an argument similar to that made by José Limón in *Dancing with the Devil*[34]), but they differed somewhat in their perceptions of the term machismo. The adult coun-selors thought that machismo was a terrible feature of Latino culture that contributed to gangs and to the abuse of women, while gang mem-bers and younger counselors saw polysemy in the term and linked being macho specifically to responsibility, reliability, and having the role of a provider. Here is a short excerpt from one of the youth counselors they interviewed:

> [Machismo] is a word Americans have totally fucked up and took out of context. As explained by my dad, you were the first male born, your role was to protect your family when your father wasn't there. It meant responsibility, watching out for brothers and sisters. Now it has been distorted to imply a cultural deformity – every Hispanic is this macho guy, "don't fuck with me," it connotes a violent person.[35]

These sentiments of responsibility and protection are echoed in one of the interviews of a youth gang member: "[Being macho means] . . . like you work and everything and being a man from the house. That's like macho. Like being a man of the house, doing all you can to feed your family and stuff."[36]

I believe that T-Rex's discourse of being macha is an extension of some of these positive valences already in play for the concept of machismo.

T-Rex and I spoke at length about being macha in a recording session which took place in my apartment one afternoon. During the session we "kicked back" (relaxed), played with makeup and clothes, and listened to Banda music for several hours. T-Rex was perceived to be such a "down" Norteña that she could wear blue when she got tired of red, listen to Banda instead of Oldies, and could wear frilly girl-clothes without jeopardizing her reputation. Below I will quote long portions of T-Rex's interview; I hope that this transcript will give you a glimpse into the discourse of being macha. As Laura Ahearn reminds us, "Attending closely to linguistic structures and practices [can reveal] how social reproduction becomes social transformation."[37]

1	T-Rex:	A girl could be more macha than some guys.
2		For example me.
3	Norma:	You think you're more macha than guys?
4	T-Rex:	I **am** more macha.
5	Norma:	What makes you macha?
6	T-Rex:	The way I act.
7		The way I don't let them step on me.
8		They way I
9		you know be tell–
10		when they do something that pisses me off I tell them.
11		I'll say oh, like, excuse me I don't like the way that you

12		you know?
13		treat me and stuff.
14		I like people to treat me like-
15		Like suppose we are at basketball right?
16	NORMA:	Uhhuh.
17	T-REX:	And they like uh say something to piss me off,
18		you know?
19	NORMA:	Mhm.
20	T-REX:	I'll step up like a guy,
21		I'll be like,
22		Fuck you.
23		[to Norma, about the makeup] That's my favorite look.
24		I like to look innocent.
25		Macha,
26		and female-type.
27	MUSIC:	Los muchachos del barrio la llamaban loca
		(The boys from the barrio called her crazy)
28	NORMA:	Now we're like trading appearance.
29		Check me out.
30		And check you out.
31		I love this fucking paño.
		(bandanna)
32	T-REX:	I like the innocent look.
33		Do you think I look innocent?
34	NORMA:	Totally innocent.
35	T-REX:	Yeah pero,
		(but)
36		that's good that females nowadays you know,
37		they don't take shit from guys.
38	NORMA:	Do you think it's changed?
39	T-REX:	Yeah, cause you know how my Mom says
40		"When you get married you have to listen to your husband,
41		do his shit-"
42	NORMA:	Yeah.
43	T-REX:	So you know
44		you have to, you know
45		cook for him
46		do this,
47		clean and stuff.
48		And I hate it because
49		we argue a lot
50		I'm like

51		you know
52		I want to be able to come home you know,
53		I'd be able to come home and
54		the guy have cooked for me and shit like that you know?
55	Norma:	So do you think your homegirls are like gonna get married and obey their husbands?
56	T-Rex:	**Hell** no.
57	Norma:	Are you sure?
58	T-Rex:	Positive.
59	Norma:	Have any of your homegirls gotten married yet?
60	T-Rex:	Uh-huh.
61		Actually,
62		now that you mention it
63		some of them do listen to their husbands.
64	Norma:	Huh.
65		So maybe it's just like they're going through a stage or something?
66	T-Rex:	No, but–
67		sincerely,
68		my type,
69		I wouldn't.
70		[. . . more about lipstick and eyeshadow]
71	T-Rex:	Sometimes [girls] get controlled
72		like the guys take
73		like advantage of them?
74		But like me,
75		I like to be my own self.
76		I like to tell a guy
77		what I like, you know
78		and I like to tell a guy
79		I don't–
80		I don't like the way you act
81		I tell them straight out without even you know
82		If something bugs me
83		I'll be like
84		I don't like the way you act
85		You know?
86		'Cause a lot of girls don't have the courage.
87	Norma:	Then how come you weren't like that with that other guy (former boyfriend)?
88	T-Rex:	See that was different. [. . .]
89		With the other guy it was because he was
90		like my first–

91		love
92		and my Mom,
93		I was following my Mom's advice.
94		Be a virgin until you get married
95		if you ever do it with somebody you have to
96		stay with them no matter what,
97		you **have** to.
98		If he plays behind your back
99		you have to stay with him no matter what.
100		So I was following my Mom's advice but the only thing was that we were not married.
101		And I was taking hella shit from him you know,
102		everything.
103		I took a lotta shit from him.
104		And um.
105		We broke up.
106		[. . .]
107		Cause my Mom's advice was,
108		you have to put up with their shit
109		so they could stay with you.
110	Norma:	But that didn't work.
111	T-Rex:	That didn't work.
112		It worked for me for a co-
113		for one month
114		actually.
115		Hunh.
116		And then I realized that
117		I'm s-
118		that I was so stupid
119	Norma:	Was he cheating on you?
120	T-Rex:	He cheated on me a few times.
121	Norma:	Fucker.
122	T-Rex:	And then
123		I used to beg him
124		I used to cry on the phone (start high-pitched voice, increased speech rate)
125		don't leave me please don't leave me
126		um
127		I'm nothing without you,
128		I'll move to (xx),
129		I'll have your baby
130		don't leave me (end high-pitched voice, return to normal speech rate)

131		I used to fucking **beg**. [...]
132		But then it came the time
133		that
134		I realized that you know?
135		That I could go on with my own self.
136		I think girls should stand up for themselves now
137		you know
138		cause like sincerely,
139		the way **I** think,
140		I want my house to be nice
141		I don't wanna be doing all the work
142		cause you know,
143		Mexican moms say that you have to obey your husband
144		like he's your master you know,
145		but I don't wanna do that.
146		I want him to come home, you know,
147		fifty fifty.
148		Hey, it's like a Sunday.
149		me and him clean the house.
150		I don't wanna do it by myself you know?
151	NORMA:	Ye::ah.
152		Does your Mom do it by herself?
153	T-REX:	Yeah,
154		my Dad don't help around the house
155		not in the kitchen.
156	NORMA:	Does he help out at all anywhere else?
157	T-REX:	In the garden and stuff
158		but that's like a guy's job.
159		That's the way they think.
160		But I just, you know.
161		My generation?
162		I wanna change it around.
163	NORMA:	Yeah?
164	T-REX:	I wanna be the boss of **my** house
165		I wanna have the <u>pantalones en la casa</u>.
		(pants in the house)
166		I wanna be able to say,
167		I don't like you when you do this
168		[...]
169		A real macha
170		is that you respect yourself
171		and you stand up for yourself

172	that's what macha **is**,
173	that is that you stand up for what you **are**.
174	Macha's not a–
175	a fucking
176	way to act.

In this long excerpt T-Rex articulates in detail her ideas on generational shift, and the past experiences in the context of which she has decided that macha is "not a fucking way to act," but instead a way to "respect yourself and stand up for yourself" (lines 169–76). Perhaps because I myself had never really understood this use of "macha" before, I ask incredulously in line 3 whether she thinks she is more macha than guys. Her response leaves no doubt that she thinks that being macha is not about being masculine, but about taking charge of one's own self (line 75) and not being controlled (line 71). T-Rex rejects the idea that I raise (line 65) that macha subjectivity might just be a stage, and articulates both a generational shift in gender norms as well as a projection of her desired outcomes later in life as a direct consequence of the macha standpoint.

There is one moment of gendered juxtaposition in the transcript, where T-Rex talks about not letting people step on her (line 7), and "stepping up like a guy" (line 20), saying "Fuck you." This use of an expletive appears in contrast to the earlier, more mitigated introduction of her hypothetical objection ". . . excuse me, I don't like the way that you . . ." (line 11). One might be tempted to analyze this as T-Rex's linking of swearing to escalation of conflict and to masculinity, were it not for the relatively frequent (six instances) use of expletives on both sides of this conversation. Mutual conversational accommodation makes direct linking of the speech form to male/female norms problematic.

On the other hand, a within-gender juxtaposition is evident in the immediately following talk (lines 24–6), where T-Rex states that her favorite look is a combination of "innocent," "Macha, and female-type." Here different types of femininity are invoked, with both innocence/naïveté/childhood and worldliness/responsibility/adulthood being juxtaposed in T-Rex's preferred "look." I believe this juxtaposition points to the way that T-Rex combines both the linguistic and symbolic resources of different kinds of femininities. In this long transcription excerpt she makes narrative sense of her own process of growing up, with the implied contrast between the innocence of childhood (being told what to do by adults and following those instructions, line 93) and the lack of innocence involved in being Macha: going "with your own self" and making your own decisions (line 135), not taking "any shit," (line 37), learning about the world, and knowing enough to take care of your own affairs.

It is this state of gendered flux within which lies the performativity of being a macha gang girl. The flux alternates between the child, listening to the advice of her Mexican Mom (lines 43, 93, 100, 108) who advocates passivity and abnegation, and the emerging independent adult. In T-Rex's narrative, this emerging adult determines that relinquishing one's personal power ("taking shit" by being controlled (line 71), bearing a disproportionate burden of the housework (lines 41–54; 141–50), and suffering a partner's infidelities (lines 120–31)) is the direct consequence of following the advice from her mother's generation.

In this excerpt T-Rex also articulates her desire for an egalitarian marriage (lines 149, 162). Her conviction about "wearing the pants in the house" (line 65) suggests that she ties some of that equality to economic power. In her adult life, she has achieved both an egalitarian relationship and economic power within it. She and her husband, Ramiro, share housework duties and the raising of their child, and they also share economic responsibilities. I think that narrating herself as "macha," as a young woman who respects herself and stands up for herself, may have had an influence in structuring T-Rex's self-actualization. Although I do not know whether she had conversations like this one with her other girlfriends, I can attest that she has reiterated these convictions over the years that I've known her, and sometimes refers to this specific conversation, orienting to themes that are consistent in time.

The narrative flux between being a young woman and a mature adult prepares T-Rex for events that follow only a few years later: her Mom becomes ill and T-Rex preserves her Mom's job by substituting for her at work; later on, Mom again has a difficult episode of depression and T-Rex takes the medical and financial reins of the whole household including providing for her ailing grandmother. In hindsight, I can see a foreshadowing of T-Rex's ability to take care of all these situations in her discourse about being macha.

As I've said in the beginning of this chapter, the premise that there is something aberrant, unfeminine, and rectifiable about girls who are involved in gangs is pervasive both in media constructions of gangs and in researchers' expectations of social injury. From T-Rex's words above, I believe there may be aspects of gendered subjectivities in the discourse of being macha that protect girls from socially injurious outcomes.

Shifting Styles in Performance

One last example from the time of my fieldwork in the 1990s that I would like to present is one of a girl whom I will call Angie. She was one of the leaders, one of the "downest" cholas, despite her diminutiveness. T-Rex said that one of the reasons that Angie was able to be a leader is because she had a really big attitude which compensated for her smallness. In other words, she wore really long eyeliner and was willing to get in a fight with anyone who'd take her up.

Angie was half Euro-American and half Mexican. Her father was Mexican, divorced from her mother when she was a toddler, so that at the time of this research Angie had always lived with her mom. She lived in a superbly wealthy part of town, in a huge, sprawling house with her mom and her stepfather, both of whom were white. All of her kin networks were homogeneously European-American. Although it is not the point of the discussion here to speculate why Angie became a chola, or why her friendship networks were almost exclusively Latina and African-American, it is interesting to note that Angie is a native speaker of both Chicano English and of the broader Euro-American Standard California English dialect. Angie style-shifted at will between the two personae. More interestingly, however, she sometimes used her broader dialect resources in the service of chola purposes. She sometimes called the principal's office and excused herself and her chola friends from school absences in the flawless California Euro-American dialect that she has been speaking from birth. Her homegirls giggled in the background when the ploy succeeded.

Was Angie in drag as a chola who was in drag as a white person? Or the opposite? Angie's many distinct styles are irreducible to impersonations of abstract idealizations. The styles of Angie, of Xóchitl and T-Rex emerged in practice, in narration, and in performance. It was an inalienable part of Angie's persona as a chola that she had resources, linguistic and otherwise, which the community found useful at various times, and which she enlisted to fulfill the aims of the cholas. She was one of the many possible characters in the daily theater of the articulation of Latina identity. I hope that this exploration of gendered style-shifting and style-making among Latina gang girls, coupled with an exploration of the discourse of "being macha," provides a counterpoint to forecasts of unavoidable socially injurious outcomes among Latina girls involved in gangs.

Notes

1 Foucault (1971: 143)
2 Puerto Rican diaspora living in and around New York.
3 Butler (1990), Turner (1982), Butler (1993)
4 Why use the concept of drag to explicate the behavior of gang girls? Am I not just using one kind of stereotype to deconstruct another? Some readers may feel uncomfortable in comparing the spectacular, carnivalesque aspects of drag queen performances to the quotidian lives of Latina girls in schools. I use this analogy carefully and want to focus attention on the common thread of *performativity* in the two identities (a review of this is Hall, 2001). My perspective on practice, more fully fleshed out in chapters 7 and 8, sees identities as continuously forged, interactive processes where individuals negotiate emergent social relations in moment-to-moment performance. It is this link on the performative and emergent aspects of gender that provides a common ground between drag queens and cholas.
5 Butler (1993: 125)
6 Turner (1982)
7 Butler (1993: 132)
8 Donovan (1993: 24)
9 Foucault's (1977) book *Discipline and Punish* provides the striking metaphor (based on Jeremy Bentham's design) of a panopticon, a prison shaped like a ring with a central guard tower. In the panopticon, guards in the tower remain unseen while prisoners know that they could be under direct surveillance at all times. This ability to see without being seen is for Foucault one of the key mechanisms of power.
10 The concept of cultural bricolage was introduced by Claude Lévi-Strauss, and later picked up by Dick Hebdige (1979). According to Lévi-Strauss (1966: 16), a *bricoleur* is someone who makes do with "whatever is at hand," and adapts existing materials to new circumstances. Hebdige takes this further by asserting that the new admixtures and combinations also change the meanings of objects and draw attention to them.

11 Chola style/makeup has been copied all the way to the catwalks of Paris, where the John Galliano for Christian Dior Ready-to-Wear Spring 2002 collection featured models made up to look like gang girls. Permission to reproduce these images is shockingly expensive, but you must see them to take in the full effect. Go to your search engine and type "Christian Dior Spring 2002 Ready to Wear".

The models sport gang-type makeup complete with eyeliner, drawn-on tears, mesh hairnets, bandannas, huge tattoos, gold-capped teeth, and to top it all off Galliano comes out at the end with an open shirt and "Dior" fake-tattooed in Old English font on his chest. The Dior "model manifesto" (presumably what models might see on the way out to the runway) reads, in huge red and black letters, with sprinkles and glitter all around them:

> AY CARAMBA!!!
> STOP THE MADNESS!
> TAKE THE STREET GANGS OFF
> THE STREET
> AND BACK INTO THE BOUDOIR
> KEEP ON KEEPIN' IT REAL – YO!
> <u>KINDLY REMAIN</u>
> UP
> ALIVE
> & SUPER ENERGETIC!!!

Helpfully guiding the interpretation of this collection, fashion critic Arman Limnander states:

> John Galliano's 'Street Chic' collection took the form of a virtual world tour, with stops that included lavishly clad Bedouins, army recruits and girls in the "hood".
> This was not the first time Dior has gone globetrotting, but Galliano injected, as always, new energy into his ethnic excursions. [. . .] Python jackets and low-slung hip-hop jeans also seem right for the moment, while the more eye-popping pieces – like the glittering pantsuit embroidered with kitschy Americana motifs – are just the thing for a starlet's weekend jaunt to Vegas.
> Galliano also showed a series of great-looking patchwork and Mexican serape-print[sic.] bathing suits, embellished with utilitarian canvas straps. (Limnander 2001)

Although the purpose of this chapter is not to examine Galliano/ Dior's products, it stands to be noted that the most common stereotypes about Latina girls in gangs are thrown together in the text of the model manifesto: codeswitching of Spanish and English in combination with features of African-American English, plus the sexualized portrayal of female gangs as having emerged from the boudoir in the first place. From the collection it is clear that, by 2002, no longer was a sarape just a "cholo blanket" as Jill had derisively complained. Now, as Limnander points out, it's become part of an "ethnic excursion" (read: safari) promoted by mainstream media, and you too can own a small, bathing-suit shaped piece of sarape for thousands of dollars and wear it on weekend jaunts to Vegas.

12 Meaning, it looks good.

13 McRobbie and Garber (1976)

14 Although the Norteñas and Sureñas of Fog City would not be a bedroom culture, the more tightly controlled "lockdown girls," the Piporras, were definitely relegated to the domestic sphere. McRobbie and Garber's (1976) analysis does endure; see for instance Melissa Hyams' (2003) discussion for an exploration of young Latinas in LA and their discourses of homeplaces and simultaneous fears of the public spaces and public freedoms, where "inside 'homeplaces' and 'homebodies' are constructed and contested as autonomous, modest, ordered, and safe, in recursive relationship to the making and resisting of 'outside' urban spaces and 'homegirl' subjectivities as dependent, indecent, violent, and vulnerable." (Hyams 2003: 537)

15 Although T-Rex liked the result, my own mother was horrified when she saw the photographs taken that day. At first she did not recognize me and complained, "Why do those girls wear so much makeup? It looks so vulgar!" Finally when I informed her they were pictures of me, she wanted to throw them out. I managed to convince her that they were for my research. Not only did the girls have to negotiate the opposition of their parents to their look, in this case the ethnographer had the same problem.

16 Here I very broadly gloss over the punk–goth–whiteness connection, but this is a complicated subject, explored further in Hodkinson (2002), who in his study of British goths remarks that they are typically white and middle class. Taylor (2006) finds goth identity in Tucson, Arizona to be more accepting of difference. I remain indebted to some Latino goth students I met at Harvard for illustrating for me the complexity in standpoint of ethnic-minority goths, as well as to Ashley Stinnett for pointing out that punks and goths often borrow Latina gang-girl makeup practices precisely for their gender-subversive associations.

17 For a discussion of food, weight and exercise issues in an American high school, see Taylor (2006).

18 Nichter (2000) provides an anthropological discussion of "Fat Talk" among adolescents, pointing out that the African-American girls she interviewed were much more satisfied with their bodies than the white girls.

19 Bordo (1993: 255)
20 Goldstein (1995: 315)
21 Thrasher (1927)
22 Curry (1998)
23 Moore (1991), Moore and Hagedorn (1996), Moore and Hagedorn (2001)
24 Moore and Hagedorn (2001: 8)
25 Moore (1991: 129)
26 Moore and Hagedorn (2001)
27 Campbell (1991)
28 Harris (1988)
29 Chesney-Lind (1993), Chesney-Lind (1995)
30 Venkatesh (1998)
31 Miranda (2003)
32 Mirandé (1998)
33 Portillos, Jurik and Zatz (1996)
34 Limón (1994)
35 Portillos, Jurik and Zatz (1996: 182)
36 Portillos, Jurik and Zatz (1996: 179)
37 Ahearn (2001: 130–1)

CHAPTER 6

SMILE NOW CRY LATER: MEMORIALIZING PRACTICES LINKING LANGUAGE, MATERIALITY, AND EMBODIMENT

Starting with the work of the Birmingham School in the 1970s, youth subculture studies has almost exclusively theorized materiality and consumption – the effect of which has been to render language invisible – in theoretical attempts to link subcultural formation and "structures of feeling."[1] Commodity fetishism à la Karl Marx[2] and commodity stylization were major features of this theoretical move, an example of which was the do-it-yourself nature of punk rock in the 1950s–70s, where an *objet trouvé* (ou cherché)[3] such as a safety pin could be incorporated into a coherent dress style via homologous signs.[4] More recent writings on the subject[5] continue to understand subcultures primarily through artifacts and commodities, though occasionally references to space and place are made as the focus shifts from local to globalized/ing youth subcultures.[6] Subcultures and scenes have been identified through larger social moral panics,[7] through musical tastes, and through consumption and the fashioning thereof, regardless of whether this fashioning takes place on the street, in the bedroom, or at raves and clubs. Conspicuously absent have been the structures of language as the vehicle for all this fashioning.[8] For Center for Contemporary Cultural Studies (CCCS) and post-CCCS scholars,[9] oppositional self-fashioning through the acquisition of *material* distinctions and their related impact on *taste* is at the core of the definition of a subculture.

Following Gary Clarke,[10] Andy Brown[11] observes that subcultures have to reach a certain critical mass before they can exist in any recognizable sense either to themselves or to others.

The objective sense of the existence of a subculture to its participants will tend to be established at the point when [. . .] a "uniform" emerges which can be purchased or modified [. . .] Some form of media-genre consumption generally plays a central role in the emergence of the subculture as well as supplying the symbolic materials that comprise the "structure of feeling" that subcultural-identifiers believe they recognize in it.[12]

In contrast to their European counterparts who have been theorizing commodities, scholars of youth (sub)cultures in the American tradition have primarily focused attention on language structure as a resource that is used by young people to create and maintain both cohesiveness and division, and as a major source for our understanding of processes of language change.[14] A strong focus on the micropatterning of language may be traced back to the work of William Labov,[15] whose linguistic studies of African-American English (AAE)-speaking children and youth,[16] including the gang-affiliated Cobras and Jets in New York City, served as the starting points for much of modern American sociolinguistics. Sociolinguistics has been a major player in studies of youth (sub)cultures in the United States for two primary reasons: on the one hand sociolinguistics has always been engaged with educational, social, and ethnoracial equity issues, and on the other hand it focuses on language acquisition, socialization, and language use through the lifespan.

Building on linguistically oriented studies of youth (sub)cultures[17], this chapter aims to show that language in its various forms is a central vehicle in the constitution of "structures of feeling." The micropatterning of language among Latina gang girls will be explored further in chapters 7, 8, and 9, but in this chapter we will see how discourse-level linguistic forms such as narratives, routinized speech forms, constraints against talk, and embodied language practices such as language games and literacy practices constitute what I call distributed memory.

An extremely important challenge for language-oriented studies of youth subcultures lies in tying language to other semiotic means for casting an identity. The notion of distributed memory allows for the working of language practices in concert with practices on different semiotic planes: circulating networks, for instance, play a crucial role in the shaping of memory. But instead of theorizing circulation as involving only material culture (drawings, photographs, poems, or commodities), we can also think of circulation as involving language practices such as first-person narratives, origin stories, and even injunctions about what kinds of speech should not circulate in a given community. This chapter also explores the various instantiations – in language, art, music, and deportment – of a concept the youth in this study called "Smile Now Cry Later," a type of moral and affective allegory, an ideology of deportment, that youth directly linked to the difficult experience of immigration itself. What can the study of linguistic and other semiotic practices of a youth subculture tell us about the persistence of subaltern identities, about history, about memory, about language, and about our understanding of the symbolic work of youth itself?

Memory and the Gang as an Institution

A proliferation of recent studies of social memory[18] have taken up the study of how memory functions in specific institutions. Institutions such as a church, a nation-state or a corporation are socially sanctioned institutions, and their processes of memorialization might involve setting up a cathedral, an archaeological museum, commissioning history books, or decorating the lobby of the company with original artifacts.

Recent work in linguistic anthropology[19] stresses the importance of narrative in both the creation and maintenance of collective memory. Charlotte Linde specifically postulates the process of narrative induction – acquisition of narrative – as one of the key ways in which institutions acquire new members and members acquire a new identity.

Linde argues that part of what is involved in belonging to any collectivity is the way that group members can tell stories. Linde specifically discusses a type of story that she calls the Non-Participant Narrative or NPN. In Linde's research, the particular grammatical and ideological stance that group members display in retelling non-participant narratives has a great deal to do with members' status within the organizational structure as well as their standing with respect to the whole institution.[20]

I will argue that narrative engages participants in processes of distributed cognition, after Edwin Hutchins'[21] study of navigation in the Pacific and in the US Navy. The central insight to be gotten from the concept of distributed cognition is that, on a ship, the knowledge for how to run the ship does not reside in any single individual, but is distributed as both archived and embodied knowledge throughout the individuals of the ship. In fact the operation of the ship is an epiphenomenal process, springing forth from embodied interaction with spaces, landscapes, texts, and instruments.

As we will see that still leaves us with the problem of how you would get distributed memory or cognition when faced with severe disincentives. Despite various disincentives, the young people involved in these gangs consciously and willfully created memory where none existed before by imagining a shared past which, as Barry Schwartz argues, provides "a stable image upon which new elements are superimposed."[22] Gang members' collective agreement on an ideologically consistent set of backward-looking references, be they in particular movies, music, or Pachuco-styles, was in fact an agreement to reinterpret the present in terms of these references, and added a layer of intertextualization to their collective understanding of new events.

The movies *Colors*[23] and *American Me*[24] emerged recurrently not as representations of origin stories, but rather as origin stories in and of themselves. In the words of Agata, "It all started in 1988 with the movie *Colors*." Although Agata didn't actually believe that her own particular gang was started by the movie, the fact that she and her homegirls collectively decided that this was their beginning reference point served an important function in restructuring what they believed about themselves, and in drawing allegories to their own lives, making predictions about their futures.

As Michel de Certeau explains in "The Jabbering of Social Life,"

> In the face of narratives of images, visible and readable productions, the spectator-observer knows perfectly well that they are but simulacra, the results of manipulations, but even so he assumes for those manipulations the status of reality, a belief that survives the denial crafted by all that we know about their manufacture.[25]

The disjunction between narratives from "the inside" (inside prison, where North/South was more strictly spatially interpreted) and narratives from "the outside" was evident to the girls, who were resigned to the fact that "the ones on the inside have their stories, and we have our stories," rendering visible a growing generational divide.

I was fortunate during this time to meet Eric Cummins, who was working on gangs inside the prison and had access to some of the major Nuestra Familia players in the California System. I asked Eric to carry a couple of questions for me, and he asked a prominent Norteño what he thought of the Norteño/Sureño dynamic and the way it was set up on the streets. The Norteño thought it was "bullshit," and that the kids would find out what "real" Norteños and Sureños were once they got inside.

Because a gang is an organization that is not sanctioned and operates under persecution, and furthermore it is not located in a single place (consider for instance transnational gang membership of Mara Salvatrucha and circular migration between gang members in the US and El Salvador), gangs operate under different constraints and affordances for memory.

Among the girls, there were many disincentives for memory and memorialization: the danger of police investigation; social constraints against gossip and tattling; speech acts of provocation; and the lack of stable physical premises for the storage of artifacts. The accumulation of material related to being in a gang has been legislated to be evidence of gang involvement, and starting with the presidency of Bill Clinton, this automatically converted the smallest infraction into a felony. Meanwhile, youth in this community had very little privacy, often sharing close quarters with siblings and other live-in relatives. The few things that they might want to keep, like the original bandanna from their induction ceremony, for instance, often got thrown out by unsympathetic parents. Despite this lack of privacy (often even a lack of personal space at all, as was the case when youth ran away from home), there was a distribution network of artifacts and narrative knowledge that could not be archived in one place. Both artifacts and narratives were copied, passed around, and shared, belonging to no one in particular.

These resources allowed for a powerfully binding memory, instantiating a type of distributed cognition that connected groups of young members to each other and to their elders. This type of memorialization was reinforced on many levels, and yet unlike a museum or an archive it lacked the quality of having a single storage place. The lack of premises for storage meant two things: 1) there was no "official" authorized version of any given narrative, and 2) no one person or entity could hold all the pieces to this memory. Every individual had a slightly different collection of personal artifacts, and everyone's version of "history" varied. This instantiates what I call distributed memory, connecting individual identity to group identity and stabilizing it over time.

Discourse Practices: Tattling, "Talking Shit," and the Inherent Untrustworthiness of Non-Participant Narratives

In his work on anti-languages, M. A. K. Halliday[26] describes an anti-language as equivalent in function to the language proper: both languages and anti-languages have reality-generating properties, but anti-languages are structured to support and maintain the anti-societies from which they spring. Halliday's set of anti-language examples consists of argots, slangs, and occasional creoles tied to groups or identities (prostitutes, vagabonds, criminals, homosexuals, etc.) whose activities are construed as oppositional and subversive by the larger mainstream. *Grypserka*, for instance, was a language created by prisoners in Poland to render their communication obscure to their guards by altering aspects of Polish vocabulary and morphology.[27] Other examples of intentionally obfuscatory language games include Sheng,[28] Polari,[29] and French Verlan.[30] 'Backwards speech' is a distinctive ironic speech mode in Smith Island, Maryland.[31] Just as an anti-society is, according to Halliday, a conscious alternative to society proper, an anti-language is a conscious, marked alternative to the mainstream language. Discourse practices around tattling, "talking shit," and other language games illustrate some of the anti-linguistic properties of communicative practices in this community.

Tattling

Words and ownership of one's words emerged as an element of crucial importance for membership among both the Norteñas and the Sureñas. In this broader illicit community, being quiet had exalted value, while talking too much was associated with being untrustworthy or tattling to the police.

One of the ways in which social hierarchy was continually tested and settled was through a speech act that I call "talking shit," after the terminology that was used by the girls themselves.[32] Talking shit is quintessential gossip, except that it has an optional confrontational *dénouement* at the end. It is either a third-person account where the speaker portrays the third party unfavorably, or a narrative where one brags about one's own factual or imaginary victory against an absent one. This type of bragging is intended to aggrandize one's own reputation, but if it should get back to the other party, as it most assuredly will, it can be considered a provocation and grounds for fighting.

Marjorie Goodwin describes a very similar speech routine which she terms He-Said-She-Said among a group of young African-American girls in Philadelphia,[33] while Amy Shuman also documents what she terms "storytelling rights" in a multi-ethnic high school in Philadelphia.[34] I have augmented Goodwin and Shuman's descriptions with my own below:

> *A says X about B in the presence of C*
> *C tells B that A said X*
> *Which causes B to confront A*

> *B then says: C said that you said X about me*
> *At which point A can deny it and say that C is a liar*
> *(and then B can tell C that A said that)*
> *or*
> *A can admit it, lose face with B, and then later confront C.*
> *Alternatively B can choose not to confront,*
> *and lose face with both A and C.*[35]

Consider this example, from an interview with fourteen-year-old Patricia, a codeswitching Sureña with a no-good boyfriend, Fernando:

PATRICIA: The next day me <u>habla una de sus amigas:</u>
                   (I get a call from one of his friend:)
              "Hey bitch why are you talking shit?"
              "What are you talking about?"
              "Fernando <u>me dijo</u> that you said that I was a bitch."
                   (told me)
              <u>le digo</u> "Oh yeah?"
              (I say)
              <u>le hace "Sí"</u>
              (She goes "Yeah")
              <u>le digo</u> "Ok fine,"
              (I say)
              <u>le digo</u> "I said it,"
              (I say)
              le digo, "Pero tráemelo aquí para que me lo diga en mi cara."
              (I say, "But bring him here so he can say it to my face.")
              And since that day <u>nunca lo he visto.</u>
                   (I haven't seen him again.)

Social control here hinges on the assumption that the party being gossiped about won't find out. In this case, Fernando, the errant boyfriend of Patricia, is caught in a talking-shit triangle and depicted as exiting the situation by not owning up to his own words. The implication here is that Fernando was somehow afraid of facing Patricia personally or not brave enough to bear the consequences of his words. Note how this short narrative itself aggrandizes Patricia by showing that when she talks shit she owns up to it, and that her undeserving boyfriend doesn't.

Let's look at another example. In this instance we are going to hear from T-Rex, a Norteña, describing an instance of bragging gone wrong. As it turned out, the braggart talked shit about T-Rex to her own brother, who didn't claim any gang affiliation and had only recently arrived from Mexico.

T-REX: He was sitting in tutorial one day
           and there's Sureñas you know
           talking to him you know
           and you know
           his sister- I'm a Norteña in the other group right?
           So you know I come in tutorial you know
           I just-
           'cause every time I come in
           everybody like
           turns around and looks at me
           and says hi you know whatever
           so I came in you know
           I like you know
           like went like this to him
           like you know whassup you know
           and walked out.
           So then this girl right
           she's a Sureña
           she's all
           "Yeah, you see that <u>ruca</u> right there?
                                (girl)
           I beat her ass."
NORMA: !!!
T-REX: "You know,
           she was CRYING.
           you know I beat her ASS
           you know I made her CRY."

and then um
and then my brother goes:
"Oh you DID?"

NORMA: Heh.

T-REX: And then
and then she's all
"Yeah, man."
You know,
they don't–
she don't fuck with ME.
and she a–
(.)
and then my brother goes
"oh that's really weird
she never told me that"
and then she turns around she's all
"what
you talk to her?
what–
you a Norteño?"
he's all
"No I just got here from Mexico
but you know
I mean she's my sister."

NORMA: Huh-huh.

T-REX: And then she's all hu::hhh
and then she's all
"Oh
I gotta go to class."
She's all
"Oh you know
you believed me huh?
I was just playing."
you know
and he came and told me
and I was just like cracking up you know
and like
you know it's like
you know when you're in a gang
it's funny how people could make things up
you know it's like
um
it's like um

it's like
"Oh yeah you know what?
I got rushed by the scraps you know?"[36]
and sometimes they be cutting themselves
you know
just to make trouble you know?

Exaggerated accounts of one's own exploits are deeply mistrusted among members of both gangs. As Michel de Certeau states:

> Storytelling has a pragmatic efficacy. In pretending to recount the real, it manufactures it. It renders believable what it says, and it generates appropriate action . . . The voices of narration transform, reorient, and regulate the space of social interaction.[37]

We can see in the examples from the girls that *it is precisely their mistrust of the manufacture of reality that is at stake.* Great weight is placed on personal recollection rather than on citation and recitation, and within that, 1st Person Narrative (where the speaker was present) or 2nd Person Narrative (where the interlocutor was present) rather than 3rd Person Narrative (where neither was present) or Non-Participant-Narratives (where the speaker was not present but narrates as though they have the storytelling right, for instance a police officer (or an anthropologist) telling the history of the gang even though they were not a participant). We can thus construct an implicational hierarchy of emergent evidentiality:

1PN< 2PN< 3PN< NPN

where first person narratives are by far the most trusted and "true," while non-participant narratives are assigned lesser value and more instability. This situation not only has the outcome of creating an evidential hierarchy in a language without much evidential marking,[38] but it can further lead us to understand how, in this particular group, projected consequences and responsibility for them take the form of the constraints against gossip. Why should it be that the circulation of artifacts (drawings, poems, bandannas, etc.) is practiced with great anonymity, while in order to circulate stories young people must make careful attributions? Part of the answer seems to lie in the potential anonymity of circulated material culture, whereas the traceability of stories, their cite-ability and their potential use as evidence both within the school structure and in the legal system demands greater standards of evidence.

Language Games, Clowning and Albur

An embodied innovation of the sort that is only acquired through intensive practice is that of word games (also known as secret languages or play languages) that depend both on fluency in the language and on practice in the form of the game. English-speaking readers may have grown up with a word game called Pig Latin, which relies on syllable suffixation as well as segment transposition, and Mexican Spanish-speaking readers will recognize *hablar en su* as a widespread children's code in Mexico. The use of secret word games has been well documented by linguists and folklorists in argots[39] and young people's speech all around the world, with examples ranging from Verlan in French (which relies on reversing the order of syllables (l'envers → verlan), to Kibalele, a secret creole in Bukabu, Zaire whose contributing languages are Swahili, Lingala, Shi, English, and French,[40] and which exhibits syllabic permutation. Here I'd like to use Tim Ingold's[41] notion of continuous embodied innovation, where participants seek to direct or influence others' engagement with the environment. The Sureña girls, most of them quite fluent in Spanish, were able to convey messages to each other in school through the use of phonological word games, establishing an exclusive practice where mere participation in such games required a high degree of fluency.

For example, one popular game involved the insertion of a dummy syllable before or after each syllable in the base. In the game of *hablar en su* ("speaking in su"), the phonological syllable /su-/ is prefixed before each syllable of the word. The base and the result look like this:

¿Como estás?
(How are you?)
Base: /**ko mo es tas**/
Result: /su **ko** su **mo** su **es** su **tas**/

Games of increasing phonological complexity make the original base string much more opaque and difficult to recover in online parsing.

For instance, the girls thought that a more difficult recovery involved the prefixation of the syllable /su-/ combined with the suffixation of the syllable /-che/

/su **ko** che su **mo** che su **es** che su **tas** che/

Avoidance of CC (consonant-consonant) sequences yields the final result:

[su **ko** che su **mo** che su **eø** che su **taø** che]

The most opaque strings are produced through a combination of highly marked affixational segments (suffixes, prefixes, and less frequently in-fixes) and sheer speed. Skill in production of these secret performat-ive codes is prized, and speakers who dominate them can easily agree on a sophisticated linguistic rule to use *just for one single day*. Thus, they could walk down the hallway, having a secret conversation, completely unperturbed, and shed this complex embodied practice the very next day.

Among youth who were more fluent in English (and less fluent in Spanish) and unable to participate in the *hablar en su* routines, I observed a different kind of practice that was called *clowning*, extended examples of which have been discussed in chapter 2. Also known in the linguistic literature as ritual insults or 'playing the dozens,'[42] this type of creative joking canonically involves a frame of the following type:

Your (possession/relation of the interlocutor) **is so** (unflattering adjective) **that** (outrageous result).

Here is an example I overheard at the lunch counter reflecting an intercultural jest element:[43]

Your *mama* ***is so*** *tiny* ***that*** *she could hang-glide on a Dorito.*

The retort to a clown is ideally a better, funnier, more creative and daring clown, created on the spot, riffing on the interlocutor's less-desirable qualities. Clowning battles could go on for a while, and usu-ally ended when the last target could no longer think of something to say, or when the mock-insult has finally caused real offense.[44] Well known in the literature on African-American English, the practice of clowning among English-speaking Chicano youth at first glance points to the interdigitation of the two communities. And yet there is another, less obvious source of influence: vernacular Mexican Spanish boasts another type of verbal art which involves "topping" another person's insult: the *albur*. *Albur*[45] is a type of casually uttered double entendre that exploits lexical ambiguity or potential rhymes to entrap an unsuspecting interlocutor into a sexually explicit verbal game. Here is an example that was common in the school:[46]

> Asked innocently: Te gusta ver gotas y no mojarte?
> Trans 1: *Do you like to watch [rain]drops without getting wet?* (ver gotas)
> Trans 2: *Do you like huge penises without getting stained?* (vergotas)

If the interlocutor suspects that they are being made the potential target of an *albur*, he or she will take an out-of-the-blue utterance like this and reanalyze it on the spot to unscramble possible sexual innuendos (as in translation 2). The trick of an *albur* is of course to "*alburear*" one's target, that is to say, to direct an ambiguous sexual innuendo and have the target reply to the surface meaning without registering the sexual meaning, thus outwitting them and demonstrating both the target's innocence and one's superior cunning and verbal skill. In a group of Spanish-speaking Mexican youth in language game mode, being the target of an *albur* is a constant risk, and the very best (most skillful) *albures* are considered to occur when the target does not notice the innuendo (the *albur* in this case does not sound out-of-the-blue), and the target responds to it earnestly, while the overhearers all "get it."

Sometimes rhymes can also be *albures*, as in the following, constantly used to taunt a blond girl at the school:

> Güera, güera, ¿Quién te encuera?
> *Blondie, Blondie who'll disrobe you?*

This rhyme eventually became so popular at the school that Güera considered changing her moniker: just the utterance of her name with a particular intonational contour was enough to recall the *albur*.

Secret language games, *albur* in Spanish and clowning in English are practices that are simultaneously on display and secretive, and whose successful oral performance depends in the most crucial way on embodiment: in the repetition and practice, either to acquire the fluency to be able to instantly analyze the syllabic/semantic structure of language in the case of *hablar en su* and *albur,* or in the ability to analyze the social situation to think of ritual insults with just the right amount of insult, codeswitching and jest that do not overshoot perceived community norms. Note that the competitive aspects of these games mirror the dynamics of talking shit as well.

I'll end this section with a joke that I found written in my field-notebook. This joke blends elements of both clowning and *albur* with its layered ambiguity:

> *Why did the Norteña come back to school pregnant?*
> *Cause her teacher told her to go home and write an essay.*

Did you get it? (ride an *ese* (another word for a guy in a gang, syn. *cholo, vato*)); it's another example of intercultural jest, depending as it does on unexpected codeswitching.

Secret Literacies: Poetry Notebooks

Although some teachers complained about students' literacy skills, it was evident that students were not displaying their full range of literacy capacities under the structured chronometer of school assignments. Earlier I pointed out how often the texture of the community involved the circulation of objects that were not the property of a single person and that could be added to or modified. One example of these practices was the circulation of poetry notebooks in Spanish, circulated mostly by Sureña girls.

Poetry notebooks were simply small notepads where different girls wrote poems, often in a strict quatrain form, of the form ABAB or ABCB, with seven or eight syllables in each line:

> Me gusta la fresa
> *I like strawberries*
> Me gusta el helado
> *I like ice-cream*
> Pero lo que mas me gusta
> *But my favorite thing*
> Es estar a tu lado
> *Is being close to you*

Often the poems would offer commentary on the nature of love and its associated problems, and occasionally they could be racy:

> De aquel lado del cerro
> *On the other side of the hill*
> Hay muchas flores pa' escoger
> *There are many flowers to be chosen*
> Tu no tienes ni pa' cigarros
> *You don't have enough money for cigarettes*
> Y quieres tener una mujer.
> *And you want to have a wife.*

Sometimes the poems were in the form of anagrams, spelling out the name of the beloved or other words:

> En la calle de la **A**
> *On **L** street*
> Me encontre a la **M**
> *I found **O***
> Y me dijo que la **O**
> *Who told me that **V***
> Era amiga de la **R**
> *Was friends with **E**.*

Sometimes girls' poems were longer and free form, involving reflections on family, death or growing up. Remarkably the poetry notebooks, as far as I could tell, really did not belong to anyone at all. All the poems were unsigned (though of course participants knew each others' handwriting), some of the poems were written in code, and many of them involved commentary on current friendships or romances that circulation network members already knew about. Thus, if a notebook were intercepted by a teacher (an occasional event and always a risk with classtime distribution), identities were not revealed, and words in this case did not get participants into trouble (a major feature of talking shit, as described above). After school, the notebooks might be taken out and read aloud, their contents memorized, and further poems would be composed and added.

Anonymous poetry notebooks circulating among the Sureñas shared numerous characteristics with documented popular literatures that emerged in Spain in the seventeenth century, among which were *aleluyas*, illustrated broadsheets inscribed with news of the day, general advice, messages for children, and religious sayings.[47] Spanish aleluyas were widely distributed for popular consumption and were one of the first forms of popular newspapers, demarcating one point of transition between orality and widespread literacy. Aleluyas' contents were recited by criers, itinerant bards, and traveling storytellers who were often blind. The verse forms, the illustrations, and the tendency for girls to memorize and recite their own written material production parallel both the form and use of these longstanding historical literacy practices in the Spanish-speaking world. Striking similarities between Sureñas' poetry notebooks and aleluyas are that a) the two are in exactly the same eight-syllable verse form; b) they serve as a way to reach broad audiences and inform them of current events. Another poetic form in popular Mexican literature and folklore that shares these characteristics is the *corrido* or folk ballad.[48] What is remarkable here for scholars of youth is that illustrated aleluyas served as the earliest vehicles of children's literature, and had a tremendous impact on its subsequent development. Not only did aleluyas allow children and youth to engage the public sphere (albeit as addressees), but the production of poetry notebooks by SJHS Sureñas provides evidence of the continuity of such engagement historically, with new forms of public sphere participation utilizing traditional forms (classical octosyllabic quatrains) and technologies (aleluya-like circulating sheets), yet appropriating agency for their production and modifying technologies in accordance with internal norms (no gossip, no tattling, no talking shit).

Just by being shown the notebooks, I was granted an honorary and short-lived membership into the poetry circulation network. When in the second year of fieldwork I broke up with my then-boyfriend Rob, poems of sympathy and solidarity started appearing in two different notebooks, instructing me on ways to get over heartbreak, or providing humorous descriptions of the former boyfriend's flaws or an enumeration of other fish in the sea. Only then was I able to experience firsthand the social support function that the notebooks served, and the ways in which they served as forums for public advice-giving and problem-solving. The circulating notebooks were in line with the face-saving functions of not "talking shit," and served as a non-face-threatening way to communicate questions and to give advice that may be embarrassing or difficult to deal with in direct speech acts. They also echoed discussions that we will see below, of smile now cry later, providing an escape valve for both direct confrontation and difficult feelings. The notebook allowed heartbreak to be shared, advice to be given, and support to be felt under the pretense of anonymity.[49]

Here is a poem that was composed on the spot for me on that occasion:

> Cuando veas mi pañuelo
> *When you see my handkerchief*
> Acuérdate de mí
> *Remember me*
> Para que despues no digas
> *So that you won't say later*
> Que por mi culpa te perdí
> *That through some fault of mine I lost you*
>
> Si porque te perdí
> *If because I lost you*
> Voy a dejar de amar
> *I were to stop loving*
> Pero lo que no sabes
> *You are not yet aware*
> Es que me he vuelto a enamorar
> *That I have found another.*

I have briefly alluded to the use of codes in the notebooks and in kids' notes to each other.[50] Because the girls knew that I was interested in literacy practices, they often passed on to me their code practice sheets. Codes were extremely common in handwritten notes, meant to be passed in class, with different codes in simultaneous use, and new codes being invented continuously. Codes, poetry, secret language games, talking shit, and clowning all form part of oral and literate performative linguistic practices that involve high degrees of embodiment. A young gang girl, by virtue of her involvement in the symbolic production of this type of community, becomes more and more adept at the implementation of these underground linguistic skills.

Smile Now Cry Later

Shown in Figure 6.1 is another example of anonymous circulation of artistic material at the high school. This black-and-white pen drawing was given to me in 1995 by a Norteño boy who knew of my interest

Figure 6.1 Drawing: "Smile Now Cry Later."

in collecting circulating materials. It was unsigned.

In the top center area of the drawing is an image of the Virgen de Guadalupe, the patron saint of Mexico, her top half emerging Venus-like from a stylized heart-shape. Clad in a halo and the robes that she has worn for 400 years since appearing to the Mexican Indian Juan Diego on the mount of Tepeyac, she gazes downward at the heart from which she springs. Both sides of the heart are pierced with flagpoles, and blood drips slowly from the wounds; the right one bears an intricately detailed eagle and serpent in a field of red, white, and green: the Mexican flag. On the left flagpole is an American flag, also drawn from a model – the number of stars, stripes, and the spacing of stars are regulation-perfect. Above each flag and on either side of the Virgin float emblematic hats, a straw hat with "MEXICO" on the brim on the right and an Uncle-Sam-star-spangled top hat above the US flag. On the Mexican side, peeking out in profile from the heart is the crying thespian mask of tragedy, two tears dripping just below the ventricular blood. On the US side is the thespian mask of comedy, laughing but vacant-eyed. In the very center bottom is a large Arabic numeral "14," and on the US side a shooting star with the letter N emblazoned on it, indicating that this is a Norteño drawing. The original drawing had the neighborhood and barrio names inscribed; I have removed those for the sake of maintaining privacy and confidentiality. After making a copy of the drawing and without altering the original I returned it to the person who gave it to me, who set it back into recirculation.

Later on I asked kids to interpret for me the meaning of the iconography found on the drawing. Everyone understood it to be a Norteño drawing, because of the 14 and the shooting stars (Norteños are commonly called Estrellas – stars). One girl told me that this drawing represented the suffering of Chicanos and what happened to people when they immigrate: that they immigrate because of poverty in Mexico so that they can find a better life in the US. T-Rex explained to me that Chicanos are laughing on the outside and crying on the inside, and that this is why you have to be tough and not let anyone in at first. Everyone agreed that they way to read the theater masks was "Smile Now Cry Later," and some mentioned a song by that name.[51] The polyreferential symbol "Smile Now Cry Later" is at once referring to the song, to theatricality, to hiding one's emotions (portraying the economy of affect, recall muscled-up Manuel and his reluctance to talk about his tattoos), and to an ideology of deportment (acting "hardcore," "don't ever smile"). For more clues to the economy of affect, we can turn to the lyrics of the song, often played at parties and given to me on a tape the week following my inquiry:

> SMILE NOW CRY LATER
> SUNNY & THE SUNLINERS
> Smile now, cry later (oo-oo-oo)
> Smile now, cry later (for you-ou, for you-ou)
> My friends tell me
> You could never belong to me
> So I'll smile for my friends and cry later
> I'm gonna (smile for my friends and cry later)
> Yeah, smile for my friends and cry later
> For you-ou, for you-ou
>
> I wouldn't be crying if I didn't love you so
> I'll smile for my friends and cry later
> (Smile for my friends and cry later)

Yeah, smile for my friends and cry later
For you-ou, for you-ou
(Smile for my friends and cry later)
Yeah, smile for my friends and cry later
(Smile for my friends and cry later)

Tell me that you love me
That you put nobody else above me
[Fade]⁵²

The homology links the lyrics of the song and the economy of affect outlined therein, metaphorically to the suffering of immigration in the passage from one country to another. Another kid mentioned to me that the song and the drawing referred to "Mexican Masks," which – intentionally or unintentionally – alludes to Octavio Paz' famous explanation of the Mexican national psyche as nihilistic, hiding behind masks.⁵³

Whether or not the young interpreter in question had read Paz, or whether he was referring to the classical symbols of theater, performativity, and artifice (keenly understood by gang members), there is no question that the thespian masks are ubiquitous. Girls wear smile now cry later earrings, with one mask in each ear (Sita the Sureña from India believes that this is something Norteñas started), and an entire line of clothing (SNCL clothing) is devoted to selling t-shirts with the masks. I have also remarked that girls tattoo or draw with eyeliner tears on their faces, representing the pain of having had someone close to them die, literally or figuratively. All of these elements contribute to the reinforcement of norms of behavior (especially as linked to speech and silence, and to affect).

It is additionally important to note that the Smile Now Cry Later symbol in the drawing (Figure 6.1), and symbols of and references to clowns in general, are in a very important sense an abstraction. They are abstractions of a particular kind of sadness and tragedy. In the drawing, SNCL is a fiction of a particular story of immigration, and not an actual instance of anyone's particular immigration story.

I want to make an analogy here to a process that was observed by Janet Carsten in her article on the Politics of Forgetting.⁵⁴ Carsten worked on the Malay peninsula island of Langkawi, reinterpreting what has been called collective amnesia by Geertz and Geertz.⁵⁵ Carsten traces remarkable consistency in the way that Langkawi people talk about migration despite their varied origins, and the patterns of her data reveal that forgetting the particular details of immigration and aligning one's story with a unified narrative (in that case, of a shared experience of poverty) is an important part of identity construction. Instead of seeing forgetting as a negative in terms of a loss, she considers it a crucial part of the way identity is acquired.

Similarly, among the Latina girls, and more broadly the Latino kids of Foxbury, particular immigration narratives are not highlighted, but rather common senses of belonging based on hemispheric localism and on the difficult experience of immigration itself are made salient.

Circulation Networks Extend Through Material Artifacts

In my second year of fieldwork at the high school it became clear to me that I needed a staff ID card. I wanted to get into the basketball games, picnics, and other activities that the school kids were engaged in. Besides, I thought, a high school staff ID would give me some legitimacy just in case the police became irked that gang-related handshapes were coming from my car. Sometimes on school trips, youth would tease the cops and throw signs out the windows. In my capacity as school tutor, sometimes I would be in charge of chaperoning minors and driving them around on school trips.

The school photographers came and I duly scheduled a picture session. Bad luck and timing conspired: I showed up in front of a worn gray pull-down screen at the gym shortly after receiving an unflattering and very short bob that made me look younger. When the school pictures came back, instead of getting my legitimating document, I found that I had been assigned the student package instead: one large, 8 × 10 head shot, four smaller portraits and about thirty-two miniatures, all with the same dreadful hairdo and a vague smile. Shortly after receiving my portraits, I was walking by the gym when Athena approached me to exchange pictures and gave me one of her tiny portraits. In it, her long hair was flipped back and she had an expressionless face. On the other side she quickly scribbled in edgy letters: "To NoRMa: WhuSSUP, hom3gurl! LeT'S k33p kiCkiN iT and don't Chang3. Lov3 Athena." I admired the picture and put it in my pocket, and gave her one of mine. I have no idea what I wrote on it.

That whole week, school photographs were exchanged at dizzying speed. Most of the girls I was close to did not smile in the pictures but stared ahead glumly, while on the verso they scrawled hearts, smiley faces, special codes, or Old English font messages. I exchanged tiny head-shots with almost every girl I knew, and quickly exhausted my own supply. A few days after all the activity had subsided, Athena casually asked me if I had her picture.

"Yeah," I said. "it's at home."

She frowned and quizzed me. "Why is it at home? Why aren't you carrying it – did you lose it?" "No," I said, "I just have it at home, it's in my drawer."

She humphed impatiently through her nose as if to say "I see," and pulled out a foldout plastic photo wallet with at least twenty picture slots. Right there in a little plastic jacket in the middle of the set was my picture, along with pictures of Athena's homegirls. Current homegirls, former homegirls and their boyfriends, homegirls' kids: all were there in a genealogy that traced Athena's social network: active members and people who were long gone from the gang, special occasions (proms and *quinceañeras*), and best-friendships all were meticulously documented. How could I not be carrying my pictures? What was I thinking? I resolved to get a wallet next time, and gave myself a break by thinking of how over and over in fieldwork researchers discern social norms by violating them.[56] If Jean Briggs was ostracized and subtly ignored for months for expressing inappropriate anger in the Canadian Artic Circle (and she recovered her standing in the Utku community), I could pull through.[57]

The girls had in effect inverted the school's panoptical device for tracking individual presence in the institution.[58] Turning the apparatus of school surveillance on its head, they used the forced photograph sitting as an opportunity to create portable genealogical galleries, making people walking repositories of memory. That, in addition to the practice of taking out and frequently comparing wallet photographs, constituted a mechanism for bracing against the way in which society deprived them, literally, of their possessions and with them of their memories.

Later on I saw girls going in groups to the local Sears to sit for additional glum portraits, cementing best-friendships (two or three to a picture), social networks (which can be deduced by who is in multiple sets of pictures), and announcing new arrivals, where mothers and babies posed together.

Pretty soon after I bought the first wallet of my life I realized that in fact I needed two wallets with a complementary distribution of

Figure 6.2 Bedroom culture: Autographing pictures.

pictures, one for Norteña pictures and one for those of Sureñas; it seemed definitely a bad idea to put both sets of pictures into the same wallet since I might be asked to show it. After I arranged the pictures in my wallets it struck me that only the babies were smiling, and that all sorts of artfully struck poses were now evident: full body shots boasted the stick-straight postures over which mothers universally cajole their children. Legs together, one knee tucked behind the other to have the feet in the shape of a "T" or a "V." Aristocratically elevated chins, Renaissance poses which, to modify Joaneath Spicer's[59] phrasing, created "an explosion of female elbows."

One late afternoon after school I got a phone call from T-Rex, Angie, and Mosquita. They were at T-Rex's house exchanging pictures and wanted me to come over and take some more pictures with their other homegirls, posing at night in the park. T-Rex needed pictures to turn in for a school assignment in the following weeks, and everyone thought it would be a great idea to have some group photos taken. I arrived at her house while it was still light, and after fixing and eating quesadillas we sat in T-Rex's room while all of them got ready. Varying combinations of outfits followed, all in shades of black, red, and burgundy: sweatshirts, bandannas, t-shirts and workmen's pants. Everything except the socks was ironed and sported careful creases. T-Rex wanted to wear Dickies and she tried out three different black ones. The winning pair was matched with a black denim vest and a white undershirt with a crease down the middle, topped off by a red bandanna. T-Rex couldn't decide whether to wear it on her head or folded and hanging from the center of her vest. We took pictures both ways.

Mosquita settled on a deep wine sweatshirt with her moniker splashed across the back in white Old English lettering:

𝕷𝖆 𝕸𝖔𝖘𝖖𝖚𝖎𝖙𝖆
𝖉𝖊
𝕱𝖔𝖌 𝕮𝖎𝖙𝖞

it read. She also wore cutoff Dickies with white knee high socks and Chinese Mary Jane flats, good for running in case the cops showed up. In Figure 6.3 Mosquita, T-Rex, and Angie have arranged themselves into a visual pyramid, with Mosquita and Angie at the bottom holding one and four roses respectively. 14 = Norte. This is one of my favorite picture series since it also includes various shots of T-Rex's white and

Figure 6.3   T-Rex hangs a bandanna from her vest, while Angie and Mosquita spell out "14" with red roses.

red teddy-bears, and red paper hearts sitting in the background incongruously, as well as T-Rex's wall of dedicated photographs.

Once it got dark we walked over to the park, and I felt strangely self-conscious in my all-black outfit topped by a black blazer. I looked so Stanford, and wondered what I would do if the police showed up. Now I didn't even have the staff ID – not that it would help when walking in a darkened park with girls who were dressed to the nines in gang getup. The park was one of the places that police and kids seemed to encounter each other. Five girls and two boys were waiting for us already, milling about smoking cigarettes, joking and talking animatedly about the poses that they wanted to have in the photographs. They agreed beforehand on who was to take up what position, and argued about the handshapes and neighborhoods that would be represented in the photographs. I took a couple of candid snapshots of them talking about their arrangement (Figure 6.4) and they protested, no, no, no, don't take pictures just like that, we need to pose!

After conferring, the girls picked a spot framed by an open metal gate, kicked the boys off their picture and started posing. They stared with upward pointing chins, dead serious and at the same time matter-of-fact, making X's, I's, and V's with their arms; ones and fours with little downward-pointing fingers; and N's with both hands. One of the girls

Figure 6.4   A candid snapshot. The pose is being planned: "Should we do an XIV?"

Figure 6.5 Norte Park pose.

was drunk and giddy and could barely make her assigned handshape, and T-Rex stopped the photo session to wait for her to quit laughing.

When I had only two pictures left, they called the boys into their pictures and I took my last shots of the whole group. With my roll finished, all the kids politely said good night, thanked me and everyone walked home. I returned duplicates for all of them through T-Rex the following week. I can imagine that those pictures were circulated as I had seen done with the school photographs.

A couple of years after I had published an article on makeup (an earlier version of chapter 5 in this book), I found out that the article was circulated into the prison system through one of T-Rex's uncles. Not only was my article circulated, but the silly smiling photograph with the bad hair was circulated as well, and I received the following letter from an inmate named Felipe:

Dear Norma,

Hola espero que cuando recivas estas cuantas letras te encuentres gosando de caval salud, usted y su familia.

Primeramente que todo dejame presentar me. Mi nombre es Jose Y si usted gusta nos podriamos escrivir para tener una amistad. He recivido una foto de usted y me pareses simpatica, Te voy a describir Un poco de mi persona, hedad 32 soltero peso 180 lb., Estatura 6 F., Personalidad simpatico

Pero si tú piensas que escribirle a una persona como llo, En las sircunstacias en las que me encuentro no es vien visto. Te comprendo. Conserba esta flor de recuerdo de un admirador túllo.

Bueno mija no me despido sino asta luego.

ps. Y si no save Español, Pues Ingles, For the next. With love, Felipe.

Dear Norma,

I hope that when you receive these words you are enjoying good health, you and your family.

First of all let me introduce myself. My name is Jose and if you wish we can write to each other so that we may have a friendship. I have received a picture of you and I think you are charming. I will describe myself a bit, age 32 single weight 180 lb., height 6ft., good personality.

However if you feel that writing to a person like me, given the circumstances that I am in is not well looked upon, I understand.

Please keep this flower as a souvenir from an admirer.

Alright mija (little one) I won't say goodbye but see you later.

Ps. And if you don't know Spanish, well then English for the next. With love, Felipe.

Starting at the lower left-hand corner and extending halfway up the page was a hand-drawn red rose. It reminded me of Güera's boyfriend's love letters from the pen. T-Rex told me that Felipe was going to be locked up for another seven years but that he was a really nice guy. Although I didn't write back to Felipe, the surprise of having my own picture circulated showed me another aspect of these transactional networks: circulation extends much more widely than I had previously thought, and the memorialization and memory work that is done by photographic exchange radiates out over a wider sphere. Prison inmates' material work faces some of the same constraints that gang girls do in the preservation of memory; with the skyrocketing incarceration rates of Latino and African-American men, it would not be surprising if the photographic circulation network served also to link inmates to their loved ones on the outside.

Conclusion

By showing continuities between narrative, literacy, drawings, and photographs I have tried to trace the ever-widening circles of distribution of material artifacts, and the degrees to which the widening of these circles is related to differential kinds of embodiment. In situations that are governed by preferences for first and second person interactions, embodiment is most saliently taught in those contexts.

These circles have a paradoxical quality in that they allow for more far-reaching contact and greater anonymity at the same time, removing aspects of the immediate context of embodiment and yet allowing long-distance embodiment and structures of feeling to emerge.[60]

This chapter has had a threefold purpose: one is to describe how particular anti-linguistic practices (talking shit, clowning, secret word games, and poetry notebooks) come to accompany broader participation in gang-affiliated networks in a community of high school students in Northern California. The second purpose has been to argue that despite the greater emphasis given in subculture studies to materiality and media consumption, analysis of youth linguistic practices is crucial in providing a more complete picture in our understanding of youth subcultures. The third purpose has been to expand the analytic lens under which we can tie linguistic analyses to the analyses of circulation of commodities. Under the concept of distributed memory, I argue that language-based practices, through their links with embodiment and their reinforcement of material practices, create and extend social memory for youth groups. Norteñas and Sureñas are an example of a youth subculture that is literally prevented by parents, teachers, and the police from holding onto much of the material culture they generate. Distributed memory in the form of discourse and literacy practices reflects the forging of subaltern youth identities; these forms allow us a glimpse into the history of youth literacy (*albures, aleluyas*) and into the degree of contact with language practices of other youth groups (clowning adopted from African-American youth). Focusing on language as part of youth practices can tell us what material practices sometimes cannot, explaining the emergence of unspoken rules (don't tattle) and how these create solidarity over time.

Ephemeral embodied practices such as language are thus linked to other systems of symbolism that rely on levels of increasing repetition and conventionalization.[61] Young Sureñas and Norteñas combined commercially available resources such t-shirts, cars, Oldies music, rap music, and even commercial toys, with locally meaningful practices such as gang colors, hand signs, makeup, drawings, poetry, and narrative conventions. *That* is how homegirls remember, by combining different semiotic levels, always including language and embodiment as well as commercially available, though often illicit, material culture.

Notes

1 Williams (1977)
2 Marx (1981)
3 Found (or searched, sought) object.
4 Hebdige (1979: 107)
5 McRobbie (1986), Thornton (1995), Brown (2007)
6 Nayak (2003), see also papers in Muggleton and Weinzierl (2003)
7 Cohen (1972)
8 Striking UK counterexamples include Hewitt (1986), Rampton (1995), Rampton (1999), Moore (2004), Stuart-Smith et al. (forthcoming)
9 The 1970s British subcultural theory had its beginnings at the University of Birmingham. Major texts outlining their assumptions include Hall and Jefferson (1976), Willis (1978), Hebdige (1979).
10 Clarke (1981/1990: 92)
11 Brown (2007)
12 Brown (2007: 64)
13 Bucholtz (2002)
14 Eckert (1988)

15 Labov (1972a), Labov (1972d)
16 Labov (1969)
17 Bucholtz (2002)
18 Swidler and Arditi (1994), Berliner (2005)
19 Ochs and Capps (1996), Linde (2000), Capps and Ochs (2001), Rymes (2001)
20 Linde (2000)
21 Hutchins (1995)
22 Schwartz (1991: 231)
23 *Colors*, motion picture release (1988).
24 *American Me*, motion picture release (1992).
25 de Certeau (1986b: 148), for further reading on simulacra see Baudrillard (1994).
26 Halliday (1976)
27 Halliday (1976)
28 A combination of Swahili, English, and Kikuyu spoken by youth in Kenya, Abdulaziz and Osinde (1997).
29 British "gayspeak," a form of pidginized Anglo-Romanian, Hancock (1984).
30 Lefkowitz (1991), Tetreault (2000)
31 Schilling-Estes (2005)
32 See also same description by youth described in Morrill, et al. (2000: 537)
33 Goodwin (1990)
34 Shuman (1986)
35 Goodwin (1990), Shuman (1986)
36 To be *rushed by scraps* means to be suddenly attacked by a group of people, scraps in this case being Sureñas from T-Rex's perspective.
37 de Certau (1986: 200)
38 Linguistic evidentiality refers to language-specific mechanisms for marking how a speaker has come to know what they know, or how much confidence they have in their utterance. English doesn't have a system of morphological evidentials with prefixes or suffixes, though we can optionally mark evidentiality in discourse with markers such as "apparently," or "obviously."
39 An argot is considered to be specialized slang.
40 Goyvaerts (1996)
41 Ingold (2001a), Ingold (2001b)
42 Labov (1972a)
43 Paredes (1993)
44 Labov (1972a)
45 Gutiérrez Gonzalez (1993), Moreno-Álvarez (2001), Cardeña (2003)
46 Also attested in Tepito, Mexico City by Cardeña (2003).
47 Martín (2005), I owe this insight to Salvador García.

48 Paredes (1993)
49 Thanks to A. Ashley Stinnett for this discussion.
50 As has Shuman (1986)
51 A 1966 Oldies hit by Tex-Mex Doo-wop star Sunny Ozuma and the Jetliners.
52 Reproduced with the kind permission of Glad Music Publishing.
53 In *The Labyrinth of Solitude*, 1950.
54 Carsten (1995)
55 Geertz and Geertz (1964)
56 J. Briggs (1970), C. Briggs (1986), Agar (2000)
57 J. Briggs (1970)
58 Foucault (1977)
59 Spicer (1992)
60 Williams (1977)
61 Or ritualization as per Haiman (1998).

CHAPTER 7

ICONS AND EXEMPLARS: ETHNOGRAPHIC APPROACHES IN VARIATIONIST SOCIOLINGUISTICS

Fighting Words

Walking through the corridor of Sor Juana High School on a Monday morning, Patricia wore head-to-toe blue and glowered from under heavily made-up eyelids, the end of her eyeliner extending well into her temples. She had been ritually inducted over the weekend by three Fog City Sureñas, and having performed relatively well in the short but scrappy fight staged for the purposes of testing her mettle and teaching her the basics of street moves, she was feeling extra tough for the beginning of study hall that Monday.

"¿Qué me ves?" *(What are you looking at?)* said Lupe defiantly, receiving Patricia's stare through a narrow eye-slit under a red bandanna covering her forehead and obscuring the upper half of her field of vision. In order to see her opponent, Lupe had thrown her head back and thrust her chin up, her neck hidden into her shoulders. All Patricia could see were the dark shadows hiding her eyes. T-Rex had called that "looking in." Also of Mexican extraction, Lupe was likewise heavily made-up, but dressed entirely in red, instantly recognizable as a Norteña.

"Tschhh, don't EVEN talk to me in Spanish, 'cause your Spanish ain't all that," yelled Patricia, *in English*. Fighting words, since both Norteñas and Sureñas had a claim to authentic Mexican-ness, and both understood Spanish to be symbolic of that claim. The switch to English was intended to circumscribe the boundary of the right kind of Spanish, and to imply that Lupe could not speak it well enough.

Lupe threw the first punch, and only after it landed she snapped, "You wanna box me?" When Patricia responded by testing a newly learned jab, other students began gathering around and egging them on. The hall monitor waddled over to break it up, and both girls were sent to the principal. There they talked their way out of trouble by explaining to him, coolly and lightheartedly, "You believed us, huh? We were just joking! We've known each other since elementary school! Ha ha ha! You know, Mexicans just TALK LOUD!" Incredibly, their skillful manipulation of stereotypes got them out of trouble that day. On their way out of the school administrative offices, they sneered and cursed each other under their breath. "I'm gonna get you bitch. Just watch your back."

Later that morning, I ran into Patricia, whom I hadn't seen since the previous Friday at school.

"Whassup?" I said to her.

"Nothing [noṯiŋ]," she replied, "just got in a fight with that bitch Lupe." By this point I had been doing ethnographic fieldwork in Sor Juana High School for two years, collecting dozens of hours of audio-taped interviews with and interactions among students, including Patricia. On hearing Patricia's utterance of the word "nothing" I was floored. Her pronunciation was different from what I'd heard on numerous prior recordings of her, and patterned more closely with the way that inducted, "core" gang members sounded in their recordings. Her previously fricative [θ] had fortitioned and dentalized into a [ṯ] and the following vowel was now a high, tense [i]. Both of these features were associated with the defiant girls forming the core gang group who, though native speakers of English and perfectly able to produce the fricative /θ/ and lax /I/, chose to draw upon the symbolic repertoire of Spanish phonology as part of their linguistic production. I was aware that Patricia had been associating loosely with some of the core members of the Sureñas, but now I could tell that something had changed. That one word, [noṯiŋ], combined with her heavier makeup and new upright-ponytail hairstyle, severe in its orderliness, pushed my curiosity over the edge of discretion. I had to ask.

"Patricia," I said, "Did you get jumped in?"

Her eyes widened. "How did you know? Did someone tell you?"

"No, no. It's just the way you talk . . . and your hair. They're, um . . . really different."

"Huh." She said in puzzled resignation, "Well, I hope my mom can't tell."

Linguistic Variation in Communities of Practice

One of the most remarkable features about the Norteña/Sureña gang dynamic is its status as a local distinction, powerful enough to organize individuals' daily practice and yet so fine-grained that it would easily be missed by an observer orienting to some of the most common assumptions one might make about Latinas and Latinos in the United States. Sociologists and newspaper columnists alike ponder whether this diverse and disparate group of Latinas/os or "Hispanics" (as the group is designated on the US government census) is most usefully understood by subdividing that population according to country of origin, socioeconomic class, citizenship status, union or party membership, linguistic fluency, or perhaps by generational status, with ever thinner slices of the sociodemographic pie served up as a way of trying to scrutinize and predict behavior. According to any of these criteria, Lupe the Norteña and Patricia the Sureña are identical: they grew up in the same neighborhood, their parents hold similar blue-collar jobs, they attend the same church, went to the same elementary and middle schools, are both 1.5 generation, and both speak Spanish and English.

And yet social badges (Norteña/Sureña gang membership) deemed important enough to start a fight between the two girls are meaningful only according to the shared repertoire of local distinctions.[1] Patricia and Lupe were not only orienting to each other's status as rival gang-dynamic participants, but even more subtly to the distinction between ritually inducted core members and peripheral members. Lupe had "read" Patricia's bandanna, looking-in posture, and eyeliner from afar as signifying a change in status, and asserting a claim of distinction. Such dynamic and malleable indices of distinction are found not only in dress, makeup, and hair, but in the deployment of linguistic variables like those involved in the production of the pronominal item *nothing*.

Every macro-level social construct, such as class, ethnicity, gender, or language, is composed of countless micro-level phenomena, instantiated in the behavior of individuals. Through the analysis of quantitative linguistic variation, I explore how low-level semiotic phenomena such as the implementation of vocalic repertoire are involved in forging higher-level symbolic organization. If we agree that expressions of collective identity such as nationalism, ethnicity, or gender are epiphenomenal, emergent constructs that can be understood by studying individual agents engaged in the moment-to-moment performance of acts of identity, then it behooves us to identify as well an intermediate level, some sort of mediating ground between individual language agency and macro-level social constructs. The articulation of the linkages between macro- and micro-, between social structure and linguistic agency, is a crucial step if we are to understand the "scaling up" of linguistic repertoires and language ideologies,[2] and of the linked, overlapping, and recursive meanings that might take us from Patricia's innovative utterance of "nothing" to understanding how her innovative use of one particular variant, in its context, may connect to the broader understandings of Norte and Sur, and their attendant relations of hemispheric localism.

In the rest of the book I explore the community of practice as constitutive of such an intermediate level that allows us to link situated activities and practices with larger constructs. I argue, after Penelope Eckert, that in sociolinguistic variation this intermediate level functions through iconic speakers and their use of particular linguistic variables, replete as they are with indexical values and language ideologies.[3] Iconic speakers are socially salient individuals toward whom others orient, and who become salient and imitated as a result of their extreme behavior, centrality within their group, and broad social ties. These factors give them greater weight in the definition of styles.[4] T-Rex, one of the key informants of this study, has the status of an iconic speaker, and, as we will see in chapters 8 and 9, is one of the leaders in the raising of /I/ and the use of the distinctive discourse markers.

In this chapter, both communities of practice and exemplar theory will be invoked as theoretical backdrops orienting our case study of variation among Latina youth in Sor Juana High School. Among the core Norteñas and Sureñas, the wannabe's, the Disco girls, and the Latina Jocks, membership in different communities of practice sheds light on the differences in their linguistic behavior.

What is a Community of Practice?

All of us participate in *communities of practice*,[5] that is to say, communities of co-present, joint engagement centered on specific activities that provide us with structured action, and through which we craft social meaning. Within the fields of sociolinguistics and linguistic anthropology, the framework of communities of practice has been helpful in understanding how day-to-day practices between people engaged in talk-in-interaction help to shape both language and society. Precisely because such practices are mundane, shared, frequent, meaningful, recurrent, and salient for participants, they texture our lives and shape our habits. A community of practice might be a group of close-knit friends sharing in-group jokes; a family; a group of work colleagues who see each other and have water cooler conversations every day; a Buddhist temple that prays together; or a handball club that engages in intense practice and competition. Within communities of practice, distinctions emerge that, though salient in the local social landscape, may not be in alignment with common analysts' categories. In my retelling of Patricia and Lupe's encounter, participants displayed the three hallmarks of a community of practice:[6] 1) mutual engagement – in this case not harmonious, but engagement still; 2) a jointly negotiated enterprise (the production of gang identities); and 3) a shared repertoire (mutually recognizable makeup, hairstyle, and linguistic practices).

A community of practice is an aggregate of people who, united by a common enterprise, develop and share "ways of doing things, ways of talking, beliefs, values, power relations – in short practices emerge in the course of this mutual endeavor."[7] A community of practice can develop out of a formally or informally constituted enterprise; once launched it has its own life and develops its own trajectory. The development of shared practices emerges as participants make meaning of their own enterprise. The community as a whole constructs a sense of itself through its relation between its practices and those of other communities. Because the center of gravity of a community of practice is local rather than extra-local, participants' behaviors are interpreted first and foremost in a local context. In many respects, a community of practice is similar to a close-knit social network, and for our purposes, I expect many of the predictions made about communities of practice to apply to dense and multiplex social networks.[8] One of the differences between communities of practice and social networks, however, is that practices and their attendant ideologies allow the emergence of what some scholars have termed "iconic speakers/participants,"[9] who develop personae[10] that serve to influence and pattern others' behavior. These iconic speakers, by virtue of their influence in their communities, can be accelerators and leaders of linguistic change, as shown in studies of Chinese yuppies,[11] Detroit-area burnout girls,[12] and Glaswegian working-class girls.[13] Within communities of practice, iconic speakers are not necessarily the *sources* of innovation,[14] but they are the ones who put together a style that is salient, identifiable, and indeed recognizable and prone to imitation by others.

In this study of the linguistic variation found among Latina girls, we see that the iconic speakers are individuals who display both the greatest token frequencies and the most innovative grammatical usage of a particular construction – the Th-Pro lexical set (thing, something, nothing, anything) that carries the variable in question. It is no accident that the girls whose frequencies of /I/-raising tokens are highest and whose degree of grammatical innovation was most pronounced are also central individuals in the community of practice, in this case recognized as leaders of their respective gang-groupings. In creating personae that are stylistically prominent relative to those of others in the community of practice, they manufacture distinction.

An Exemplar-Based Approach to Language and Social Identity

Insofar as a _linguistic variable_ is "a construct that unites a class of fluctuating variants within a language set,"[15] it reflects a decision point at which a speaker chooses between alternative ways of saying the same thing. The conservative and prestigeful Standard California English pronunciation of _nothing_ as [noθɪŋ] denotes the same referent as the innovative and somewhat stigmatized pronunciation [noṭiŋ]. They are technically two ways of saying the same thing, the very definition of a sociolinguistic variable. Both of these variants are available to Patricia and Lupe, since they are both native speakers of English and have heard both growing up. And yet when one of them arrives at a decision point where there are alternate ways of saying the same thing, in the action of favoring one variant over another, she is crafting social meaning that goes beyond the purely referential.

It is precisely by studying these decision points that we find, to borrow the phrasing of Robert LePage and Andrée Tabouret-Keller,[16] that language is replete not only with orderly patterning but with _acts of identity_. But how do speakers make such decisions? Asserting that speakers perform acts of identity is neither a complete explanation, nor can it give speakers unlimited agency. All sociolinguistic acts of identity take place, as we will see, within the historical trajectory of the linguistic variable in question, a history containing the traces of the routinized speech of those before us, as Bakhtin[17] would have it. Sociolinguistic innovation takes place within the limits of the system of language production and perception, constraints that determine whether a particular variant can be produced relative to motor principles of effort and habituation, and whether it can be interpreted relative to the limits of psycholinguistic processing, the linguistic history of the variable, and that particular community of practice.

We all use the continuum of variation to align with others and display affiliation, or to display rejection, contestation, or resistance. Socially meaningful variation such as the dropping of a pronoun, the shortening of a vowel, or the switching of a register or code (English to Spanish, for example) are continually interpreted as figure against ground, always relative to the orderly patterning of the speech in the entire community. Speakers are even able to manipulate interpretation by drawing on knowledge of a hearer's imputed perceptions of variation, as Patricia and Lupe so cleverly played on what they knew to be perceptual stereotypes by insisting to the principal: "You know how Mexicans just TALK LOUD!"

What is Exemplar Theory?

Exemplar theory is emerging as unifying model in linguistics, especially within probability-based frameworks used in morphology,[18] phonetics and phonology,[19] historical linguistics and grammaticalization,[20] language acquisition,[21] and syntax,[22] as well as sociolinguistics.[23] In other work[24] I have suggested that we might expand the horizons of exemplar theory by positing sociolinguistic rubrics *(social saliency, agency)* that may, in conjunction with current findings on the importance of frequency, serve to strengthen current exemplar theoretic models.

Exemplar theory is a model for language learning and use based on the notion that multimodal, detail-preserving episodic memory underlies the cognitive representation and processing of language.[25] In the lexicon, for instance, it is not merely words that are stored: Talker-specific characteristics such as gender and voice quality have been shown to be retained by listeners, facilitating access to lexical representations.[26] Episodic memory traces include linguistic material as well as social and contextual information. Perceptual categories, whether they be grammatical (phonemes, morphemes, etc.), social (female, working class, etc.), or contextual (i.e., lexical neighborhood, genre, etc.) are not a priori givens that are acquired early on by the learner and to which input is then matched. Rather, categories are epiphenomenal, emerging anew with each comparison–matching task. The current token-to-be-matched is compared not only to all past experiences of tokens in the input, the token itself increments the categories to which it is eventually assigned and provides a new set of potential matching data. This is consistent with sociolinguistic and linguistic anthropological understandings of language both reflecting and constructing social reality.[27]

Although exemplar theory is uniquely compatible with current sociolinguistic understandings of the social construction and performance of identity,[28] its primary thrust has been in providing evidence that frequency of tokens in the input and the organization of such frequency in time serves the purposes of category organization:[29] this type of evidence questions the need for innate categories, parameters, and strictly categorical accounts.[30] Exemplar theoretic accounts then rely on distributional characteristics and covariation in the input to explain emergent patterns. Input frequency and recency/priming are two well-adumbrated areas of inquiry within psycholinguistically oriented exemplar theory and other models of phonological, lexical, and semantic competitive activation;[31] less well understood are social mechanisms through which attention and other factors can be modeled. Since clearly not all input into the speech learning system is given equal weight in terms of output, researchers have independently suggested mechanisms such as attributes of attention,[32] various types of weighting,[33] and stereotyping[34] in perception. But how are these probabilistic input and memory accounts reconciled with sociolinguistic evidence?

Members of any kind of linguistic community are exquisitely attuned to the frequencies of language phenomena in their surroundings. As babies, we are born with a sensitivity to the rhythmic patterns that characterize language,[35] an ability which serves us greatly in the process of its acquisition. As early as a few months, babies in auditory discrimination tasks prefer to listen to the sounds of the ambient language rather than a language they haven't yet been exposed to. Later on, we are sensitive to the frequency with which linguistic segments are used,[36] and interpret new utterances against our experiential database of how that person and others commonly utter the same string. More robust categories are created for frequently used lexical items, for more frequently occurring morphological and phonological collocations, and for more frequently occurring grammatical constructions. Exemplars are stored, made robust in perception and activated in production on the basis of quantitative frequency information in our input. Communities of practice are the theaters that provide the opportunities for our usage, and social-indexical words are the vehicles that carry these frequencies, forming what Pierre Bourdieu in his analysis of practice calls *habitus*, the powerful automatic dispositions (including what psycholinguistics would call perceptual biases), the bodily and mental habits that structure our presence in the world.[37] My own sensitivity to the variable frequency in the tapes I had been listening to is how I could tell that Patricia had changed social networks, and is the same reason that her mom will not be able to distinguish these changes – she does not have enough access to that experiential database.

A Short History of Sociolinguistics: From Stratification to Ethnography

I proceed with this chapter by providing a few reference points in variationist sociolinguistics, a field of quantitative linguistic study that distinguishes itself not only through its primary reliance on multivariate statistical analysis but also through its development of a specialized kind of research methodology called the *sociolinguistic interview*. In this chapter we will review the sociolinguistic interview as a methodological construct, and pay special attention to research syntheses that seek to illuminate the linguistic patterning gleaned from quantitative study with the qualitative understandings gained from long-term ethnographies. I will concentrate on developments beginning with what has come to be known as the Labovian tradition, referring the reader to the work of earlier scholars and historiographies of the field where appropriate.

The Labovian Tradition

Language is key to the definition of identity, to the relationship of individuals to larger social constructs. We recognize as part of identity formation the daily drama that unfolds as students interact and coalesce into groups, each group with its own unique imprint and seemingly a language all its own, weaving a tapestry of distinct styles that is difficult for outsiders to decipher. But what defines these styles? What are the elements that all of us use to shape and define, perform and cement our identities? Ethnography-based variationist studies such as this one now advance the claim that, as meaning-making individuals, we utilize not only language but also symbolic elements at many different levels (gesture, historical references, dress, music, and other aspects of material culture) to craft our stylistic practice. Although this may sound like a rather commonsense statement, especially to poetics- and performance-oriented folklorists,[38] this view actually represents a radical shift in variationist sociolinguistics, a field that has spent the past forty years seeking to 1) demonstrate language variability in speech communities at an abstract level, 2) understand the intricate quantitative patterning internal to language, and 3) correlate that patterning to analyst pre-determined categories such as "age," "sex," "class," or "ethnicity." This last effort has led to a kind of correlational imperative, where groups are pre-emptively divided into sociodemographic categories and their linguistic behavior explained by appeal to these same categories. In contrast, a community of practice approach starts from the ground level, with ethnography, talking to speakers and attempting to find out what *their* relevant social ordering and categories might be.[39]

Sociolinguistics and linguistic anthropology both saw their beginnings in the writings of early anthropologists and ethnologists. Bronislaw Malinowski,[40] Raymond Firth[41] and Leonard Bloomfield,[42] for example, all played important roles in developing the role of language study in anthropology, while Dell Hymes,[43] Charles Ferguson,[44] and John Fischer[45] emerge as early figures who used quantification strategies to investigate linguistic behavior of speech communities.[46]

It was not until the late 1960s that quantitative sociolinguistics would split off and become a bona fide branch of its own. The paradigm-forming events were the publication of William Labov's work on Martha's Vineyard, as well as his book *The Social Stratification of English in New York City*. The latter established not only the sociological method and stratificational aims of early sociolinguistics, but also developed a specific interview methodology that would serve to nourish the statistical demand for the collection of robust quantities of speech data.

Labov[47] investigated the centralization of /ay/ and /aw/ in Martha's Vineyard, a place where the local identity of the fisherfolk comes into daily contact with the social, cultural, and economic capital of tourists coming from the mainland. Labov found that in interviewing people on the island, a relationship emerged between younger interviewees' professed orientations toward staying on the island or leaving it and their use of variants tied to islander identity. Centralization of the nuclei of /ay/ and /aw/ (the diphthongs in "right" and "house") correlated strongly with islander identity; they did so to such an extent that the social meaning of the centralized diphthongs could be understood as "traditional Vineyarder." The more standard variants of the diphthongs, on the other hand, were correlated in interview narratives with expressions of desire to leave the island for the mainland. This early ethnographic exploration of a system of social indices provided much inspiration for future sociolinguistic work, as well as a radical departure from the dialectology paradigm that focused on item-by-item elicitations from a few (usually elderly male) individuals.

The new field of sociolinguistics, instead of focusing on the speech of a few "pure" dialect speakers, sought to model the behavior of entire speech communities by utilizing representative random samples, balanced numerically by age-groups, social classes, ethnicities, and other social categories thought to be relevant. Utilizing a representative sample has been thought to bear the potential of transcending the limitation of time and allowing us to see linguistic change in progress.

The understanding of social variation as central to the problem of historical change continues to be reflected in current work. Modern sociolinguistics is firmly grounded in the belief that the propulsion for language change lies *within* social variation, where innovative speakers push the envelope of pre-existing changes, always abstracting from and simultaneously scaffolded and constrained by linguistic structural factors. Thus we can restate the dual goals of modern quantitative sociolinguistics as:

1 Understanding speakers' acts of identity against the backdrop of the "orderly heterogeneity" of language,[48] and
2 Understanding how the collectivity of those individual acts results in large-scale change in language.

Sociolinguistic Constructs: Apparent-Time and Real-Time

Rather than looking only at the synchronic state of the language represented in a single recording of one speaker, an age-stratified sample affords analysts a window into the past. Working from the assumption that adults acquire the bulk of their phonology as children in the critical period of language acquisition, it follows that the differentially aged subsets of the population have acquired slightly different systems which reflect ongoing stages of change in the language. Thus, looking at the speech of an eighty-year-old in the year 2010 would reflect the phonology that she acquired in the 1930s. Comparing her speech to that of a sixty-year-old, a forty-year-old, and a twenty-year-old would allow us to look at graduated time-slices of sixty years' worth of language change. This type of comparison rests on the *apparent-time* hypothesis, which states that changes in apparent time as inferred from speakers' ages accurately reflect those occurring in *real time* during speakers' life spans. Many of the classic works of sociolinguistics follow this type of paradigm, stratifying informants based on age and other social characteristics, and finding that linguistic change is gradual and spreads through a population in a predictable way.[49] Some of the hallmarks of a typical linguistic change are: a period of "initial stasis, a rapid rise, and a leveling off" that together give shape to an S-curve, one of the most frequently observed patterns in diffusion of all kinds.[50] This is the pattern which is now considered a basic template for the modeling of linguistic change.[51]

The apparent-time hypothesis relies on the assumption that a speaker's repertoire is static after childhood, the critical period of language acquisition. But is it really the case that speakers do not change their phonology as teens or adults? Although urban surveys and apparent-time studies have yielded an accepted methodology as well as a wealth of knowledge on patterns of change occurring cross-linguistically, studies of single speakers are now beginning to provide a robust challenge to these underlying assumptions.

Patricia Cukor-Avila and Guy Bailey[52] make a compelling case that the speech of individuals undergoes considerable change as individuals' life-circumstances change. Especially striking is the example of a Texan teenager pseudonymed Sheila. Sheila (born 1979) was a young African-American woman from Springville (pop. 180), a small town in Texas. She was interviewed from ages nine until twenty, while Cukor-Avila and Bailey tracked the occurrence of four syntactic features of African-American English in her speech. They were able to observe that significant life events, such as Shelia's beginning to spend the summers in the nearby city of Wilson (pop. 100,000), had a dramatic effect on her linguistic usage. As she developed new friends, new interests, and new networks, Sheila also modified her speech to include more variants that were indicative of her new city identity. One of the variables studied was *had* + past used as simple past; Bailey cites this example of its usage: *when I was workin' at Billups me an' the manager had became good friends.*[53]

For the *had* + past variable, Shelia went from *zero* usage at the age of nine when she lived in Springville to 75 percent after beginning to spend the summers in Wilson to 82 percent after finally moving there. What is remarkable about this example is not only the dramatic change in Sheila's grammar, where she essentially replaced one verbal form (simple past) with another (*had* + past), but also the implications that it has for the study of language change. Given a situation of low stability or of changing social allegiances, individuals can effect quite dramatic changes in their speech that do not necessarily correlate with patterns of change in the language, but rather with a change in the personal circumstances of the individuals.

A striking example of a real-time change that has been recently documented in an adult is found in the speech of Queen Elizabeth II of the United Kingdom, whose Christmas addresses of the past forty years were collected and studied by Jonathan Harrington, Sallyanne Palethorpe, and Catherine Watson.[54] This is an unusual sample of a single speaker, varying only by age but engaging in the same speech event, saying almost the same words in the same sequence. This is as close as we can come to a natural experiment: the Christmas address is delivered to the nation every year in almost exactly identical circumstances. It takes place around the same date, lasts approximately ten minutes, and has approximately the same degree of formality. Harrington found that in real-time, Elizabeth II did something quite unexpected: the phonetic implementation of her phonology gradually changed to converge closely with the speech of her subjects on several key variants. Harrington et al. hypothesize that her real-time shift from Received Pronunciation (RP) to Estuary English (EE) may be due both to sociopolitical, populist pressures on the monarchy and to the influence of younger royals who were more likely to have moved in wider circles and thus been carriers of innovations that could be picked up by the Queen. Despite a great deal of stability in the Queen's social position and geographic location, changes in the communities of practice of members of her network appear to have had a remarkable effect on her speech. We would assume that the Queen retains the ability to speak the most restricted RP, and that she is making strategic but not altogether conscious decisions about how to portray herself to her subjects.

We can postulate the following summary observations:

1 Ethnographic studies and studies of single individuals provide enough detail for us to see the effect of individuals' communities of practice and personal social milestones on their linguistic biographies. Patricia's induction into the gang of the Sureñas and Sheila's move to the city of Wilson are illustrative of rapid change in response to specific events, while the Queen's gradual shift from RP to EE is the real-time response to sustained social pressure. These small-scale studies have the advantage of allowing us to craft more sophisticated social-theoretic explanations for individual linguistic behavior, and directly relate these explanations to sociocultural factors as we understand them to be experienced by participants in communities of practice.

2 By contrast, it is in the domain of surveys and apparent-time studies that we can abstract from individual differences to draw large-scale inferences about language change and its impact on geographic and social dialects. This also allows us to form and test certain kinds of quantitatively based hypotheses.[55] Large-scale studies have the advantage of allowing greater generalization. Both real-time and apparent-time studies are thus needed to understand the social history of language at different levels of granularity.

3 Because they rely on quantitative data collection, both methods share the features of replicability, recountability, and reanalysis. For a specific data sample (for example, my recordings of Patricia), any researcher could go back and recount/reclassify/reanalyze the tokens to further investigate inherent linguistic or social patterning in the data. With large-scale, random-sample urban studies, there is even the possibility of replicating a study.[56]

Because the collection of data is crucially shaped by the relationship between the interviewer and interviewee (as per the observer's paradox, explained below), I stated in chapter 2 that it may be impossible to replicate a long-term ethnographic study, since the interactions and the resulting linguistic data are product of a long-term relationship between the participants and the researcher. Researchers and participants in ethnographic situations actively co-construct identities for each other. Depending on the social situation, T-Rex and Patricia would introduce me as a fictive cousin, their teacher, or their friend. In the example given in the beginning of this chapter, I (un)consciously converged with Patricia's speech patterns, greeting her with a "whassup?" not completely uncharacteristic of my speech, but much more commonly heard in Patricia's friendship networks. My convergence in turn has the possibility of reinforcing Patricia's production norms. Furthermore, my own status as a 1.5 generation bilingual Mexican immigrant in her mid-twenties had sustained effects on our interactions.

The Sociolinguistic Interview

The Labovian tradition has primarily relied on a specific data collection method called the *sociolinguistic interview*. It consists of a one-time, face-to-face conversation between relative strangers (the interviewer and the interviewee), with a reading of a prepared paragraph and word-lists/minimal pairs at the end. Researchers were aware very early on of the *observer's paradox*. The very act of observing language can change the object of observation in dramatic ways. If I had asked Patricia, out of the blue, to pronounce into a tape recorder the word "nothing" for me, she would have produced a formal-sounding quotation form quite unlike the one she produced spontaneously. The awareness of knowing that someone is observing or recording one's speech can have such a strong effect that it may mask some of the contextual effects (variation according to linguistic or social context) that a sociolinguist is trying to capture.

The "solution" that was devised to the paradox of observation (to lessen attention paid to speech by working for interest and involvement through the elicitation of narratives) also contributed to researchers' willingness to forget themselves as instruments of data collection. Consider the following case from my fieldwork.

Although I was able to form close friendships and record interviews and naturally occurring interactions in all kinds of settings with Latina girls, doing narrative interviews and naturalistic interaction recording among teenage Latino boys proved quite difficult for me precisely because of my age and gender, and the fact that I am Latina. This combination of status characteristics made me interpretable as a potentially more intimate member of their group. Despite having gone through the research protocols requesting permissions, and despite having obtained consent forms from parents and assent from the participants, I began to notice hesitation from different groups about my doing interviews with boys.

When I realized that boys' girlfriends might begin to mistrust me, I understood that the free-flowing conversations that were possible with girls were simply not going to happen with boys. And although I do have data from those initial interviews with boys, I am hesitant to analyze it and compare it with the girls', simply because I think they do not reflect the same level of comfort or familiarity, and these factors can greatly affect variable speech production. On the other hand, it can be argued that a young male Latino fieldworker might be able to gather Latino male gang member data of the relatively forthcoming sort that I was able to collect from the girls, at which point a comparison of boys' and girls' linguistic data might be warranted.

Canonically, a one-shot sociolinguistic interview begins with some demographic questions about the interviewee's background, and proceeds to ask questions of common human experience designed to elicit storytelling on the part of the interviewee (some of the questions will be exemplified below). Although the nature of the questions depends partly on the speech community under study, the protocol as practiced by many sociolinguists aims for some uniformity, with the aim of comparing questions across individual speakers and across communities by replicating the structure of other sociolinguistic interviews.

Field methods instruction for sociolinguists[57] has included such principles as the importance of "entering fresh, as a stranger" (to avoid the sampling bias of one's pre-existing networks); beginning with those who have "nothing to do"; asking for help and identifying oneself on a local dimension; avoiding talking directly about language (for fear of exacerbating the observer's paradox and arousing normative linguistic behavior); introducing recording equipment openly and securing full permissions (on ethical grounds – frankly, light-years ahead of its time in terms of the treatment of human subjects); and beginning the interview by resting one's case on a general truth with which everyone agrees:
✳ *It seems like kids don't learn very much in school nowadays.*[58]

Questioning the Sociolinguistic Interview

The critique of this type of methodology has almost as long a history as the methodology itself.[59] Nessa Wolfson[60] argues that the interview as a speech event elicits a particular kind of speech that may in no way be understood either as natural or as the speech that members of the community use with each other. In a related vein, Charles Briggs[61] details some of his own communicative blunders, incisively showing how the assumptions that researchers commonly bring to interviews cloud their interpretive frameworks.

We will further note that Labov's dictate to enter as a stranger would appear to preclude the considerable insights that can be gained by native or activist linguistic anthropologists. By implying that only outsiders with nonexistent networks are suited to the study of a community's language, an injunction that has the intention of controlling the contextual variable of interviewer familiarity indirectly reproduces the colonialist and capitalist relations of domination between researchers and subjects that have so plagued the fields of linguistics and anthropology.[62] Advocates of the sociolinguistic interview might answer this claim by arguing that within the stratificational program there is in fact an attempt to cover all social classes, not just the subordinated ones, and that this interview protocol might well be used in "studying up." However, critiques of the effects of the sociolinguistic enterprise on subordinated populations abound,[63] while studies of privileged populations are very few – access is more easily gained by prestigious academics to subordinated populations, as they are the ones that may be considered by researchers as having "nothing to do."

The Danger of Death and the Vernacular

One of the most famous and controversial questions in the classic sociolinguistic interview protocol is the so-called *danger of death question*. This question is normally introduced by the interviewer well into the interview, after the expected initial period of discomfort and habituation to the equipment. After some informal introductory queries about neighborhood background, childhood games, and perhaps about basic oppositions of local interest (small town vs. large city, people vs. government, etc.), the interviewer, working for interest and personal involvement, may introduce a question laden with an affective component. It is hoped that this question will result in the speaker focusing more on the content and less on the linguistic form of her response. *Have you ever been in a situation where you thought you were going to die, where you said to yourself, "This is it?"* The goal of this question is to elicit from the interviewee a narrative, in the telling of which the speaker might become less self-conscious, and their speech might better reflect their *vernacular*. The danger-of-death question has elicited many narratives, all across the world, of suspenseful, death-defying acts, of tragedies, of good fortune and sheer luck. According to Faegin,[64] it also has elicited furrowed brows in Norwich, England,[65] the unemotional narratives of those used to danger in Belfast,[66] and uncomprehending pauses in Anniston, Alabama,[67] where questions such as *What were you doing when that tornado hit in 1954?* were much more effective in the elicitation of narratives.

Obviously, depending on the field situation, some questions will prove more effective than others in eliciting narratives – the danger-of-death question itself is quite culturally specific, and highly inappropriate, even taboo in some contexts. Can you imagine asking Manuel the tattooed veterano in the laundromat about his "danger of death" experiences? He presumably had "nothing to do" because he was just folding laundry.

In my own fieldwork among gang members, danger-of-death questions were outright *faux pas*, along with questions I unwittingly asked Manuel such as the meaning of tattoos. Questions of this nature are highly suspicious to gang members and indicative of "snitch-type" behavior associated with police informants. Even outside of those suspicions, the answers to these questions are understood to be very personal, and only to be told to trusted friends. It was about a year into my fieldwork when speakers spontaneously began telling me such narratives and explaining their tattoos.

During the informal portions of the interview (defined as the vernacular as per the definition above), analysts have found that on the whole the speech of an individual systematically shifts toward the most innovative speech forms in her system, the forms that are advancing linguistic changes. When confronted with minimal-pair elicitation, one's speech systematically shifts toward more conservative, standard, and prestigeful forms that reflect greater planning and self-awareness. It is in excited, purposeful narratives (rather than in demographic questions answered for the benefit of a formal, stilted, and possibly untrustworthy interviewer) that speakers display the most innovative forms in their range. The tremendous regularity of this finding, combined with the unequitable and differential distribution of linguistic resources in any single population, means that notwithstanding the caveats above, sociolinguists have been able to use the sociolinguistic interview as a tool for the investigation of linguistic stratification. Much of the gang data that I have presented to this point in the book has relied on ethnographic observations as well as over forty hours of tape-recorded naturalistic conversations and multi-party interactions that I gathered during the time I was actively doing fieldwork in the high school. In order to take the next step, that of uncovering and analyzing systematic linguistic variation, it is important to control for interlocutor effects and to compare speech that has been gathered in similar conditions. I will turn in the next two chapters to the data that I gathered in controlled, sociolinguistic interview situations from twelve individual girls representing the different social categories in the high school.

In summary, although the sociolinguistic interview paradigm suffers from the caveats outlined throughout, it has yielded replicable results that allow us to contextualize variation in a broader context. These results must be both accounted for and elaborated upon in the new wave (the third wave, as Penny Eckert calls it) of ethnographically based sociolinguistic approaches.

Coming Full Circle: From Stratification Back to Ethnography

After more than a quarter century of studying communities almost exclusively according to sociological categories, variation scholars are now bridging the gap between analysts' and participants' categories through a strengthening trend toward ethnographic studies which look at situated practices and at participants' explicit interactional orientations. The fact that some of the earliest studies in quantitative sociolinguistics were oriented to participant categories has prompted some scholars to point out that sociolinguistics seems to have returned to its ethnographic roots.[68]

Sociolinguistic researchers commonly analyze interview data as a coherent whole made up of quantifiable parts (tokens of linguistic variables of interest), ignoring the social history of the linguistic forms themselves, and the symbolic context surrounding the interview as a culturally-specific speech event. Ethnographic approaches often point to the history of the linguistic forms, so that Zhang[69] traces the development of speech personae among Beijing speakers of Mandarin Chinese, highlighting clusters of variables that give rise to different styles: the Beijing alley saunterer, the Beijing smooth operator, and the Chinese transnational yuppy who uses phonological variables influenced by Hong

Kong Chinese. These personae that arise in the time-slice of her data in turn have a long history within Chinese culture; the first two are characters found in Chinese literature, while the transnational yuppy is a relatively new speech persona linked to the dramatic economic transition of China since the 1970s due to globalization.

Ethnography has allowed variation studies a focus at the level of participant-defined activity systems. John Rickford's study of Canewalk, Guyana,[70] famously called for a reanalysis of sociolinguists' approaches to social class, and a consideration of the locally relevant categories which in the Guyanese case turned out to be estate class vs. non-estate class. The copious ethnographic work taking place since Labov's Martha's Vineyard study has given rise to research that orients to categories of practice arising from the speakers, categories such as poker-game player on the outer banks of North Carolina;[71] participation in activities such as cruising in a car on a Saturday night in Detroit;[72] being a doctor by day and gay diva on weekends;[73] being a Pakeha (European-extraction) woman with strong friendship networks among Maori or Polynesian men in New Zealand;[74] orienting toward sports or being "alternative" as a male adolescent in Glasgow;[75] or even having been a farmer when one is now a retired senior.[76]

Community of practice studies have taken up the challenge of mapping speakers' ground-level social groupings, and of attending to the fine-grained patterning of sociolinguistic variation that reflects and enacts social order. The focus on the speech of adolescents has allowed for the investigation of temporary alliances and for the tracing of the sensitivity of sociolinguistic variables to these alliances, while a cultural/historical focus has allowed for the scaling of local indexical relations to broader levels of representation. Exemplar theoretic concerns such as item frequency, as well as ethnographically derived understandings of social saliency and the legibility of social indices, are the foci of chapters 8 and 9 of this book.

Notes

1   See Irvine (2001) on style and distinction.
2   Schieffelin, Woolard, and Kroskrity (1998)
3   Eckert (2000), Eckert and Wenger (2005)
4   Other researchers to explore the dynamics of individuals in language change are Labov (2001) and Milroy (1985).

5   Lave and Wenger (1991), Eckert and McConnell-Ginet (1992), Eckert and Wenger (2005); community of practice theorists build on the cultural and literary-theoretic approaches of Bourdieu (1977), Bakhtin (1981), and Bourdieu (1992).

6   Wenger (1998)

7   Eckert and McConnell-Ginet (1992: 464)

8   Those that have many links not only between ego and other members but among members, as well as links that cut across different contexts.

9   Eckert (2000), Labov (2001)

10 Eckert (2000), Zhang (2005)

11 Zhang (2005)

12 Eckert (2000)

13 Stuart-Smith et al. (forthcoming)

14 A status that has been claimed by Milroy (1985, 1987) to belong rather to individuals in the social network with loose ties to many social networks. Similar arguments appear in Labov (2001: 360).

15 Wolfram (1991: 23)

16 Le Page and Tabouret-Keller (1985)

17 Bakhtin (1981)

18 Bybee (2001)

19 Bybee (1994), Johnson (1997), Pierrehumbert (2003)

20 Papers in Bybee and Hopper (2001), Bybee (2002), Phillips (2007)

21 Díaz-Campos (2004), Foulkes and Docherty (2006)

22 Bresnan and Hay (2007)

23 Mendoza-Denton, Hay, and Jannedy (2003), Khattab (forthcoming)

24 Mendoza-Denton (forthcoming)

25 Johnson (1997)

26 Goldinger (1997)

27 cf. Goodwin and Duranti (1992)

28 Strand (1999), Mendoza-Denton, Hay, and Jannedy (2003), Johnson (2006)

29 Dell (2000), see also papers in Bybee and Hopper (2001), Díaz-Campos (2004), Bybee (2001).

30 Carter (2003), Goldinger and Azuma (2003)

31 Metsala (1997), Beckman and Pierrehumbert (1993), Luce and Pisoni (1998)

32 Nosofsky (1987)

33 Smith and Zárate (1992)

34 Niedzielski (1999), Strand (1999)

35 Petitto et al. (2001)

36 Pierrehumbert (2003), Zamuner, Gerken, and Hammond (2004)

37 Bourdieu (1977)

38 i.e., Abrahams (1968), Hymes (1971), Bauman (1975), Hymes (1977), Limón (1982), Bauman and Briggs (1990)

39   See also Mendoza-Denton (2002), and Mendoza-Denton, Hay, and Jannedy (2003) for a more detailed discussions of sociolinguistic history and quantification.

40   Malinowski (1964, 1937)

41   Firth (1964)

42   Bloomfield (1933)

43   Hymes (1964)

44   Ferguson (1996)

45   Fischer (1958)

46   For excellent accounts of this history see Chambers (1995), Duranti (2001), Chambers (2002).

47   Labov (1972c)

48   Weinreich, Labov, and Herzog (1968: 100)

49   Trudgill (1974), see also references in Bayley (2002).

50   Chambers (2002: 359)

51   Chambers (2002: 360)

52   Cukor-Avila and Bailey (2001)

53   Bailey (2002: 320)

54   Harrington, Palethorpe and Watson (2000)

55   For an application of the apparent-time construct in narrative and history, see Boum (2006).

56   Trudgill (1988) replicated Trudgill's famous (1974) study of Norwich, England; and Blake and Josey (2003) replicated Labov's Martha's Vineyard study.

57   Most famously disseminated through Labov's (1972b) *Some Principles of Linguistic Methodology*, as well as through unpublished reading packets from his courses at the University of Pennsylvania.

58   See Labov (1972b), for general discussion of principles of approaching the community.

59   Wertheim (2006)

60   Wolfson (1976)

61   Briggs (1986)

62   See Bourdieu (1992) for discussion on power and language; also see Linda Tuhiwai Smith (1999) for discussion on power, colonization, and research.

63   See Morgan (1998), Rickford (1997) for excellent accounts of the relationship between the African-American community and language researchers.

64   Faegin (2001)

65   Trudgill (1974)

66   Milroy (1985)

67   Faegin (2001: 26)

68   Eckert (2000), Bayley (2002: 135)

69   Zhang (2005)
70   Rickford (1986)
71   Wolfram and Schilling-Estes (1996)
72   Eckert (2000)
73   Podesva (2006)
74   Meyerhoff (1999)
75   Lawson (2005)
76   Rose (2006)

CHAPTER 8

VARIATION IN A COMMUNITY OF PRACTICE

By looking at the subtle patterning of behavior at the phonetic level, sociolinguists and more specifically socio-phoneticians approach communities from a perspective that is complementary to other perspectives that focus on macro-language (like code choice) and on beliefs that people hold about language (language ideologies). In chapter 4, for instance, I discussed how code choice contributed to the attributes that young people considered constitutive of membership in the Norteñas (use of Chicano English, African-American English) and Sureñas (use of Mexican Spanish and sometimes Chicano English), in Piporras (use of rural Mexican Spanish) and Fresas (use of urban, middle-class Latin American Spanish varieties). We examined the intricate links between language and beliefs about race, about class, about nations, and about authenticity.

To briefly summarize the findings around language and other symbolic practices: we started at the macro-level where we have analyzed ideologies and stereotypes around language choice in chapters 1 through 4; we moved through embodiment and material culture in chapters 5 and 6, and also looked in chapter 6 at the discourse level through interactional routines such as clowning and *albur*, where we also examined literacy practices such as the creation of secret alphabets and the circulation of poetry notebooks. All of these different symbolic levels are levels at which youth interact and repeatedly engage in routinized, structured activities – practices – the pursuit of which organizes members into communities. Patterns of practices make group members known to each other while simultaneously signaling who they might be to outsiders. In the last chapter I presented the broader field of ethnographic socio-linguistics and situated the contribution of this work within the field.

The current chapter will move toward a finer level of detail in the examination of the indexing of social meaning. This level is just as important because micro-level actions (like the raising of a vowel) are the building blocks for implementing macro-level constructs.[1] From race, to nationalism, to gender, all of the constructs that we are accustomed to considering as part of the repertoire of societies are implemented thorough the building blocks of micro-level "acts of identity."[2] Both the interpretation and the continuation of existing linguistic structures and social constructs are the accomplishments of speakers, though these are only partially visible in the limited perspective of outside observers as they unfold in interaction.[3]

How speakers pronounce their words says a lot not only about the identities that they wish to project, but also about the history of the language(s) that they speak. The history of English and the history of its contact with Spanish are actively reflected in Chicano English speakers' largely automatic linguistic patterning. Sociolinguistic studies routinely show how the linguistic behavior that speakers and listeners display is just as much influenced and constrained by the structures of language as it is by the structures of society. In this view language and society are mutually constitutive, each one updating the other and determining the other's possibilities.[4]

Consider the case of the Norteñas and the Sureñas of Foxbury: as we've seen in the chapter on ideology and language choice, Spanish and English play an important role in the explanations that members give in interviews about their behavior, and in the sense that they make of other speakers' linguistic choices. And yet there were inconsistencies: sometimes speakers' self-report of monolingual Spanish or English use did not match their use or observed competence. This was the case in chapter 1 with Güera's claims of not speaking English, where on closer examination she exhibited both literacy skills and translation skills. Junior, in chapter 4, viewed his own English skills as a functional necessity, but switched codes flawlessly when necessary and was doing well in an advanced math class in English. Ernesto spoke of rural migrant boys he knew putting on the accent of Mexico City because they perceived their own accent as rural and embarrassing. The fake-accent boys could get away with this deception either because they acquired some basic strategies for sounding like they came from Mexico City, or because interlocutors, though noting the mismatch, chose to go along with the fictional identities.

Projecting an Accent, Casting an Identity

How is it that speakers implement linguistic choices in connecting their usage to the larger structures of society around them? Part of the answer lies in the details of how people present themselves; the numerous small habits of self-presentation, including the particulars of how speakers choose the moment-to-moment execution of their accent.

Working from recorded speech data from native English-speaking girls at Sor Juana High School, the rest of this chapter explores the factors that determine the variable phonetic raising of the mid lax phoneme /I/. This is the vowel sound in words like *bit* and *thing*. As we've taken some time in the last chapter to review the history of sociolinguistics and position this study within that enterprise, we will take some time now to define the variable under study, and what we mean by "raising" and "lowering." We'll also review some of the background literature on California English and on Chicano English, the speech varieties that we hypothesize are used meaningfully by the English-speaking girls we have encountered all the way through this book.

Up until now I have spent some time describing the social landscape of Latinas/os at Sor Juana High School, including descriptions of groups who were an integral part of the landscape and who speak mostly Spanish (like the Fresas and the Piporras, discussed in chapters 1, 2, and 4). For the remainder of this analysis, I focus only on the groups for which I identified speakers that could be considered native speakers of English. This is important because in order to carry out a study of sociophonetic variation, we need to isolate a *variable*, "different ways of saying the same thing," as per William Labov's classical definition[5] Comparing girls' Spanish sound production with their English sound production would be like comparing proverbial apples and oranges, given that the two languages have entirely different systems. In order to carry out a quantitative, comparative analysis, I had to select speakers who could be thought to be doing the same thing.

One way of showing how the Norteñas, Sureñas, and other groups of girls are positioned in the social landscape is by trying to understand how they vary with respect to each other in their use of the same elements in the sound system of language. Throughout this chapter and the next I introduce figures with bar charts depicting statistical relationships that emerged from patterns of English language use in the interviews that I conducted with the girls; these figures appear in the chapter text and are provided as an aid in the visualization of relationships in the numerical data. The tabular data displays in the appendix provide a fuller accounting of the statistical results, and should be consulted for a more detailed picture. The patterns that are described in these graphical displays allow us to make inferences about social structures (frozen as they are by our analytic lens), about individuals and their standings in groups, and about phenomena that are internal to language. We will find surprising commonalities between the Norteñas and Sureñas, as well as reflexes in the girls' behavior of long-established discourse processes in the history of English.

I begin by explaining some of the terms I will be using, and presenting the results for the patterning of the girls' groups with respect to the linguistic variable in question. In the next chapter we follow these sociophonetic findings into the discourse system to understand how low-level variation finds its way up into increasingly larger levels (such as discourse and conversation) where speakers can deploy relatively small changes to participate, with variations in stance and style, in their communities of practice.

Raising and Lowering: Some Visual Evidence

The terms "raising" and "lowering" refer to the relative positions of the tongue in the vocal tract when we produce different vowels. For example, consider the magnetic resonance imaging photograph of a normal adult saying the vowel iota [I] (Figure 8.1). An example of this vowel would be the 'standard' pronunciation of the word "bit".

We call this vowel a *high, front, lax* vowel. These are its properties on the height dimension, the front–back dimension, and the tense/lax dimension. Shown in Figure 8.2 is the vowel chart for American English, arranged on these dimensions.

The vowels we will be considering in this study are the vowels [i] and [I], both of which are described phonetically as high and front. The crucial distinction in these vowels lies in their laxness: [i] is front and tense, higher, with the tongue muscle tensed up, while for [I] the tongue body is lax. The magnetic resonance imaging (MRI) photographs shown in Figure 8.3 illustrate the difference between the two vowels that are at the heart of this study. Notice that the tongue in the case of [i] is higher than for [I]; you can see what we mean with the

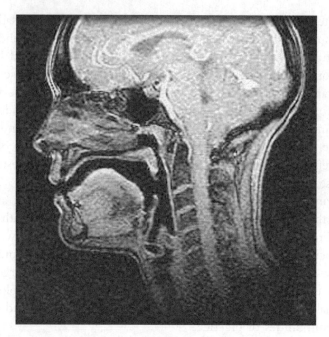

Figure 8.1   The vowel "iota": [ɪ]. MRI images courtesy of Diana Archangeli.

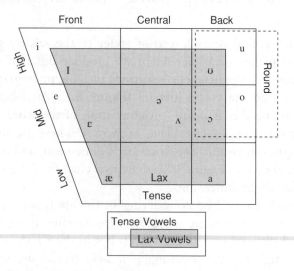

Figure 8.2   The vowel sounds of American English.

234   Variation in a Community of Practice

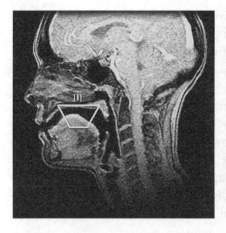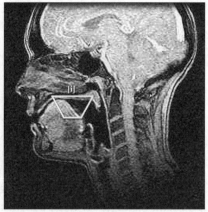

Figure 8.3   MRI images: Front, high, lax [ɪ] vs. front, high, tense [i].

parallelogram of vowel sounds (commonly called a "vowel triangle": imagine it upside down and with the base at the roof of the mouth) as it is superimposed on the oral cavity, viewed in cross section.

Figure 8.3 shows the difference in the space between the tongue and the palate in the two vowels. In English the tense [i] appears in words such as *beet*, and the lax [ɪ] in words like *bit*; they represent two different **classes** of sounds, phonemes which we annotate with slashes /i/ vs. /ɪ/. Historically in English, all of the words rhyming with *beet* belonged to one class of sounds, while the words rhyming with *bit* belonged to another. They are considered different phonemes.

Phonemes are the idealized representations of how sounds are organized mentally for speakers. In actual production we recognize distinctions in pronunciation (you could pronounce the same phoneme slightly differently on different occasions), and we annotate these as phonetic expressions with square brackets [I]. The **phoneme** (in slashes) is considered to be the idealized mental representation and the **allophone** (in square brackets) is the actual phonetic realization.

So for a word like *nothing*, there is only one possible sequence of phonemes /nʌθɪŋ/, corresponding to its historical identity as an English word, but pronunciations with several different allophones for the /ɪ/ and the /θ/ and the final /ŋ/:

/nʌθɪŋ/   →   [nʌθɪŋ] here the allophones are the same as underlying phonemes
          →   [nʌθɪn] here final [n] is substituted for underlying /ŋ/

[nʌfɪn] same as above but with medial [f] for /θ/, common in Scottish English and other UK varieties[6]

→ [noʔn̩] attested for Puerto Rican and African-American English[7]

The entire premise of this chapter is that there exists considerable, socially organized variation in how the young Chicano English speakers in this study pronounce the vowel in the class /ɪ/. Pronunciations range all the way up and down the height dimension, from high front [i] all the way to low mid [æ]. Mapping these differences will add to what we know about Chicano English and about the use of these sociophonetic distinctions to signal social structure and forge social meaning.

Analyzing Vowel Differences Statistically

Using the variable rule methodology and specifically GoldVarb,[8] a statistical analysis tool for the analysis of sociolinguistic variation developed by David Rand and David Sankoff,[9] I present a multivariate analysis of 1,800 instances of the utterance of /I/ in its various forms. Each one of these is called a **token** of the variable /I/. The /I/ tokens were extracted from recordings of interviews with twelve selected members of the community of Latina girls at Sor Juana High School. Multivariate analyses[10] such as those performed by the GoldVarb software allow us to look at the influence of multiple factors in the patterning of language, making it possible to establish which factors are the most important in the analysis of the variable in question. Is it important for the analysis of the variable /I/ to take into account the social group? Does it matter if speakers were codeswitching near the utterance? Is it important what type of sound preceded or followed the /I/? Which of these factors might be more important? Can we rank them in order of importance? These are the kinds of questions that a multivariate analysis can help us to address.

I show that the phonetic raising of the phoneme /I/ in Chicano English is governed by a combination of linguistic and social factors, crucially the speaker's position within her social group. An important lexical subset of the tokens, Th-Pro (consisting of pronominal elements which share the semantic and morphological element *thing*, i.e., *anything*, *something*, *nothing* and *thing*) is identified for further analysis, showing results that closely parallel and serve to illuminate those of the larger data set.

I begin by summarizing prior research findings on the status of /I/ in California. Next I outline the methodology used for selecting the speakers and coding the data, and finally present the variable rule analysis and conclude the chapter with a discussion of the implications of the data.

The Story of Chicano English /I/ in California

Researchers working on Chicano English[11] have identified one of the features of Chicano English to be a variable raising and tensing of the mid lax front vowel /I/ to a high front variant [i]. The study of /I/ among Chicano English speakers in California, however, would be incomplete without an understanding of prior studies of this variable in the region.

California as a dialect region was until recently relatively understudied; the first study to even consider California English as a distinctive dialect was done by David De Camp in 1949. His classic, "The Pronunciation of English in San Francisco," provides the most detailed information available on the California English pronunciation of sixty years ago. De Camp documents /I/ among Californians being realized primarily as the Standard American [I] in most environments, and slightly centralized and lowered [I] before laterals.[12]

Almost forty years later and across the San Francisco Bay, a group of UC Berkeley linguists led by Leanne Hinton[13] conducted a study on the speech of native Californians, and found that among the many new sound changes taking place since the 1950s, /I/ now exhibited raising before nasals (as did the other front vowels studied, /ε/, and /æ/), and some lowering and backing in other environments.[14] Interestingly, the same speakers that exhibited the highest scores for raising (African-American, Hispanic, and rural speakers), also exhibited the lowest scores for fronting of /ow/, the flagship variant most commonly recognized as part of urban "California Style".[15] The fronting of /ow/ in this study is almost exclusively the domain of Euro-American and Asian-American speakers in Northern California. From Hinton and colleagues' study, it appears that much has changed in the pronunciation of English in California since the time of De Camp. California has developed a real distinctiveness in terms of language variation, with different sub-communities leading with respect to different changes, so that what constitutes California Style to one may be systematically different for another. As Penny Eckert and I observed in our overview of California English,[16] the stereotyping of the speech of Californians as "valley girls" and "surfer dudes" (stereotypes with strong ethnicity and class connotations) could not be further from the truth: the nearly 34-million strong population of California has no clear majority: 11 percent is Asian American, 16 percent African-American, 32 percent Latina/o, and 47 percent white. All of these groups may have their own ethnic English varieties in continuum with what we might call a Standard California English variety, and all of them engage in contact-induced phenomena such as "crossing," a type of language-mixing of both codes and styles practiced by linguistic outsiders.[17]

Penny Eckert has described what she calls the Northern California Shift in the speech of Euro-American and Latina girls from the same dialect area as the speakers in this study. Figure 8.4 is based on her Northern California shift diagram.

The preceding frameworks point to interesting questions that may be pursued to deepen our understanding of the sociolinguistic processes that underlie Chicano English. While other researchers have studied the nature of generational effects and gender within Chicano communities, there have been few sociolinguistic studies that focus on the construction of particular Chicana/o identities through language, though relevant among these is Carmen Fought's[18] study of gang/non-gang/tagger groups in Los Angeles, where the focus was on negative con-

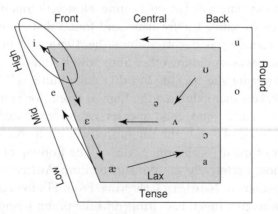

Figure 8.4 Northern California shift: Highlighting raising of /ɪ/.

cord, and some features of the phonology including realizations of /u/ and /ae/.[19]

In the last chapter, we reviewed how traditional sociolinguistic methodology relies on the classification of informants according to fixed and "objective" criteria, such as income level, gender, educational background, and ethnicity. Data from informants that have been classified into one group are often manipulated in concert and cross-compared with data from other similarly grouped informants. Some of these criteria are also combined to produce reified categories like "the lower middle class," "working-class males," and so on to levels of increasing abstraction.[20] While large-scale demographic studies are both useful and necessary to understand the broad picture of linguistic variation in different communities, especially for comparative purposes, we also need to take a magnifying glass, as it were, to understand variation *in situ*, as it unfolds in the everyday lives of individual speakers. Variation studies are just now beginning to develop frameworks that describe and analyze *members' categories* – the categories according to which speakers from the community divide up their own social world.[21] Following up on our discussion in chapter 7 about communities of practice, these categories may be as disparate as speaking Hungarian,[22] being a high-school Burnout,[23] being part of a fishing community,[24] or being a soccer fan.[25] All of these categories have something in common: they represent people engaged in common pursuits that are meaningful to them and texture their lives.[26] Not every community of practice may be the repository of linguistic difference, and yet communities of practice are the building blocks of our social, and thus linguistic, interactions. This study is meant to explore in depth one such community of practice and contribute to our understanding of variation already based on large-scale survey-based research.

The Study

The quantitative linguistic portion of this study seeks to understand whether the members of the communities of practice that we have talked about at Sor Juana High School show in their quantitative behavior the social distinctions that they themselves draw in discourse and in practice.

In order to investigate how these questions might be resolved in the speech of native English-speaking Northern California Chicanas, I collected a sufficiently large sample of the /I/ variable (1,800 tokens, all bearing primary or secondary stress) to make fine-grained distinctions in vowel quality, as well as to make results robust when I extracted subsets of words that bear this variable.

I approached the data set with no prior binary assumptions.[27] The coding procedure consisted of coding in the beginning as many different degrees as possible for the phonetic realizations of the variable, and analyzing these for consistent patterning. For /I/, this revealed movement in both directions: there was *both* substantial raising and lowering in the sample, and this motivated two separate analyses. Here I will focus only on the analysis of raising, but readers who wish to know about lowering may refer to my dissertation reporting those results.[28]

Methodology and Speakers

From a total sample of forty-four individual interviews in the high school, I chose twelve speakers to do a close analysis of their realizations of /I/, and grouped them into six distinct and mutually exclusive groups reflecting the communities of practice to which they belonged at Sor Juana High School. To some extent this was a combination of analyst categories and members' categories, since I made the final categorization by triangulating three separate sources of information on each girl's membership in distinct groups:

1   *Self-reported membership.* In each of the interviews, I asked speakers' judgments and opinions on what the social groups in the school were, as well as their assessment of what group(s) they belonged to and why. I found great consistency between different girls' representations of the social structures in the school; most accounts were fairly articulate in the description of group differences and of symbolic features that characterized each group.

2   *Other-reported membership.* In conjunction with self-reported membership, in the context of the interviews I also inquired about each girl's assessment of others' group membership. Often the question was phrased in the following manner: "What other groups of Latina students do you think there are here at Sor Juana High School, and who do you know that might be in these groups?" Inspired

by Lesley Milroy's discussion of social networks,[29] and by Penny Eckert's diagrams of Jock and Burnout networks at Belten High,[30] I also periodically asked the girls to draw pictures of their network diagrams. I elicited these drawings by first illustrating my own friendship network diagrams at Stanford, and then asking the girls to draw their network diagrams. This exercise was extremely useful: girls drew on their knowledge of the communities not only to articulate what the differences were between each of the social groups, but also to point out to me the complexities of membership and non-membership in each of the groups.

3 *Ethnographic observation.* The last criterion that I used to select the girls in this part of the study was consistent ethnographic observation of their participation in those specific communities of practice, as reflected in my fieldnotes. Membership in the different groups at the high school level was relatively fluid, rising and ebbing with the strength of friendships, rites of passage, and different life circumstances of the members of the group. In trying to compare different girls of various ages, I aimed to identify those whose membership in the various groups within the school was relatively stable. In other words, all the girls in this part of the study were observed to a) affirm that they belonged to a certain group, b) be affirmed by others of belonging to that group, and c) have consistently maintained strong links to the group throughout the time of my study. By identifying individuals in this way, I have delimited this study to exclude girls who were *shifters* – those who frequently changed group membership. This is not to say, however, that shifters are necessarily peripheral. Indeed, sometimes girls who have shifted into a group achieve quick status and notoriety in the group. In this study, however, standardization of the stability of the girls' network practices allows for some measure of control, so that for example, I have been able to systematically avoid grouping recently inducted Norteñas (some of whom may be shifted ex-Sureñas) with long-time, well-established members of the group. Thus, if there are differences to be found between Norteña and Sureña speech, I have opted to look for them in the speech of those group members who are the most stable within as well as the most loyal to their respective groups. In Table 8.1, I've listed the speakers and the groups into which I eventually divided them, though the table itself underwent final inspection by several different girls who approved of the categorization.

Table 8.1 The speakers: Sor Juana High School Latina adolescents

Social group	Name	Age
Norteñas	T-Rex	18
	Raisa	18
Norteñas Wannabe's	Mariana	16
	Cati	15
Disco Girls	Yadira	16
	Veronica	15
Jocks	Jill	16
	Yolanda	17
Sureña Wannabe's	Jackie	14
	Tina	15
Sureña	Sadgirl	15
	Reina	17

Data collection for the variable rule portion of this study involved identifying and extracting from tape-recorded sociolinguistic interviews with each speaker 150 stress-bearing tokens of the variable.[31] Interviews with the speakers generally took place fairly early in my relationships with them. This ensured that the speakers had approximately the same level of familiarity with the interviewer. Although there are advantages to interviewing speakers with whom one has had a long personal history,[32] I believe that in an ethnographic setting where different eventual degrees of familiarity with different speakers is unavoidable, it is best to select interviews where the speakers have approximately the same level of familiarity with the interviewer. While much of the information that I have discussed in earlier chapters was gathered over a period of years, the first interviews with each speaker were the ones that were used for this portion of the study, thus avoiding the potentially problematic confound of speakers' mutual speech accommodation over a long period of time.[33]

The interviews for this study were conducted in low-noise environments, such as enclosed classrooms and open-air, low-wind settings in the school, to ensure that the sound quality of the resulting recording would be reasonably good. A SONY Walkman Pro, WM-D6C Stereo cassette-recorder, and a SONY lavaliere microphone were used for the sociolinguistic interviews.

The variables

I coded one dependent and ten independent variables[34] in my corpus of /I/ tokens. They are listed and explained below:

1 *Speaker individuation (Independent)*: This factor group consisted of coding the twelve speakers individually, each speaker having her own unique factor. An important rationale for coding the data this way is that it might allow the emergence of individual patterns and different group configurations from speakers that were initially grouped together by social affiliation.

2 *Social affiliation (Independent)*: Each token was coded according to the social group membership of the speaker, based on Table 8.1 and following the membership categorization methods outlined above.

3 *Realization of the phoneme (Dependent)*: Extraction and coding of each token took place in three phases. The first phase involved digitizing the speech data from the interviews with *Xwaves*, a speech synthesis and analysis program. *Xwaves*, like other programs designed to manipulate speech signals, digitized the sound signal and enabled its conversion into visual representations of formant frequencies that are useful to phoneticians. Using a UNIX workstation, I digitized the speech from the interviews into computerized speech files and displayed them on the screen in the form of speech waveforms. The second phase involved listening to the interviews to find the relevant places where the phoneme /I/ had been realized, and inspecting the waveforms and spectrograms made from each of those utterances to determine the range of phenomenon. From the waveforms and spectrograms, I was able to train myself to hear the variation of the sound consistently over time, and with the help of the instrumental measures I was additionally able to revisit previous auditory measurements I had made to ensure consistency with current measurements. This in effect provided a built-in reliability check on the coding of the data.

Having established an internally consistent and temporally reliable auditory scale with which to measure the tokens, the third phase of coding took place as I auditorily coded the remainder of the corpus, occasionally referring again to the waveforms of particular tokens for a reliability check.

After much auditory and instrumentally guided coding, I settled on a five-point scale to capture the gradience of the phonetic realization of the phoneme. I distinguished two degrees of raising (numbers 1 and 2 in Table 8.2), two degrees of lowering (numbers 4 and 5), and one baseline (number 3) /I/ value. The points on this scale are represented in Table 8.2; they constitute a trajectory from lower to higher values of F1 (F1 values are calculated based on acoustic data reported for children by Gordon Peterson and Harold Barney.[35]

4   *Preceding and following phonological segment (two factor groups, Independent)*: Phonological segments preceding and following the target vowel were coded within and across syllables and words. Each segment was coded with a unique code corresponding to its phonological value, rather than with a pre-ordered set of generalized phonological codings (i.e., lateral, obstruant, etc.). This was done in order to ensure that the results would capture generalizations as well as possible interactions within the various features of each segment.

5   *Preceding and following phonetic segment (two factor groups, Independent)*: Phonetic realizations of the phonological environments were also coded in separate factor groups. This was done in the hope of being able to distinguish the strength of effects of phonetic realization vs. the underlying phonemic representation.

6   *Preceding and following prosodic boundaries (two factor groups, Independent)*: Following Richard Sproat and Osamu Fujimora,[36] who found that prosodic boundary strengths had consistent effects on the realization of /l/, I coded preceding and following boundaries to investigate their effects on realization of the target phoneme. Prosodic boundaries were coded with a three-way distinction assuming the framework for English syllable structure developed by Elizabeth Selkirk.[37]

7   *Th-Pro status (Independent)*: Upon first listening to the tapes collected in fieldwork, I was immediately struck by a lexical class whose pronunciation seemed to differ greatly from Standard English pronunciations: they were those for the group of pronominal compounds ending in *-thing*, such as anything, something, nothing, and thing (which will be henceforth referred to as **Th-Pro**). This factor group coded whether the particular word in question was a Th-Pro. Later I separate out these pronominal forms from the rest of the data set and consider them in an independent analysis.

8   *Phrase-level and topic-level codeswitching (two factor groups, Independent)*: Recognizing the possibility, raised by Letticia Galindo,[38] that bilingualism may be a good predictor of use of Chicano English variables,

I decided to test whether codeswitching would make a difference in the on-line processing of variation. In other words, is a raised phonetic realization of the variable more likely to occur in the vicinity of a foray by the speaker into Spanish? Some of the speakers in my sample are frequent, fluent codeswitchers. Does codeswitching affect the realization of the variable, all other things being equal? The procedure that I used attempts to distinguish two different kinds of codeswitching: phrase-level and topic-level.

I coded a phrase-level codeswitch in the instances where the variant in question occurred in the same informational phrase as an instance of codeswitching. According to John Gumperz and Norine Berenz, "an informational phrase can be described as a stretch of speech that falls under a single intonational contour or envelope and ends in an intonational boundary marker."[39] For every token collected, then, I ascertained whether it fell within the range of a single informational phrase, and additionally whether it fell within the boundary of a single conversational topic, since codeswitching (as well as styleshifting) has been shown to be sensitive to topic shifts.[40] As most of the time the interview was driven by questions from the interviewer, conversational topic was essentially determined by the questions that the speaker was answering. Occasionally, the speaker would introduce a new topic, and in that case I would code it as such.

I used these eleven (ten independent, one dependent) factor groups to perform a multivariate logarithmic analysis on the data set of 1800 tokens, the results of which are discussed below.

Table 8.2 First formant frequency values for coded phonetic values of /I/[1]

IPA symbol	Description	1st formant frequency (F1, in Hz)
1. [i]	cardinal vowel #1	370
2. [ɪ̝]	raised iota	450
3. [ɪ]	iota	530
4. [ə]	schwa	560
5. [ɛ]	epsilon	700

[1] Based on Peterson and Barney (1952).

The results

In order to investigate the question of whether Chicana speakers might be raising or lowering /I/, or both, I conducted separate analyses for raising and lowering and, although the results reported here are only for raising (the largest part of the sample), I will describe how the 1,800 tokens were divided into subsets for analysis. Based on the possibility that raising and lowering might be governed by different constraints, the two groups of tokens were run separately through the Goldvarb statistical program while excluding tokens that exhibited variation in the opposite direction. Thus, the results reported here are those of the raised subset of tokens of stressed /I/, all compared with the baseline value [I]. In addition, I have extracted a particular lexical subset of tokens – those containing the Th-Pro forms – and analyzed that separately. I conclude by summarizing the results as a prelude to the analysis of discourse usage of Th-Pro.

Figure 8.5 displays the relative proportions of raised, lowered, and baseline tokens in the overall data. Note that the largest proportion of tokens is in the baseline category. In fact, the existing variation is heavily weighted toward the raising end of the continuum, though a small but substantial (9.7 percent) proportion of tokens is lowered.

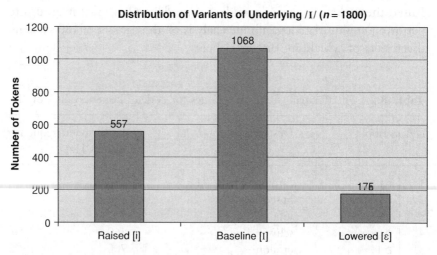

Figure 8.5 Distribution of variants of underlying /I/.

Raising

Two separately coded factors were collapsed together (raised iota [ɪ], and the high front cardinal vowel [i]) in the raising category in order to consider it against the baseline tokens. Thus extreme and moderate raising were considered as raised, and lowering values were excluded from the computations. This is the reason that the following figures and charts are less than 1,800 tokens – 1,800 was the total number of tokens, both raised and lowered, and the charts only refer to the 1,625 tokens considered in the raising-only analysis.[41]

Variable rule analysis makes the mathematical assumption of an ideal data set with cross-cutting factor effects but without significant inter-actions, where all the factors are independent of one another.[42] Certain factors in this data set, however, have an extremely high likelihood of interaction with others, thus only factors that could be assumed to be fairly independent of each other were run together. One example of this type of problem is the codeswitching factor, which interacts with the social group factor because most of the codeswitching was done by members of one or two social groups (the Sureñas and the Sureña Wannabe's), whereas the other social groups exhibited very little codes-witching. Thus, including codeswitching in a single run with the social groups factor "bleeds" the significance of the social groups, rearranges the cells, and gives different results. To avoid this, interacting factors are treated individually in separate runs.

Figures 8.6 and 8.8 show the two factor groups that emerged as significant in a step-up step-down analysis[43] in GoldVarb. The factor groups are discussed in order of their importance in predicting vari-ation in the data. The first factor group is that of following phonetic segment, and the second factor group discussed is that of social categ-ory. This statistical run included all factor groups except the individu-ation factor group (which interacts with the social category factor group) and the codeswitching factor group.

The most significant predictive factor group was a purely linguistic one: phonetic realization of the following segment. As shown in Figure 8.6, engma, [ŋ], is the strongest favoring factor[44] affecting the likelihood of raising of /I/ to [i]. Engma was coded separately from the other nasals because from the beginning of the coding process it became clear that it might have a special role (as part of Th-Pro).

The high level of significance ($p < 0.000$) of this result allows us to say that most of the variation in the data set of words containing the mid

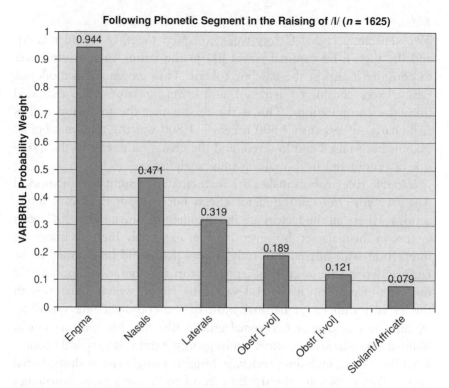

Figure 8.6 Following phonetic segment is most significant factor in raising of /ɪ/.

Most sonorous   >   >   >   >   Least sonorous

Vowels > Glides > Liquids/Nasals > Sibilant/Affricate > Voiced Obstr. > Voiceless Obstr.

Figure 8.7 Sonority hierarchy ranking; cf. Selkirk (1984b), Santa Ana (1996).

front vowel is conditioned first and foremost by the phonetic segment following the variable. Nevertheless, the groupings are essentially consistent with a sonority hierarchy ranking segments from most sonorous to least sonorous, as shown in Figure 8.7. As an important parameter of phonology, sonority then governs the following phonetic segment. In Figure 8.8, the three least sonorous groups, with weights that are quite similar, are those least favoring raising. The laterals and nasals are more favoring than the obstruents, but are far outstripped by the lone engma at 0.944 probability weight.

Table 8.3 Constraint ordering and probability weights for raising of /I/

Galindo 1987		Mendoza–Denton 2007	
Nasal	0.818	Engma	0.944
Liquid	0.791	Nasal	0.471
Stop	0.478	Lateral	0.319
Fricative	0.33	Voiceless Obstruent	0.189
Sibiliant	0.278	Voiced Obstruent	0.121
Affricate	0.253	Sibilant/Affricate	0.079

From these results, we see that raising is generally disfavored by all factors except engma. This is consistent with the findings of Leanne Hinton et al.,[45] who discovered substantial raising before nasals (which were taken together as a class, and thus we are unable to recover the results for individual members of the class, e.g., engma), but very little raising elsewhere.[46] In fact, raising prior to nasals scored 69 on an 80-point scale devised for that study, showing very extreme raising, while elsewhere it only scored 24 on the scale.

These results also support those of Letticia Galindo's study in Austin, Texas (see Table 8.3) and although the specific probability weights differ, especially with respect to liquids/laterals, the constraint ordering here is very consistent with her rankings for the same variable.[47] Both sets of results point to an analysis of the following segment in a sonority hierarchical configuration. It should be noted that Galindo's results represent a much more gradual transition in the probability weights from more to less sonorous. Although there is no obvious explanation for this difference of patterning in the same variable, I believe that part of the abrupt shift in the data that I have collected results from most of the variation being accounted for through a single, related set of forms (Th-Pro) which are used in meaningful ways in the community and which I argue serve as ethnic discourse markers.

The other significant factor group, second in importance in predicting the raising of /I/, was the social group of the speakers. The ranking of the social groups according to their likelihood of raising is given in Figure 8.8.

Surprisingly, from what we know about their social stance toward each other, the core Norteñas and the core Sureñas together had almost

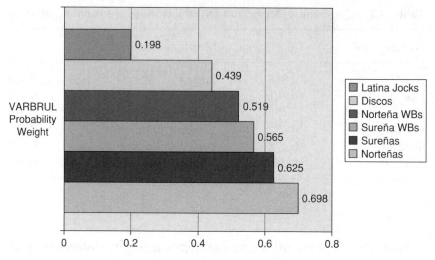

Figure 8.8   Social grouping is second most significant factor in raising of /ɪ/.

identical rates of application and very similar favoring probability weights. They clearly led the rest of the groups in favoring raising. Immediately behind them and also very similar to each other in application values are the Norteña and Sureña Wannabe's, who have very slightly favoring probability weights. Still behind them, though now on the disfavoring side of the divide (below 0.5 probability weight) are the Disco girls. At the very lowest end, with a probability weight extremely disfavoring raising, are the Jocks. It is worthwhile to point out here that while the first five groups are different from each other, their probability weights decrease in relatively small steps. When we finally arrive at the Jocks, the difference between their probability weight and the next most favoring, that of the Discos (.241) is roughly the same as the range of difference spanning all the other groups (.259). This means that while the core gang girls, the Wannabe's and the Discos, pattern close to each other, the Jocks are clearly at the other end of the spectrum. We might even ask ourselves whether they are part of the same system.

Both linguistic and social factors proved to be predictive in the raising of /ɪ/. The ordering of the social factor group, however, appears a bit more puzzling, almost counterintuitive, at least from the ethnographic point of view. Chapter 2 chronicles the great rivalry between Norteñas and Sureñas at Sor Juana High School. Norteñas "feel" themselves Chicanas, Sureñas "feel" themselves Mexican, and are both opposed to and in intense competition with each other in every aspect of their symbolic existence. The latter are frequent Spanish users and code-switchers, while the former prefer to use English. They are sworn enemies and fight at any opportunity, and yet their percentages of application and probability weights are nearly identical. And immediately behind them in the ordered rankings are the Wannabe's of each gang. Jocks, as might be expected from the strength of their social ties with Euro-Americans, are at the bottom of the rankings in this hierarchy of /I/ raising.

In this particular case, and in contrast with Letticia Galindo's study,[48] it is the girls who are the *least* bound to traditional mores and the home who are the leaders in the raising of /I/. The gang girls from opposing gangs, with their nontraditional gender habits of fighting, staying out late, and horrifying parents, are quite nearly the antithesis of the homebound, traditional girls that led in the relative weight rankings in Galindo's study. It appears also that reported Spanish use and ideology are *not* strongly predictive of variation, since the Norteñas and Norteña Wannabe's, with a strong Chicano-English-Only ideology, rank high in raising of /I/.

One possible explanation is that the raising of /I/ is somehow indexical, not of traditional mores, but of a broader Latina-based identity, and that since both of these gangs are ultimately and unequivocally about highlighting some variety of Latina identity, they would be the most likely to use the raised variant. This would also explain why the Wannabe's are close to, but not as advanced as, the leaders. On the one hand, they could be "following" them in the direction of variation, but in this strictly hierarchical group, extreme frequency of raising might also be construed as an "having an attitude." More than once I have heard core gang girls' criticizing Wannabe's and especially shifters for inconsistent ideological posturing – here I quote T-Rex's words about a Sur-to-Norte shifter: "That bitch doesn't know what to be, one day she's Mexican and the next day she thinks she's Norteña." Also up for commentary are those who use extreme variants – "she's acting tough," "she was talking all chola." It is possible, then, that higher probability weights for *phonetic* variables might be interpreted as socially meaningful, bringing above the level of consciousness variation which has traditionally been thought to be below the level of consciousness.[49] Whatever the explanation, the data in Figure 8.8 point to a delicate patterning of variation according to the social group of the speaker.

Such overt linguistic evaluation of speakers ("she's talking all <u>chola</u>"), point to language ideologies that, though normally recognized for phenomena like lexical choice, are not usually recognized in the study of very fine-grained phonetic variation. As we saw in chapters 1, 2, and 4, language ideologies extend all the way into ideologies on the practices of codeswitching. Although many of the girls share linguistic resources, there is an unspoken set of community norms, based on past practice, ideology, and expectations, dictating who is entitled to use different resources. For instance, Disco girls occasionally criticized Jocks for codeswitching. If it should ever occur to a Latina Jock girl to index her Latina identity by codeswitching, Disco girls mocked her. When Valerie, a Latina Jock who almost exclusively identified with Euro-American students, once said the word "chisme" *(gossip)* to a Disco girl-friend of hers, Yadira and Cati later joked about it sarcastically: "Whoa, a Spanish word. What an accomplishment!" I have dubbed this type of dynamic "codeswitching rights," meaning the crystallization and reification of speech community norms that keep speakers, literally, in their linguistic place. Extend this to "variation rights" – who is *supposed to*, and *allowed to*, have the highest, frontest, most non-standard [i]; who has not only the prerogative but the expectation of sounding Latina, and who has the option to signal this identity through dramatically high probability weights for raising.

Factor groups that were included in this analysis but did not emerge as significant predictors of variation were preceding and following phonological segments, preceding phonetic segments, and preceding and following prosodic boundaries.

But what of the other factors not included in this run? Perhaps they can reveal in more detail the workings of variation with respect to engma, particularly in Th-Pro words.

Second run: individuation, Th-Pro, and codeswitching

The second run for raising includes the factors that were excluded in the first run because of interactions: Individuation, Codeswitching (phrase-level and topic-level), and Th-Pro status. Together in a separate run (and boosted by the absence of the main predictive factors from the preceding run), all of these factor groups were significant, and are shown in Figures 8.9, 8.10, and 8.11.

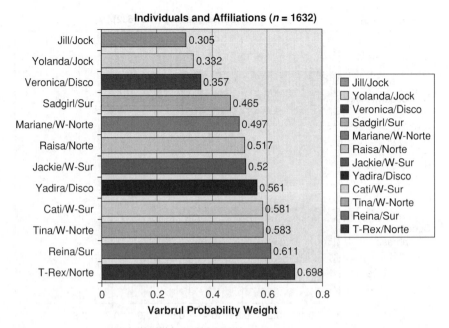

Figure 8.9   Individuation is most significant factor, second run.

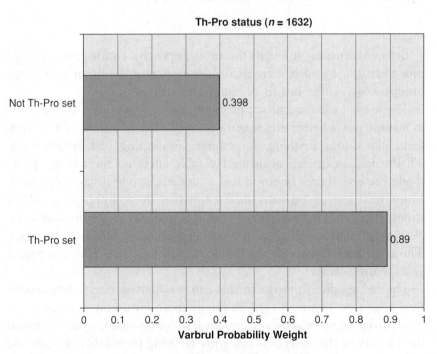

Figure 8.10   Th-Pro status is second most significant factor, second run.

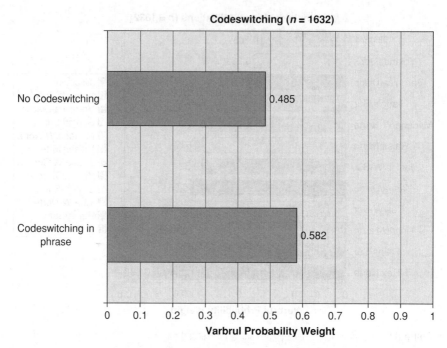

Codeswitching (n = 1632)

Figure 8.11   Codeswitching is third most significant factor, second run.

Before discussing at length the most important factor group, that of individuation, I will briefly discuss the results of the other two factor groups which came out to be significant in this run.

The second most significant predictive factor group after speaker individuation was whether the token occurred in the context of a Th-Pro form like thing, anything, something, or nothing (see Figure 8.10). Th-Pro had an extremely strong favorable effect on the raising of /I/, while the elsewhere condition had a similarly strong disfavoring effect. In the next section I discuss the exemplar-theoretic implications of the strong effect of Th-Pro, but for now it is interesting to note that a *single class of words* can have such a strong patterning effect on the data. This is no doubt related to the significance of following phonetic engma as a favoring factor.

The last predictive factor in this run was that of phrase-level codeswitching (see Figure 8.11). Although topic-level codeswitching was thrown out as not significant, phrase-level codeswitching occurring in the vicinity of the token had a slightly favoring probability weight, and the lack of occurrence of codeswitching a slightly disfavoring effect on the expression of raising. This very interesting result appears to confirm that of Galindo for the same variable, where she found that Spanish use influenced the use of Chicano English vernacular variables in Texas.[50] Earlier, however, we had observed how *reported* Spanish use did not appear to predict raising of /I/, since Norteñas and Norteña Wannabe's, whose ideology reinforces the use of English, scored very high in the relative weights for raising of /I/. This result shows that the effects of reported and actual use may be different. On the one hand, the lack of correlation of reported use would lead us to believe that this was not a significant factor in the data set, whereas observations of the effect of specific instances of codeswitching within the scope of the phrase appear to support the claim that Spanish use influences vernacular Chicano English variable use. This somewhat puzzling result raises interesting questions, and is a possible subject for further study, about the correspondence of actual vs. reported use and how those might best be represented by the researcher when trying to link them with variation.

Returning to Figure 8.9, the most significant factor group was that of individuation, and here we can see the differences that were collapsed under "group membership" in the earlier run. While it is not the aim of variation studies to explain the exact probability weight of variation for each speaker (nor is this fully possible, since there are always factors in the situation that are not captured or not adequately captured in the analysts' categories), we can nevertheless note how individuals fit into the overall patterning of the data and try to provide further explanation, especially within the framework of an ethnographic study where much more is known about speakers and their microsocial relationships to each other than would normally be possible in a large-scale survey study.

In Figure 8.9, we can see for instance that Jocks and Discos generally pattern lower on the raising scale than the core gang girls and their respective Wannabe's. It is the absolute leaders of each gang, the icons, that have the highest scores for raising. T-Rex and Raisa are widely acknowledged to be the "downest," most committed cholas, the most extreme in their nonstandard behavior. Another thing that they have in common is simply their outrageousness. Of all the gang girls and Wannabe's in this group, they were the only ones to have fought boys (both won), and they were similarly the ones who have the strongest links to actual prison gangs in the area. T-Rex, the vociferously committed Norteña whom I consider an iconic speaker, led all the other girls in raising. She was especially conscious of her heightened status and was often the community voice that performed social and linguistic evaluation of all the other girls. This is not to say that there is some sort of correlation between prison contacts and raising of the vowel, but only to indicate that the most extreme behavior in the vocalic system corresponds to community members who had the most extreme behavior in the social system.

The exceptional girls, Yadira (a high-raising Disco) and Sadgirl (a low-raising core Sureña), both have histories that may help us understand their behavior with respect to the other girls.

It is common practice for Disco girls to go out with Norteño boys, and thus to develop close ties to the Norteño community of practice. Yadira is a Disco girl whose past two boyfriends have been Norteños, and so we can hypothesize that she may have had some influence in her phonetic realizations from her association with Norteño boys. This does not mean that Yadira is outrageous, or that she would have access to the core Norteñas and their phonology, but she may be able to share in the most salient of their resources through other channels. Gang boys are very attractive to different groups of girls (including Euro-American girls), I assume because they embody some sort of broader American youth ideal of disgruntled rebelliousness and danger. In addition, each gang group exhibits customary exogamy (so that the gang groups *do* cross-date, shocking until we realize that members of the same gang regard each other as quasi-siblings).

As far as Sadgirl is concerned, I believe she is a great example of variability and of the latitude that one can have as a gang girl. Sadgirl was a very religious girl whose whole family was Apostolic. She was not allowed to (nor did she want to) wear makeup or pants, and so she was a bit unusual in this respect. She grew up primarily in a gang-dominated neighborhood, so these were mostly the social networks she knew as a child. She didn't drink or smoke, and nobody pressured her to do otherwise. She was definitely a core gang girl by virtue of her sustained membership, how often other girls mentioned her as a leader, and the degree to which her opinion and contribution was respected in the community – yet she was also different. Sadgirl dramatically illustrates that makeup, baggy Dickies pants, and high realizations of /I/ are typical but not necessary markers of membership in the group of core gang girls.

Because raising is much more frequent than lowering, members of the community (and others) would have increased perceptual saliency of raising as a marker for highlighting this particular ethnic identity. An example of awareness in the general population of raised [i], and especially of [t̪iŋ], as a marker of Latina/o identity is a Spring 1996 performance of *Fires in the Mirror*, a play by the award-winning actress and Stanford professor Anna Deavere Smith. In the play, Smith performs a one-woman show where she impersonates a series of characters, her impressions of persons whom she interviewed in relation to the LA riots. In her impression-performance of a young Chicano, Smith uses precisely the tensed and raised variant of [i], combined with fortition of theta, to produce a hyper-hispanicized and dramatic [t̪iŋ], presumably to make her character come alive. This generalized awareness of [i] as a Chicano English feature may be what is driving both the pattern of variation for the core girls and its following by the Wannabe's.

The study of Th-pro

In this section I analyze a subset of tokens extracted from the original larger set of stress-bearing /I/ tokens ($n = 1,800$). This data set consists of what I have called Th-Pro, the set of tokens sharing the underlying morphophonological shape /θɪŋ/ and acting semantically as pronominal material. The members of this lexical set are the lexical items *anything*, *something*, *nothing*, and *thing*.

A total of 195 tokens of Th-Pro were extracted from the original 1,800-token data set. The rationale behind extracting these tokens for a separate VARBRUL run is that when they were coded as a factor group in the larger data set they were significant in predicting raising (see Figure 8.10). When the word bearing the /I/ token was part of the Th-Pro set, the favoring probability weight for raising was extremely high, at 0.890. If the word bearing the token was not part of the Th-Pro data set, then the probability weight indicated that raising was disfavored at 0.398. Since the Th-Pro data set also contains the following phonological engma (which in many cases is realized as phonetic engma), then this means that two of the most strongly favoring conditions for raising were subsumed in the class of Th-Pro.

The analysis of Th-Pro as a free-standing data set also serves to shed some light on the workings of the variable in general. As was previously mentioned, there were some interesting issues arising as a result of coding sequential tokens of the same variable from the speakers. Word frequency was one of these thorny issues. It is common practice in variation analytical methodology to exclude tokens that do not vary, or that are extremely common and vary unidirectionally, lest the results be skewed. For instance, Walt Wolfram in his study of copula absence among Detroit African-American English speakers gives the following rationale for excluding the "invariant" second-person singular *am* from his count of copula tokens: "In the quantitative measurement of copula absence, it is essential to separate environments where there is no variability from those where there is legitimate variation between the presence and absence of the copula."[51] It is only recently that researchers have begun to question the methodological ramifications of not counting some parts of the data set,[52] and the issue is compounded by the fact that the predominant and accepted tool of sociolinguistics, the VARBRUL statistical analysis package in its various forms, does not support the analysis of factor groups that have 0 percent or 100 percent rates of application. These categorical applications are known as "knockouts," and they are not acceptable for inclusion in binomial or multinomial analyses. Thus, the predominant methodology within the field itself discourages researchers from investigating certain types of variation.

This issue became important in my research on /I/ because the Th-Pro forms had two characteristics, 1) very high frequency among certain groups (notably the gang girls), and 2) among those groups, the forms were often realized nearly categorically as extreme raising. This pointed to a special status for Th-Pro within the data set, and also to the possibility that the Th-Pro items were "skewing" the variation results due to their high frequency. In order to disentangle some of these effects, I ran a separate variation analysis on the Th-Pro subset, with the following results.

Methodology, Speakers and Variables

As this study is an offshoot of the larger study presented above, the methodology and speakers remain the same. The coding used for the larger data set was also retained here, with the exception of codings that were redundant. The independent variables for this study then are individuation, social groups, preceding and following phonetic realizations, and phrase-level and sentence-level codeswitching. The dependent variable was the coding for vowel height.

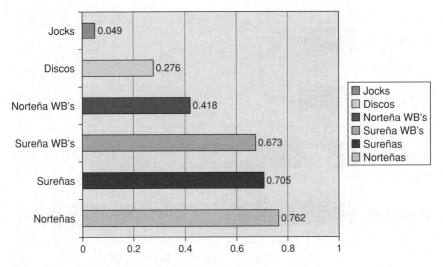

Figure 8.12   Social group is most significant factor in Th-Pro.

Results

The results obtained for this study will be presented below as raising, with no analysis of lowering. It should be noted that the Th-pro data set mostly exhibited raising (81 percent) and very little lowering (2 percent). The three variables that emerged as significant in the patterning of the raising of /I/ within Th-Pro were (in order of predictive power) social grouping, preceding phonetic realization, and following phonetic realization. Figure 8.12 ranks the social groups in order of most favoring probability weight to least favoring probability weight.

As in the results for raising of the entire data set of /I/, Norteñas and Sureñas lead on the favoring side of the probability weights, while Discos and Jocks disfavor. Also in parallel to the larger data set, the Jocks trail far behind the others. In this study, however, the Discos are ranked much closer to the Jocks in disfavoring (0.276 versus 0.439 in the larger data set), which could indicate that while the Discos are disfavoring the tensing of /I/, they disfavor it much more in this environment than the other groups. Later I will argue that the core and Wannabe gang-girl groups are participating in a complex grammatical innovation involving Th-Pro. This would explain why other groups so disfavor the use of raised /I/ in Th-pro constructions.

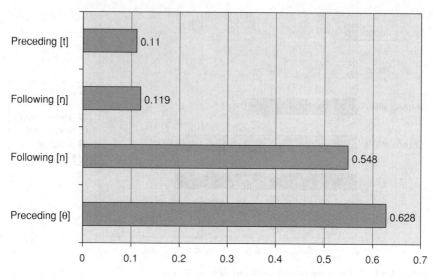

Figure 8.13 Phonetic factors are second most significant in Th-Pro.

As far as the other significant factor groups, this is a place where it might be possible for us to discern the effect of Th-pro versus segmental effects in the larger data set. Figure 8.13 shows phonetic segments and their probability weights. As we can see from the table, phonetic [t] and phonetic engma favor raising while phonetic theta and phonetic [n] disfavor it. This of course means that once a girl has begun the utterance of a Th-pro item with a theta, we have an extremely low likelihood of encountering a raised /I/ after it. Also nearly mutually exclusive are phonetic [n] and the raising of /I/. This is especially interesting because most of the variation of engma has been studied in relation to the variation between apical and velar variants of *-ing*, that is to say between forms like *going* and the vernacular *goin'*. By focusing exclusively on the consonantal and morphonological aspects of *-ing*, most researchers have left untouched both vocalic variation in *-ing* forms and variation in forms like Th-Pro, which are normally considered to be invariant.[53]

Conclusion

This chapter has explored the delicate patterning of phonetic variation according to subtle distinctions obtaining within specific communities of practice. Variation in the realization of /I/ distinguishes core girls (iconic speakers) from peripheral members in the community of practice, and points to some unexpected similarities: girls of opposing gangs pattern quite similarly with respect to their linguistic practices. We've traced the variation from the segmental level up to the lexical level, focusing on the especially frequent use of the pronominal item Th-Pro. This family of pronouns is the main vehicle linking variation at the phonological level to that at the discourse level. For the relationship of the patterning of Th-Pro words in variation, we must especially consider the role that they might be playing in discourse to serve functions of signaling identity. Different individuals and groups use allomorphs of Th-Pro that vary in terms of grammatical function. Do these different grammatical functions correlate with social functions? And how do the social groups pattern with respect to what we know of their phonological behavior? These are the questions we will explore in the next chapter as we look further at the use of Th-Pro in discourse.

Notes

1 My perspective is indebted not only to the variationist sociolinguistic tradition of William Labov and his contemporaries Peter Trudgill, Walt Wolfram, and his students Penny Eckert and John Rickford, but also historically to the intellectual legacy of early interactional sociologists and ethnomethodologists (among them George Herbert Mead, Alfred Schutz, Harold Garfinkel, Erving Goffman, and Harvey Sacks). One of the earliest scholars thinking along these lines, Georg Simmel, believed that society is pieced together in the "interspersed effects of countless minor syntheses." Simmel wrote, ". . . the whole gamut of social relationships, that play from one person to another, and that may be momentary or permanent, conscious or unconscious, ephemeral or of grave consequence, . . . all these [interactions] incessantly tie men together. Here are the interactions among the atoms of society. They account for all the toughness and elasticity, all the color and consistency of social life, that is so striking and yet so mysterious" (Simmel [trans. by Wolff, K.] 1950: 9–10). Note that this perspective is in tension with ideas of distributed cognition referred to earlier. Both must simultaneously hold true: individual acts add up to construct larger social structures, and yet the whole system in itself has emergent orderliness and properties as well.

2 This wording comes from the title of the book *Acts of Identity* by creolists Robert Le Page and André Tabouret-Keller (1985).

3   Here I modulate a position held by ethnomethodologists (like Harold Garfinkel (1967)) and classic conversation analysts (Emanuel Schegloff (2000)). In that tradition, analysts are constrained to the phenomena that are oriented to by speakers and where such orientations are evident from the data collected by the analysts. While I share the broad belief that speakers are actively constructing society in interactions, I believe that the observer (linguists and anthropologists) and our instruments are relatively impoverished: we are constrained by the kinds of data that we can obtain, as well as by the granularity of our instruments and our analysis. We must assume that speakers are orienting to other aspects, unseen by the observer, of their personal or group histories, and that we are lucky if and when we do find such an orientation evident in our data. Our observations are thus always radically partial and fundamentally incomplete.

4   Bakhtin (1981), referencing Bahktin's notion of centrifugal and centripetal forces of heteroglossia.

5   Labov (1969). For an interesting problematization of the definition of the linguistic variable, see Wolfram (1991).

6   Lawson (2005)

7   Wolfram (1974)

8   GoldVarb is a multivariate analysis program, http://www.york.ac.uk/depts/lang/webstuff/goldvarb.

9   Rand and Sankoff (1990) developed software in the 1970's specifically for the analysis of linguistic data. An alternative to this is the common ANOVA program, which some find more difficult to use for linguistic data (see explanations in Mendoza-Denton, Hay and Jannedy (2003)).

10 For a detailed account of the history and uses of variable rules please see Wolfram (1991), Bayley (2002), and Mendoza-Denton, Hay, and Jannedy (2003).

11 Metcalf (1979), Peñalosa (1980), García (1984), Godinez and Maddieson (1985), Penfield and Ornstein-Galicia (1985), Galindo (1987), Merrill (1987), Veatch (1991), Fought (2003), Eckert (2006)

12 De Camp (1971: 554)

13 Hinton et al. (1987)

14 Hinton et al. (1987: 121–2)

15 Hinton et al. (1987), Mendoza-Denton and Iwai (1993), California Style Collective (1993)

16 Eckert and Mendoza-Denton (2006: 139–40)

17 Rampton (1995), Lo (1999), Chun (2001), Bucholtz (2003), Bucholtz and Hall (2005)

18 Fought (2003)

19 Fought (2003)

20 Eckert and McConnell-Ginet (1992)

21 Rickford (1986), Sacks (1992)
22 Gal (1993)
23 Eckert (1989)
24 Labov (1964)
25 Milroy (1985)
26 Lave and Wenger (1991), Eckert and McConnell-Ginet (1992)
27 In contrast with many phonological variation studies, this one does not group the linguistic phenomena into binary categories. That is to say, many studies of variation utilizing the VARBRUL methodology are (by the very nature of the program) studies of applications and non-applications, and as such encourage the researcher to approach and set up the problem in a binary way. Did the phenomenon happen (application of the "rule")? Or did it not happen (non-application of the "rule")? In the case of the variable /I/, the rule would be a raising rule, raising underlying /I/ to [i]. An application would be coded as a 1, a non-application as a 0, and we would generate a string of 1,800 0's and 1's which could then be analyzed for their multivariate patterning.
28 Mendoza-Denton (1997)
29 Milroy (1987: 105–12)
30 Eckert (2000)
31 This prevented the inclusion of de-stressed tokens of /I/ that might be completely reduced and not appropriate for comparison with stress-bearing, potentially raising tokens.
32 Labov and Harris (1986)
33 I have discussed some of the implications of interviewer-interviewee accommodation in Mendoza-Denton (2002).
34 The dependent variable is the item whose behavior we are trying to predict: in this case, our main interest is in investigating the realization of /I/. That is our dependent variable. The independent variables are the factors that we are considering as possibly influencing the dependent variable, so we may consider the girls' group membership or whether they have codeswitched as possible factors that will affect our dependent variable. Those factors that we believe may affect the dependent variable are our independent variables.
35 Peterson and Barney (1952)
36 Sproat and Fujimura (1993)
37 Selkirk (1984 a,b)
38 Galindo (1987)
39 Gumperz and Berenz (1993: 99)
40 Rickford and McNair-Knox (1994)
41 Further discrepancies of a handful of tokens are present because occasionally GoldVarb will present knockout factors (all-or-nothing conditions)

that prevent the program's operation. One way to get around knockout factors is to carefully collapse categories or to judiciously omit single tokens whose absence would not have a great effect on the final distributions.

42 Sankoff (1988: 4–19)

43 Varbrul analysis (and the particular program used in this study, GoldVarb) follows a statistical formula for deciding which factor groups to "keep" as significant and which to "throw out." Every time an analysis of a particular data set is done with more factors, the fit of the model to the data improves, since the model now has more parameters to work with. However, the only improvements in fit that should be retained are those of a statistically significantly better fit. This is determined by GoldVarb in the step-up-step-down procedure, whereby the most significant factor is found first and then other factors are added, one at a time, and only kept so long as they do not significantly worsen the overall model. The procedure is then repeated in reverse by starting with all the factors together and then throwing out, one by one, the factors that do not significantly detract from the overall likelihood of the model. Severe interactions between factor groups result in discrepancies between the results of the step-up and step-down routines, where ideally the same factors that were chosen to be added on the step-up are the ones that are not thrown out on the step-down. It is through these discrepancies that interactions between factors in this data set were discovered and controlled for.

44 In this model a disfavoring probability weight is one that falls below 0.5, with the closer to zero it is the more strongly disfavoring it is. Similarly, favoring values are mildly favorable beginning at 0.5 and strongly favorable as they approach the 1.0 asymptote value.

45 Hinton et al. (1987)

46 Hinton et al. (1987: 122)

47 Galindo (1987: 62)

48 Galindo (1987)

49 Labov (1990)

50 Galindo (1987)

51 Wolfram (1969: 166)

52 Rickford et al. (1991)

53 Houston (1985: 50)

CHAPTER 9

"THAT'S THE WHOLE THING [t̪ɪŋ]!": DISCOURSE MARKERS AND TEENAGE SPEECH

In order to understand how symbolic practices connect individual participants to larger communities, I analyze in this chapter a variably occurring discourse marker in the speech of the Latina gang girls and other girls who are part of the extended Chicano English-speaking community of practice in the school. Chicano English here refers to an ethnic contact dialect previously described as occurring in zones of contact between Spanish and English speakers, primarily in areas where Mexican-descent communities form tightly knit social networks. Chicano English linguistic features include a number of phonological, syntactic and semantic features that distinguish this contact variety from other dialects.[1]

For the purposes of this chapter, I will focus on the innovative discursive use of the lexical set that I have dubbed Th-Pro, consisting of *anything*, *something*, *nothing*, and *thing*. The girls in this study take the conventionally referring pronominal expressions that these lexical items denote and superimpose an innovative grammatical function of *discourse marking*.[2] According to Laurel Brinton:

> Discourse markers are generally considered to have little or no meaning . . . no grammatical function . . . [They] appear with high frequency . . . but are stylistically deplored . . . they are "short" items which occur either outside the syntactic structure or loosely attached to it . . . they seem to be optional rather than obligatory features.[3]

In this chapter I explore the discourse-marking uses of Th-Pro expressions in the interviews that I conducted with the girls. All the interviews come from the same body of data as the tokens of /I/ discussed in the last chapter.

Some of the questions that arise with regard to Th-Pro forms in this context are:

- What is the distribution and patterning of Th-Pro forms in discourse?
- Is there any social conditioning to this distribution?
- What are the characteristics of Th-Pro expressions that they should form a unified class, and why would they be carriers of significant social and phonetic variation?
- Are Th-Pro forms social markers, and if so, what is it that allows them to function in this way?

To answer these questions, we will examine first some of the current research on Th-Pro forms, starting with their historical uses.

The History and Uses of -*thing*

In her sweeping study of the variable (ING), Ann Houston identifies the Th-Pro set as the only words in her study that are monomorphemic in origin, all others bearing -*ing* as a separate morphological affix.[4] *Everything*, *anything*, *something*, and *nothing* are attested in Old English as separate forms, e.g., *euery thyng* (ca. 1440). According to Houston, *thing* is common to Old English, Old German, and Old Norse, originally having the meaning of a legal process or an assembly, and later developing into *that which is said*, or *that which exists*.[5]

Houston consistently finds Th-Pro forms to behave differently from other tokens of -*ing*. One of her findings is that *of all the grammatical categories*, Th-Pro exhibits the highest probability and percentage of velar application ([ŋ] as opposed to [n]) in all the American and British dialects that she investigated.[6] Based on this strong pattern in her data, she asserts that Th-Pro has a special grammatical status separating it from all other instances of -*ing*, and further theorizes that there is a co-occurrence relationship between a high front vowel, a velar application, and Th-Pro.[7] The latter point is highly consistent with the results for the data set presented in chapter 8, where it was found that following /ŋ/ favors raising while following [n] disfavors it.

In defining (ING) as a sociolinguistic variable, linguists have traditionally only considered unstressed -*ing*.[8] Houston follows this procedure, and classifies Th-Pro forms as either secondarily stressed (*anything*, *everything*) or unstressed (*something, nothing*) since they constitute part of three- or two-syllable compounds. Chicano English dialects, however, have a stress-shift rule which affects the production of compounds like *nothing*, assigning primary stress on the second syllable rather than on the first. This observation has been corroborated by other researchers studying /I/ and -*ing* in Chicano English.[9]

Adding to the historical evidence, Th-Pro (*everything, something, nothing, anything*, and *thing*) is also considered to be a unified lexical set by Randolf Quirk et al., who describe *everything, something, anything*, and *nothing* to be compound pronouns that are composed of a determiner morpheme *some-, every-, no-, any-*, and a nonpersonal nominal morpheme, -*thing*.[10]

Quirk et al. consider the compound pronouns to be "the least problematic of all indefinite pronouns, since they behave like noun phrases of very general meaning."[11] As unproblematic as Quirk et al. may believe they are, these forms are found to be highly stigmatized by speakers for being "vague" and "inarticulate."[12]

Prior Studies and Stuff Like That

Elizabeth Dines includes *and everything* in a quantitative study of what she calls "sentence marking tags," unified by an apparent functional equivalence in discourse. She asserts that clause terminal tags of the form:

AND/OR [PRO-FORM] (LIKE THAT)
(e.g., *and stuff like that, and everything, or something, and that*)

are surface expressions serving a unified function, specifically that of "marking the preceding element as a member of a set."[13]

Dines further hypothesizes that speakers can variably choose to refer directly to "wholes" without reference to "parts," where the force of the tag is to generalize the specific noun phrase or verb phrase preceding the tag. "In every case the function is to *cue the listener to interpret the preceding element as an illustrative example of some more general case.*"[14] The following example comes from one of her interviews with a working-class woman:

B: Does your husband drink much?
A: Not much. He'll have a drink at **a party an' that**.

In this example, according to Dines, *party* is meant to stand for "a class of occasion characterized by infrequency and bonhomie," and additionally the listener is "cued in" to extract the more general meanings of "He's a social drinker," and "He's an occasional drinker."[15]

Dines finds a strong correlation between lower socioeconomic status and a tendency to use "general reference" as opposed to "particularistic reference." She finds that in her sample of Australian women, working-class women are much more likely than middle-class women to use set-marking tags for general reference, and as such are stigmatized for using "inexplicit" or vague language. She concludes by pointing out that charges of inexplicitness as opposed to implicitness are only valid if the speaker has misjudged the degree to which she shares assumptions with the listener.

In an article entitled "The Semantics and Pragmatics of *And Everything*," Gregory Ward and Betty Birner argue that *and everything* conveys "only that the variable is to be instantiated by at least one other member of some inferable set."[16] This interpretation of *and everything* is fairly close to that of Dines. Ward and Birner give the following example:

> We may do some things with just keyboards, or we may do a full-blown big band arrangement with **horns and everything**.[17]

Ward and Birner suggest replacing *horns and everything* with a variable that is instantiable with at least one member of some set of which horns is a member, presumably other members of the set of other big band instruments. Acceptable instantiations might be "horns and piano," or "horns and drums," but not "horns and cello."

The resulting prediction here is that there is a truth-conditional meaning that requires 1) horns, and 2) some other member from the set of which horns is a member, to both be present in order for the sentence to be true. I examine this prediction in light of their examples (a) and (b) below:

(a) They served beer at the party.
(b) They served **beer and everything** at the party.

Ward and Birner claim that (a) and (b) are truth-conditionally distinct along the following lines: if beer and nothing else was served at the party, (a) would be true while (b) would be false. Although this seems to make sense given their claims and from the surface form of the sentences, let us imagine a different context. Picture a situation where I am a prudish person who only attends parties where there is no beer, no music, and no "bonhomie," as Dines would have it. Within that context, I utter the following sentence to my friend Prudette:

(c) They served **beer and everything** at the party.

Sentence (c) above as uttered to Prudette can be true even if only beer and nothing else was served at the party. My use of *beer and everything* serves as a meta-instruction from me to Prudette to access assumptions about parties where beer is served. It could indeed mean something like, "They served beer and did other morally unacceptable things at the party."

This meta-instruction use of *and everything* to access common frames partially sabotages strict truth-conditionality, since frames dynamically index relationships, shared knowledge, and shared assumptions between speaker and hearer that are bound to vary from one context to the next. It is this particular usage of *and everything* which appears repeatedly in my data.

Discourse Marking -*thing* Among California Latina Girls

The difficult issue of reference comes up repeatedly in discourse studies of Th-Pro forms, part of what Maryann Overstreet calls "general extenders"[18] because they are both generic and because they extend grammatically complete utterances, similar to the definition of discourse markers above. The complexity of the problem is illustrated by the following example from the corpus, where four instances of *everything* are used, and each one serves a different function and denotes a different referent. This example is taken from my interview of Jackie, a Sureña Wannabe, who tells a long story about dallying with other boys besides her regular boyfriend. In fact she has several different boyfriends, but is so bad at concealing this fact that she is always getting caught. In this excerpt she tells of being caught spending time with a boy named Juan. Let's assume her main boyfriend is named Pedro.

1	JACKIE:	There was a <u>feria</u> on Foxbury street, <u>y yo estaba con</u> Juan,
		(fair) *(and I was with)*
2		I saw him there and I was with him all the time.
3		Somehow he [Pedro] found out about that,
4		and about other stuff. He found out **everything**.
5		He did. He did.
6	NORMA:	You got somebody watching you.
7	JACKIE:	He found out **EVERYTHING**.
8		Well not **everything**.
9		But I mean like about shit down here **and everything**.

In the first instance (line 4), *everything* refers to Jackie's being with Juan at the fair "and . . . other stuff." This example fits Quirk et al.'s definition of a pronoun, since *everything* is substituting for a noun phrase.[19]

In the second instance (line 7), Jackie puts emphatic stress on *everything*, implying that Pedro found out not only about her being at the fair with Juan but also about what they might have done there (in fact he found out that Juan and Jackie had kissed). This example is also pronominal, but depends on the discourse context to select its referent. Here it is clear that *everything* in line 4 is a subset of *EVERYTHING* in line 7.

In line 8, "Well not *everything*," Jackie still further delimits the scope of her previous utterance, because she does not mean to say that Pedro found out about her other boyfriends besides Juan (of whom he was unaware at the time), but only "about shit down here." This third (line 8) instance of *everything* is still another superset of the second.

The last occurrence of *everything*, in (line 9), is even more opaque than the others. Without a clear referent, *and everything* is typical of forms that I argue are within the realm of discourse markers. The meaning of these units cannot be derived merely from the local language context; they are discourse marking units that are expressly designed for recipients,[20] and index interlocutors' shared knowledge.

The Data Set

The examples that I have collected all come from the interviews that I conducted as described previously in chapter 8. The data set is the subset of tokens identified and analyzed as Th-Pro ($n = 195$), also in chapter 8. See Table 9.1a in Appendix.

In what follows I present a discourse analytic picture of the functional differences in the usage of the various examples of Th-Pro. I have isolated and classified the examples of words containing the sequence "thing" and divided them into two classes, according to the description outlined by Quirk et al.[21]: referentially given Th-Pro, and referentially new Th-Pro. I have also added an additional category of discourse-marking Th-Pro. I present the distribution of the examples based on these ideal categories. Because "given" versus "new" are actually endpoints on a continuum, and because the token numbers are too few to make statistical claims, the distributional figures should be taken with a grain of salt. After presenting the distribution in order to get a rough handle on the contours of the data, I show pervasive ambiguities of interpretation between the referentially given and the referentially new examples, and between the referentially new tokens and the discourse markers, suggesting a possible path in the development of the latter.

Referentially Given vs. Referentially New

In an influential article on givenness, contrastiveness, and information flow, Wallace Chafe defines given information as "that knowledge which the speaker assumes to be in the consciousness of the addressee at the time of the utterance," and new information as "what the speaker assumes he is introducing into the addressee's consciousness by what he says."[22] Any token of Th-Pro in this data set was considered to be referentially given if its referent could be completely recovered from the foregoing discourse. An example of a referentially given token is the following by Yolanda, a Jock girl who wants to be a sports trainer and talks about a situation where sports medicine would be involved:

> YOLANDA: One or two girls might get hurt, and they think it_1's really minor, but it_1 turns into **something$_1$** really big, and they keep using it_1 and using it_1, and then finally it_1 turns really big . . .

In this example, *something* refers to the particular injury or injuries suffered by the players. Although *something* is indeterminate as to the exact definite description (it could be an elbow or a knee injury), it refers to an injury that has been previously mentioned in the discourse. It is coreferential with *it*, as shown by the indices. I consider this pro-form to be an example of given information.

Referentially new pro-forms were judged to be so if they introduced any new or previously unmentioned referents in the discourse. One example of new reference in the form of Th-Pro occurs in the discourse of Reina, a Sureña who tells of going to a popular hangout spot for her group and being bored by it:

> REINA: I go to the restaurant like three times a week. <u>Pero me aburro</u>
> *(I get bored)*, cause you don't do **anything**, you just like talk,
> you see the same people in school.

In this example, *anything* is informationally a completely new indefinite pronoun that does not derive its reference from any other part of the discourse. In effect, "you don't do *anything*" is the nonassertive pronominal first mention of what happens at the restaurant.

Discourse Markers

There is no clear consensus among researchers of discourse markers as to their definition. Also known under various aliases such as discourse connectives, pragmatic markers[23] and conversational markers, discourse markers have only recently been conceptualized as separate, patterned, units of talk. Stephen Levinson suggests that one of the features of discourse markers is that they "indicate the relationship between an utterance and the prior discourse," and that they "resist truth-conditional treatment."[24] The conceptualization of discourse markers as *primarily* serving to indicate sequential relations between units of talk is one that has dominated the research since Levinson's original observation.

Deborah Schiffrin defines discourse markers as "sequentially dependent elements which bracket units of talk."[25] These brackets can be initial, medial, or final in position, but they always serve to signal both anaphoric and cataphoric relations between the units of talk. By "sequential dependence," it is meant that these units work with reference to the larger discourse coherence level, and are thus dependent for their meaning on sequencing of clauses. The meaning of discourse markers (DMs henceforth) is consequently independent from the syntactic, semantic, or phonological levels of talk. For instance, devices like *well, now, but, right,* and *you know,* "make no syntactic predictions but they do allow some predictions about discourse content."[26]

An example of a discourse marker use of *and everything* can be found in the speech of Sadgirl below. In this interview, collected after I had interviewed quite a few of Sadgirl's friends, we are discussing how the girls from different gangs look at each other in order to pick fights.

1	NORMA:	They say that the Norteñas look you up and down and Sureñas will look you in the eye.
2	SADGIRL:	Well I guess it depends on the person
3		because one person will look at you **and everything**,
4		but they'll kind of be scared at the same time.
5		'Cause they'll probably say, oh, look at her **and everything**,
6		and if the girls turns back **and everything**,
7		they could either back down or back up,
8		and go, "hey, what's on," you know?
9		Then she can look at you up and down **and everything**, you know,
10		go around you know?
11	NORMA:	<u>Como despectivo?</u> *(Like with contempt?)*
12	SADGIRL:	Aha.

The examples on lines 3, 5, 6, and 9 above are what I have classified as discourse-marking occurrences of Th-Pro. They fit almost every one of Brinton's[27] definitional criteria, given at the beginning of the chapter: they are short, high in frequency, are loosely bound by the syntactic structure, and are optional rather than obligatory features. These examples are not referentially given pronouns because their reference cannot be recovered from anything in the preceding discourse. Neither are they even pronominal since they do not actually pick out any referent whatsoever. The discourse markers do, however, serve important pragmatic functions that help to construct mutual understanding between speaker and hearer. We will notice as we begin to look closely at more tokens that most but not all of the discourse-marking instances of Th-Pro are of the con/disjunctive form *and everything, or something, or nothing, or anything,* and that these forms may occasionally be discontinuous and in those cases they are ambiguous with referentially new pronominal expressions.

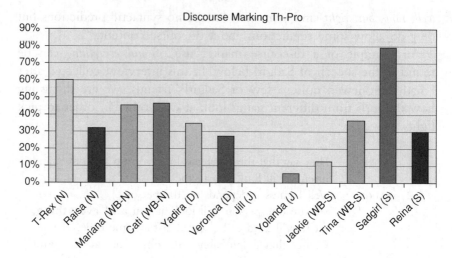

Figure 9.1 Distribution of 195 tokens of discourse-marking Th-Pro organized by speaker and social group.

Now that we have classified the tokens by means of functionally based criteria, let us return to the representation of the distributional facts for the Th–Pro data. Table 9.1a in the appendix illustrates the distribution of the 195 total tokens of Th–Pro, which together accounted for 10.83 percent of the data on /I/. Although some of the examples in the data set exhibited a degree of ambiguity between categories, I applied the strictest possible definitions of new, given, and discourse marking. If there was any new information in the noun phrase that could not be recovered from the context, then it was new. If all the information could be recovered or inferred, then it was given. Similarly, the discourse marking classification was used when the examples simply did not fit into either the new or given categories, and appeared to have a different function altogether. This was done with the purpose of finding overall patterning and structure in the data according to strict criteria.

I have listed next to the token count the percentage of that speaker's total that each category accounts for. Since these percentages are based on low token counts, they are strictly for rough comparisons within the data but not for the purpose of drawing statistical or probabilistic conclusions.

One of the most noticeable features of this chart is the wide range in the total number of tokens per speaker, which ranges from as few as 4 to as many as 34 tokens (each speaker's total token count of /I/ was 150). Since these tokens were collected over 150 consecutive occurrences for each speaker of the token /I/, the counts above reflect of how much each speaker was using a particular form over the 150 token spread.

Figure 9.1 shows only the distribution of discourse-marking Th-Pro as organized by speaker and social group. See Table 9.1a in the Appendix for the full numerical values and token counts for given, new, and discourse marking Th-Pro. Note that in the distribution of tokens the smallest percentages of discourse-marking Th-Pro occurrences are among the Jocks. Even though Yolanda uses quite a few referentially new instances of Th-Pro, her usage of the discourse marker Th-Pro consists of only one token. Compare this to T-Rex and Sadgirl, who are core gang girls and whose usage of Th-Pro is the highest of anyone on the list.

This disparity in raw numbers between the different girls returns us to a problem that we dealt with in the later part of chapter 8: to what extent does the relative frequency of some forms over others affect our interpretation of the data? As was mentioned above, in variation analysis extremely frequent, categorical tokens are often excluded from the data sets in which they are "over-represented" for fear that they will skew the results. In this case the Th-Pro tokens account for a fairly robust part (just under 10 percent) of the whole data set, considering that they belong in a single lexical category. And yet within that lexical category some of the social groups are clearly not producing the item as frequently as the others. It is possible that another analyst might have thrown out the Th-Pro tokens in the first place as being too frequent and rather skewed in one direction of variation (90 percent of them are raised), but I believe that an important part of the social life of /I/ would go unnoticed. It goes without saying that when listeners perceive a stream of speech they do not edit out too-frequent or categorical tokens, and perceptions about other groups' speech often consist of forms that are perceived as frequent in the group's production (as per exemplar theory). For these reasons I believe that it is essential for us to examine the categorical and high-frequency tokens qualitatively even if they cannot be fit into our statistical models.

In the variation analysis of the phonetic realization of /I/ in Th-Pro in chapter 8, we were unable to obtain results broken down by individual speaker because some of the speakers were "knockouts" as a result of having categorical applications in raising or in lowering (see expanded discussion in chapter 8). Some of the core gang-girl speakers had 100 percent application of raising in Th-Pro, while one of the Jocks had 0 percent application of raising. And yet some of the disparities in rates of application even appear happenstance. Table 9.1a in the Appendix shows that Yolanda's total usage of Th-Pro forms is as much as or even more than some of the core gang girls. If we look closely at her distribution though, we find that most of her tokens are in the new referential category and not in the discourse marking category that is heavily favored by some of the gang girls (as shown in Figure 9.1). Upon closer examination of the actual tokens I noticed that Yolanda's high use of new referential indefinite pronouns was prompted by my asking her vague questions about her career plans. She proceeded to tell me that she wanted to study sports medicine, and explained to me her skill as a sports trainer using indefinite expressions:

YOLANDA: I know a lot about physical therapy, I know when **things** are sprained. I have the natural talent of knowing when **something's** hurting you.

The examples above show how Yolanda's use of new reference with Th-Pro might have been prompted by an open-ended query about her future plans. Despite Yolanda's frequent use of the Th-Pro forms, from the previous statistical analysis of phonological variation in the same data set, we know that only three out of her total of eighteen tokens of Th-Pro were raised. Even though there is a possibility that her frequency of Th-pro forms was boosted by the conversational situation, she uses *only one* discourse-marking Th-Pro and does not adopt the wider Latina community practice of raising before engma [ŋ].

Having discussed some of the distributional facts and examined the questions that they raise about the nature of the data, I would now like to turn to the discourse-analysis part of this chapter, where we can investigate the ambiguities between categories and how they blend into one another.

Discourse Analysis of Th-pro

How might referentially given or new examples of Th-Pro have come to be used in discourse-marking positions? In this section, I examine how ambiguities in the function of the pronouns might give rise to new distinctions, and specifically how certain referentially new instances of the pronouns might develop into discourse markers through well-known paths of grammaticalization. Note that I am not claiming that the discourse-marking usage of Th-Pro historically follows from the more conventional "pronoun" usage. All three of the categories are represented in the young speakers from my sample, and have surely been coexisting in many dialects of English for a long time. What I am investigating is the way in which the central, pronominal meanings of Th-Pro are contiguous with the more unusual, peripheral, discourse-marking usages. What do they have in common? All pronouns exploit listeners' ability to infer.

One of my main assumptions here is that when a speaker asks a listener to draw an inference, she is in fact drawing on the frames that the two may have in common. The concept of frame is one with a long tradition in sociology, anthropology, and linguistics.[28] Deborah Tannen describes a frame as "a structure of expectation based on past experience . . . which helps us to process and comprehend stories [and which] serves to filter and shape perception."[29] This general definition of a frame encompasses both knowledge about the world and shared history that the speaker and her interlocutor may have with each other. When in conversation, a speaker may already share with her interlocutor overlapping frames that guide her in interpretation. Even speakers who are not familiar with each other will have structured expectations about the kind of speech act that they are engaged in and what is appropriate within it: "service interaction," "polite conversation," "job interview," "ordering a meal." All of these situations access common-knowledge frames that we acquire simply as a result of our socialization in the culture. These shared knowledge structures, scripts about the world we live in and what our role in it should be, guide our interpretation of every speech act and communicative behavior from another being, with whom we automatically assume to share at least some of the most general frames. For instance, H.P. Grice's conversational maxims[30] are one specialized subset of social frames that we can assume that we share with each other as participants in the same culture. The maxims themselves are even worded in the form of expectations, as are any set of rules for a new situation for which we may not yet have a frame. Frames guide our understanding of what may be inferred from a situation.

In the case of two interactants who may know each other well and who share more than only a general socialization-frame, the structures of expectation are very complex, since interactants will assume greater common knowledge of situations. Our structures of expectation for any given situation are dynamic and incrementally changing with each new experience. Interactants take this into account in communication, exploiting shared frames through shared communicative acts that might be indecipherable to those who do not share the same frames. Inside jokes, technical jargon, and knowing looks are all communicative acts that exploit structures of shared knowledge.

In the following sections I use the concept of frames to argue that the discourse-marking meaning of Th-Pro, though related to the pronominal meanings, takes a meaning of its own as a signal that the speaker gives to the interlocutor to access frames of common knowledge.

Ambiguities in Referentially Given vs. New

Among the examples in my corpus there exist ambiguities in reference where it is not clear from the context whether these instances should be taken as new or given. Let us look at an example of quasi-given[31] information where a euphemistic, nonspecific reference results in an obvious inference.

In the following example Reina (a core Sureña) and I are talking about another girl, Lisa, who is particularly outrageous in her swearing practices and always talks about her sexual exploits. Later in the conversation it surfaces that Reina also talks like that with some of her friends.

1	REINA:	Lisa <u>siempre quiere andar de</u> crazy like that.
		(always wants to act)
2		"<u>Que ese vato, que me lo agasajo.</u>"
		("Oh, that guy, I have sex with him.")
3		She's <u>bien</u> nasty to talk, like that.
		(really)
4		<u>Es bien, no sé como,</u> very perverted.
		(She's, I don't know,)
5	NORMA:	So you guys don't talk like that?
6	REINA:	Oh we do. <u>Pero depende de con quienes andamos.</u>
		(But it depends who we're with.)
7		If we know that the girls are crazy like that,
8		<u>o si sé</u> that they've done **things**,
		(or if I know)
9		that we have done together,
10		<u>o que lo mismo tenemos</u> in common,
		(or that we have the same)

11	that we have done the same **things**,
12	¡entonces sí nos ponemos a hablar!
	(then we'll start talking!)

In line 7, Reina explains the context of a situation in which she might talk explicitly about sex with girls whom she doesn't know very well. She uses the purposefully vague "If I know that they've done *things*" in line 8, not only so as not to go into the details of what those presumably sexual matters might be, but also because the social context of our interaction in some ways prevents her from being too explicit about it with me. I am older than she is, and at the time not her close friend (although she does uses the *tú* form with me, signaling some degree of familiarity), so she is socially constrained and cannot talk about sex openly. Rather than refusing to discuss the subject altogether with me (which she could have done, by steering the topic away), and rather than talking overtly about a taboo subject, she chooses to use the referential but nonspecific pro-form *things* to refer to sex. The reference of *things* has not been introduced prior to this example, but it is certainly accessible in the discourse, so it is neither completely new nor completely given. The vagueness of the pro-form *thing* where the context demands a noun signals to me, the addressee, that this might be a noun which will need an inference to be accessed. This is an example of what I call the meta-instructional use of Th-Pro, where the speaker instructs the addressee to access the most relevant shared information. This use of meta-instructional Th-Pro is one of the steps through which the strictly pronominal and referential Th-Pro might come to be de-linked from its strict referentiality and thus able act as a discourse marker, explicitly negotiating information and invoking the relationship between speaker and hearer.

Ambiguities in Referentially New vs. Discourse Marker

Even though we might think of the discourse-marking Th-Pro usages as not being strictly referential in the way that a classically defined pronoun would be, there exists nevertheless continuity between the referentially new and the discourse marking usages. Let us recall that one of the main clues to the presence of discourse marking with Th-Pro is the presence of the conjunction *and* or the disjunction *or*. In the Latina girls' corpus there are examples where the disjunction is discontinuous with the Th-Pro, as the following example:

1 REINA: Those girls who are from India, yeah,
2   they wanna be Sureñas **or they wanna be something**,
3   and they're always dressed like us <u>pero nadie las pela</u>.
                                  (but no one pays attention to them.)

In this example, "They wanna be Sureñas or they wanna be something," roughly would mean "they wanna be Sureñas or they wanna be some other kind of gang girl." Here the status of *something* is both referentially new and derivable as an item belonging to the set of which Sureñas are a part. Thus, this particular example fits both the description of the discourse-marking usage found in Dines[32] and the descriptions for referentially new information found in Chafe.[33] The semantic under-specification of Th-Pro as well as the gradual continuity between referentially given, referentially new, and discourse marking uses allows the form to serve a number of semantically and referentially diverse functions. Note that given and new referential Th-Pro can function as the subject or object of a clause, while the grammaticalized Th-Pro has lost its ability to occupy those slots within the sentence, and is the subject of increased morphosyntactic fusion between the con/disjunction and the Th-Pro. This type of ossification or idiomatization is typical of increased grammaticalization,[34] while a restriction in possible syntactic slots to those that are extrasentential is typical of discourse markers. Reina's example is an excellent intermediate example that shows us the path that Th-Pro takes on its way to becoming less strictly referential and more discourse-like.

In the next section I will discuss the varieties of discourse-marking usages of Th-Pro and their relationship to the invocation of shared frames.

Varieties of Discourse-Marking Th-Pro

Set-marking tags

By set-marking Th-Pro, I refer to the functions of *and everything* identified by Dines[35] and Ward and Birner,[36] where the tag is theorized to be an instantiation of a variable referring to a whole set.

In the example below, line 2 could be expanded as "his parents are from Vacaville, or some other place like Vacaville," (i.e., small and rural, and unlike the urban place where Reina lives).

1 REINA: He was born in the United States
2   but his parents are from Vacaville **or something like that**.

This usage can be also seen below, where Yadira, a Disco girl with a high frequency of discourse markers, tells me about her father's successful career in soccer prior to his emigration from El Salvador to the US.

1 YADIRA: I mean he was good **and everything**, you know, he WAS.
2   He should have stayed in El Salvador instead
3   cause he was like in newspapers, interviews.
4   This and this and that **and everything**, you know, he had
             it made.

In line 1, the meaning of *and everything* is restricted by the prior description *good*, so that possible instantiations of the variable might be "good and famous," or "good and talented," and not "good and unsuccessful." It even appears that this example could be truth conditional, true just in case the item following *good* belongs in the same set. Line 4, however, poses a problem, because there is no possible instantiation of this variable that could be considered to be in the same set as the highly unspecific *this and this and that*. So although we do find the set-marking usages described in the literature, there are examples that simply cannot be fit to that model. Let's examine more examples that do are not dependent on the set invoked.

Meta-Instructional

The examples of discourse-marking Th-Pro that I call "meta-instructional" are those which are not strictly dependent on set relationships as was the example in line 1 of Yadira's speech. Meta-instructional discourse markers involve the negotiation of information between speaker and hearer and the accessing of common frames. These meta-instructional examples exploit prior shared experiences in the relationship between speaker and hearer, and simply could not be decoded unless these shared experiences were invoked.

Some discourse markers, notably *well*[37] and *you know*[38] have been analyzed as markers of insufficiency, acting as signposts to tell that the speaker has left something out of the discourse, and telling the interlocutor to find the most relevant context and "fill in" the necessary information. Meta-instructional examples work in a similar way, except that the instruction to the speaker hinges on relevant shared experience. In the following example, Sadgirl, a core Sureña, is in the middle of a list of the defining characteristics of Norteños:

1   SADGIRL: The Norteños usually they all have them cars
2   and they'll fix em up **and everything**, you know, rims.
3   NORMA: Aha. <u>Como</u> . . . the lowriders?
                (Like)
4   SADGIRL: Yeah.

Here Sadgirl tells me that Norteños "fix [their cars] up and everything, you know, rims." Her use of *and everything* here is both anaphoric (since it refers back to "fix em up" and cataphoric, since it adds further elaboration with "you know, rims." She is trying to be maximally informative, and since I am an outsider to her social group, it is not obvious to her whether or how much I know about cars that have been fixed up to look like lowriders. To ensure my comprehension, she mentions rims, which are one of the most salient features of a fixed-up lowrider car. I finally catch on, and request confirmation: "Like . . . the lowriders?" This negotiation between the speaker and hearer to ensure the hearer's comprehension would have been completely unnecessary if I had been a Sureña, or some other kind of person with a broader base of knowledge of Latino youth culture. In this example it appears that Sadgirl's accurate assessment of my lack of contextual knowledge prompted her to elaborate on her previously inference-invoking *and everything*.

Another example where the meaning of the discourse marker is meta-instructional and not dependent on previous set invoked is in line 6 of the following excerpt, again from the interview with Sadgirl:

1   SADGIRL: I think that these gangs were for like, the Mexican people,
2   and here I see that white people are getting into it,
3   and black people too you know?
4   NORMA: And you don't agree with that.

5 SADGIRL: It's not that . . . it's just that, wait,
6   weren't these only supposed to be for Mexican people
                    and everything you know?

In this example, *and everything* does not refer to some element in the
same set as Mexican people. Rather, in this context it means "Mexican
people and only Mexican people," just like all the other gangs in the
school that are segregated by ethnicity/nationality. Her use of *you know*
after the Th-Pro is a further sign that she is putting out a signpost for
me to interpret this in the context of what I know and what we share
in terms of knowledge about gangs in this particular high school.

Left-dislocated or S-initial

Work on grammaticalization has consistently traced the development
of certain kinds of sentential material to peripheral clause positions.[39]
The left-dislocated position outside of the English sentence has been
shown to be a host for grammaticalized material (like the discourse
markers *well, indeed*) that dates to Indo-European.[40] There are a few
examples in my data set of discourse-marking Th-Pro appearing in the
left-operator, peripheral slot, either standing intonationally outside the
main clause that follows it, as in the example below, or completely by
itself.

    In this excerpt, Yadira is telling the story of how her parents met.
She reveals a surprising detail:

1 YADIRA: That's how it started.
                    But the **thing** [tɪŋ] is that, my dad was engaged in El
                    Salvador.
                    But he called the wedding off because he wanted to get
                    married to my mom.
2 NORMA: h!hh! Oh my God. [2.73 seconds]
3 YADIRA: **And everything**, and like umm so like my mom . . . she
                    decided to marry him.

After Yadira tells me that her father broke off his engagement, I react
with surprise. After she has told me the surprising detail, and without
interrupting her, I take a long in-breath, exclaim, "Oh my God," and
2.73 seconds later Yadira begins her next utterance with "And everything," setting it off from the rest of the clause with an intonational

contour, much like the one found on other sentence-initial markers of stance like *indeed, frankly*. The pause in this utterance is very signi ficant. The fact that the *and everything* stands by itself, outside of either of the utterances around it, lends support to the idea that this point was intended by the speaker as the beginning of the next logical sequence in her narrative, rather than the *and everything* in the beginning resulting from an interruption of the previous clause. In some ways this type of usage might resemble that of *indeed*, which serves to mark the speaker's attitude. In this case, *and everything* emphasizes all the negative conse-quences in the cultural context of Yadira's father breaking off his engage-ment. In this position it appears to serve the function of an utterance like *Can you believe it?*

In the next example, Raisa gives her perspective on how Sureños dress. Not very well, according to her:

1	RAISA:	Some of the Sureños dress pretty nice,
2		but some of them look like their pants haven't been ironed,
3		or their shirts,
4		or they got ugly shoes **or something**.
5		**Or something**, you know, you can usually tell the difference.

The phrase-initial *or something* in line 5 leaves little doubt as to its dis-tinctness from that on line 4. It is unambiguously part of a different phrase. It comes after a pause, bears a different intonational contour, and it starts on the higher overall pitch which normally signals the begin-ning of a new sentence. Unless it were interpreted as the beginning of a new phrase it would have to be interpreted as a repetition, of which there are none elsewhere in this data set. But what does it mean, if it is in the beginning of the phrase? Does it denote an alternative refer-ent that is a member of the set of ugly shoes, unironed pants or unironed shirts? Not necessarily. It would also make sense if it were referring to a member of the superset of "behaviors that Norteños disapprove of," and not only to the set of clothing by which Norteños think they can tell Sureños apart. This phrase-initial *Or something* accesses the com-mon frames of knowledge between the speaker and interlocutor, not adding anything to the truth conditionality of the statement but stress-ing the speaker's point: there is always some unfavorable way to tell Sureños apart from Norteños.

Discourse-Marking Th-Pro is an Ethnic Marker

To summarize the findings so far, we have reviewed evidence suggesting that:

- much of the variation in the realization of /I/ among the girls I interviewed is attributable to the use of the Th-Pro set (Figure 8.10);
- there is a social conditioning of its use, generally with core gang girls using it more (Figure 9.1);
- there are interactional, meta-instructional uses of a subset of the elements of Th-Pro, all of which are grammatically innovative and more frequent among precisely the subset of girls who lead the variation in raising of /I/ (Table 9.1a, in Appendix).

A larger question that arises here is *why* is it precisely the set of Th-Pro that serves as the vehicle for linguistic variation and as a social marker?

Dines[41] claims that the clause-terminal tags are regarded disfavorably by her middle-class informants, and are stigmatized for their association with working-class speech. Although this study did not measure attitudes concerning the discourse-marking Th-Pro forms, it is clear that discourse markers in general suffer from an image problem. California speech especially is stereotyped as consisting of few elements other than discourse markers,[42] to wit the Saturday Night Live performances of California speech, roughly consisting of:

[nɛːʷ wɛ˩. wɛ˩. yɑ ʃi wʊz ɑl tʰɛʷt'li laykʷ˩ ɛʷ mˊ gʰɑ'd]
No way. Way. Yeah, she was all totally like, "oh my God."

Discourse markers have consistently drawn prescriptive criticism,[43] even when those doing the criticizing are prolific users themselves![44] Californian vowel qualities and use of discourse markers are a sort of American prescriptivist *cause célèbre*, pastime for both language grinches and language comedians.[45]

It is possible that the salience of Th-Pro elements as discourse markers, as well as their prescriptive (i.e., teacher- and adult-) stigmatization might help to motivate an explanation of these tags as youthful ethnic markers. Howard Giles has noted that while in the broader American population small increments in Mexican features of English were associated with gradually less favorable impressions of the speaker,

Mexican Americans themselves were among the few who would favorably perceive the use of Mexican phonological markers in English.[46]

Let us return to our driving question in this section: Why should it be that the Th-Pro forms serve as ethnic markers in the speech of California Latina girls? From the preceding discussion it is possible to extrapolate a few points:

1   Because of their high frequency among certain ethnic subgroups (like the core gang girls) and because they are generally stigmatized in their function as discourse markers, the Th-Pro forms already have some potential for being refashioned into a covert prestige form. Frequency plus stigmatization may contribute to saliency.
2   The Th-Pro forms pack a multiple punch, as it were, since they contain several opportunities for marking ethnicity, vernacularity, and general divergence from the standard dialect variety. Not only is the vowel available for play within a large vowel space, but the immediately preceding consonant can undergo fortition as well. In addition to these phonetic-realization factors, the very utterance of Th-Pro forms with stress on the last syllable [ɛvri'ṭiŋ] is ethnically marked, a distinctive Mexican-American innovation that is not even shared by other Spanish-language-background groups.[47] Furthermore, with some forms there exists the possibility of negative concord, so that for instance using *nothing* instead of *anything*, becomes a possibility: "I didn't do **nothing**!"

    Although this process is itself variable in the community of Chicano English speakers (it's not done in all contexts by all speakers), it is nevertheless widely used among other ethnic minorities (a variable rule for African-American English speakers, according to William Labov),[48] and sharply diverges from the Standard Euro-American dialect of the area.
3   The impersonal and nonspecific semantics of the Th-Pro forms, inherent in their core meaning, not only invite but dictate that some sort of inference take place. The more frequent the use of the form, the greater the number and amount of inferences that must take place. But why would speakers violate the Gricean Maxim of Quantity which compels them to make their contribution exactly as informative as is required (and no more informative than is required)? Why would they perversely require inference and processing time from their listeners at the end of many of their clauses? In fact, they do not. I show that the underspecificity of the Th-Pro forms is

precisely what allows in-group inferential processes to take place. As Diane Blakemore argues, speakers do not invite inferences if they do not have grounds for thinking that the hearers can access the information.[49] We may recall that Sadgirl clarified her utterance "Norteños have them cars and they fix em up *and everything*, you know, rims" on the grounds that I did not have enough information about lowriders to process the inference-inviting sentence tag. The invitation of the inference specifically directed at the relevant in-group can be made apparent if we imagine that the discourse is directed at a variety of different addressees with different characteristics.

Let us imagine that two girls, Marga and Thalia, are talking about old boyfriends, and Marga says to Thalia:

(a)   I was walking around the other day and Jose stopped to talk to me and everything.

Now let us imagine that the same girl recounts the incident to her current boyfriend, in which case she might say:

(b)   I was walking around the other day and Jose just stopped to talk to me.

Although the sentences in (a) and (b) have identical truth-conditions, that is they are true and false in exactly the same cases (true if Marga was walking around and Jose stopped to talk to her), in fact they have very different implicatures. In (a), Jose stopping to talk might be the *least* that happened. This utterance invites the interlocutor, Thalia, to draw an inference about what else may have happened. In (b), Jose stopping to talk to Maricela is the *most* that happened, and the use of "just" actually blocks any inference by the new boyfriend from taking place. So strong are these connotations, that (a) sounds like Maricela is bragging (it could easily be augmented by "He still likes me") while (b) sounds like she's apologizing (and could be augmented by "It wasn't my fault."). It is precisely this kind of addressee-oriented quality that is so significant in the interpretation of *and everything*, contributing to its function as an in-group marker of ethnicity. In some ways it is like an in-group code, an argot of inferences, since only those speakers who have full access to the assumptions and knowledge of the group will be able to properly interpret *and everything*. To out-group listeners, this would of course sound decontextualized and "inarticulate." This explanation is in some ways a reinterpretation of Basil Bernstein's notions of "restricted code" vs. "elaborated code";[50] however, I avoid the assumption that these are correlated in any way with social class. Rather it seems that every community of practice[51] would have its own basis for establishing assumptions and shared background, and thus would differ on precisely what elements could be restricted and which ones may be elaborated.

From the preceding discussion it seems that we may be able to explain why the Th-Pro forms in this community have become a magnet for variation, carrying not only the greatest weight of the vocalic variability, but also allowing speakers latitude in accessing in-group inferences which at every turn affirm and reconstitute membership in this community of practice.

Conclusion: The Stigma of Discourse Markers

The speech produced by youth is often stereotyped as inarticulate, linked not only with the use of discourse markers such as *like* and *dude*,[52] but also with intonational contours (like so-called "uptalk"),[53] as well as with slang.[54] These judgments of "inarticulateness" and "bad language" go hand in hand with moralistic representations, enforcing what Deborah Cameron has called "verbal hygiene,"[55] the social tendencies to regulate, legislate, and otherwise clean up language for moral purposes.

Since 2003, a wildly popular British TV sketch comedy show called "Little Britain" has featured a character named Vicky Pollard, purportedly a teenager (played by middle-aged male comedian Matt Lucas) who is supposed to be a "chav," embodying a stereotype of a young working-class British person who speaks "inarticulately" and with a nonstandard accent. Vicky Pollard is a teenage mom who has flunked out of school, gotten in fights, traded in one of her six kids for a CD, and is constantly getting caught trying to steal things from stores. The typical dialog when she gets caught goes something like this:

STOREKEEPER: "Did you take that?"
VICKY: "Yeah-but-no-but-yeah-but-no-but I didn't. 'Cause I couldn't have, even if I wanted to. I don't know **or nothing**."

Vicky is a dramatic example, halfway across the world, of representations of working-class youth as inarticulate and also another example of the social stigmatization of the use of the discourse marking Th-Pro elements *or something* and *or nothing*. The pervasiveness of verbally hygienic efforts aimed at the speech of teens and young adults is remarkable, especially given that these teens grow up to be adults that still use discourse markers, albeit possibly different ones (*apparently*, *evidently*, *etcetera*).

This chapter has attempted to highlight three main elements in the use of stigmatized discourse-marking Th-Pro in the speech of Latina girls at Sor Juana High School:

- A connection was drawn to the socially-patterned variation of [I] and [i], which as we saw in the last chapter enriched our understanding of the Norteñas and Sureñas as participating in similar stylistic practices in their English variation (and not only in the symbolic oppositions of localism/ethnicity/makeup as seen earlier);
- The special status of the Th-Pro set is attested in historical linguistic accounts, and the girls are acting and innovating upon on these historical trends by picking up these elements as centerpieces of their variation;
- Th-Pro combines elements of frequency and saliency to pack an especially powerful discursive punch, giving it covert prestige and allowing it to function as an ethnic marker. Because these grammatically innovative elements were being employed by socially iconic speakers, Th-Pro could serve as a locus for the display of being part of the "in-group," as with the story of Patricia in the beginning of chapter 7.

I have discussed in some of my other linguistic work on exemplar theory[56] how notions of frequency and saliency can play a part in larger linguistic models. So far most of that work has been conducted in laboratory settings. It is my hope that this ethnographic study, conducted with speakers who have collaborated in drawing out the social categories in the landscape, will spur more ethnographic variationist research that tries to draw out the complex relations between language and other symbolic systems.

While displaying affiliation, language and other symbolic resources (makeup, dress, music) also signal differentiation. The young Latinas in this study deploy various linguistic mechanisms to subvert normative expectations, for example, on the part of the institution of the school.

Much as in the prior vilification of discourse markers such as *like*[57] – which was/is negatively linked with California "Valley Girl" speech – the use of innovative markers *anything, something, nothing* is despised by teachers and yet links the girls with wider Chicano English speech communities, as well as with historical developments in the history of English.

Notes

1   Mendoza-Denton (1999), Fought (2003)
2   Fraser (1988)
3   Brinton (1990: 46–7)
4   Houston (1985: 165)
5   Houston (1985: 165)
6   Houston (1985: 152–4, 354)
7   Houston (1985: 142)
8   Labov (1972a), Houston (1985)
9   García (1984), Galindo (1987)
10 Quirk, et al. (1985: 377)
11 Quirk, et al. (1985: 378)
12 Norrby and Winter (2001), Jucker, et al. (2003)
13 Dines (1980: 23)
14 Dines (1980: 34)
15 Dines (1980: 22)
16 Ward and Birner (1993: 205)
17 Ward and Birner (1993: 207)
18 Overstreet (1999)
19 Quirk et al. (1985)
20 Goodwin (1981)
21 Quirk et al. (1985)
22 Chafe (1976: 30)
23 Roth-Gordon (forthcoming)
24 Levinson (1983: 87)
25 Schiffrin (1987: 31)
26 Schiffrin (1987: 102)
27 Brinton (1990)
28 Bateson (1972), Goffman (1974), Tannen (1993), inter alia
29 Tannen (1993: 53)
30 Grice (1989: 26)
31 Chafe (1976: 34)
32 Dines (1980)
33 Chafe (1976)

34 Traugott (1995), Traugott (2003)
35 Dines (1980)
36 Ward and Birner (1993)
37 Jucker (1993)
38 Schiffrin (1994)
39 Schiffrin (1991) on *then*, Mendoza-Denton (1993) on *concerning*, Traugott (1995) on *indeed*.
40 Kiparsky (1995)
41 Dines (1980)
42 Preston (1986)
43 Quirk, et al. (1972: 105), Brinton (1990: 47)
44 Dines (1980: 24)
45 cf. "Surfer Chick" by Whoopi Goldberg (1985), cited and analyzed in Hinton et al. (1987).
46 Giles (1979a)
47 cf. Wolfram's (1974) attestation of Puerto Rican [noʔn̩] in New York City.
48 Labov (1972d: 236)
49 Blakemore (1987: 236)
50 Bernstein (1971)
51 Lave and Wenger (1991), Eckert and McConnell Ginet (1992)
52 Kiesling (2004)
53 McLemore (1991)
54 Roth-Gordon (forthcoming)
55 Cameron (1995)
56 Mendoza-Denton (forthcoming)
57 See Buchstaller (2001) on grammaticalization of "like".

CHAPTER 10

CONCLUSION

A Small Note about Phonetic Awareness

One of the questions people commonly ask about this research is whether the young people in this study were aware of all this fine-grained phonetic variation of the sort that I describe in Chapters 7–9. This question has a complex answer.

I occasionally asked girls for meta-linguistic judgments on specific features, and most of the time this exercise was met with puzzled looks. On the other hand, occasionally quite explicit judgments that tied pronunciations to attitudes and even to perceptions of prejudice were articulated. Let me give you an example.

The following transcription excerpt comes from a car ride that Rob and I took with T-Rex and her then-boyfriend Mimo. We were talking and bantering in Rob's car, taking in the Bay Area sights. I had previously asked and they had allowed the presence of a tape recorder as we took a long drive into another of the Bay Area cities. We began talking (unprompted by me) about what Ben Rampton calls "crossing,"[1] speaking in a language variety that "belongs" to another group. T-Rex begins to comment on Americans' exaggerated pronunciations of Spanish words.

T-Rex: [riyow][græendey]
That's fucking what?
NMD: Mock Spanish.

T-Rex:	It would be [buRiṭo] [granḏe]
	Not [bəɹirow:ː] [grændey:ː]
Norma:	So how do you feel about Americans who have strong American accents in Spanish? How do you think they sound?
T-Rex:	They're making- they're exaggerating.
	They're making fun of our fucking language!
Rob:	Oh yeah? What if they can't do any better?
T-Rex:	Then it would be serious, not like they a:lways do on T.V.
	they always like pretend,
	or they say it lo:ng,
	with lo:ːng fucking things [ṭiŋs]
	you know?
	They [spɪːːkʰ].
Rob:	You know I'm not quite sure where exactly I'm going . . .
T-Rex:	You're gonna make a right here.

When T-Rex objects to hyperanglicized pronunciations of Spanish, I invoke Jane Hill's concept of Mock Spanish,[2] a type of language use that participates in a system of semantic derogation whereby whiteness is elevated and Latinos are derogated by the inappropriate use of elements from Spanish. T-Rex's sensitivity to the use of quite subtle linguistic variants is evident here, as well as the explicit links between the use of those out-of-place elements and the intention to offend. This sensitivity extends even to American accents in Spanish, much to the dismay of Rob, who was a native English-speaking, second-language learner of Spanish. But T-Rex's point is even more subtle: she uses her characteristic Th-Pro [ṭiŋs] and immediately juxtaposes it to the out of place token of "speak" which is uttered with an [I] instead of the normative [i]. Not only is she making quite subtle distinctions in sub-segmental phenomena in both languages, but the utterance of [spɪk] leaves open the possibility that she is referring also to the slur word "spic," a derogatory term for Mexicans presumably derived from their attributed inability to pronounce "speak." The distinctions are subtle here, and telling. Whereas a point-blank question on the [I] segment produced little information, its spontaneous emergence in the ethnographic context makes it possible to say that speakers do indeed orient to these microphenomena in their fashioning of linguistic and cultural stances.

Concluding Remarks

The mutually constitutive relationship between language and the body – embodied, materialized language – is one of the most striking aspects of the tattoos, makeup, and other symbolic practices used by young Latinas who consider themselves gang members. In the preceding chapters I've analyzed how semiotic elements of speech, bodily practices, and symbolic exchanges are employed to signal social affiliation, coming together to form styles – specifically the "Norteña" and "Sureña" gang girl styles of Northern California.

This work is drawn from ethnography I conducted from 1993 to 1997 in a Silicon Valley, California high school and its surrounding Latino immigrant community. I've presented transcriptions and analysis of speech data gathered during the research, and brought in supporting documents from the government, the police, the school, and community sources. I've analyzed the connection of language behavior and other symbolic practices (the semiotics of the body and the circulation of material artifacts) with larger social processes of hemispheric localism, nationalism, racial/ethnic consciousness, and gender identity. I believe that one crucial aspect in presenting this information is also to invite the reader to interrogate and examine the researcher's role in data collection; I have tried to provide signposts to let you know where I think my subjectivity affects how I interpret and analyze the data.

Viewing girl gang groups through the framework of communities of practice[3] emphasizes the fluidity of stylistic processes. Case studies of key participants have demonstrated how the dynamic manifestation of distinctive styles expressed participants' varied and shifting engagements with the sociopolitical systems of Mexico and the United States. These sociopolitical stances with respect to the two countries, and their projection onto the two hemispheres, have crystallized into gang ideologies, creating an elaborate division where homologous relationships are constructed among physical topography (North and South), deportment, language practices, and the body.

Homegirls is the first monograph-length ethnographic study of the Norteña/Sureña youth gang dynamic. It focuses on issues specific to the key participants as those issues emerged in their everyday lives and their ongoing linguistic and material practices. I situate these issues as much as possible in the transcripts of the interviews I did with them, identifying especially a discourse of "being macha" that I argue serves one girl, T-Rex, in thinking about and working through her future life options. These gender-transgressive moments are part of what I believe sets apart girls who may avoid potential "social injury" from their association with the stigmatizing gang identity.

This book is also one of the only studies to document in detail aspects of a gang dynamic other than violence, control of territory, or the traffic of drugs, factors routinely considered as paramount in both police intervention and gang research. I have tried to expand the boundaries of the gang literature by investigating a dynamic (Norteña/ Sureña) that is defined primarily through the deployment of symbolic capital. Linguistic (English/Spanish) and ethnic-nationalistic ideologies (US/Mexico) create a system of oppositions and loyalties that lends structure to a complex system of signs operating at many levels of representation.

Some of the questions that have guided this work are the following: How did the individual girls in their communities of practice come to create styles that indexed complex, ideology-based identities? What were the elements of material, linguistic, and interactional practice that entered into their bricolage of style? How did members learn which elements should be used? What role did phonetic and low-level discourse phenomena play in the definition of styles? This study found that frequency and saliency in the use of discourse-marking pronominal expressions with distinct phonetic shapes were important in the construction of stylized identities. Core Norteñas and Sureñas extended the established meanings of these pronominal expressions to new contexts, paying special attention to the distribution of their use that showed a difference in the type and frequency of usage. This patterned use distinguished not only among the Norteñas and the Sureñas, but also among other Latina girl youth groups, such as the Latina Jocks and the Disco girls. By understanding the participation of low-level features of language in cultural dynamics of group function and group affiliation, I hope to lend a new dimension to studies of youth styles, showing them to be innovative not only in terms of dress, music, and appearance, but also as crucially participating in processes of language variation and change.

To understand the articulation of linguistic and other symbolic elements into embodied styles, *Homegirls* has linked material practices to the analysis of micro-level language patterning that locates each participant within broader communities of practice. By linking the macro- and micro-analysis of practices, I invite readers to consider the possibilities of embodied language as a participant in the semiotic system created on the body's surface.

Notes

1 Rampton (1995)
2 Hill (1998)
3 Lave and Wegner (1991), Eckert (2000)

REFERENCES

Abdulaziz, M. H., and K. Osinde (1997) Sheng and Engsh: Development of Mixed Codes among the Urban Youth in Kenya. *International Journal of the Sociology of Language*, 125: 43–63.

Abrahams, R. (1968) Introductory Remarks to a Rhetorical Theory of Folklore. *The Journal of American Folklore*, 81(320): 143–58.

Abu-Lughod, L. (1991) Writing Against Culture. In: R. G. Fox (ed.) *Recapturing Anthropology: Working in the Present*. Santa Fe, NM: School of American Research Press, pp. 137–62.

Acuña, R. (1996) *Anything but Mexican: Chicanos in Contemporary Los Angeles*. (Haymarket series) London; New York: Verso.

Adams, K. L., and A. Winter (1997) Gang Graffiti as a Discourse Genre. *Journal of Sociolinguistics*, 1(3), 337–60.

Adamson, C. (2000) Defensive Localism in White and Black: A Comparative History of European-American and African-American Youth Gangs. *Ethnic and Racial Studies*, 23(2): 272–98.

Agar, M. (1984, 2000) *The Professional Stranger*. New York: Academic Press.

Ahearn, L. (2001) Language and Agency. *Annual Review of Anthropology*, 30: 109–137.

Alonso, A. M. (1995) *Thread of Blood: Colonialism, Revolution, and Gender on Mexico's Northern Frontier*. Tucson, AZ: University of Arizona Press.

Alonso, A. M. (2004) Conforming Disconformity: "Mestizaje," Hybridity, and the Aestyhetics of Mexican Nationalism. *Cultural Anthropology*, 19(4): 459–90.

Althusser, L. (1971) Ideology and Ideological State Apparatuses. In: *Lenin and Philosophy and Other Essays*. New York: Monthly Review Press, pp. 127–86.

Anzaldúa, G. (1987) *Borderlands/La Frontera: The New Mestiza*. San Francisco, CA: Aunt Lute Books.

Arizona Department of Education (2007) State Intervention. Site Visit Findings: Naylor Middle School, Tucson, AZ.

Augustine, A. [St Augustine, Bishop of Hippo] (1993) *Confessions*, trans. F. J. Sheed. Indianapolis, IN: Hackett Publishing Company.

Auletta, K. (1982) *The Underclass*. New York: Random House.

Aunger, R. (1995) On Ethnography: Storytelling or Science? *Current Anthropology*, 36(1): 97–130.

Bailey, B. H. (2002) *Language, Race, and Negotiation of Identity: A Study of Dominican Americans*. New York: LFB Scholarly Publishing.

Bailey, G. (2002) Real and Apparent Time. In: J. K. Chambers, P. Trudgill, and N. Schilling-Estes (eds.) *The Handbook of Language Variation and Change*. Malden, MA: Blackwell Publishing, pp. 312–32.

Bakalaki, A. (1997) Students, Natives, Colleagues: Encounters in Academia and in the Field. *Cultural Anthropology*, 12(4): 502–26.

Bakhtin, M. M. (1981) Discourse in the Novel. In *Dialogic Imagination*, trans. Emerson, C. and M. Holquist. Austin: University of Texas Press, pp. 259–422.

Barrios, L. (2003) The Almighty Latin King and Queen Nation and the Spirituality of Resistance: Agency, Social Cohesion, and Liberating Rituals in the Making of a Street Organization. In: L. Kontos, D. Brotherton, and L. Barrios. (eds.) *Gangs and Society: Alternative Perspectives*. New York; Chichester [England]: Columbia University Press, pp. 119–35.

Bateson, G. (1972) *Steps to an Ecology of Mind*. New York: Ballantine Books.

Bauman, R. (1975) Verbal Art as Performance. *American Anthropologist*, 77(2): 290–311.

Baudrillard, J. (1994) *Simulacra and Simulation*. Ann Arbor, MI: University of Michigan Press.

Bauman, R., and C. Briggs (1990) Poetics and Performance as Critical Perspectives on Language and Social Life. *Annual Review of Anthropology*, 19: 59–88.

Bayley, R. (2002) "The Quantitative Paradigm." In: J. K. Chambers, P. Trudgill, and N. Schilling-Estes (eds.) *The Handbook of Language Variation and Change*. Malden, MA: Blackwell Publishing, pp. 117–41.

Beckman, M. and J. Pierrehumbert (1993) Interpreting "Phonetic Interpretation" Over the Lexicon. In: J. Local, R. A. Ogden, and R. Temple (eds.) *Phonetic Interpretation: Papers in Laboratory Phonology VI*. Cambridge: Cambridge University Press, pp. 13–37.

Behar, R. (1993) *Translated Woman: Crossing the Border with Esperanza's Story*. Boston, MA: Beacon Press.

Berliner, D. (2005) The Abuses of Memory: Reflections on the Memory Boom in Anthropology. *Anthropological Quarterly*, 78(1): 197–211.

Bernstein, B. (1971) *Class Codes and Control I*. London: Routledge.

Bettie, J. (2003) *Women without Class: Girls, Race, and Identity*. Berkeley, CA: University of California Press.

Bexley, L. (1994) Even Unintentional Racism Hurts. *Sor Juana Times*. Foxbury Hills, CA: Sor Juana High School.

Bishop, W. (1992) I-Witnessing the Composition: Turning Ethnographic Data into Narratives. *Rhetoric Review*, 11(1): 147–58.

Blake, R., and M. Josey (2003) The /ay/ Diphthong in a Martha's Vineyard Community: What Can We Say 40 Years After Labov? *Language in Society* 32(4): 451–85.

Blakemore, D. (1987) *Semantic Constraints on Relevance*. Oxford: Blackwell.

Bloomfield, L. (1933) *Language*. Chicago, IL: The University of Chicago Press.

Bordo, S. (1993) *Unbearable Weight: Feminism, Western Culture and the Body*. Berkeley, CA: University of California Press.

Boum, A. (2006) *Muslims Remember Jews in Southern Morocco: Social Memories, Dialogic Narratives, and the Collective Imaginations of Jewishness*. Unpublished PhD Dissertation, The University of Arizona.

Bourdieu, P. (1977) *Outline of a Theory of Practice*, trans. R. Nice. Cambridge: Cambridge University Press.

Bourdieu, P. (1992) *Language and Symbolic Power*. London: Polity Press.

Bresnan, J., and J. Hay (2007) *Gradient Grammar: An Effect of Animacy on the Syntax of give in New Zealand and American English*. http://www.stanford.edu/%7Ebresnan/anim-spokensyntax-final.pdf. Accessed February 1, 2007.

Briggs, C. L. (1986) *Learning How to Ask: A Sociolinguistic Appraisal of the Role of the Interview in Social Science Research*. Cambridge: Cambridge University Press.

Briggs, J. (1970) *Never in Anger: Portrait of an Eskimo Family*. Cambridge, MA: Harvard University Press.

Brinkhoff, T. (2006) *The Principal Agglomerations of the World*. http://www.citypopulation.de, 2006-11-22. Accessed February 12, 2007.

Brinton, L. (1990) The Development of Discourse Markers in English. In: J. Fisiak (ed.) *Historical Linguistics and Philology*. Berlin: De Gruyter, pp. 45–76.

Brotherton, D. C. (2003) Education in the Reform of Street Organizations in New York City. In: L. Kontos, D. Brotherton, and L. Barrios (eds.) *Gangs and Society: Alternative Perspectives*. New York; Chichester [England]: Columbia University Press, pp. 136–58.

Brotherton, D. C., and L. Barrios (2004) *The Almighty Latin King and Queen Nation: Street Politics and the Transformation of a New York City Gang*. New York: Columbia University Press.

Brotherton, D. C., and C. Salazar-Atias (2003) Amor de Reina!: The Pushes and Pulls of Group Membership among the Latin Queens. In: L. Kontos, D. Brotherton, and L. Barrios (eds.) *Gangs and Society: Alternative Perspectives*, New York; Chichester [England]: Columbia University Press, pp. 183–210.

Brown, A. (2007) Rethinking the Meaning of the Subcultural Commodity: Exploring Heavy Metal T-Shirt Culture(s). In: P. Hodkinson and W. Deicke (eds.) *Youth Cultures: Scenes, Subcultures and Tribes*. London: Routledge.

Bucholtz, M. (2000) The Politics of Transcription. *Journal of Pragmatics*, 32: 1439–65.

Bucholtz, M. (2002) Youth and Cultural Practice. *Annual Review of Anthropology*, 35: 525–52.

Bucholtz, M. (2003) Sociolinguistic Nostalgia and the Authentication of Identity. *Journal of Sociolinguistics*, 7(3): 398–416.

Bucholtz, M., and K. Hall (2005) Identity and Interaction: A Sociolinguistic Approach. *Discourse Studies*, 7(4–5): 585–614.

Buchstaller, I. (2001) He Goes *and* I'm like: *The New Quotatives Re-visited*. Paper presented at New Ways of Analyzing Variation (NWAV 30), Raleigh, N.C.

Burris-Kitchen, D. (1997) *Female Gang Participation: The Role of African-American Women in the Informal Drug Economy and Gang Activities*. Lewiston, UK: The Edwin Mellen Press.

Bustamante, J. (1994) *Ernesto Galarza's Legacy to the History of Labor Migration*. Stanford, CA: Stanford Center for Chicano Research.

Butler, J. (1990) *Gender Trouble: Feminism and the Subversion of Identity*. New York: Routledge.

Butler, J. (1993) *Bodies that Matter: on the Discursive Limits of "Sex."* New York: Routledge.

Bybee, J. (1994) A View of Phonology from a Cognitive and Functional Perspective. *Cognitive Linguistics*, 5: 285–305.

Bybee, J. (2001) *Phonology and Language Use*. Cambridge: Cambridge University Press.

Bybee, J. (2002) Cognitive Processes in Grammaticalization. In: M. Tomasello (ed.) *The New Psychology of Language. Cognitive and Functional Approaches To Language Structure*. New Jersey: LEA.

Bybee, J., and P. Hopper (2001) *Frequency and the Emergence of Language Structure*. Amsterdam: Johns Benjamins.

California Department of Education (1995) *California Education Code*. Sacramento, CA: Legislative Counsel of California.

California Department of Justice (1995) *Gangs 2000: A Call to Action. The Attorney General's Report on the Impact of Criminal Street Gangs on Crime and Violence in California by the Year 2000*. Sacramento, CA: Division of Law Enforcement, Bureau of Investigation, California Department of Justice.

The California Style Collective (1993) *Personal and Group Style*. Paper presented at NWAVE22.

Camarillo, A. (1985) *Chicanos in California: A History of Mexican Americans in California*. San Francisco, CA: Boyd & Fraser.

Cameron, D. (1995) *Verbal Hygiene*. London: Routledge.

Campbell, A. (1984) *The Girls in the Gang: A Report From New York City*. New York: Basil Blackwell.

Campbell, A. (1987) Self Definition by Rejection: The Case of Gang Girls. *Social Problems*, 34(5): 451–66.

Campbell, A. (1991) *The Girls in the Gang: A Report from New York City* (2nd edn). Cambridge, MA: Basil Blackwell.

Capps, L., and E. Ochs (2001) *Living Narrative: Creating Lives in Everyday Storytelling.* Cambridge, MA: Harvard University Press.

Cardeña, I. (2003) On Humour and Pathology: the Role of Paradox and Absurdity for Ideological Survival. *Anthropology and Medicine,* 10(1): 115–42.

Carrera, M. M. (2003) *Imagining Identity in New Spain: Race, Lineage, and the Colonial Body in Portraiture and Casta Paintings.* Austin, TX: University of Texas Press.

Carsten, J. (1995) The Politics of Forgetting: Migration, Kinship and Memory on the Periphery of the Southeast Asian State. *Journal of the Royal Anthropological Institute,* 1: 317–35.

Carter, P. (2003) Extrinsic Phonetic Interpretation: Spectral Variation in English Liquids. In: J. Local, R. A. Ogden, and R. Temple (eds.) *Papers in Laboratory Phonology VI: Phonetic Interpretation.* Cambridge: Cambridge University Press, pp. 235–49.

Cepeda, A., and A. Valdez (2003) Risk Behaviors among Young Mexican American Gang-Associated Females: Sexual Relations, Partying, Substance Use, and Crime. *Journal of Adolescent Research,* 18: 90–106.

de Certeau, M. (1986a) *Heterologies: Discourse on the Other.* Trans. B. Massumi. Minneapolis, MN: University of Minnesota Press.

de Certeau, M. (1986b) The Jabbering of Social Life. In: M. Blonsky (ed.) *On Sign.* Baltimore, MD: Johns Hopkins University Press, pp. 146–54.

Chafe, W. (1976) Givenness, Contrastiveness, Definiteness, Subjects, Topics and Point of View. In: C. Li (ed.) *Subject and Topic.* New York: Academic Press, pp. 25–55.

Chambers, J. K. (1995) *Sociolinguistic Theory: Linguistic Variation and its Social Significance.* Oxford: Blackwell.

Chambers, J. K. (2002) Patterns of Variation Including Change. In: J. K. Chambers, P. Trudgill, and N. Schilling-Estes (eds.) *The Handbook of Language Variation and Change.* Malden, MA: Blackwell Publishing, pp. 349–72.

Chesney-Lind, M. (1993) "Girls, Gangs, and Violence: Anatomy of a Backlash." *Humanity and Society,* 17(3): 321–44.

Chesney-Lind, M. (1995) Girls, Delinquency and Juvenile Justice: Toward a Feminist Theory of Young Women's Crime. In: B. Price and N. Sokoloff (eds.) *The Criminal Justice System an Women* (2nd edn). New York: McGraw-Hill, pp. 71–88.

Chesney-Lind, M., and J. Hagedorn (1999) *Female Gangs in America: Essays on Girls, Gangs, and Gender.* Chicago, IL: Lake View Press.

Chesney-Lind, M., and L. Pasko (2004) *The Female Offender: Girls, Women, and Crime.* Thousand Oaks, CA: Sage Publications.

Chesney-Lind M., R. G. Shelden, and K. A. Joe (1996) Girls, Delinquency and Gang Membership. In: C. R. Huff (ed.) *Gangs in America* (2nd edn). Thousand Oaks, CA: Sage, pp. 185–204.

Chiquita Brands, L. L. C. (2006) *Our Story.* http://www.chiquita.com/. Accessed September 30, 2006.

Chun, E. W. (2001) The Construction of White, Black, and Korean American Identities through African American Vernacular English. *Journal of Linguistic Anthropology*, 11(1): 52–64.

Clarke, G. (1990/1981) Defending Ski-Jumpers: A Critique of Theories of Youth Subcultures. In: S. Frith and A. Goodwin (eds.) *On Record: Rock, Pop and the Written Word.* London: Routledge, pp. 81–96.

Cohen, A., and E. Taylor (2000) *American Pharaoh: Mayor Richard J. Daley, His Battle for Chicago and the Nation.* New York: Little Brown and Company.

Cohen, S. (1972) *Folk Devils and Moral Panics.* London: MacGibbon and Kee.

Comaroff, J., and J. Comaroff (1991) *Of Revelation and Revolution: Christianity, Colonialism, and Consciousness in South Africa. Vol. 1.* Chicago, IL: University of Chicago Press.

Coupland, N. (1980) Style-Shifting in a Cardiff Work Setting. *Language in Society*, 9(1): 1–12.

Covey, H. C. (2003) *Street Gangs Throughout the World.* Springfield, IL: Charles C. Thomas.

Cukor-Avila, P., and G. Bailey (2001) The Effects of the Race of the Interviewer on Sociolinguistic Fieldwork. *Journal of Sociolinguistics*, 5(2): 254–70.

Cummings, S., and D. J. Monti (1993) *Gangs: The Origins and Impact of Contemporary Youth Gangs in the United States*, Albany, NY: State University of New York Press.

Curry, G. D. (1998) Female Gang Involvement. *Journal of Research in Crime Delinquency*, 35(1): 100–18.

Curry, G. D., R. Ball, and R. Fox (1994) Gang Crime and Law Enforcement Record Keeping. Washington, DC: US Department of Justice, Office of Justice Programs, National Institute of Justice.

Curry, G. D., and I. A. Spergel (1988) Gang Homicide, Delinquency, and Community. *Criminology*, 26(3): 381–405.

Curry, G. D., and I. A. Spergel (1992) Gang Involvement and Delinquency among Hispanic and African-American Adolescent Males. *Journal of Research in Crime and Delinquency*, 29: 273–29.

Dawley, D. (1973) *A Nation of Lord: The Autobiography of the Vice Lords.* Garden City, NY: Anchor.

Daniels, D. H. (2002) Los Angeles Zoot: Race "Riot," the Pachuco and Black Music Culture. *The Journal of African American History*, 87: 98–118.

Davis, M. (1990) *City of Quartz: Excavating the Future in Los Angeles.* New York: Vintage Books.

De Camp, D. (1971) The Pronunciation of English in San Francisco. In: J. Williamson and V. Burke (eds.) *A Various Language: Perspectives on American Dialects*. New York: Holt, Rhinehart and Winston, pp. 549–69.

De Los Santos, N. (1999) LAPD Crusades Against Homies. *Hispanic*, 12(12): 20.

Dell, G. (2000) Acquisition and the Lexicon. In: M. Broe and J. Pierrehumbert (eds.) *Papers in Laboratory Phonology V.* Cambridge: Cambridge University Press, pp. 335–48.

Díaz, L. (2000) *Cuando sea grande me voy pál norte. La migración como contexto de socialización infantil en Ucácuaro, Michoacán.* Tesis de Maestría en Estudios Rurales, El Colegio de Michoacán.

Diaz-Campos, M. (2004) Acquisition of Sociolinguistic Variables in Spanish: Do Children Acquire Individual Lexical Forms or Variable Rules? In: T. Face (ed.) *Laboratory Approaches to Spanish Phonology*. Berlin: Mouton de Gruyter, pp. 221–36.

DiChiara, A., and R. Chabot (2003) Gangs and the Contemporary Urban Struggle: An Unappreciated Aspect of Gangs. In: L. Kontos, D. Brotherton, and L. Barrios (eds.) *Gangs and Society: Alternative Perspectives.* New York; Chichester [England]: Columbia University Press, pp. 77–94.

Dines, E. (1980) Variation in Discourse – "and Stuff Like That." *Language in Society*, 9: 13–39.

Domínguez, V. (1997) *White by Definition: Social Classification in Creole Louisiana.* New Brunswick, NJ: Rutgers University.

Donovan, J. (1992) California's Chicano Gang Subculture: The Journey from Pachuco "Sadistic Clowns" to a Norteno Society of Houses. *Latino Studies Journal*, 3(3): 29–44.

Donovan, J. (1993) An Introduction to Street Gangs, In: N. C. G. I. Association (ed.) *1993 Gang Training Seminar Handbook.* Sacramento, CA: Northern California Gang Investigators Association.

Duffy, M., and S. Gillig (2004) *Teen Gangs: A Global View.* Westport, CN: Greenwood Press.

Duranti, A. (2001) *Linguistic Anthropology: A Reader.* London: Blackwell.

Eckert, P. (1988) Adolescent Social Structure and the Spread of Linguistic Change. *Language in Society*, 17: 183–208.

Eckert, P. (1989) *Jocks and Burnouts: Social Categories and Identity in the High School.* New York: Teachers College Press.

Eckert, P. (2000) *Linguistic Variation as Social Practice: The Linguistic Construction of Identity in Belten High.* Oxford: Blackwell.

Eckert, P. (2006) *California Vowels.* www.stanford.edu/~eckert/vowels.html. Accessed October 15, 2006.

Eckert, P., and S. McConnell-Ginet (1992) Think Practically and Look Locally: Language and Gender as a Community-Based Practice. *Annual Review of Anthropology*, 21: 461–90.

Eckert, P., and N. Mendoza-Denton (2006) Getting Real in the Golden State (California). In: W. Wolfram and B. Ward (eds.) *American Voices: How Dialects Differ From Coast to Coast*. Malden, MA: Blackwell, pp. 139–43.

Eckert, P., and E. Wenger (2005) What is the Role of Power in Socio-linguistic Variation? *Journal of Sociolinguistics*, 9(4): 582–89.

Erlanger, H. (1979) Estrangement, Machismo, and Gang Violence. *Social Science Quarterly*, 60(2): 235–48.

Esbensen, F., and D. Huizinga (1993) Gangs, Drugs, and Delinquency in a Survey of Urban Youth. *Criminology*, 31: 565–89.

Espinoza, F. G. (1984) *A Historical Perspective on the Growth of Hispanic Gangs in Los Angeles County*. Long Beach, CA: California State University.

Faegin, C. (2001) Entering the Community: Fieldwork. In: J. K. Chambers, P. Trudgill, and N. Schilling-Estes (eds.) *The Handbook of Language Variation and Change*. Malden, MA: Blackwell Publishing, pp. 20–39.

Farr, M. (2003) Oral Traditions in Greater Mexico. *Oral Tradition*, 18(2): 159–61.

Ferguson, C. (1996) *Sociolinguistic Perspectives: Papers on Language in Society, 1959–1954*, T. Huebner, ed. Oxford: Oxford University Press.

Firth, J. R. (1964) On Social Linguistics. In: D. Hymes (ed.) *Language in Culture and Society: A Reader in Linguistics and Anthropology*. New York: Harper & Row, pp. 66–72.

Fischer, J. L. (1958) Social Influences on the Choice of a Linguistic Variant. *Word*, 14: 47–56.

Flege, J. (forthcoming) Language Contact in Bilingualism: Phonetic System Interactions, In: J. Cole and J. I. Hualde (eds.) *Papers in Laboratory Phonology 9*. Berlin: Mouton de Gruyter.

Fleisher, M. S. (1998) *Dead End Kids: Gang Girls and the Boys They Know*. Madison, WI: Wisconsin University Press.

Fleisher, M. S., and J. L. Krienert (2004) Life-Course Events, Social Networks, and the Emergence of Violence among Female Gang Members. *Journal of Community Psychology*, 32: 607–22.

Flores Farfán, J. A. (1999) *Cuatreros Somos y Toindioma Hablamos: Contactos y Conflictos En Nahuatl y el Espanol en el Sur de Mexico*. Mexico City: Centro de Investiggatgion Estudios Superiores en Antropologia Social (CIESAS).

Foley, D. E. (1990) *Learning Capitalist Culture: Deep in the Heart of Texas*. Philadelphia, PA: University of Pennsylvania Press.

Foucault, M. (1971) *Dits et Écrits vol II*. Paris: Gallimard.

Foucault, M. (1977) *Discipline and Punish: The Birth of the Prison*. New York: Pantheon Books.

Fought, C. (2003) *Chicano English in Context*. London: Palgrave.

Foulkes, P., and G. Docherty (2006) The Social Life of Phonetics and Phonology. *Journal of Phonetics*, 34(4): 409–38.

Fraser, B. (1988) Types of English Discourse Markers. *Acta Linguistica Hungarica*, 38: 19–33.

Frias, G. (1989) *Barrio Patriots: Killing and Dying for America*. Los Angeles, CA: G. F. Guerrero.

Fusco, C. (1994) The Other History of Intercultural Performance. *The Drama Review*, 38(1): 143–67.

Gal, S. (1978) Peasant Men Can't Get Wives: Language Change and Sex Roles in a Bilingual Community. *Language in Society*, 7(1): 1–43.

Gal, S. (1993) Diversity and Contestation in Linguistic Ideologies: German Speakers in Hungary. *Language in Society*, 22: 337–59.

Gal, S., and J. Irvine (2000) Language Ideology and Linguistic Differentiation. In: J. Irvine, S. Gal, and P. Kroskrity (eds.) *Regimes of Language*. Santa Fe, NM: School of American Research Press, pp. 35–84.

Galindo, D. L. (1987) *Linguistic Influence and Variation of the English of Chicano Adolescents in Austin, Texas*. PhD Dissertation, University of Texas at Austin.

García, M. (1984) Parameters of the East Los Angeles Speech Community. In: J. Ornstein (ed.) *Form and Function in Chicano English*. Rowley, MA: Newbury House, pp. 85–98.

García Saíz, M. C. (1989) *Las Castas Mexicanas: Un Género Pictórico Americano*. Milan, Italy: Olivetti.

Garfinkel, H. (1967) *Studies in Ethnomethodology*. Englewood Cliffs, New Jersey: Prentice-Hall Press.

Gaudio, R. (2001) White Men Do It Too: Racialized (Homo)Sexualities in Postcolonial Hausaland. *Journal of Linguistic Anthropology*, 11(1): 36–51.

Geertz, H., and C. Geertz (1964) Teknonymy in Bali: Parenthood, Age-Grading and Genealogical Amnesia. *The Journal of the Royal Anthropological Institute of Great Britain and Ireland*, 94(2): 94–108.

Gibson, M. A. (1988) *Accommodation without Assimilation: Sikh Immigrants in an American High School*. Ithaca, NY: Cornell University Press.

Gibson, M. A. (1997) Conclusion: Complicating the Immigrant/Involuntary Minority Typology. *Anthropology & Education Quarterly*, 28: 431–54.

Gibson, M. A., and J. U. Ogbu (1991) *Minority Status and Schooling: A Comparative Study of Immigrant and Involuntary Minorities*. New York: Garland.

Giles, H. (1979) Ethnicity Markers in Speech. In: K. R. Scherer and H. Giles (eds.) *Social Markers in Speech*. Cambridge: Cambridge University Press, pp. 251–89.

Gilmore, P. (1985) Gimme Room: School Resistance, Attitude and Access to Literacy. *Journal of Education*, 167: 111–28.

Godinez, M., and I. Maddieson (1985) Vowel Differences between Chicano and General Californian English. *International Journal of the Sociology of Language*, 53: 43–58.

Goffman, E. (1974) *Frame Analysis: An Essay on the Organization of Experience*. New York: Harper and Row.

Goldinger, S. (1997) Words and Voices: Perception and Production in an Episodic Lexicon. In: K. Johnson and J. W. Mullenix (eds.) *Talker Variability in Speech Processing*. San Diego, CA: Academic Press, pp. 33–66.

Goldinger, S., and T. Azuma (2003) Puzzle-Solving Science: The Quixotic Quest for Units in Speech Perception. *Journal of Phonetics*, 31: 305–20.

Goldstein, J. (1995) The Female Aesthetic Community. In: G. Marcus and F. Myers (eds.) *The Traffic in Culture: Refiguring Art in Anthropology*. Berkeley, CA: University of California Press, pp. 310–29.

Gomez-Peña, G. (2006) *On the Other Side of the Mexican Mirror*. Pochanostra. http://www.pochanostra.com/antes/jazz_pocha2/mainpages/otherside.htm. Accessed September 1, 2006.

Goodwin, C. (1981) *Conversational Organization: Interaction between Speakers and Hearers*. New York: Academic Press.

Goodwin, C., and A. Duranti (eds.) (1992) *Rethinking Context: Language as an Interactive Phenomenon*. Cambridge: Cambridge University Press.

Goodwin, M. H. (1990) *He-Said-She-Said: Talk as Social Organization among Black Children*. Bloomington, IN: Indiana University Press.

Goodwin, M. H., C. Goodwin and M. Yaeger-Dror (2002) Multi-Modality in Girls' Game Disputes. *Journal of Pragmatics*, 34: 1621–49.

Gould, S. J. (1996) *The Mismeasure of Man*. New York: W.W. Norton.

Gouldner, A. G. (1957) Cosmopolitans and Locals: Toward An Analysis of Latent Social Roles. *Administrative Science Quarterly* 2, pp. 444–80.

Gowen, A. (2002) Latino Toys Criticized as Stereotypes: "Homies" Spark Uproar over Impact on Children. *Washington Post*, June 18, p. B01.

Goyvaerts, D. L. (1996) Kibalele: Form and Function of a Secret Language in Bukavu (Zaire). *Journal of Pragmatics*, 25: 123–43.

Gramsci, A. (1971) *Selections from the Prison Notebooks*. New York: International.

Grice, P. (1989) *Studies in the Way of Words*. Cambridge, MA: Harvard University Press.

Gumperz, J. (1958) Dialect Differences and Social Stratification in a North Indian Village. *American Anthropologist* (New Series), 60(4): 668–82.

Gumperz, J. (1971) *Language in Social Groups*. Stanford, CA: Stanford University Press.

Gumperz, J., and D. Berenz (1993) On Data Collection. In: J. Edwards and M. Lampert (eds.) *Talking Data: Transcription and Coding in Discourse Research*. Hillsdale, NJ: Erlbaum, pp. 91–121.

Gutiérrez Gonzalez, N. (1993) *Qué Trabajos Pasa Carlos: La Construcción Interactiva del Albur en Tepito*. Tuxtla Gutiérrez: Instituto Chiapaneco de Cultura.

Haeri, N. (1996) *The Sociolinguistic Market of Cairo: Gender, Class, and Education*. Cairo; New York: Kegan Paul International; New York: Columbia University Press.

Hagedorn, J. (1988) *People and Folks: Gangs, Crime and the Underclass in a Rustbelt City*. Chicago: Lakeview Press.

Hagedorn, J. (2007) Gangs and Politics. In: L. Shaerrod (ed.) *Youth Activism and International Encyclopedia.* http://gangresearch.net/GangResearch/Policy/gangsinpolitics_files/youthact_files/gangsinpolitics.html. Accessed February 12, 2007.

Haiman, J. (1998) *Talk is Cheap: Sarcasm, Alienation, and the Evolution of Language.* New York: Oxford University Press.

Hale, C. (1996) Mestizaje, Hybridity, and the Cultural Politics of Difference in Post-Revolutionary Central America. *Journal of Latin American Anthropology,* 2(1): 34–61.

Hall, K. (2001) Performativity. In: A. Duranti (ed.) *Key Terms in Language and Culture.* Malden, MA: Blackwell, pp. 180–83.

Hall, S. (1985) Signification, Representation, Ideology: Althusser and the Post-Structuralist Debates. *Critical Studies in Mass Communication,* 2(2): 91–114.

Hall, S., and T. Jefferson (eds.) (1976) *Resistance Through Rituals: Youth Subcultures in Post-War Britain.* London: Hutchinson.

Halliday, M. A. K. (1976) Anti-Language. *American Anthropologist,* 78(3): 570–84.

Hancock, I. (1984) Shelta and Polari. In: P. Trudgill (ed.) *The Languages of the British Isles.* Cambridge: Cambridge University Press, pp. 384–403.

Harrington J., S. Palethorpe, and C. Watson (2000) Monophthongal Vowel Changes in Received Pronunciation: an Acoustic Analysis of the Queen's Christmas Broadcasts. *Journal of the International Phonetic Association,* 30(1–2): 63–78.

Harris, M. (1988) *Cholas: Latino Girls and Gangs.* New York: AMS Press.

Haskins, J. (1974) *Street Gangs: Yesterday and Today.* New York: Hastings House.

Hazlehurst, K., and C. Hazlehurst (eds.) (1998) *Gangs and Youth Subcultures: International Explorations.* New Brunswick: Transaction Publishers.

Hebdige, D. (1979) *Subculture: The Meaning of Style.* London: Methuen.

Hegel, G. W. F. (1996) *Dialectic of Desire and Recognition: Texts and Commentary,* J. O'Neill, ed. Albany, NY: SUNY Press.

Hendrickson, L. R. (2004) *"Thirdspace" Re-figurations of Kinship and Hybrid Ethnicity in the Works of Josefina Pelayo Mendoza, Alma Lopez, and Noni Olabisi.* Madison, MN: UW-Madison Chicana/o Studies Program.

Hewitt, R. (1986) *White Talk Black Talk: Interracial Friendship and Communication amongst Adolescents.* Cambridge: Cambridge University Press.

Hill, J. H. (1998) Language, Race, and White Public Space. *American Anthropologist,* 100(3): 680–9.

Hilliard, J. (1983) *Observations of Rural Chicano Youth Gang Graffiti: Their Meanings and Implications.* Unpublished MA Thesis, Fresno, California State University.

Hinton, L., B. Moonwomon, S. Bremner, C. Luthin, et al. (1987) It's Not Just the Valley Girls: A Study of California English. *Berkeley Linguistic Society,* 13: 117–28.

Hodkinson, P. (2002) *Goth: Identity, Style, and Subculture*. Oxford: Berg.

Hondagneu-Sotelo, P. (2001) *Doméstica: Immigrant Workers Cleaning and Caring in the Shadows of Affluence*. Berkeley, CA: University of California Press.

Hopwood, K. (1999) *Organised Crime in Antiquity*. London: Duckworth.

Horrox, R. (1994) *The Black Death*. Manchester: Manchester University Press.

Houston, A. (1985) *Continuity and Change in English Morphology: The Variable (ING)*. Unpublished PhD Dissertation, University of Pennsylvania.

Huff, R. G. (ed.) (2002) *Gangs in America III*. Thousand Oaks, CA: Sage Publications.

Hunt, G., and K. Joe-Laidler (2001) Situations of Violence in the Lives of Girl Gang Members. *Health Care for Women International*, 22: 363–84.

Hunt, G., K. Joe-Laidler, and K. Evans (2002) The Meaning and Gendered Culture of Getting High: Gang Girls and Drug Use Issues. *Contemporary Drug Problems*, 29: 375–415.

Hunt, G., K. Joe-Laidler, and K. Mackenzie (2005) Moving into Motherhood: Gang Girls and Controlled Risk. *Youth & Society*, 36: 333–73.

Hunt, G., K. Joe-Laidler, and K. Mackenzie (2000) "Chillin," Being Dogged and Getting Buzzed: Alcohol in the Lives of Female Gang Members. *Drug Education and Prevention Policy*, 7: 331–53.

Hutchins, E. (1995) *Cognition in the Wild*. Cambridge, MA: MIT Press.

Hyams, M. (2003) Adolescent Latina Bodyspaces: Making Homegirls, Home-bodies and Homeplaces. *Antipode*, 35(3): 536–58.

Hymes, D. (ed.) (1964) *Language in Culture and Society: a Reader in Linguistics and Anthropology*. New York: Harper & Row.

Hymes, D. (1971) Competence and Performance in Linguistic Theory. In: R. Huxley and E. Ingram (eds.) *Language Acquisition: Models and Methods*. London: Academic Press, pp. 3–24.

Hymes, D. (1977) *Foundations of Sociolinguistics: An Ethnographic Approach*. London: Tavistock.

Ingold, T. (2001a) From the Transmission of Representations to the Education of Attention. In: H. Whitehouse (ed.) *The Debated Mind: Evolutionary Psychology Versus Ethnography*. Oxford: Berg, pp. 113–53.

Ingold, T. (2001b) Beyond Art and Technology: the Anthropology of Skill. In: B. Schiffer (ed.) *Anthropological Perspectives on Technology*. Albuquerque, NM: University of New Mexico Press, pp. 17–31.

Irvine, J. (2001) "Style" as Distinctiveness: the Culture and Ideology of Linguistic Differentiation. In: P. Eckert and J. Rickford (eds.) *Style and Sociolinguistic Variation*. Cambridge: Cambridge University Press.

Irvine, J., and S. Gal (2000) Language Ideology and Linguistic Differentiation. In: P. V. Kroskrity (ed.) *Regimes of Language: Ideologies, Polities, and Identities*. Santa Fe, NM: School of American Research, pp. 35–84.

Jacobs-Huey, L. (2006) *From the Kitchen to the Parlor: Language and Becoming in African American Women's Hair Care*. Oxford: Oxford University Press.

Joe, K. A., and M. Chesney-Lind (1995) "Just Every Mother's Angel": An Analysis of Gender and Ethnic Variations in Youth Gang Membership. *Gender & Society*, 9: 408–30.

Joe-Laidler, K. A., and G. Hunt (2001) Accomplished Femininity among the Girls in the Gang. *British Journal of Criminology*, 41: 656–78.

Joe-Laidler, K. A., and G. Hunt (1997) Violence and Social Organization in Female Gangs. *Social Justice*, 24: 148–69.

Johnson, K. (1997) Speech Perception without Speaker Normalization: An Exemplar Model. In: K. Johnson and J. W. Mullennix (eds.) *Talker Variability in Speech Processing*. San Diego, CA: Academic Press, 145–65.

Johnson, K. (2006) Resonance in an Exemplar-Based Model: The Emergence of Social Identity and Phonology. *Journal of Phonetics*, 34(4): 485–99.

Jucker, A. (1993) The Discourse Marker *well*: A Relevance-Theoretical Account. *Journal of Pragmatics*, 19: 435–52.

Jucker, A., Smith, S. W., and T. Ludge (2003) Interactive Aspects of Vagueness in Conversation. *Journal of Pragmatics*, 35(12): 1737–69.

Kamil, M., J. A. Langer, and T. Shanahan (1985) *Understanding Reading and Writing Research*. Boston: Allyn and Bacon.

Katzew, I. (1996) Casta Painting: Identity and Social Stratification in Colonial Mexico. In *New World Orders: Casta Painting and Colonial Latin America. Exhibition Catalog*. New York: America Society Art Gallery.

Katzew, I. (2000) *Ordering the Colony: Casta Painting and the Imaging of Race in Eighteenth Century Mexico*. PhD Dissertation, NYU, New York.

Khattab, G. (forthcoming) Variation in Vowel Production by English-Arabic Bilinguals. In: J. Cole and J. I. Hualde (eds.) *Papers in Laboratory Phonology 9*. Berlin: Mouton de Gruyter.

Kiesling, S. F. (2004) DUDE. *American Speech*, 79(3): 281–305.

Kiparsky, P. (1995) Indo-European Origins of Germanic Syntax. In: A. Battye and I. Roberts (eds.) *Clause Structure and Language Change*. Oxford: Oxford University Press, pp. 140–70.

Klein, M. (1968) *From Associate to Guilt: The Gangs Guidance Project in Juvenile Gang Intervention*. Los Angeles, CA: Youth Studies Center, University of Southern California.

Klein, M. (1995) *The American Street Gang: It's Nature, Prevalence and Control*. New York: Oxford University Press.

Klor de Alva, J. (1996) Mestizaje from New Spain to Aztlán. In: I. Katzew and J. A. Farmer (eds.) *New World Orders: Casta Painting and Colonial Latin America*. New York: Americas Society Art Gallery, pp. 58–71.

KOLD News 13 (2006) Tucson Police Strengthens Gang Unit. Broadcast September 20, 2006, 10 p.m. News.

Kondo, D. (1986) Dissolution and Reconstitution of Self: Implications for Anthropological Epistemology. *Cultural Anthropology*, 1: 74–88.

Kondo, D. (1990) *Crafting Selves: Power, Gender, and Discourses of Identity in a Japanese Workplace.* Chicago: University of Chicago Press.

LaBrack, B., and K. Leonard. (1984) Conflict and Compatibility in Punjabi-Mexican Immigrant Families in Rural California, 1915–1965. *Journal of Marriage and the Family,* 46(3): 527–37.

Labov, W. (1964) Phonological Correlates of Social Stratification. *American Anthropologist,* 66(6): 164–76.

Labov, W. (1969) Contraction, Deletion, and Inherent Variability of the English Copula. *Language,* 45: 715–62.

Labov, W. (1972a) *Language in the Inner City: Studies in the Black English Vernacular.* Philadelphia, PA: University of Pennsylvania.

Labov, W. (1972b) Some Principles of Linguistic Methodology. *Language in Society,* 1: 97–120.

Labov, W. (1972c) *Sociolinguistic Patterns.* Philadelphia, PA: University of Pennsylvania Press.

Labov, W. (1972d) Negative Attraction and Negative Concord in English Grammar. *Language,* 48(4): 773–818.

Labov, W. (1990) The Intersection of Sex and Class in the Course of Linguistic Change. *Language Variation and Change,* 2: 205–54.

Labov, W. (2001) *Principles of Linguistic Change: Social Factors.* Oxford: Blackwell Publishing.

Labov, W., and W. Harris (1986) De Facto Segregation of Black and White Vernaculars. In: D. Sankoff (ed.) *Diversity and Diachrony.* Amsterdam: John Benjamins.

Laidler, K. J., and G. Hunt (1997) Violence and Social Organization in Female Gangs. *Social Justice,* 24(4): 148.

Lave, J., and Wenger, E. (1991) *Situated Learning: Legitimate Peripheral Participation.* Cambridge: Cambridge University Press.

Lawless, E. (1992) "I was afraid someone like you . . . an outsider . . . would misunderstand." Negotiating Interpretive Differences between Ethnographers and Subjects. *The Journal of American Folklore,* 105(417): 302–14.

Lawson, R. (2005) *Sociolinguistic Constructions of Identity in a Glasgow High School.* Unpublished Masters of Philosophy Thesis, Department of English Language, University of Glasgow.

Leach, E. (1954) *Political Systems of Highland Burma: A Study of Kachin Social Structure.* London: Athlene.

Leibniz, G. W. (1985) *Monadology and Other Philosophical Writings.* New York: Taylor & Francis.

Lee, B. (1999) *Chinese Playground: A Memoir.* San Francisco, CA: Rhapsody Press.

Lefkowitz, N. (1991) *Talking Backwards, Looking Forwards: The French Language Game Verlan.* Tubingen: Narr.

Leonard, K. (2006) *The Battle for Los Angeles: Racial Ideology and World War II.* Albuquerque, NM: University of New Mexico Press.

Le Page, R. B., and A. Tabouret-Keller (1985) *Acts of Identity: Creole-Based Approaches to Language and Ethnicity.* Cambridge: Cambridge University Press.

Levinson, S. C. (1983) *Pragmatics.* Cambridge: Cambridge University Press.

Lévi-Strauss, C. (1966) *The Savage Mind.* Chicago, IL: University of Chicago Press.

Levy, J. (1975) *Cesar Chavez: Autobiography of La Causa.* New York: Norton.

Limnander, A. (2001) *Spring 2002 Ready-to-Wear: Christian Dior Runway Review.* http://www.style.com/fashionshows/collections/S2002RTW/review/CDIOR. Accessed February 1, 2007.

Limón, J. (1994) *Dancing with the Devil: Society and Cultural Poetics in Mexican-American South Texas.* Madison, WI: University of Wisconsin Press.

Linde, C. (2000) The Acquisition of a Speaker by a Story: How History Becomes Memory and Identity. *Ethos*: Special Issue on History and Subjectivity, 28(4): 608–32.

Lindel, B. (1991) In Yuba City: Traces Remain of Fading Mexican-Hindu Culture. *Sacramento Bee*, November 11, p. B1.

Lo, A. (1999) Codeswitching, Speech Community Membership, and the Construction of Ethnic Identity. *Journal of Sociolinguistics*, 3(4): 461–79.

López Castro, G. (2005) Niños, Socialización y Migración a Estados Unidos en Michoacán. *CMD Working Paper #05-02d.* Princeton, NJ: Center for Migration and Development.

Lucas, T. (1998) Youth Gangs and Moral Panics in Santa Cruz, California. In: T. Skelton, and G. Valentine (eds.) *Cool Places: Geographies of Youth Cultures* London: Routledge, pp. 145–60.

Luce, P., and D. Pisoni (1998) Recognizing Spoken Words: The Neighborhood Activation Model. *Ear & Hearing*, 19(1): 1–36.

Lyotard, J.-F. (1984) *The Postmodern Condition.* Manchester: Manchester University Press.

Madrid, D. (2006) *Like It Or Not, Gangs Are San Jose's Social Movements.* http://www.siliconvalleydebug.com/story/062205/stories/notgangs.html. Accessed August 8, 2006.

Main, F. (2006) Gangs Claim Their Turf in Iraq: Experts See More Members in Uniform, Warn of Effect at Home. *Chicago Sun-Times*, May 11, p. 16.

Malinowski, B. (1937, 1964) The Dilemma of Contemporary Linguistics. In: D. Hymes (ed.) *Language in Culture and Society: A Reader in Linguistics and Anthropology.* New York: Harper & Row, pp. 63–72.

Manilow, B., B. Sussman, and J. Feldman (1978) *Copacabana: At the Copa.* Kamakazi Music Corp. BMI.

Mankekar, P. (2002) 'India Shopping': Indian Grocery Stores and Transnational Configurations of Belonging. *Ethnos*, 67(1): 75–97.

Marcus, G., and M. Fischer (1986) *Anthropology as Cultural Critique: An Experimental Moment in the Human Sciences.* Chicago, IL: University of Chicago Press.

Martín, A. (2005) Historia de las Lecturas Infantiles. Las Aleluyas: Primera Lectura y Primeras Imagines Para Niños (Siglos XVII–XIX). *CLIJ: Cuadernos de Literatura Infantil y Juvenil*, 179: 44–53.

Marx, K. (1981) *Capital: A Critique of Political Economy*. London: Penguin.

Mascia-Lees, F., P. Sharpe, and C. Ballerino Cohen (1989) The Postmodernist Turn in Anthropology: Cautions from a Feminist Perspective. *Signs*, 15(1): 7–33.

Maseko, Z., et al. (1998) *The Life and Times of Sara Baartman* [videorecording]: "The Hottentot Venus." New York: First Run Icarus Films.

Maseko, Z., and G. Smith (2003) *The Return of Sara Baartman* [videorecording]: "The Hottentot Venus." New York: First Run Icarus Films.

Matute-Bianchi, M. E. (1986) Ethnic Identities and Patterns of School Success and Failure among Mexican-Descent and Japanese-American Students in a California High School. *American Journal of Education*, 95: 233–55.

Matute-Bianchi, M. E. (1991) Situational Ethnicity and Patterns of School Performance among Immigrant and Nonimmigrant Mexican-Descent Students. In: J. U. Ogbu and M. A. Gibson (eds.) *Minority Status and Schooling*. New York: Garland, pp. 205–47.

McCorkle, R., and T. Miethe (2002) *Panic: The Social Construction of the Street Gang Problem*. Upper Saddle River, NJ: Prentice-Hall, Inc.

McLemore, C. (1991) *The Pragmatic Interpretation of English Intonation: Sorority Speech*. Unpublished PhD Dissertation, University of Texas at Austin.

McRobbie, A. (1986) *Feminism and Youth Culture* (2nd edn). Basingstoke: Macmillan.

McRobbie, A., and J. Garber (1976) Girls and Subcultures. In: S. Hall and T. Jefferson (eds.) *Resistance Through Rituals*. London: Routledge, pp. 208–22.

Mendoza, R. (2005) *Mexican Mafia: From Altar Boy to Hit Man*. Corona, CA: Whitley & Associates.

Mendoza-Denton, N. (1993) *On Concerning*. Paper presented at Koln-Berkeley Stanford Workshop on Grammaticalization.

Mendoza-Denton, N. (1995) "Oyes Tú": Linguistic Stereotyping as Stance and Alliance. In: J. Loftin and P. Silberman (eds.) *SALSA II: Proceedings of the Second Annual Symposium about Language and Society – Austin*. Austin, TX: Department of Linguistics, University of Texas.

Mendoza-Denton, N. (1996) "Muy Macha": Gender and Ideology in Gang Girls' Discourse about Makeup. *Ethnos*, 61(1–2): 47–63.

Mendoza-Denton, N. (1997) *Chicana/Mexicana Identity and Linguistic Variation: An ethnographic and Sociolinguistic Study of Gang Affiliation in an Urban High School*. PhD Dissertation, Stanford University Linguistics.

Mendoza-Denton, N. (1999) Fighting Words: Latina Girls, Gangs, and Language Attitudes. In: L. Galindo and N. Gonzalez-Vasquez (eds.) *Speaking Chicana*. University of Arizona Press, pp. 39–56.

Mendoza-Denton, N. (2002) Language and Identity. In: J. K. Chambers, P. Trudgill, and N. Schilling-Estes (eds.) *The Handbook of Language Variation and Change.* Malden, MA: Blackwell Publishing, pp. 475–99.

Mendoza-Denton, N. (forthcoming) Sociolinguistic Extensions of Exemplar Theory. In: J. Cole and J. I. Hualde (eds.) *Papers in Laboratory Phonology 9.* Berlin: Mouton de Gruyter.

Mendoza-Denton, N., Hay, J., and Jannedy, S. (2003) Probabilistic Socio-linguistics: Beyond Variable Rules. In: R. Bod, J. Hay, and S. Jannedy (eds.) *Probabilistic Linguistics.* Boston, MA: MIT Press, pp. 98–138.

Mendoza-Denton, N., and M. Iwai (1993) "They Speak More Caucasian": Generational Differences in the Speech of Japanese Americans. In: Queen and Barrett (eds.) *SALSA 1: Proceedings of the First Annual Symposium About Language and Society ~ Austin.* Austin, TX: Department of Linguistics, University of Texas, pp. 58–67.

Mendoza-Denton, R. (in press) Stigma. In: W. A. Darity (ed.) *International Encyclopedia of the Social Sciences* (2nd edn). Farmington Hills, MI: Thomson Gale.

Merrill, C. (1987) *Mexican-American English in McAllen, Texas: Features of Accentedness in the English of Native Spanish Bilinguals.* PhD Dissertation, Department of Linguistics, The University of Texas at Austin.

Merton, R. K. (1938) Social Structure and Anomie. *American Sociological Review,* 3(5): 672–82.

Merton, R. K. (1949) *Social Theory and Social Structure: Toward the Codification of Theory and Research.* Glencoe, IL: Freepress.

Messing, J. (2003) *Ideological Multiplicity in Discourse: Language Shift and Bilingual Schooling in Tlaxcala, Mexico.* Unpublished Thesis, University of Arizona.

Meranze, M. (1966) *Laboratories of Virtue: Punishment, Revolution, and Authority in Philadelphia, 1760–1835.* Chapel Hill, NC: University of North Carolina Press.

Metsala, J. L. (1997) An Examination of Word Frequency and Neighborhood Density in the Development of Spoken-Word Recognition. *Memory & Cognition,* 25(1): 47–56.

Metcalf, A. (1979) *Chicano English.* Arlington, VA: Center for Applied Linguistics.

Meyerhoff, M. (1999) Sorry in the Pacific: Defining Communities, Defining Practices. *Language in Society,* 28: 225–38.

Miller, J. (2001) *One of the Guys: Girls, Gangs and Gender.* New York: Oxford University Press.

Miller, J. and R. K. Brunson (2000) Gender Dynamics in Youth Gangs: A Comparison of Male and Female Accounts. *Justice Quarterly,* 17(3): 801–30.

Milroy, L. (1985) *Language and Social Networks.* Oxford: Blackwell.

Milroy, L. (1987) *Observing and Analyzing Natural Language: A Critical Account of Sociolinguistic Method.* London: Basil Blackwell.

Mintz, S. (1985) *Sweetness and Power: The Place of Sugar in Modern History.* New York: Penguin.

Miranda, M. (2003) *Homegirls in the Public Sphere.* Austin, TX: University of Texas Press.

Mirandé, A. (1998) *Hombres y Machos: Masculinity and Latino Culture.* Boulder, CO: Westview Press.

Modan, G. (2006) *Turf Wars: Discourse, Diversity and the Politics of Place.* London: Blackwell Publication.

Modan, G., and Mendoza-Denton, N. (2005) The Afterlife of Research. Presented at the Amer. Anthropological Association.

de Montaigne, M. (1991) *The Complete Essays.* Trans. M.A. Screech. New York: Penguin.

Monti, D. (1994) *Wannabe: Gangs in the Suburbs and Schools.* Oxford: Oxford University Press.

Moore, E. (2004) *Explaining the Correlation between Social Identity and Language Use: The Community of Practice.* Paper delivered at the BAAL/CUP Language and Identity Seminar. University of Reading.

Moore, J. (1978) *Homeboys: Gangs, Drugs, and Prisons in the Barrios of Los Angeles.* Philadelphia, PA: Temple University Press.

Moore, J. (1991) *Going Down to the Barrio: Homeboys and Homegirls in Change.* Oxford: Blackwell.

Moore, J. (1994) The Chola Life Course: Chicana Heroin Users and the Barrio Gang. *International Journal of Addictions*, 29: 1115–26.

Moore, J., and J. Hagedorn (1996) What Happens to Girls in the Gang? In: C. R. Huff (ed.) *Gangs in America* (2nd edn). Thousand Oaks, CA: Sage Publications, pp. 205–18.

Moore, J., and J. Hagedorn (2001) *Female Gangs: A Focus on Research.* Office of Juvenile Justice and Delinquency Prevention. Washington, DC: US Department of Justice, Office of Justice Programs.

Moore, J., and D. Vigil (1993) Barrios in Transition. In: J. Moore and R. Pinderhughes (eds.) *The Barrios: Latinos and the Underclass Debate.* New York: Russell Sage Publications, pp. 27–50.

Moore, J., D. Vigil, and R. García (1983) Residence and Territoriality in Chicago Gangs. *Social Problems*, 31(2): 182–94.

Moraga, C., and G. Anzaldúa (1983) *This Bridge Called My Back: Writings by Radical Women of Color.* New York: Kitchen Table, Women of Color Press.

Morgan, M. (1998) More than a Mood or an Attitude: Discourse and Verbal Genres in African-American Culture. In: S. S. Mufwene, J. Baugh, and J. R. Rickford (eds.) *African American English: Structure, History, Usage.* London: Routledge, pp. 251–81.

Moreno-Álvarez, G. (2001) *El Uso del Albur en La Frontera.* Unpublished MA Thesis, New Mexico State University, Las Cruces.

Morrill, C., et al. (2000) *Telling Tales in School: Youth Culture and Conflict Narratives. Law & Society Review*, 34(3): 521–65.

Movimiento de Jóvenes Encuentristas (1999) *Jóvenes Sedientos de Amor: Voces de Ilobasco.* El Salvador: JME, Impresos Gráficos.

Mowry, J. (1992) *Way Past Cool.* New York: Farrar, Straus and Giroux.

Muggleton, D., and R. Weinzierl (2003) *The Post-Subcultures Reader.* Oxford: Berg.

Muniz, M. (1993) *Nondelinquent and Nonviolent Group Activities: A Comparison of Gang and Nongang Latino Youths.* Unpublished MA Thesis, California State University, Long Beach.

Myers-Scotton, C. (1995) *Social Motivations for Codeswitching.* Oxford: Oxford University Press.

National Coalition of Advocates for Students (1988) *New Voices: Immigrant Students in U.S. Public Schools.* Boston, MA: National Coalition of Advocates for Students.

National Institute of Justice, US Department of Justice (1995) *Research in Brief, Prosecuting Gangs: A National Assessment.* Washington, DC: U.S. Department of Justice, National Institute of Justice.

Nayak, A. (2003) *Race, Place and Globalization: Youth Cultures in a Changing World.* Oxford: Berg.

Nichter, M. (2000) *Fat Talk: What Girls and Their Parents Say about Dieting.* Cambridge, MA: Harvard University Press.

Niedzielski, N. (1999) The Effect of Social Information on the Perception of Sociolinguistic Variables. *Journal of Language and Social Psychology,* 18: 62–85.

Norrby, C., and J. Winter (2001) *Affiliation in Adolescents' Use of Discourse Extenders.* Proceedings of the 2001 Conference of the Australian Linguistic Society.

Nosofsky, R. (1987) Attention and Learning Processes in the Identification and Categorization of Integral Stimuli. *Journal of Experimental Psychology: Learning, Memory, and Cognition,* 13: 87–108.

Northern California Gang Investigators Association (1993) *Gang Training Seminar Handbook.* Sacramento, CA: Northern California Gang Investigators Association.

Nurge, D. (2003) Liberating Yet Limiting: The Paradox of Female Gang Membership. In: L. Kontos, D. Brotherton, and L. Barrios (eds.) *Gangs and Society: Alternative Perspectives.* New York; Chichester [England]: Columbia University Press, pp. 161–82.

Oboler, S., and A. Dzidzienyo (2005) *Neither Enemies Nor Friends: Latinos, Blacks, Afro-Latinos.* New York: Palgrave MacMillian.

Ochs, E. (1979) Transcription as Theory. In: E. Ochs (ed.) *Developmental Pragmatics.* New York: Academic Press, pp. 43–72.

Ochs, E. (1981) Indexing Gender. In: A. Duranti and Goodwin, C. (eds.) *Rethinking Context: Language as an Interactive Phenomenon,* Cambridge: Cambridge University Press.

Ochs, E., and L. Capps (1996) Narrating the Self. *Annual Review of Anthropology,* 25: 19–43.

Ogbu, J. U. (1999) Beyond Language: Ebonics, Proper English, and Identity in a Black American Speech Community. *American Educational Research Journal,* 1(2): 147–84.

Orenstein, P. (1994) *Schoolgirls.* New York: Doubleday.

Overstreet, M. (1999) *Whales, Candlelight, and Stuff Like That.* Oxford: Oxford University Press.

Padilla, F. (1992) *The Gang as an American Enterprise.* New Brunswick, NJ: Rutgers University Press.

Paredes, A. (1993) *Folklore and Culture on the Texas-Mexican Border.* Austin, TX: University of Texas Press.

Park, R. E. (1928) Human Migration and the Marginal Man. *American Journal of Sociology,* 33(6): 881–93.

Park, R. E. (1952) *Human Communities: the City and Human Ecology.* Glencoe, IL: The Free Press.

Patai, D. (1994) Sick and Tired of Scholars' Nouveau Solipsism. *The Chronicle of Higher Education,* 40: 25.

Paz, O. (1950) *El Laberinto de la Soledad.* Mexico City: Cuadernos Americanos. *pelon408* (2006) V.T.V., http://www.youtube.com/watch?v=eGUfKW7cogY&feature=PlayList&p=4662C048C89FDA99&index=3. Accessed August 8, 2006.

Penfield, J., and J. Ornstein-Galicia (1985) *Chicano English: An Ethnic Contact Dialect.* Amsterdam: Benjamins.

Peñalosa, F. (1980) *Chicano Sociolinguistics: A Brief Introduction.* Rowley, MA: Newbury House.

Perlmann, J. (1988) *Ethnic Differences: Schooling and Social Structure among the Irish, Italians, Jews and Blacks in an American City.* Cambridge: Cambridge University Press.

Peterson, G. E., and H. L. Barney (1952) Control Methods Used in a Study of the Vowels. *Journal of the Acoustic Society of America,* 24: 175–84.

Petitto, L. A., et al. (2001) Language Rhythms in Baby Hand Movements. *Nature,* 413(6851): 35.

Pierrehumbert, J. (2003) Probabilistic Phonology: Discrimination and Robustness. In: R. Bod, J. Hay, and S. Jannedy (eds.) *Probability Theory in Linguistics.* Cambridge, MA: MIT Press, pp. 177–228.

Pinsky, M. (1987) The Mexican-Hindu Connection: In a Search for their Roots, Descendants Discover a Moving Tale of Loneliness and Racism, by Mark I. Pinsky. *Los Angeles Times,* December 21, pt. V, pp. 9–12.

Philips, S. (1998) Language Ideologies in Institutions of Power: A Commentary. In: B. Schieffelin, K. Woolard, and P. V. Kroskrity (eds.) *Language Ideologies: Practice and Theory.* Oxford: Oxford University Press, pp. 211–25.

Phillips, B. (2007) *Word Frequency and Lexical Diffusion.* Basingstoke: Palgrave Macmillan.

Phillips, S. A. (1999) *Wallbangin': Graffiti and Gangs in L.A.* Chicago, IL: University of Chicago Press.

Podesva, R. (2006) *Phonetic Detail and Sociolinguistic Variation: Its Significance and Role in the Construction of Social Meaning.* PhD Dissertation, Stanford University.

Portes, A., & R. G. Rumbaut (1996) *Immigrant America: A Portrait* (2nd edn). Berkeley, CA: University of California Press.

Portillos, E. (1999) Women, Men and Gangs: The Social Construction of Gender in the Barrio. In: M. Chesney-Lind and J. Hagedorn (eds.) *Female Gangs in America: Essays on Girls, Gangs and Gender.* Chicago, IL: Lakeview Press, pp. 232–44.

Portillos, E., N. Jurik, and M. Zatz (1996) Machismo and Chicano/a Gangs: Symbolic Resistance or Oppression? *Free Inquiry in Creative Sociology,* 24: 175–84.

Pratt, M. L. (1986) Fieldwork in Common Places. In: J. Clifford and G. E. Marcus (eds.) *Writing Culture: The Poetics and Politics of Ethnography.* Berkeley: University of California Press, pp. 27–50.

Preston, D. (1986) *Perceptual Dialectology: Nonlinguists' View of Areal Linguistics.* Dordrecht: Foris.

Purnell, T., W. Idsardi, and J. Baugh (1999) Perceptual and Phonetic Experiments on American English Dialect Identification. *Journal of Language and Social Psychology,* 18(1): 10–30.

Quicker, J. C. (1983) *Homegirls: Characterizing Chicana Gangs.* San Pedro, CA: International University Press.

Quirk, R., S. Greenbaum, G. Leech, and J. Svartvik (1972) *A Grammar of Contemporary English.* London: Oxford University Press.

Quirk, R., S. Greenbaum, G. Leech, and J. Svartvik (1985) *A Comprehensive Grammar of the English Language.* New York: Longman.

Rampton, B. (1995) *Crossing: Language and Ethnicity among Adolescents* (Real Language Series). London; New York: Longman.

Rampton, B. (1999) Sociolinguistics and Cultural Studies: New Ethnicities, Liminality and Interaction. *Social Semiotics,* 9(3): 355–73.

Rand, D., and D. Sankoff (1990) GOLDVARB: A Variable Rule Application for the Macintosh, Version 2. Montreal: Center for Mathematical Research, University of Montreal.

Rawlings, L. (1999) *Condottieri and Clansmen.* In: K. Hopwood (ed.) *Organised Crime in Antiquity.* London: David Brown Book Company, pp. 97–127.

Rickford, J. R. (1986) The Need for New Approaches to Social Class in Sociolinguistics. *Language and Communication,* 5(3): 215–21.

Rickford, J. R. (1991) Sociolinguistic Variation in Cane Walk: A Quantitative Case Study. In: J. Cheshire (ed.) *English Around the World: Sociolinguistic Perspectives.* Cambridge: Cambridge University Press, pp. 609–16.

Rickford, J. R. (1997) Unequal Partnership: Sociolinguistics and the African American Speech Community. *Language in Society,* 26: 161–97.

Rickford, J., A. Ball, R. Blake, R. Jackson, and N. Martin (1991) Rappin on the Copula Coffin: Theoretical and Methodological Issues in the Analysis of Variation in African American Vernacular English. *Language Variation and Change*, 3: 103–32.

Rickford, J., and F. McNair-Knox (1994) Addressee- and Topic-Influenced Style Shift: A Quantitative Sociolinguistics Study. In: D. Biber and E. Finegan (eds.) *Sociolinguistic Perspectives on Register*. New York: Oxford University Press, pp. 235–76.

Ritzer, G. (2003) Rethinking Globalization: Glocalization/Grobalization and Something/Nothing. *Sociological Theory*, 21(3): 193–209.

Rodriguez, L. (1993) *Mi Vida Loca: Gang Days in L.A.* New York: Touchstone.

Roscoe, P. B. (1995) The Perils of "Positivism" in Cultural Anthropology. *American Anthropologist*, 97(3): 492–504.

Rose, M. (2006) Language, Place and Identity in Later Life. PhD Dissertation, Stanford University.

Roth-Gordon, J. (forthcoming) Youth, Slang, and Pragmatic Expressions: Examples from Brazilian Portuguese. *Journal of Sociolinguistics*.

Rymes, B. (2001) *Conversational Borderlands: Language and Identity in an Alternative Urban High School*. New York: Teachers College Press.

Sacks, H. (1992) *Lectures on Conversation*. Cambridge, MA: Blackwell Publishing.

Sánchez-Jankowski, M. (1991) *Islands in the Street: Gangs and American Urban Society*. Berkeley, CA: University of California Press.

Sanday, P. (1990) *Frat Gang Rape: Sex, Brotherhood, and Privilege on Campus*. New York: New York University Press.

Sankoff, D. (1988) Sociolinguistics and Syntactic Variation. In: F. Newmeyer (ed.) *The Cambridge Survey, IV: Language: The Socio-cultural Context*. Cambridge: Cambridge University Press, pp. 140–61.

Santa Ana, O. (1991) *Phonetic Simplification Processes in the English of the Barrio*. PhD Dissertation, University of Pennsylvania.

Santa Ana, O. (1996) Sonority and Syllable Structure in Chicano English. *Language Variation and Change*, 8: 63–90.

Sartre, J.-P. (1948) *Anti-Semite and Jew*, trans. George L. Becker. New York: Schocken Books.

Sawin, P. (2002) Performance at the Nexus of Gender, Power, and Desire: Reconsidering Bauman's Verbal Art from the Perspective of Gendered Subjectivity as Performance. *Journal of American Folklore*, 115(455): 28–51.

Schegloff, E. (2000) Overlapping Talk and the Organization of Turn-Taking in Conversation. *Language in Society*, 29: 1–63.

Scheper-Hughes, N. (1993) *The Academic and The Witch*. New York Times Book Review, September 5, p. A1.

Schieffelin, B., K. Woolard, and P. V. Kroskrity (eds.) (1998) *Language Ideologies: Practice and Theory*. Oxford: Oxford University Press.

Schiffrin, D. (1987) *Discourse Markers*. Cambridge; New York: Cambridge University Press.

Schiffrin, D. (1991) Anaphoric Then: Aspectual, Textual, and Epistemic Meaning. *Linguistics*, 30: 753–92.

Schiffrin, D. (1994) *Approaches to Discourse*. Oxford: Blackwell.

Schilling-Estes, N. (2005) *"Backwards Talk" in Smith Island, MD: Linguistics Forms and Social Functions*. Paper presented At SECOL LXXII. Raleigh, North Carolina.

Schwartz, B. (1991) Social Change and Collective Memory: The Democratization of George Washington. *American Sociological Review*, 56: 221–36.

Selkirk, E. O. (1984a) *Phonology and Syntax: the Relation between Sound and Structure*. Cambridge, MA: MIT Press.

Selkirk, E. O. (1984b) On the Major Class Features and Syllable Theory. In: M. Halle, M. Aronoff, and R. T. Oehrle (eds.) *Language Sound Structure: Studies of Phonology*. Cambridge, MA: MIT Press, pp. 107–13.

Shalet, A., G. Hunt, and K. Joe-Laidler (2003) Respectability and Autonomy: The Articulation and Meaning of Sexuality among the Girls in the Gang. *Journal of Contemporary Ethnography*, 32: 108–43.

Shankar, S. (2005) *Absolutely FOBulous: Performing Multicultural Day at Silicon Valley High Schools*. Paper presented at American Anthropological Association.

Shakur, S. (1994) *Monster: The Autobiography of an L.A. Gang Member*. New York: Penguin.

Short, J., and L. Hughes (2006) *Studying Youth Gangs*. Lanham, MD: AltaMira Press.

Shuman, A. (1986) *Storytelling Rights: The Uses of Oral and Written Texts by Urban Adolescents*. Cambridge: Cambridge University Press.

Silverstein, M. (1976) Shifters, Linguistic Categories and Cultural Description. In: K. H. Basso and H. A. Selby (eds.) *Meaning in Anthropology*. Albuquerque, NM: University of New Mexico Press, pp. 11–55.

Simpson, C. (2005) *Inside the Crips: Life Inside L.A.'s Most Notorious Gang*, New York: St. Martin's Press.

Smith, A. L. (2006) *Colonial Memory and Postcolonial Europe: Maltese Settlers in Algeria and France*. Bloomington, IN: Indiana University Press.

Smith, C. (1974) Economics of Marketing Systems: Models from Economic Geography. *Annual Review of Anthropology*, 3: 167–201.

Smith, E., and M. Zárate (1992) Exemplar-Based Model of Social Judgment. *Psychological Review* 99(1): 3–21.

Smith, L. T. (1999) *Decolonizing Methodologies: Research and Indigenous Peoples*. New York: St. Martin's Press.

Smith, R. (2005) *Mexican New York: Transnational Worlds of New Immigrants*. Berkeley, CA: University of California Press.

Smitherman-Donaldson, G. (1986) *Talkin' and Testifyin': The Language of Black America*. Detroit, MI: Wayne State University Press.

Spergel, I. (1990) Youth Gangs: Continuity and Change. *Crime and Justice*, 12: 171–275.

Spicer, J. (1992) The Renaissance Elbow. In: J. Bremmer and H. Roodenburg (eds.) *A Culture History of Gesture: From Antiquity to the Present Day.* Ithaca, NY: Cornell University Press, pp. 84–128.

Spivak, G. C. (1990) *The Post-Colonial Critic: Interviews, Strategies, Dialogues.* New York: Routledge.

Sproat, R., and O. Fujimura (1993) Allophonic Variation in English /l/ and Its Consequences for Phonetic Implementation. *Journal of Phonetics*, 21: 291–311.

Steele, C. (2003) Stereotype Threat and African American Student Achievement. In: T. Perry, C. Steele, and A. Hilliard III (eds.) *Young Gifted and Black: Promoting High Achievement among African-American Students.* Boston, MA: Beacon Press, pp. 109–30.

Strand, E. (1999) Uncovering the Role of Gender Stereotypes in Speech Perception. *Journal of Language and Social Psychology*, 18: 86–99.

Stuart-Smith, J., C. Timmins, and A. Wrench (forthcoming) Empirical Evidence for Gendered Speech Production: /s/ in Glaswegian. In: J. Cole and J. I. Hualde (eds.) *LabPhon 9: Change in Phonology.* Berlin: Mouton De Gruyter.

Stumphauzer, J., et al. (1977) East Side Story: Behavioral Analysis of a High Juvenile Crime Community. *Behavioral Disorders*, 2(2): 76–84.

Suarez-Orozco, C., and M. Suarez-Orozco (2002) *Children of Immigration.* Cambridge, MA: Harvard University Press.

Swidler, A., and J. Arditi (1994) The New Sociology of Knowledge. *Annual Review of Sociology*, 20(1): 305–29.

Tannen, D. (1993) *Framing in Discourse.* Oxford: Oxford University Press.

Taylor, C. (1993) *Girls, Gangs, Women and Drugs.* East Lansing, MI: Michigan State University Press.

Taylor, N. (2006) *Constructing Gendered Identities through Discourse: Body Image, Exercise, Food Consumption, and Teasing Practices among Adolescents.* Unpublished PhD Dissertation, University of Arizona.

Tetreault, C. (2000) *Adolescents, Multilingual Punning and Identity Play.* Paper delivered at the American Anthropological Association.

Thomas, W. I., R. E. Park, and H. Miller (1971, 1921) *Old World Traits Transplanted.* Montclair: Patterson Smith.

Thomas, W. I., and F. Znaniecki (1920) *The Polish Peasant in Europe and America, Vol. 5: Organization and Disorganization in America.* Boston, MA: Badger.

Thornton, S. (1995) *Club Cultures: Music, Media and Subcultural Capital,* Cambridge: Polity Press.

Thrasher, F. (1927) *The Gang: A Study of 1,313 Gangs in Chicago.* Chicago, IL: University of Chicago Press.

Traugott, E. (1995) *On the Role of the Development of Discourse Markers in a Theory of Grammaticalization.* Presented at ICHL XII, Manchester.

Traugott, E. (2003) Constructions in Grammaticalization. In: B. Joseph and R. Janda (eds.) *A Handbook of Historical Linguistics*. Oxford: Blackwell, pp. 624–47.

Trudgill, P. (1974) *The Social Differentiation of English in Norwich*. Cambridge: Cambridge University Press.

Trudgill, P. (1988) Norwich Revisited: Recent Linguistic Changes in an English Urban Dialect. *English World-Wide* 9: 33–49.

Turner, V. (1982) *From Ritual to Theater: The Human Seriousness of Play*. New York: PAJ Publications.

United States Department of Justice – Office of Legal Policy (1985) *The Prison Gangs: Their Extent, Nature, and Impact on Prisons*. Cambridge, MA: Harvard Press.

United States Government, 109th Congress (2005) *Alien Gang Removal Act of 2005, H.R. 2933. Hearing before the Subcommittee on Immigration, Border Security, and Claims, June 28, 2005*. Washington, DC: US Government Printing Office.

United States Government, 109th Congress (2005) *Gangs and Crime in Latin America: Hearing Before the Subcommittee on the Western Hemisphere of the Committee on International Relations, April 20, 2005*. Washington, DC: US Government Printing Office.

United States Government, 109th Congress (2005) *Gang Deterrence and Community Protection Act of 2005, H.R. 1279. Hearing Before the Subcommittee on Crime, Terrorism and Homeland Security, April 5, 2005*. Washington, DC: US Government Printing Office.

Villaraigosa, A. R. (2007) *Mayor Villaraigosa, Chief Bratton, and Federal Law Enforcement Agencies Announce Major Crackdown on LA Street Gangs*. Official Press Release.

Valdés, G. (1994) *Bilingualism and Testing*. Norwood, NJ: Ablex.

Valdés, G. (1996) *Con Respeto: Bridging The Distances between Culturally Diverse Families And Schools: An Ethnographic Portrait*. New York: Teachers College Press.

Valdés, G. (2001) *Learning and Not Learning English*. New York; London: Teachers College Press.

Valle, V., and R. Torres (2000) *Latino Metropolis*, Minneapolis, MN: University of Minnesota Press.

Vasconcelos, J., and M. Gamio (1926) *Aspects of Mexican Civilization*. Chicago, IL: University of Chicago Press.

Veatch, T. (1991) *English Vowels: Their Surface Phonological Structure and Phonetic implementation in Vernacular Dialects*. PhD Dissertation, University of Pennsylvania.

Venkatesh, S. A. (1998) Gender and Outlaw Capitalism: A Historical Account of the Black Sisters United "Girl Gang." *Signs*, 23: 683–709.

Venkatesh, S. A. (2000) *American Project: The Rise and Fall of a Modern Ghetto*. Cambridge, MA: Harvard University Press.

Venkatesh, S. A. (2003) A Note on Social Theory and the American Street Gang. In: L. Kontos, D. Brotherton, and L. Barrios (eds.) *Gangs in Society: Alternative Perspectives*. New York: Columbia University Press, pp. 19–30.

Venkatesh S. A., and S. D. Levitt (2000) Are We a Family or a Business?: History and Disjuncture in the Urban American Street Gang. *Theory and Society*, 29: 427–62.

Vigil, J. D. (1988) *Barrio Gangs: Street Life and Identity in Southern California*. Austin, TX: University of Texas Press.

Vigil, J. D. (2002) *A Rainbow of Gangs: Street Cultures in the Mega-City*. Austin, TX: University of Texas Press.

Villa, R. H. (2000) *Barrio-Logos: Space and Place in Urban Chicano Literature and Culture*. Austin, TX: University of Texas Press.

Villenas, S. (1996) The Colonizer/Colonized Chicana Ethnographer: Identity, Marginalization, and Co-optation in the Field. *Harvard Educational Review*, 66(4): 711–31.

Wade, P. (1997) *Race and Ethnicity in Latin America*. London: Pluto Press.

Ward, G., and B. Birner (1993) The Semantics and Pragmatics of *and everything*. *Journal of Pragmatics*, 19: 205–14.

Weinreich, U., W. Labov, and M. I. Herzog (1968) Empirical Foundations for a Theory of Language Change. In: W. Lehmann and Y. Malkiel (eds.) *Directions for Historical Linguistics*. Austin, TX University of Texas Press, 95–195.

Weismantel, M., and S. Eisenman (1998) Race in the Andes: Global Movements and Popular Ontologies. *Bulletin of Latin American Research*, 17(2): 121–42.

Wenger, E. (1998) Communities of Practice: Learning, Meaning, and Identity. Cambridge: Cambridge University Press.

Wertheim, S. (2006) Cleaning Up for Company: Using Participant Roles to Understand Fieldworker Effect. *Language in Society*, 35(5): 707–27.

Williams, R. (1977) *Marxism and Literature*. Oxford: Oxford University Press.

Willis, P. (1977) *Learning to Labor*. New York: Columbia University Press.

Willis, P. (1978) *Profane Culture*. London: Routledge & Kegan Paul.

Willrich, M. (2003) *City of Courts: Socializing Justice in Progressive Era Chicago*. Cambridge: Cambridge University Press.

Winton, R., and P. McGreevy (2007a) *L.A. Shifts Tactics Against Gangs*. LA Times.com. http://www.latimes.com/news/local/la-me-gangs10jan10, 0,6060324.story?coll=la-home-headlines. Accessed February 28, 2007.

Winton, R., and P. McGreevy (2007b) *Will LA's Strategy to Battle Gangs Work?* LATimes.com. http://www.latimes.com/news/local/la-megangs11feb11,0, 3897626.story?coll=la-home-local. Accessed February 28, 2007.

Wolff, K. (ed.) (1950) *The Sociology of Georg Simmel*. Glencoe, IL: The Free Press.

Wolfram, W. (1969) *A Sociolinguistic Description of Detroit Negro Speech*. Washington, DC: Center for Applied Linguistics.

Wolfram, W. (1974) *Sociolinguistic Aspects of Assimilation: Puerto Rican English in New York City.* Arlington, VA: Center for Applied Linguistics.

Wolfram, W. (1991) The Linguistic Variable: Fact and Fantasy. *Journal of American Speech*, 66(1): 22–32.

Wolfram, W., and N. Schilling-Estes (1996) On the Social Basis of Phonetic Resistance. In: J. Arnold, et al. (eds.) *Sociolinguistic Variation: Data, Theory and Analysis: Selected Papers from NWAV 23 at Stanford*, Stanford, CA: CSLI Press, pp. 69–82.

Wolfson, N. (1976) Speech Events and Natural Speech: Some Implications for Sociolinguistic Methodology. *Language in Society*, 5(2): 189–209.

Woolard, K., and B. Schieffelin (1994) Language Ideology. *Annual Review of Anthropology*, 23: 55–82.

Yablonsky, L. (1997) *Gansters: Fifty Years of Madness, Drugs and Death on the Streets of America.* New York: New York University Press.

Zamuner, T., L. Gerken, and M. Hammond (2004) Phonotactic Probabilities in Young Children's Speech Production. *Journal of Child Language*, 31(3): 515–36.

Zentella, A. C. (1998) *Growing up Bilingual.* London: Blackwell.

Zhang, Q. (2005) A Chinese Yuppie in Beijing: Phonological Variation and the Construction of a New Professional Identity. *Language in Society*, 34(3): 431–66.

Discography

Café Tacuba (1994) *La Chica Banda.* EMI Music.

Gene Chandler (1962) *Duke of Earl.* Vee Jay.

Mackenzie, L., G. Montgomery, W. Wirges, and J. Althouse (1984, 1945) *Chiquita Banana Jingle.* Delaware Water Gap, PA: Shawnee Press.

Ozuna, I. (1963) *Smile Now Cry Later.* Teardrop Records.

Rosie and the Originals (1960) *Angel Baby.* Ace Records.

War (1975) *Lowrider.* Avenue Records.

Filmography

Hopper, D. (1988) *Colors.* Metro Goldwyn Mayer, MGM Studio.

Olmos, E. J. (1992) *American Me.* Universal Pictures, YOY Productions, Sean Daniel Company, Olmos Productions.

APPENDIX

Table 8.4a Significant factor group in the raising of /I/: following phonetic segment (*n* = 1625)

Following segment	% Application	Tokens	**Probability weight**
Engma	83	526	**0.944**
Nasal	27	222	**0.471**
Lateral	14	58	**0.319**
Voiceless Obstruent	8	538	**0.189**
Voiced Obstruent	5	119	**0.121**
Sibilant/Affricate	3	162	**0.079**
Input 0.244	*Log Likelihood = −551.910*		*Significance = 0.000*

Table 8.5a Social grouping second most significant factor in raising of /I/ (*n* = 1625)

Social group	% Application	Tokens	**Probability weight**
Norteñas	43	261	**0.698**
Sureñas	42	267	**0.625**
Sureña WB's	39	280	**0.565**
Norteña WB's	35	277	**0.519**
Discos	30	265	**0.439**
Jocks	18	275	**0.198**
Input 0.244	*Log Likelihood = −551.910*		*Significance = 0.000*

Table 8.6a Individual subject probability weights ($n = 1632$)

Name/Affiliation	% Application	Tokens	Probability weight
T-Rex/Norte	49	127	0.698
Reina/Sur	46	125	0.611
Tina/W-Norte	38	138	0.583
Cati/W-Sur	39	135	0.581
Yadira/Disco	38	144	0.561
Jackie/W-Sur	39	144	0.520
Raisa/Norte	37	134	0.517
Mariane/W-Norte	31	134	0.497
Sadgirl/Sur	38	146	0.465
Veronica/Disco	20	130	0.357
Yolanda/Jock	19	139	0.332
Jill/Jock	17	136	0.305
Total tokens		1632	
Input 0.327	*Log Likelihood = −874.522*		*Significance = 0.002*

Table 8.7a Th-Pro status is second most predictive factor ($n = 1632$)

Word bearing the token was part of Th-Pro set: (consisting of thing, something, anything, nothing)	% Application	Tokens	Probability weight
Th-Pro set	79	269	.890
Not Th-Pro set	26	1363	.398
Total tokens		1632	
Input 0.327	*Log Likelihood = −874.522*		*Significance = 0.002*

Table 8.8a Codeswitching is third most predictive factor ($n = 1632$)

Presence of codeswitching	% Application	Tokens	Probability weight
Codeswitching in phrase	43	244	0.582
No Codeswitching	33	1388	0.485
Total Tokens		1632	
Input 0.327	*Log Likelihood = −874.522*		*Significance = 0.002*

Table 8.9a Social group is most significant factor in Th-Pro ($n = 158$)

Social group	% Application	Tokens	**Probability weight**
Norteñas	95	40	**0.762**
Sureñas	93	41	**0.705**
Sureña WB's	96	26	**0.673**
Norteña WB's	81	21	**0.418**
Discos	71	24	**0.276**
Jocks	27	6	**0.049**
Input 0.909	*Log Likelihood = −52.296*		*Significance = 0.018*

Table 8.10a Phonetic factors are second most significant in Th-Pro ($n = 158$, derived by adding preceding environments *or* following environments)

Phonetic realization	% Application	Tokens	**Probability weight**
Preceding [t]	92	143	**0.628**
Following [ŋ]	83	147	**0.548**
Following [n]	65	11	**0.119**
Preceding [θ]	38	15	**0.110**
Input 0.909	*Log Likelihood = −52.296*		*Significance = 0.018*

Table 9.1a Distribution of 195 tokens of discourse-marking Th-Pro organized by speaker and social group ($n = 195$)

Social group	Name	Given Th-Pro		New Th-Pro		Discourse marking Th-Pro		Total	
		Tokens	%	Tokens	%	Tokens	%	Tokens	%
Norteñas	T-Rex	3	15%	5	25%	12	60%	20	100%
	Raisa	9	40.90%	6	27.30%	7	31.80%	22	100%
Norteñas Wannabe's	Mariana	4	36.30%	2	18.20%	5	45.50%	11	100%
	Cati	4	26.60%	4	26.60%	7	46.60%	15	100%
Disco Girls	Yadira	7	30.40%	8	34.80%	8	34.80%	23	100%
	Veronica	5	45.50%	2	18.10%	3	27.30%	11	100%
Jocks	Jill	2	50%	2	50%	0	0%	4	100%
	Yolanda	5	27.70%	12	66.60%	1	5.55%	18	100%
Sureña Wannabe's	Jackie	6	37.50%	8	50%	2	12.50%	16	100%
	Tina	3	27.30%	4	36.40%	4	36.40%	11	100%
Sureñas	Sadgirl	2	5.90%	5	14.70%	27	79.40%	34	100%
	Reina	3	30%	4	40%	3	30%	10	100%

INDEX

Bloods *see also* street gangs
Bloomfield, L. 216
body
  image 27, 157–8
  size 158
Bordo, J. 159
Boum, A. 228n
Bourdieu, P. 214, 227n
Briggs, C. 41n, 223
Brinton, L. 264, 273
Brotherton, D. 77–9, 85
Brown, A. 176
Bucholtz, M. 262n
Butler, J. 150
Bybee, J. 227n

California
  demographics 238
  as a dialect region 237
California Department of Justice
  91
California Youth Authority 91, 94
Cameron, D. 288
Campbell, A. 162
capital flow, as definitional of gangs
  58, 78
Carrera, M. 119
Carsten, J. 195
castas 118–22
categories
  linguistic 214
  social 216
CCCS (Centre for Contemporary
  Cultural Studies) 154, 176
Central American Spanish 28
Chabot, R. 76, 79
Chafe, W. 271
Chambers, J. 228n
cheerleading 30
Chesney-Lind, M. 106, 162
Chicano English 28, 231
  comparison across dialects of
  249

description 265
  as ethnic dialect 61
Chicano gangs, educational research
  on 90
Chicano Rights Movement 86, 94
child migrants 22
children 129–30
Chiquita Banana 11
chola(s) 62, 151
circular migration 22, 65
circulation,
  of drawings 193
  of narratives 186–9
  of photographs 196–8, 201–4
  of poetry 190
city, sociological notion of the
  76–7
Clarke, G. 176
class 125–7, 132
  backgrounds brought from
    Mexico 21, 87
  mobility 19, 21
  reproduction 21
Clinton, W. J. 180
clothing *see also* symbolic markers of
    gang identity
  and profiling 93
  as source of intimidation 57
clowning *see also* speech acts
codeswitching/code choice
  108–10, 140, 182, 207, 244,
  254–5
college preparatory courses, and
  immigrant students 34–5
colonialism 118–22
Colors 179
colors *see also* symbolic markers of
  gang identity
Comaroff, Jean and John 59
commodity fetishism 176, 210–12,
  214, 220, 239
conflict resolution, efforts by school
  111

Euro-Americans   28
evidentiality   185, 205n
exchange students   132
exemplar theory   212–15, 289
  sociolinguistic rubrics   213
eyeliner *see also* symbolic markers of
  gang identity   152–5

Faegin, C.   224
farmer, as an appellation   94
Farr, M.   40n
faux-pas, in the fieldsite   112–14,
  224
female liberation hypothesis   150,
  162
femininity   149–53, 160–1, 169
Ferguson, C.   216
fighting   142, 207
  between MS-13 and Sur   139
  provocation   61
Firth, R.   216
Fischer, J.   216
Fluent English Proficiency (FEP) *see
  also* ESL   34
food, attitudes toward   158
Foucault, M.   151, 148, 172n
Fought, Carmen   238, 290n
Foulkes, P.   227n
fractal recursivity *see also* recursivity
framing, in discourse   277
fraternities   77
frequency *see also* exemplar theory
  258, 275, 286, 289
Fresas *see also* social groups in high
  school
  definition   11
  language use   29
  musical tastes   14
Frias, G.   94
Fujimora, O.   244

Gal, S.   115, 263n
Galindo, D. L.   249

Galliano, J.   173n
games, language *see also* language
  games
gang members / membership
  career aspirations of youth   64
  competition for notoriety among
    80
  core vs. peripheral   209
  disparities in perceptions   58
  incarcerated   113
  intergenerational   112
  wannabe's   57
gang(s)
  adult patronage of youth   84–5
  African-American   84
  Chicago   84–5
  as defined in the literature   58
  definition   77–8
  girls in   77, 85, 93
  historical dimensions   77, 84–6
  international structure   77
  Northern California   78
  as organizations   180
  political activities of   77, 86
  prison *see also* prison gangs   94
  pro-social activities of   77
  signs   67
Garber, J.   154
García, R.   83
García, S.   205n
Garfinkel, H.   261n, 262n
Gaudio, R.   41n
Geertz, C.   195
gender
  among different groups of
    immigrants   19
  interaction with class   20
  and language expectations   20
generational differences   169–70
Geraldo Show, The   148–50
Gerken, L.   227n
Gibson, M.   41n
Giles, H.   285

probabilistic approaches, in
    linguistics   210–15
pronouns, Th-Pro   209, 236, 253,
    257, 266
  data set   270, 274
  as discourse markers   273, 276,
    280, 285
  as ethnic markers   285–8
  frequency   275, 286
  grammaticalization   277, 280,
    283
  history   266–7
  varbrul analysis   259–60
Proposition 187   10–11, 142
punk(s)   132, 157, 176
Purnell, T.   114

Quirk, R.   271

race
  ideas of, in Latin America
    118–22
  ideas of, in the United States
    121
  and language   21
racism see also skin color   134
  as a factor in gang formation
    86
  in Mexico   119, 134
  as perceived by students   36
Ragen's Colts gang   85
Rampton, B.   292
real-time, language change in   219
Received Pronunciation (in Britain)
    219
recursivity see also fractal recursivity
    78, 114–17
relajo   26n, 40
replicability   48, 220
representations of gang members, by
    police   81
Rickford, J.   226, 228n, 261n
rites of passage   129

Rivera, G.   148
Roth-Gordon, J.   290n

Sacks, H.   261n
salience   212–13, 256, 289
Salvadorans see also El Salvador
San Jose, California   96
Santa Ana, O.   248
sayings see also speech acts
Schegloff, E.   262n
Scheper-Hughes, N.   73n
Schieffelin, B.   226n
Schiffrin, D.   272
Schutz, A.   261n
Schwartz, B.   178
segregation   25
self-report, inconsistencies with
    behavior   231
Selkirk, E.   248
semantics   286
set-marking tags   267–9, 280
sexism   163
sexual innuendo, in jokes see also
    speech acts   67–8, 71–2
sexual orientation, as discussed by
    youth   70
shifters see also switching gangs
Shuman, A.   182
Simmel, G.   261n
skin color see also phenotype, racism
    20, 116–25
  and makeup   157
slurs   61
  coconut   30
  mari-macha   163
  pocho   116
  spic   293
  wetback/mojado   108, 143
  whitewashed   30
smiling   156, 194
Smith, R.   40n
social factors, in the linguistic
    analysis   249

SHAKESPEARE'S PROBLEM PLAYS

SHAKESPEARE'S PROBLEM PLAYS

E. M. W. TILLYARD, *1889-1962*
LITT.D.

1971
UNIVERSITY OF TORONTO
PRESS

PUBLISHED BY
University of Toronto Press
Toronto and Buffalo

ISBN 0-8020-5005-0 (clothbound)
ISBN 0-8020-6026-9 (paperback)

London: Chatto & Windus Ltd

Printed in Great Britain

First Published 1950
Reprinted 1951, 1957, 1961, 1964, 1968, 1971

PREFACE

THIS study of four of Shakespeare's plays was written for delivery as the Alexander Lectures at the University of Toronto for the academic year 1948-9. Professor W. J. Alexander, who died in 1944, held the chair of English at University College Toronto from 1889 to 1926, and the lectureship was founded as a tribute to his distinction as teacher and scholar. The first series was delivered in 1929-30.

I wish to thank the Toronto authorities for honouring me by their invitation to give these lectures, and I am particularly grateful to Professor A. S. P. Woodhouse for his kindness and help in arranging the details of their delivery.

No student of Shakespeare's Problem Plays can fail to be indebted to W. W. Lawrence's *Shakespeare's Problem Comedies* (New York 1931). This book not only tells us things about these plays which we did not know or did not heed before, but by its vigour and charm induces us to read them with fresh eyes. As usual I have got much profit and stimulus from the relevant portions of Mark Van Doren's *Shakespeare* (New York 1939), even when I disagree (as I do immoderately over the style of *Troilus and Cressida* for instance). The brief critical remarks in Peter Alexander's *Shakespeare's Life and Art* (London 1939) have made me think and have helped me greatly. A memorable lecture by Hardin Craig on Shakespeare's bad poetry, delivered at Stratford-on-Avon in August 1947 and printed in the first volume of *Shakespeare Survey* (Cambridge 1948) has given me courage and authority to speak boldly on certain topics about which I might have been timid. For associating *Hamlet* with the three plays I mainly treat and not with *Othello* and the other later tragedies I can invoke the precedent of F. S. Boas in his *Shakespeare and his Predecessors*. It is but too easy to take E. K. Chambers's *William Shakespeare* (Oxford 1930) quite for granted: a kind of institution, used but not talked of. I make the effort not to take it for granted, and I record my debt to its constant utility.

Other debts will be acknowledged in the notes at the end of the different chapters.

E. M. W. T.

CONTENTS

INTRODUCTION

THE three plays I originally set out to discuss, *Troilus and Cressida*, *All's Well that Ends Well*, and *Measure for Measure*, have been called "dark comedies" and "problem comedies", while the first has been called a "satirical comedy". Though not fond of any of these names, I recognise that the plays make a group and that a common name is needed. As a choice of evils "problem comedies" gives least offence. But, finding, however reluctantly, that *Hamlet* goes with these plays (or at any rate with *Troilus and Cressida*) more aptly than with the three undoubted tragedies usually grouped with it, I cannot use "problem comedies" for all four plays; and "problem plays" is the only available term.

It is anything but a satisfactory term, and I wish I knew a better. All I can do now is to warn the reader that I use it vaguely and equivocally; as a matter of convenience. The warning is the more necessary because "problem play" can mean something reasonably definite. L. J. Potts in his forthcoming book on comedy says of the problem play that it "treats the situations that arise in society simply as moral or political problems, in the abstract and without reference to the idiosyncrasies of human nature", and he cites *Everyman*, *Troilus and Cressida*, and the plays of Galsworthy. This is a good definition, but for my present purposes too good and too precise; for though it may include *Troilus and Cressida* it does not extend to *All's Well*. To achieve the necessary elasticity and inclusiveness, consider the connotations of the parallel term "problem child".

1

There are at least two kinds of problem child: first the genuinely abnormal child, whom no efforts will ever bring back to normality; and second the child who is interesting and complex rather than abnormal: apt indeed to be a problem for parents and teachers but destined to fulfilment in the larger scope of adult life. Now *All's Well* and *Measure for Measure* are like the first problem child: there is something radically schizophrenic about them. *Hamlet* and *Troilus and Cressida* are like the second problem child, full of interest and complexity but divided within themselves only in the eyes of those who have misjudged them. To put the difference in another way, *Hamlet* and *Troilus and Cressida* are problem plays because they deal with and display interesting problems; *All's Well* and *Measure for Measure* because they *are* problems.

In sum, the term problem play can have a wide meaning, and if in using it I have to be equivocal I had rather be so than not use it at all.

One large matter I had better mention at once and get rid of summarily. Many readers have found in the Problem Plays a spirit of gloom, disillusion, and morbidity that exceeds dramatic propriety and demands some extrinsic explanation in Shakespeare's private life at the time. Others on the contrary think that such readers have unconsciously begun from Shakespeare's supposed biography and have insisted on reading that biography into this group of plays. Between these two extremes there may be many intermediate positions. I need not be concerned with them in these lectures. The whole matter has been thoroughly aired, and all I need do is to take sides. And I take it with those who think such personal explanations superfluous, or at least too uncertain to be worth anything. I agree here with Sisson [1] on the mythical

---

[1] C. J. Sisson, *The Mythical Sorrows of Shakespeare*, British Academy Shakespeare Lecture for 1934.

sorrows of Shakespeare and with R. W. Chambers [1] in his prefatory remarks on *Measure for Measure* concerning the early years of James I, and the small need Shakespeare had to be unhappy just then, or with this sentence of W. W. Lawrence:

> Critics have been too much inclined to emphasise one or more possible explanations of the problem comedies—personal misfortune or bereavement, disappointment in friendship or in love, the degeneration of the age, the demands of the theatre, the influence of prevailing literary and dramatic fashions, haste and carelessness.

However, though it may be vain to conjecture from external evidence how Shakespeare's emotions were behaving at this period, we can infer from the plays themselves that he was especially interested in certain matters. Some of these occur in all the plays, some in at least three; and, when pointed out, they will serve to make a genuine group of the four plays which so far I have separated into two pairs.

First, Shakespeare is concerned throughout with either religious dogma or abstract speculation or both. It may be retorted that so he was also when he wrote his later tragedies. Yet there is a difference, in that dogma and speculation are less completely absorbed into the general substance of the Problem Plays; they are felt rather more for their own and rather less for the drama's sake, as if, in this form at least, they were new and urgent in Shakespeare's mind, demanding at this point statement and articulation rather than solution and absorption into other material. Hamlet is powerfully aware of the baffling human predicament between the angels and the beasts, between the glory of having been made in God's image and the incrimination of being descended from fallen

---

[1] R. W. Chambers, *The Jacobean Shakespeare and Measure for Measure*, British Academy Shakespeare Lecture for 1937.

Adam. Gertrude in re-marrying in haste appeared to him worse than a beast wanting discourse of reason. Again, if man was the glory of the world he might still be aghast at being allowed to crawl between heaven and earth. In *All's Well* the wretched insufficiency of natural man is pointed to at a most emphatic place in the play (IV. 3. 24).

> *A.* Now, God lay our rebellion! as we are
> ourselves, what things are we!
> *B.* Merely our own traitors.

When in *Measure for Measure* Isabella speaks of the atonement,

> Why, all the souls that were were forfeit once;
> And he that might the vantage best have took
> Found out the remedy,

she is indeed speaking in character, and the doctrine has been quite assimilated into the dramatic context; but there is so much theological lore elsewhere in the play on the relation of Justice and Mercy (and less assimilated into the dramatic context) that we need not doubt that the doctrine of the forfeit soul was present in Shakespeare's own mind at that time. In *Troilus and Cressida* there is little or no theology but abundance of speculation, for instance on the question whether worship can be only of a worthy object or whether it can invest the object with a worthiness not its own.

Other instances must wait till I treat the separate plays, but I believe the above to be fair samples and to show Shakespeare in a mood of uncommon abstraction and speculation.

Thoughtfulness about man's estate and about religious dogma must be serious to be worth anything but it need not be pessimistic. And the mood of these plays is serious but not black. In *Hamlet* Shakespeare glories in his sense of the wonder and the diversity of life, which though it

4

can be terrible is not bad. There is much satire in *Troilus and Cressida*; but the play is not fundamentally satirical, implying that things can, not must, go like that. By far the most melancholy of the four plays is *All's Well*, but not because Shakespeare treats his subject cynically. Certainly Helena is too sombre and Bertram too unpleasant to be heroine and hero of normal comedy; but neither character is satirised. They are realistic, and Shakespeare was interested in the detailed workings of their minds. The play is unusual, difficult to label, but not pessimistic. On the other hand the pervading melancholy suggests that Shakespeare was tired when he wrote and that he forced himself to write. In *Measure for Measure* the themes of mercy and forgiveness are treated in all sincerity with no shadow of satire. There is much good and much evil presented in the play; but no hint that evil is the rule. Any failure it argues in Shakespeare is not of morale but of technique. The plays then are powerfully united by a serious tone amounting at times to sombreness; they show a strong awareness of evil, without being predominantly pessimistic.

I mentioned the realistic characterisation of Helena and Bertram; and this exemplifies a second large quality of the Problem Plays: an acute interest in observing and recording the details of human nature. Such an interest exists of course through the whole series of Shakespeare's plays, but in very different ways and degrees. In the early History Plays the realism peeps out fitfully in the minor characters, like Cade's followers, but it is there just as surely as anywhere else. In the last plays, though held in absolute control, it is often subordinated to the symbolic presentation of characters, as in the statue scene in the *Winter's Tale*. Now in the Problem Plays Shakespeare was interested in observing and recording the details of human nature for its own sake in a way not found elsewhere. It is as if at that time he was freshly struck by the fascination of the human spectacle as a spectacle and that he was more content than at other times merely to record his observation without subordinating it to a great overriding theme. The beginning of this fresh interest may perhaps be seen in *Henry IV*. If so, it is suspended in *Julius Caesar*. But certainly by the time of *Othello* observation, though acute and brilliant, is held in strict subordination. In the interim Hamlet, Troilus, Bertram, and Angelo are all of them characters embodying their author's powerful interest and pleasure in the varieties and the possibilities of the human mind.

It is these two interests—in speculative thought and in the working of the human mind—pursued largely for their own sake that partly characterise the Problem Plays. And from them spring characteristic virtues and defects. They create a peculiar sense of real life but they prevent the sharp clarity of intention we are apt to demand of very great art. There is no need to follow this topic here, since I shall resume it in dealing with the separate plays.

So much for general matters: I pass to some details which the plays have in common. In each play, but in different degrees of importance, recurs the theme 'a young man gets a shock'. Hamlet, indeed, has just got his first shock when the action opens, and before long he gets another. The two shocks motivate the whole play. Claudio has just had a shock when the action of *Measure for Measure* opens, but though it sets much of the action in motion it is not a principal part, for other themes, arising indeed from it, usurp the interest. In *Troilus and Cressida* and *All's Well* Troilus and Bertram get first a smaller and then a greater shock in the course of the action. Troilus's first shock is to be separated from Cressida, his second is to witness her infidelity. Bertram's first shock is to be forcibly married, his second is to undergo a long series of surprises and alarms on the night before he leaves Florence to return to France. Shakespeare must have been specially interested at this time in different types of young men on the verge of manhood and in the harsh experiences that force them to grow up. If *Measure for Measure*, as is usually thought, is the latest, it looks as if this interest had begun to work itself out by then, for Claudio and his development are drawn but slightly. All the same we are led to think that Claudio *does* grow up. When (IV. 2. 69) the Provost shows him his death-warrant and asks where is Bernardine, he says,

> As fast lock'd up in sleep as guiltless labour
> When it lies starkly in the traveller's bones.
> He will not wake.

This cool and reflective reply shows him a different man from the hasty and unreflective lover of Juliet. So the full theme does recur in *Measure for Measure*, even if not very emphatically.

If Claudio is slightly drawn, the other three young men are drawn in great detail. Bertram and Troilus belong to what Lafeu calls "the unbaked and doughy youth of a nation"; and it may well be that Pandarus's long moral about "tarrying the leavening, and the kneading etc." in the first scene of *Troilus and Cressida* is meant to apply not only to the process of winning Cressida but to the process of growing up. Hamlet is anything but "unbaked and doughy" in the sense that Bertram is; yet he has an emotional tenderness and a sensitive idealism that belong to adolescence and which are forcibly brought to maturity in the course of the play. Here then is a master-motive, and one that binds the four plays strongly together.

Secondly, in at least three of the plays, the business that most promotes this process of growth is transacted at night. There are so many night-scenes in Shakespeare that such an observation may amount to little. Yet the repetition is so striking that I find it difficult to believe it fortuitous. I do not mean any conscious plan, but instinctively Shakespeare staged the most critical phase of growth in darkness. If Hamlet develops at all in the play, it is principally during the night when the *Murder of Gonzago* was acted and when, having killed Polonius, he spoke out to his mother. It is in the depth of the night that Troilus, witnessing Cressida's infidelity, has years of mental growth imposed on him in a brief hour. Bertram's last night at Florence is crowded with disturbing happenings: the receipt of a severe letter from his mother; news of his wife's supposed death which upsets his equanimity over his supposed seduction of Diana; the unmasking of the man on whom he relied, Parolles. The effect of all these happenings is not disclosed till the end of the play, but we cannot doubt it. In *Measure for Measure* the case is different. There indeed the night-scene occurs, and in the corresponding place. But there is no sense of the darkness synchronising with a change in Claudio's mind. On the contrary we picture him as resigned soon after Isabella has repudiated his plea for his life. The one touch of full analogy comes when Angelo soliloquises after midnight on his supposed seduction of Isabella:

> This deed unshapes me quite, makes me unpregnant
> And dull to all proceedings. A deflower'd maid,
> And by an eminent body that enforc'd
> The law against it!

Here are some tokens of remorse and at least the chance of mental change. And Angelo, though not adolescent in years, was in some ways immature.

There is a deep propriety in these midnight crises. It is not only that thought and the dark go together, as in *Il Penseroso*, but that we naturally conceive the most significant growth to take place unseen and in silence: notions to which the darkness and stillness of night correspond.

Thirdly (and allied possibly to Shakespeare's interest in adolescence) is his interest in the old and new generations and in old and new habits of thought. It appears only in *Troilus and Cressida* and *All's Well*, but doing so in that pair and not in one of the two common pairs it is likely to represent a genuine interest belonging to the whole period. It is not new for it was very evident in Shakespeare's second historical tetralogy. There, the antique medieval world of Richard II is set side by side with the newer world of Henry IV. The same sort of contrast exists in the Trojans and Greeks in *Troilus and Cressida*. The Trojans are antique, anachronistically chivalrous, and rather inefficient; the Greeks are the new men, ruthless and, though quarrelsome and unpleasant, less inefficient than the Trojans. In *All's Well* the contrast is between age and youth. The castle at Rossillion and the court at Paris are controlled by pathetic relics of a gracious past. To these relics the new generation is sharply contrasted. It has energy and strong will, but graciousness and elegance are not among its virtues. It looks as if Shakespeare were aware at this time of the social and economic changes that were taking place. In his last plays he came to picture the new generation differently.

The matters, largely of plot and structure, common to *All's Well* and *Measure for Measure*, are too obvious to need special mention. The two plays hang together much as do *Cymbeline*, the *Winter's Tale*, and the *Tempest*. But it is worth noting that the way these two plays convey a moral norm differs from that of *Hamlet* and *Troilus and Cressida*. *All's Well* and *Measure for Measure* abound in moral statements. In the first the two French Lords and in the second Escalus and the Provost form the *punctum indifferens* in their respective plays. *Triolus and Cressida* is different. There the morality is not conveyed through any one person or set of persons. It is rather choric and to be gathered from what a number of people say when they are least themselves and most rhetorical mouthpieces. Ulysses is not a highly moral character himself; but his great speeches, choruslike, convey the principle of order which is essential for judging the play's emotional turbulence. The case is rather the same in *Hamlet*. Horatio is not strong enough to be the moral *punctum indifferens* in his own right. But there is a lot of choric morality as well.

Such are some of the common characteristics of the group. I have stated them briefly and dogmatically, postponing amplification or proof to my treatment of the separate plays.

Much has been added in recent years to our knowledge of Shakespeare's thought, of his imagery, and of his contemporary setting; and it should all be to the good. The danger is that it should blind us to the poetic logic of the actual text. For instance, in learning that a certain type of image occurs frequently in a play we may easily forget that frequency, a mere numerical thing, may mean little compared with poetic emphasis: that a certain type of image occurring once but in a poetically emphatic place may have more weight than another type that occurs ten times in less emphatic places. We need in fact a weighing-machine like that pictured in the *Frogs* of Aristophanes for the contest between Aeschylus and Euripides. But such a machine is imaginary, and the only substitute is the reader's apprehension of the total poetic effect.

Some of the criticism of the Problem Plays seems to me to incur the above danger by abstracting the thought too crudely from its dramatic context. It may not be for me to criticise, since I have probably done the same in writing of Shakespeare's History Plays. But for my present treatment I have tried to follow the poetic and not the mere abstracted significances and to allow the poetic or dramatic effect to dictate the relative emphasis. How far I have succeeded can only appear in my treatment of the plays themselves.

HAMLET

SINCE *Hamlet* is usually classed as a tragedy, I recognise my obligation to explain why I go against habit and class it as a problem play. Where you class it will depend on your notion of tragedy; so I must begin by stating my own.

No single formula will cover all those works we agree to call tragic: at least three types of feeling or situation are included in the word. The first and simplest is that of mere suffering; and it has been very well set forth by J. S. Smart.[1] Suffering becomes tragic when it befalls a strong (even a momentarily strong) nature, who is not merely passive but reacts against calamity. Then "There is a sense of wonder", and the tragic victim

> contrasts the present, weighed as it is with unforeseen disaster and sorrow, with the past which has been torn from him: it seems as if the past alone had a right to exist, and the present were in some way unreal. The stricken individual marvels why his lot should be so different from that of others, what is his position among men; and what is the position of man in the universe.

This simple conception is needed because it includes certain things which we recognise as tragic but which elude any conception more rigid or more complicated. The *Trojan Women* and the *Duchess of Malfi* are tragedies of simple suffering, where the sufferers are not greatly to blame. In fact the conception resembles the simple medieval one, with the addition that the sufferer's quality of mind causes him to protest and to reflect. *Hamlet* is cer-

[1] *Essays and Studies of the English Association*, VIII. 16.

tainly, among other things, a tragedy of this kind. Terrible things do befall its protagonist; while as a tragic hero Hamlet lacks a complication and an enrichment common in much tragedy: that of being to some extent, even a tiny extent, responsible for his misfortunes. Othello and Samson were part responsible for theirs. Even with Desdemona and her loss of the handkerchief we think faintly that perhaps she was the kind of person who might have been so careless. No one could accuse Hamlet of being the kind of person whose mother was bound to enter into a hasty and incestuous re-marriage, of being such a prig that his mother *must* give him a shock at any cost. If you read the play with a main eye to the soliloquies, you can easily persuade yourself that *Hamlet* is principally a tragedy of this first simple kind.

The second type of tragic feeling has to do with sacrificial purgation and it is rooted in religion. The necessary parties in a sacrifice are a god, a victim, a killer, and an audience; and the aim is to rid the social organism of a taint. The audience will be most moved as the victim is or represents one of themselves. The victim may be good or bad. Shakespeare's Richard III is a perfect example of a sacrificial victim carrying the burden of his country's sins; and he is bad. Once again, *Hamlet* is tragic, and in this second way. There is something rotten in the state of Denmark, and one of its citizens, blameless hitherto and a distinguished member of society, is mysteriously called upon to be the victim by whose agency the rottenness is cut away. And when Hamlet curses the spite by which he was born to be the victim and the cure, we thrill because it might be any of us. Like the first we can make this second tragic feeling the principal thing, if we narrow our vision sufficiently. But we should be wrong, for in actual fact our sense of Denmark's rottenness is much weaker than our sense of what a lot happens there. Denmark is not at all like Macbeth's Scotland, for instance, where the social and political theme is dominant. We have the liveliest sense of Malcolm destined to rule a purged body politic; no one gives a thought to Denmark as ruled by Fortinbras.

A third kind of tragic feeling has to do with renewal consequent on destruction.[1] It occurs when there is an enlightenment and through this the assurance of a new state of being. This kind penetrates deep into our nature because it expresses not merely the tragedy of abnormal suffering but a fundamental tragic fact of all human life: namely that a good state cannot stay such but must be changed, even partially destroyed, if a succeeding good is to be engendered. This paradox of the human condition, however plain and unescapable, is hard to accept: nevertheless tragedy gives us pleasure in setting it forth and making us accept it. The usual dramatic means of fulfilling this tragic function is through a change in the mind of the hero. His normal world has been upset, but some enlightenment has dawned, and through it, however faintly, a new order of things. Milton's Samson is for a second time reconciled to God, and this second reconciliation is other than the earlier state of friendship with God, which was destroyed. Othello is more than the stoical victim of great misfortune. He has been enlightened and though he cannot live it is a different man who dies. Those tragedies which we feel most centrally tragic contain, with other tragic conceptions, this third one. It is partly through failing to contain this conception that *Hamlet* is separated from the three great tragedies with which it is popularly joined. But this is a contentious statement which must be substantiated.

The main point at issue is whether Hamlet's mind

---

[1] See M. Bodkin, *Archetypal Patterns in Poetry* (London 1934) sections I and II, for this topic, psychologically elaborated.

undergoes during the course of the play a revolution comparable to that which takes place in the minds of Oedipus, or Lear, or Samson. If it does not, there can be no question of tragedy in the third sense. Till recently this point was hardly at issue, and my last paragraph would not have contradicted the general assumption. But recently a fundamental change in Hamlet's mind has been very confidently asserted. For instance, Middleton Murry sees a clear progress in the play ending with the hero's regeneration. The key-soliloquy ("To be or not to be . . .") states the master-theme, Hamlet's terror of death, and

> it is in his conquering his fear of the unknown futurity that Hamlet's victory lies. That is the central line of his progress and his growth. He has to teach himself, as it were all over again, to make a mouth at the invisible event.[1]

He has to learn to be brave with his whole mind, and not only when he momentarily forgets himself. He becomes wholly brave when just before the fencing-match he "defies augury" and immediately afterwards apologises to Laertes "with the simplicity and candour of a reborn soul". C. S. Lewis speaks of *Hamlet* largely in terms of a state of mind, the state of thinking about being dead, but he too finds the same progress in the mind of the hero:

> The world of *Hamlet* is a world where one has lost one's way. The Prince has no doubt lost his, and we can tell the precise moment when he finds it again. 'Not a whit. We defy augury. There's a special providence in the fall of a sparrow. . . .'[2]

Both writers rely for their opinions mainly on a single passage, the prose conversation between Hamlet and Horatio in V. 2 after Osric has gone out bearing with him Hamlet's acceptance of an immediate fencing-match with

---

[1] J. Middleton Murry, *Shakespeare* (London 1936) p. 248.
[2] *Hamlet, the Prince or the Poem*, British Academy Shakespeare Lecture for 1942, p. 13.

Laertes. They think this passage (containing Hamlet's "defiance of augury") marks the revolution in Hamlet's mind. If they are wrong here, their argument cannot hold. Here, therefore, it is crucial to make a decision. It is one that can be made only through our own response as we read. Amleth, Belleforest, the First Quarto, and *Der bestrafte Brudermord* are here irrelevant.

As I read it the passage shows no fundamental change in Hamlet's mind;[1] and for two main reasons.

First, any piety shown here by him was anticipated earlier in the play. He has been from the first remote from natural, unregenerate man. He is deeply religious, as the complete man of the Renaissance ought to be. And the signs of his piety and his belief that "the readiness is all" in other and earlier parts of the play argue that in the present passage he exhibits no spiritual development. When Horatio tries to restrain him from following the Ghost with "Be ruled: you shall not go", Hamlet replies "My fate cries out". What better example of "the readiness is all" turned to action? And he had already protested that the Ghost could do nothing to his soul, "being a thing immortal as itself". His sense of the glory of man as created in God's image ("What a piece of work is a' man!") and of his ignominy as a fallen creature ("Virtue cannot so inoculate our old stock but we shall relish of it") is theologically impeccable. And his words on Polonius's dead body are equally so:

> For this same lord
> I do repent: but heaven hath pleased it so,
> To punish me with this and this with me,
> That I must be their scourge and minister.
> I will bestow him and will answer well
> The death I gave him.

---

[1] For a more detailed discussion see Appendix A, p. 144.

Nothing in the "defiance of augury" speech is more pious and regenerate than this. Hamlet did not change.

But a more important reason is the tone of the passage. And this is not new and profound and significant, but elegantly conventional. Quietism not religious enlightenment is the dominant note. Hamlet is ready for anything that will come along; he has not acquired a new and liberating mastery of his own fate.

If therefore this crucial passage shows nothing new, the notions of a regenerate Hamlet, and hence of a play tragic in the fullest sense, are ruled out. Further, even though *Hamlet* is tragic in certain senses, that tragic quality is not the principal quality. If it is not the principal quality (and I do not deny its importance as an ingredient) it remains to say what those principal qualities are.

To lead up to these, I will first correct a possible false impression. In denying to Hamlet any powerful spiritual growth, any definitive spiritual revolution, I may have given the impression that his mind was quite static. This I did not intend; for the religious is not the only type of mental growth, and it is possible that Hamlet without undergoing a religious regeneration does change in some sort. Indeed it would be strange if all the things Hamlet had to suffer made no impression on his mind. Thus Theodore Spencer argues [1] that Hamlet's soliloquies show a progress in his power to convert the personal into the general, and that in the end he is above rather than in the tumult. This, I believe, is to argue from single passages in abstraction from the play. And even if Hamlet's soliloquies do show a progression from the personal, his behaviour at Ophelia's funeral, which comes after all the soliloquies, shows a very thorough relapse. On the other hand the notion that Hamlet grows older during the play

[1] *Shakespeare and the Nature of Man* (New York 1942) p. 108.

17

is surely true. Not that we should be dogmatic about Hamlet's precise age. V. Østerburg [1] has argued very sensibly that the fixing of his age at thirty on the authority of the Grave-Digger is to ignore the Elizabethan habit of speaking in round numbers that were never meant to be precise. But Shakespeare does succeed in making us picture Hamlet as an older man by Act Five, just as he did Troilus. Hamlet wrestling with Laertes in Ophelia's grave is indeed not above the tumult but he is older than his undergraduate self at the beginning. All the same such an ageing is no more than an impression appropriate to all that Hamlet has endured. It is not an independent theme, and the things that Hamlet endures are more important than the changes in himself that his endurance brings about.

On the other hand, though the things Hamlet endures may not work a spiritual revolution in him they do have their effect on the given ingredients of his mind. And that effect has its own order. Again, this order is not the principal thing in *Hamlet* but it has high importance. To speak of this importance is useless till I have made out a case for the order itself. In so doing I shall have to be highly subjective, for the order will depend less on what is stated than on the ways in which the poetic stress appears to the reader to fall. Further, to be at all brief, I shall have to be dogmatic on just those matters which have been the subject of most doubt and controversy: namely on what passes on Hamlet's mind; for what gives the order I seek to elucidate is the degree of prominence different events assume in Hamlet's mind and any action he takes to meet them.

First, I must recall Granville-Barker's timely and emphatic reminder [2] that the accepted act divisions are mis-

---

[1] *Prince Hamlet's Age* (Copenhagen 1924).
[2] H. Granville-Barker, *Hamlet* (London 1937) p. 91

leading and that the play falls naturally into three parts. The first corresponds with the first act and ends with Hamlet's acceptance of the task given him by the Ghost. The second begins with Polonius sending Reynaldo to Paris (II. 1) and ends with Hamlet's departure to England (IV. 4). The last begins with Ophelia's madness (IV. 5) and comprises the rest of the play. Between the parts there are long lapses of time. The first part presents Hamlet's state of mind, the position he is in, and the problems of action involved; the second presents the action and counter-action of Hamlet and Claudius; the third presents the consequences of what happened in the second.

Next, I must record my agreement with Waldock in the great prominence he gives to Hamlet's first soliloquy "O that this too too solid flesh would melt" and in his surprise that from Goethe and Coleridge (and one might now add from Middleton Murry and C. S. Lewis) one would not gather that before the coming of the Ghost anything had happened to trouble Hamlet. Of the import of the soliloquy Waldock writes:

> A terrific calamity has befallen Hamlet, his whole nature is upturned. And the particular origin of his trouble is made perfectly plain. It is the recent re-marriage (indecently hasty and incestuous re-marriage) of his mother. This event has changed the whole of life for him, the realisation of all that it seems to imply is poisoning his very soul.[1]

The truth of these remarks is so obvious that one can only marvel at the great need that undoubtedly existed and still exists for making them. The impression the shock left is conveyed later in Hamlet's bitter words to his mother in the third act, but the nature of the shock itself

[1] A. J. A. Waldock, *Hamlet* (Cambridge 1931) p. 15.

SHAKESPEARE'S PROBLEM PLAYS

can best be understood by Troilus's words when he has
ocular proof of Cressida's infidelity:

> This she? no, this is Diomed's Cressida:
> If beauty have a soul, this is not she;
> If souls guide vows, if vows be sanctimonies,
> If sanctimony be the gods' delight,
> If there be rule in unity itself,
> This is not she. O madness of discourse,
> That cause sets up with and against itself!
> Bi-fold authority, where reason can revolt
> Without perdition, and loss assume all reason
> Without revolt; this is and is not Cressid.
> Within my soul there doth conduce a fight
> Of this strange nature that a thing inseparate
> Divides more wider than the sky and earth,
> And yet the spacious breadth of this division
> Admits no orifex for a point as subtle
> As Ariachne's broken woof to enter.
> Instance, O instance, strong as Pluto's gates:
> Cressid is mine, tied with the bonds of heaven,
> Instance, O instance, strong as heaven itself:
> The bonds of heaven are slipp'd, dissolv'd, and loos'd;
> And with another knot, five-finger-tied,
> The fractions of her faith, orts of her love,
> The fragments, scraps, the bits and greasy relics
> Of her o'er-eaten faith, are bound to Diomed.
>
> (V. 2. 137)

Such, we may infer, was the kind of shock Hamlet received. It was a fact that his mother would hang on his
father as if increase of appetite had grown by what it fed
on; and it was another fact that within a month she had
married his uncle. And the two facts, of which he had
utter personal evidence, could not be reconciled. When
such a shock is recounted in the earliest place in the play
where Hamlet is able to reveal himself, that is his soliloquy
in the second scene, we may surely expect that the rest of

the play will deal largely with the working out of this shock. It should also be observed that in his soliloquy Hamlet says nothing about his uncle having cheated him of the succession; he thinks only of his mother's action, which has made the world ugly for him, and (in a lesser degree) of his uncle's unworthiness.

In the next scene—that is before Hamlet meets his father's ghost—we hear of his courtship of Ophelia; and I think the critics have been backward in seeing the great prominence of this motive, which occurs so early in the play and at the very time when the themes that are to prevail are being set forth. The chief value of Clutton-Brock's little book on *Hamlet* lies in his perception that Hamlet is unkind to Ophelia because he sees in her a repetition of his mother; but I believe we may go further and say that the way Act One is organised suggests that Hamlet's very first advances to Ophelia had to do with his mother's second marriage. He hoped to find in Ophelia evidence to contradict what his mother's action appeared to prove. Not that we are justified in working out a time-table for *Hamlet* (after the manner of those appendices of Bradley that read like a parody of the text of *Shakespearean Tragedy*); but the order of dramatic presentation bids us connect Gertrude and Ophelia closely and to expect that Polonius's orders to Ophelia to deny her presence to Hamlet will have a powerful bearing on the course of the play. By the end of the third scene therefore the overwhelmingly important theme is Gertrude's re-marriage, its effect on Hamlet reinforced by Ophelia's behaviour, and the probability of further consequences. Nor, if this theme was to count during the course of the play, could Shakespeare have spared making it so prominent in view of the force of the next two scenes, when Hamlet meets his father's ghost. Well, the Ghost commands Hamlet to avenge his murder and, though putting an end to the incestuous connection of Claudius and Gertrude, not to contrive anything against his mother:

> Let not the royal bed of Denmark be
> A couch for luxury and damned incest.
> But, howsoever thou pursuest this act,
> Taint not thy mind; nor let thy soul contrive
> Against thy mother aught. Leave her to heaven
> And to those thorns that in her bosom lodge
> To prick and sting her.

The words are ambiguous. It is not clear whether in upbraiding his mother as Hamlet later did he was transgressing his father's command. But at least the Ghost couples what are by now evidently the master-themes, the vengeance on Claudius and the lascivious and incestuous guilt of Gertrude. And it is the co-existence of the two themes and the contrasted ways in which Hamlet responds to them that give the play what regularity of structure it possesses. It must not be forgotten that the first act closes with the Ghost scene; and not only by modern editorial conjecture. Though there are no act divisions in the Quartos, there are in the Folio up to the end of Act Two, and it is good that the Folio confirms the obvious pause in the action, implying that the main themes have now been stated, at this point.

The second act, which begins the true second part, develops both themes without bringing them to a crisis. Hamlet's disgust at his mother had prompted his dealings with Ophelia; and her actions in their turn exacerbate his feelings against her, his mother, and all women. Hamlet's experience with his father's ghost had dealt a second shock to his mind, bringing with it the danger of derangement and prompting him to assume a fictitious derangement in addition and to express the conflict in his feelings through long soliloquies. This derangement alarms Claudius and causes him to take precautions. The next act contains Hamlet's answers to the two shocks he has suffered in the first act; and they consist of his testing the Ghost's veracity through the play, followed by his sparing Claudius immediately after, and of his upbraiding his mother. There is no interval between his dealing with Claudius and his dealing with his mother, and these should be considered jointly yet in contrast; so considered, they match the manner in which the two themes had been set forth in the first act. Interpretations of the play-scene, of the sparing of Claudius,[1] and of Hamlet's words to his mother vary and will continue to vary; but such variety will not affect the plea that the scenes must be considered together in correspondence with the master-motives as set forth in the first act, and that thus they give the play a recognisable shape. My impression is that Hamlet forces himself in his dealings with Claudius, lashing himself to hysteria but not acting with his whole heart, while he puts his whole self into his words to his mother. In the deepest sense therefore he disobeys the Ghost's commands. Hamlet's brutal words to Ophelia in the play-scene tell the same tale, for they show him thinking of his mother's action and of his disgust of womankind at the very crisis of his dealings with Claudius. While, then, in the two scenes that mainly concern Claudius Hamlet shows himself histrionic, artificially self-excited, and even hysterical, in talking to his mother he shows the full range of his character and relieves his long-suppressed feelings by speaking from his heart. Moreover in his positive advice to her he finds an outlet for the active side of his nature. This is the supreme scene of the play. Psychologically, what resolution there is in the play is mainly here. Once Hamlet can face his mother and share with her the burden of what he thinks of her, he can at least begin to see the world as something other than a prison. In the very act of

[1] For a note on Hamlet's motives see Appendix B, p. 146.

rating his mother he does a justice to Ophelia which the bleeding body of Polonius ironically renders incapable of any happy consequence. Hamlet calls his mother's re-marriage

> such an act
> That blurs the grace and blush of modesty,
> Calls virtue hypocrite, takes off the rose
> From the fair forehead of an innocent love,
> And sets a blister there.

He is of course thinking of Ophelia, of her true innocence and of his own treatment of her as if she were a harlot. (How, by the way, do those who consider Hamlet's coarse-ness to Ophelia as an undigested relic from the old play get around these lines? Surely if Shakespeare himself gives an explanation, it is idle to seek further.) It is in this scene too that Hamlet, although terrified by the Ghost, over-whelmingly vehement in denunciating the loathsomeness of his mother's sexual sin, and callous over the body of Polonius ("I'll lug the guts into the neighbour room"), shows his most winning sanity and the utmost delicacy of his sensibilities. When, on the Ghost's exit, he protests that his pulse keeps time as temperately as his mother's, the words that follow bear his protest out. What better could illustrate his sane and delicate and critical temper than the sudden interpolation into his preaching to his mother of

> Forgive me this my virtue,
> For in the fatness of these pursy times
> Virtue itself of vice must pardon beg,
> Yea, curb and woo for leave to do him good.

His final callousness over Polonius's body did not exclude his pious words quoted earlier about his deed, while his final disposition towards his mother is tender. All these exhibitions, even if they are fragmentary, of sanity and clean feeling come after Hamlet has relieved his mind of his horror at his mother's act; and, coming also after and in spite of the Ghost's interposition urging revenge, are surely meant to show us that his mother's act rather than the obligation to his dead father usurps the main part of his mind. What we learn from this most revealing scene is that Hamlet (unlike the world at large) does not really believe that it is relevant to kill Claudius: that will not bring his father back to life. To awaken Gertrude's sense of guilt is his fundamental need.

Hamlet's conversation with his mother does not cure him, does not altogether rescue him from his prison, but it does either initiate a slow healing process or render him less impatient of his burdens. His bad conscience about the revenge stirs again, on his way to take ship to England, in his last soliloquy ("How all occasions . . ."). Later, on his return, he exhibits violent passions at Ophelia's funeral. Yet these relapses do not efface the sense of Hamlet's having obtained a real relief and being more resigned. And this more resigned temper persists till the end of the play. In the third part (from Hamlet's return from England) the psychological interest, from the preponderant motives of Hamlet's mind having been revealed, shifts partly to the other characters and now counts for less compared with the interest of the plot; the details of which evolve with perfect propriety from the events recounted in the second part.

Hamlet, then, does possess a shape. The states of mind presented in the first act lead to certain actions in the second act and are tested and clarified in the third. Thus clarified they persist to the end of the play. This shape contributes substantially to the poetic quality; and mainly on the intellectual side, giving the sense of a masterly controlling brain. But psychological explication showing intellectual mastery, and spiritual action are not the same.

At most Hamlet regains some of the dignity and composure that we know to have been part of his original endowment. Out of the wreck of his affection and respect for his mother something may have been salved. By comparing what has been regained or salved with what formerly existed whole we do indeed get a pleasant sense of order. But, with no great revelation or reversal of direction or regeneration, the play cannot answer to one of our expectations from the highest tragedy.

This failure does not mean that *Hamlet* is not one of the greatest plays. On the contrary, the subtlety and the fascination of its psychological appeal (within the limits indicated) joined with the simple but firm lines of its general shaping exalt it to eminence.

Even so I do not place these matters, however important, quite among the principal things, and it remains to say which these are.

The first is the sheer wealth and vigour and brilliance of all the things that happen. In fact one of *Hamlet's* virtues resembles that of Masefield's *Odtaa*, where the sheer variety and the very lack of a rigorous type of causal logic for every detail are part of the point. In addition to the general shaping I have been at pains to describe, there are more casual sequences of detail, comparable to the way one word may suggest another. *Man—monkey— monkeypuzzle—difficulties of climbing—Alps—Swiss francs:* the sequence of thought is obvious enough. But it is a superficial sequence by means of only one out of numberless details comprised in each item. Yet its very casualness is related to life and is not alien to art. The entry of the Players in *Hamlet* is perfectly contrived and linked: yet it has just that casual character. Simply as a play of things happening, of one event being bred out of another, and of each event being described with appropriate and unwearied brilliance, *Hamlet* is supreme. Such an opinion can claim the support of Horatio, who in almost the last words of the play describes the action as having consisted

> Of carnal, bloody, and unnatural acts,
> Of accidental judgements, casual slaughters,
> Of deaths put on by cunning and forced cause,
> And, in this upshot, purposes mistook
> Fall'n on the inventors' heads.

The effect of all these events so masterly presented is primarily one of vitality. One is tempted to call *Hamlet* the greatest display of sheer imaginative vitality in literary form that a man has so far achieved. It is here we feel that Shakespeare first reached the full extent of his powers; and he gives us the sense of glorying in them. And no other play of Shakespeare gives us just that touch of sheer exultation.

The second principal matter has to do as much with the setting as with the business of the play. To explain it I will proceed indirectly. Aristotle said that poetry answered two profound human instincts: those of imitation and of harmony or rhythm. The first had to do with the desire to learn. It matters less what Aristotle in this highly compressed passage of the *Poetics* precisely meant than that he suggested a distinction of fundamental importance. Thoughtful people are puzzled by the appearance life presents to them. Their hour-to-hour experiences do not satisfy them and are felt to convey a false impression. The impression is both impoverished and unordered, and they wish to have it enlarged and interpreted. In fulfilling this wish people will do the work for themselves or obtain help from others in proportions that accord with their capacities. The great artists do a great deal of the work for themselves and offer a great deal of help to others. The help they offer will be through enrichment and through ordering or interpretation, corresponding to Aristotle's distinction between imitation and harmony or rhythm. The artists by the richness of their presentation enlarge the range of experience comprehensible by the unaided efforts of the ordinary person, and by the form of their presentation suggest some order in this range of experience. A great artist will excel in both functions. But, however great he is, he has to compromise and to adjust the scope of one function to that of the other. If he is very great, he will wish to present a variety of such compromises, for each type of compromise will express something that none of the others can.

To apply the above to Shakespeare's tragedies. *King Lear* is the play where the balance is most evenly struck. In *Othello* the content of experience is less and the emphasis falls more on the ordering. *Hamlet* is best understood as a play less of ordering than of sheer explication or presentation, as a play presenting the utmost variety of human experience in the largest possible cosmic setting.

It is strange that a play so dominated as it would seem by one character should convey so rich a sense of varied humanity and human activity. But this is what happens, and criticism has erred in treating the profundities and the paradoxes and the turnings of Hamlet's mind as the substance of the play rather than as the means of expressing another substance. It is not the interest and variety of Hamlet's mind that comes first but the wonder and variety of all human experience which his quality of mind makes peculiarly evident; just as to a psychologist lunatics are chiefly interesting not in themselves but because by isolating and exaggerating an ordinary mental proclivity they make its workings clearer and hence give new information about the workings of the ordinary mind. Hamlet, the achieved Renaissance young man of the most varied accomplishment, is in his normal self well equipped to reflect an abundant human experience: subjected to two shocks that come near to upsetting his reason, his capacities are enlarged still further and his sensibilities so worked on, that experience as now reflected in him takes on a new and terrifying intensity. Nor must we forget the abundance of humanity and of human action that reinforces the range of Hamlet's mind in suggesting multifarious existence. It is not only of minor characters such as Osric that I am thinking, but of such passages as Marcellus's description in the first scene of the preparations for war. Unnecessarily particularised for the requirements of the plot, it somehow forces one to hear the beat of hammers in the distance as the accompaniment of the scene and to bear in our minds the notion of ordinary physical life going on behind the heightened passions of the main actors.

Critics have spoken of the difficult or intractable material Shakespeare inherited from his traditional story. Difficult it may have been, but in the end perfect for his purposes. Aiming not at tidiness or homogeneity or a classical shape, he could use the antique barbaric nature of his material to contrast as sharply as possible with the modern refinement and sophistication of his hero. Moreover it is a contrast true in a double sense: in the familiar sense that refinement and civilisation are but a thin crust on a much greater mass of barbarism and disorder; and in the sense that Shakespeare's own England was a violent blend of the crude and the delicate.

Shakespeare's picture of the varieties of human experience was of course conditioned by the contemporary world picture. And I doubt if in any other play of Shakespeare there is so strong an impression of the total range of creation from the angels to the beasts. Maybe in the *Tempest* the lower stretches of the chain of being and the doubtful stretches between man and angel are more fully presented, but the angels and man's variety in his own great stretch of the chain are presented there with less emphasis. This way of looking at creation is powerfully traditional and Christian; and in *Hamlet* if anywhere in Shakespeare we notice the genealogy from the Miracle Plays with their setting of Heaven, Purgatory, and Hell, as for instance in the hero's description of himself as a fellow "crawling between heaven and earth". Indeed, one of the best analogies with the total landscape of *Hamlet* is Landland's description of the fair field full of folk at the opening of *Piers Plowman*. *Hamlet* is one of the most medieval as well as one of the most acutely modern of Shakespeare's plays. And though the theme of spiritual regeneration may be absent from the plot, the setting includes the religious consciousness most eminently.[1] But lest this medievalism remain too little qualified, let me give a second analogy: with Homer's description of the scenes on the shield of Achilles. It is a brief description, dealing mainly with ordinary life and aimed at correcting the more narrowly martial trend of the *Iliad* as a whole, but it includes the picture of the ocean and the stars, and blended with the variegated adventures in the body of the poem, sets forth Homer's surpassing awareness of the wonder and diversity of life and of the fateful conditions under which it is transacted.

I hope that the bearing of my last pages on the question whether *Hamlet* is a tragedy or a problem play has been apparent. I will end by speaking explicitly on this topic. The tragic mode is ideally very definite and formal. Motives are clear in the characters, and the spectator has no doubt where his sympathies should lie. We know that Medea has been hardly treated and also that she acted with deplorable violence. We know that Macbeth was a

[1] For the contention that in *Hamlet* Shakespeare shows himself the heir of Christian Platonism see Joseph E. Baker, *The Philosophy of Hamlet*, in the Parrott Presentation Volume (Princeton 1935) pp. 455-70

villain in having Banquo murdered. Further, in ideal tragedy life is presented in a startlingly clear and unmistakable shape: we are meant to see it indubitably so and not otherwise. When sheer explication, or abundance of things presented, takes first place, then we leave the realm of tragedy for that of the problem play. Here it is the problems themselves, their richness, their interest, and their diversity, and not their solution or significant arrangement that come first. I have argued that *Hamlet*, though containing tragedy of sorts, and though reinforced intellectually by a noble general shape, belongs principally to this type. The same is true of *Troilus and Cressida*, though it has less tragic content. And to this play I turn next.

Notes on *Hamlet*

No one is likely to accept another man's reading of *Hamlet*. Of the three weighty books that have been published in recent years on the course of the play's action (J. Dover Wilson, *What Happens in "Hamlet"*, Cambridge 1935; H. Granville-Barker, *Hamlet*, London 1937; L. L. Schücking, *The Meaning of Hamlet*, London 1937) I have found the second most congenial, though I differ completely on the matter of Hamlet's regeneration, in which Granville-Barker agrees with Middleton Murry and C. S. Lewis. More especially I have found Granville-Barker very helpful in his sections on the shaping of the plot. But I have found the best interpretation of the action of *Hamlet* in Dowden's footnotes to his edition in the Arden Shakespeare. Dowden read the text very closely and with sensitive sympathy, and his notes are better criticism than his section on *Hamlet* in *Shakespere, his Mind and Art*. This is not surprising, because Dowden's *Hamlet*, first published in 1899, is twenty-four years later than his *Shakespere*.

SHAKESPEARE'S PROBLEM PLAYS

A. J. A. Waldock's *Hamlet* (Cambridge 1931) has helped me in various ways, particularly in its encouragement not to miss the play for the critics. I agree with the respect he accords to A. C. Bradley's treatment of the play.

Though I cannot read *Hamlet* generally in the way G. Wilson Knight does (*The Wheel of Fire*, London 1930), I agree with his insistence on the fundamental irrelevance to Hamlet of killing Claudius: "What would have been the use of killing Claudius? Would that have saved his mother's honour?" (p. 33).

TROILUS AND CRESSIDA

Although the contemporary setting cannot ensure an answer to the main questions that *Troilus and Cressida* insists on posing it can help tell us the kind of play it is and, even more, is not. In Victorian times many readers refused to give it a proper chance because they thought it degraded the high Homeric treatment of the Trojan War. To-day the case is different: there are fewer readers of Homer, and of these a smaller proportion would insist on the sanctity of the Homeric tradition. Besides, the recent findings of scholarship that Shakespeare's Trojan War is medieval and not classical are beginning to penetrate the consciousness of the non-academic reader. A recent attempt to answer the main questions through associating *Troilus and Cressida* with a type of play, satirical comedy, which then enjoyed a brief vogue, does not succeed, but it does help to explain why Shakespeare chose a form that was neither tragedy, comedy, nor history through which to say the things he wished to say.

It is usual, in glossing Shakespeare's treatment of the Trojan War, to say that this war had long ceased to be heroic, that to the medieval reader the Greeks had always been the enemy and an ill-natured set, and that as time went on the Trojans too were tarnished; further, Cressida during the fifteenth and sixteenth centuries became proverbial as a wanton and a lazar, so that Shakespeare could not possibly have made her the character Chaucer made her, and finally Shakespeare's un-Homeric and apparently cynical treatment of his material was quite to be expected in view of the state in which the material reached him. Such a general conception is useful in warning us what not to expect, but I believe that Shakespeare's medieval predecessors can help us rather more than is usually allowed.

First, it is well to understand that *Troilus and Cressida* need bear no relation to those books of Chapman's Homer published in 1598. It is true that Shakespeare was very unlikely not to have read them, but it is equally true that the bulk of his material was medieval and that for the small residue he need not have gone to Chapman. Homer had long been known in Latin and was hence accessible to many readers, and the way he treated the war must have been common knowledge. There was no need of Chapman's translation to tell the Elizabethans that Thersites was a railer—Erasmus, among others, had made that clear long ago. And Shakespeare's Thersites himself, though exclusively Homeric in origin, is un-Homeric in function; he is a version of the Elizabethan Fool, and hence a privileged person. When in the second book of the *Iliad* Odysseus hits Thersites on the back with his golden staff for railing at King Agamemnon and raises a bloody weal, all the Greek leaders laugh sweetly. But Shakespeare's Achilles defends Thersites from Ajax, who had no business to hit a licensed fool for sharp words. The other matter that is at least partly Homeric and not medieval is the duel between Hector and Ajax. It is true that there was one—and a very important one—in the *Troy Book*, but it was an accidental one in a battle. The challenge, Nestor's complaint that the Greek chieftains are slack in accepting the challenge, the choice of the Greek defendant by lot, and the breaking off of the duel by heralds are all absent from the *Troy Book* and come from Homer. But even so Shakespeare makes the whole episode a very medieval affair conducted according to the rules of chivalry. Remotest of all from Homer is Hector's protest that

> He hath a lady, wiser, fairer, truer,
> Than ever Greek did compass in his arms.

The insistence on the close kinship of Hector and Ajax is also medieval. Shakespeare *may* have got some of the non-medieval details of the duel from Chapman's *Iliad* but he could have got them from Homer direct, through his small Greek, or from a Latin translation, or from hearsay. Had he taken Chapman very seriously he must have motivated Achilles's sloth as Homer does in his first book, through his anger at being bereft of Briseis. But he does not: he first lets us think that Achilles is merely proud and moody and later brings in the medieval motive, his love for Polyxena. No, we should think of Chapman only by the way and rather pay our attention to the great inherited conception of Troy as the rich and wonderful city whose fall was one of the most striking and exemplary achievements of Time and during whose flourishing so many chivalric or base or romantic deeds were transacted. Shakespeare himself had made poetry of these conceptions years before in the *Rape of Lucrece*. First, in her protest against Time and Opportunity, Lucrece describes it as Time's glory to calm contending kings, to ruinate proud buildings and smear with dust their glittering golden towers, and to feed oblivion with decay of things. This is very much the same Time, which in *Troilus and Cressida* is the arbitrator of the Trojan War, which dusts over the gilt of past deeds, and which feeds that great-sized monster, Oblivion, with their fragments. Later, Lucrece, meditating on her own sacrifice to Opportunity and Time, thinks of another ruin of Time, the city of Troy, and she describes episodes from the siege, recollecting them from a painting. Sinon, the traitor and proverbial as such in the

Middle Ages, is dwelt on, for he corresponds to Tarquin. Lucrece does not find the extreme of misery

> Till she despairing Hecuba beheld
> Staring on Priam's wounds with her old eyes,
> Which bleeding under Pyrrhus' proud foot lies.

> In her the painter had anatomised
> Time's ruin.   (1447-51)

If these lines look forward to *Hamlet*, the rest of the descriptions show that the elements of the Trojan world of *Troilus and Cressida* existed in Shakespeare's mind many years before. First, there is the guilt of Helen and Paris, the criminal weakness of Priam, and the tragedy that society should suffer for the private quarrels of a few. The passage deserves quoting in full, if only to show that Shakespeare could speak bitterly of war at a time when, according to the rules, he ought to have been feeding on the elation of the post-Armada years, untouched by the disillusion later experienced through the history of Essex. Lucrece exclaims:

> Show me the strumpet that began this stir,
> That with my nails her beauty I may tear.
> Thy heat of lust, fond Paris, did incur
> This load of wrath that burning Troy doth bear:
> Thy eye kindled the fire that burneth here;
> And here in Troy, for trespass of thine eye,
> The sire the son the dame and daughter die.

> Why should the private pleasure of some one
> Become the public plague of many moe?
> Let sin, alone committed, light alone
> Upon his head that hath transgressed so;
> Let guiltless souls be freed from guilty woe:
> For one's offence why should so many fall,
> To plague a private sin in general?

Lo, here weeps Hecuba, here Priam dies,
Here manly Hector faints, here Troilus swounds,
Here friend by friend in bloody channel lies,
And friend to friend gives unadvised wounds,
And one man's lust these many lives confounds.
Had doting Priam check'd his son's desire,
Troy had been bright with fame and not with fire.

(1471-91)

Note how Hector and Troilus are mentioned together, the
two chief Trojan heroes, against the Homeric treatment.
The other characters mentioned are Achilles, Nestor,
Ajax, and Ulysses. Achilles bears no character, but the
other three are as they were later to be in *Troilus and
Cressida*:

In Ajax' eyes blunt rage and rigour roll'd,
But the mild glance that sly Ulysses lent
Show'd deep regard and smiling government.

There pleading might you see grave Nestor stand
. . . . his beard, all silver white,
Wagg'd up and down.   (1398-1401, 1405-6)

Precisely whence Shakespeare derived his notions of
Troy we cannot know. Many may have reached him
through conversation. But the kind of tradition he was
open to is shown neatly enough in a poem he may or may
not have read, Hawes's *Pastime of Pleasure*. The pen-
ultimate chapter is on Time and his acts. And one of his
chief acts was the destruction of Troy—and no other
fallen city is mentioned:

Do not I, Tyme, cause nature to augment,
Do not I, Tyme, cause nature to decay,
Do not I, Tyme, cause man to be presente,
Do not I, Tyme, take his lyfe away,

37

> Do not I, Tyme, cause death take his say,
> Do not I, Tyme, passe his youth and age,
> Do not I, Tyme, every thynge asswage?
>
> In tyme Troye the cyte was edyfied;
> By tyme also was the destruccyon.

And casually, in the eighth stanza of the twentieth chapter comes the mention of Priam's folly in allowing the war to happen at all.

> The myghty Pryant, somtyme kynge of Troye,
> Wyth all his cyte so well fortyfyed,
> Lytle regarded all his welth or joye,
> Wythout wysdome truely exemplyfied,
> His propre death him selfe he nutrifyed;
> Agaynst his warre wysdome did reply,
> At his grete nede to resist the contrary.

Troy fell, one of the supreme works of Time, and it was the Trojans' fault, even if they were better knights than the Greeks.

In his preface Hawes mentions his "maister Lydgate, the monke of Bury, floure of eloquence"; and there is no doubt that Lydgate was one of the writers most responsible for spreading the traditions about Troy of which I have been speaking. But before I come to Lydgate's picture of the Trojan War, I must ask the question how Shakespeare is likely to have read and heeded him.

It is generally admitted that Shakespeare drew from both the main English works deriving from Guido delle Colonne's prose version of the Troy legends, Lydgate's *Troy Book* and Caxton's *Recuyell of the Histories of Troye*. I believe one may go further and say that he went to Caxton for some of his facts but that he found Lydgate much more useful in suggesting ideas and motivation. For instance, though both mention the six gates of Troy, and in the same order, it is from Caxton that Shakespeare in his prologue takes the forms of the names "Dardan and Timbria, Helias, Chetas, Troien, And Antenorides". But take the scenes in Lydgate and Caxton where Ulysses, Nestor, and Diomed try to persuade Achilles to fight, scenes which correspond to Ulysses's conversation with Achilles in *Troilus and Cressida*, III. 3, and you will find that there is nothing in Caxton that resembles Shakespeare except possibly Achilles's protest that "in the end there is no prowess but it be forgotten", while these lines of Lydgate dwelling on the need to keep renown fresh are close in sentiment though not in poetic force to Ulysses's "Time hath, my lord . . ." Ulysses appeals to Achilles

> By youre manhood, that is spoke of so ferre
> That your renoun to the worldis ende
> Reported be, wherso that men wende,
> Perpetually, by freshnes of hewe
> Day by day to encrese newe,
> That the triumphe of this highe victorie
> Be put in story and eke in memorie,
> And so enprented that foryetilnes
> No power have by malis to oppresse
> Youre fame in knyghthod, dirken or difface,
> That shyneth yit so clere in many place
> Withoute eclipsynge, sothly this no les;
> Which to conserve ye be now rekeles
> Of wilfulnes to cloude so the lyght
> Of youre renoun that whilom shon so bright,
> Youre mighty hond of manhood to withdrawe.
>
> (IV. 1770-85)

There are of course places where the debt is doubtful. Achilles kills Hector in *Troilus and Cressida* as he kills Troilus in Lydgate and Caxton; and there is no doubt that Shakespeare draws from one or the other, or from both simultaneously. But we cannot be certain which alternative to choose. Such a detail matters little compared with the general and pervasive influences. And the probability here may be settled by picturing how Shakespeare was likely to have come across his originals. Such inquiries are unusual; but it may really make a difference to know not only what his most influential original was likely to be but also whether he had acquired his material in the past, meditated on it and recollected it, or whether he came on it suddenly and for the first time and cast it into dramatic form while still fresh in his mind. It is plain from *Lucrece* that he had long known the medieval matter of Troy, and it is highly probable that he knew it primarily from Lydgate.

After having superseded Chaucer as the most popular English poet in the late fifteenth and early sixteenth centuries Lydgate gradually dwindled from that high position but became firmly established as one of the few early English classics. Right at the end of the sixteenth century and shortly before Shakespeare wrote *Troilus and Cressida* Meres wrote that "England hath three ancient poets, Chaucer, Gower, and Lydgate". Nashe in his preface to Greene's *Menaphon* (1589) mentions Chaucer, Lydgate, and Gower as ancient English poets to set up against the Italians. Three years earlier Webbe's *Of English Poetry*, in its survey of English poetical production, began with Gower and Chaucer, and went on to Lydgate and *Piers Plowman*, adding that there was nothing else to note till the reign of Henry VIII. The most popular of all poems in Shakespeare's boyhood, the *Mirror for Magistrates*, professed to continue Lydgate's *Fall of Princes*. It could never have done so unless Lydgate had been a much read poet. I have no doubt myself that Shakespeare read Lydgate as a youth, along with the other early writers or works enumerated, just as I believe he read Hall's *Chronicle*. There is no proof, and yet the probability is overwhelming unless we make Shakespeare a freak among poets. Boys and youths who feel the true urge to versify want to know what the poets of contemporary reputation have written, and habitually satisfy that want by voracious reading. Far from cramming up Gower in middle age in order to compose the choruses of *Pericles* Shakespeare must have read him in his youth as one of the English classics, venerable if quaint. And we shall never get *Troilus and Cressida* right unless we think of a Shakespeare steeped as a youth in the antique and venerable and quaint world of Lydgate's Troy.

This is not a popular supposition, for the notion of an unread Shakespeare, whose first stirrings of mind came from contact with the stage, is still widely prevalent in England. In his edition of *Macbeth* [1] (1947) Dover Wilson doubts whether Shakespeare ever looked into the *Mirror for Magistrates*, unless to read Sackville's contributions. I can only be amazed at such a sentiment. The *Mirror* was so popular in Shakespeare's youth that edition followed edition with new "tragedies" often added. Even with a lukewarm taste for poetry Shakespeare could hardly have kept aloof. It may be that in America, where so much work has been done on the conditions in which he must have grown up, the notion of Shakespeare in his youth reading what was then thought to constitute the English poetical classics will not appear improbable.

What would Shakespeare have found in Lydgate's *Troy Book* and in a more factual and less moralised form in Caxton's *Recuyell*? First of all a world antique yet familiar, rather ridiculous but still, as literature, useful; a version of the world of medieval chivalry. The city that Priam built on the ruins of the old city of Laomedon surpassed in glory anything actually on earth. Priam himself was a peerless king, tall, bold, just, musical, incorruptible, an

[1] In the New Cambridge Shakespeare, p. xliv, note 3.

early diner, and above all a cherisher of worthy knights. His sons too were peerless. Hector was the first knight in the world, the spring and well of knighthood, the ground, root, and crop of chivalry. Paris was the handsomest man and the best archer in the world. Troilus, it is true, could not be peerless because of Hector, but he was nearly as formidable. Polyxena (in spite of Helen) was peerless, and when Nature created her she put forth a unique effort to make her excel all other women in beauty and in morals. In scope Lydgate is lavish. The tale of Troy as we think of it extending from the rape of Helen to the sack of the city is preceded by the story of how Laomedon's city was destroyed by Hercules (with the adventures of the Argonauts included) and is followed by the adventures of the Greek chieftains up to the death of Ulysses. Romantic excess prevails in the Trojan War proper. Hector twice kills a thousand Greeks single-handed in one battle. When Hector has been killed, Troilus takes his place as the first Trojan hero and performs similar prodigies. Fighting on the Trojan side was a monstrous archer (or sagittary). He was man down to his middle and horse below, but he neighed like a horse. He had a fiery face and flaming breath; and he did great execution among the Greeks until Diomed killed him.

But Lydgate, as well as transmitting this romantic material, is its critic. He is a courageous and original moralist. In a most prominent place, near the beginning of Book Two which opens the main Trojan War, he condemns that war and many others too as springing from a trivial cause.

> We trewly may adverten in oure thought
> That for the valu of a thing of nought
> Mortal causes and werris first by-gonne;
> Strif and debate here under the sonne
> Wer meved first of smal occasioun

That caused after gret confusioun,
That no man can the harmys half endite.
For, for a cause dere y-nowghe a myte
Eche is redy to distroien other;
A man for litel will strive with his brother:
Blood is unkynde, whiche gretly is to drede.
Allas, whi nyl thei taken better hede?
For olde Troye and afterward the newe
Thorughe smal enchesoun, who the trothe knewe,
Wer finally brought to distruccioun.

(II. 123-37)

For all Priam's many virtues Lydgate blames him sharply
for being responsible for the war. After Priam had rebuilt
Troy he lived in peace and prosperity until envy stirred
him to avenge the detention of Hesione by the Greeks. It
was malice that

Made him wery to lyven in tranquille
And mevid him, of his iniquite,
Upon the Grekis avenged for to be.

And it was Priam who stirred up his sons to vengeance.
Through the mouth of Cassandra Lydgate insists on the
sin of abducting Helen and the punishment Troy will get
from it:

O wrechid Troye, errying in this cas
Withinne thi silfe to suffre this trespas,
For to concent unto swyche folye
In sustenyng of foule avoutrye
That Paris shulde takye unto wyve
The quene Eleyne whos husband is alyve.

(II. 4195-200)

And as well as saying that the war offends the sanctity of
marriage, she reiterates the Trojans' folly in having stirred
up trouble when they were prosperous. Nor is Hector
himself blameless, for his death was due to his sin of

43

covetousness. Seeing a Greek knight wearing jewelled armour, he forgets prudence in coveting this armour. He kills the knight, and the better to strip him puts his shield on his back. This gives Achilles the chance of a treacherous attack. Lydgate reprimands Hector severely:

> Desyre of havynge, in a gredy thought,
> To highe noblesse sothly longeth nought,
> Nor swiche pelfre, spoillynge, nor robberie
> Apartene to worthi chivalrye;
> For covetyse and knyghthod, as I lere,
> In o cheyne may not be knet y-fere.
>
> (III. 5361-6)

Not only that, but Hector was culpably negligent in not accepting the gifts of fortune. In the first great battle after the Greeks established the bridgehead the Trojans were victorious. Hector killed Patroclus and carried the battle into the Greek ships. Then he had a duel with his kinsman Ajax, who persuaded him for friendship sake to call off the day's battle. Hector imprudently yielded, and fortune's favours were over for good. Caxton, for once, is as strong a moralist as Lydgate when he describes this episode, though he bases his criticism more solely on the folly of refusing fortune's favour and does not put it in terms of mistaken chivalry. Here is his piece of moralising:

The unhappy Hector accorded to him his request and blew an horn and made all his people to withdraw into the city. Then had the Trojans begun to put fire in the ships of the Greeks and had all brent them, ne had Hector called them fro thence, whereof the Trojans were sorry of the rappeal. This was the cause wherefore the Trojans lost to have the victory to the which they might never after attain ne come; for fortune was to them contrary. And therefore Virgil saith *Non est misericordia in bello*: that is to say, there is no mercy in battle. A man ought not to take misericord, but take the victory who may get it.

If the Trojans are to blame, though in the main chivalrous, the Greeks are worse. Ulysses and Diomed on an embassy to Troy behave arrogantly and misdeliver their message. Achilles is a downright villain through the treachery he uses to procure the deaths of the two chief Trojan warriors, Hector and Troilus.

Such, then, are the general features of the Lydgate tradition. We must further remember that Shakespeare probably knew Chaucer's *Troilus and Criseyde* at an early age. This poem was regarded as Chaucer's masterpiece in the sixteenth century. Erasmus mentions it approvingly in the *Praise of Folly*, Sidney in his *Defence of Poetry* mentions it alone of Chaucer's works. Now when Cressida appears in the *Troy Book* she is already Troilus's plighted lover; and Lydgate expressly excuses himself from treating their earlier history by saying that Chaucer has already dealt with it. So Shakespeare would perforce take his conception of the pair, in their capacity of lovers, from Chaucer. Now Chaucer treats his theme as a comedy and never gets nearer to authentic tragic feeling than to pathos. But in Lydgate Troilus is anything but a comic figure. He is indeed a model of constancy as in Chaucer; but this constancy goes beyond fidelity in love and includes a ruthless resolution:

> He was alwey feithful just and stable,
> Perseveraunt and of wil inmutable
> Upon what thing he onys set his herte,
> That doubilnes mygth hym nat perverte.
>
> (II. 4879-82)

Above all he was a fierce fighter and no Trojan chief came near him as such except Hector.

It would take too long to enumerate further details of Shakespeare's inheritance, but enough has been said to show that it contained a number of paradoxes. The Trojan

War was both romantic and fought for an unworthy cause. Some of the fighters were true knights but committed moral errors: some were ignoble. Troilus was both a comic and a grim figure. Cressida was a faithless woman, but the course of her infidelity and the state of mind dictating it could vary very widely. The story of Troilus and Cressida was an integral part of the story of Troy.

Even if we discount the supposed influence of Chapman's *Iliad*, there is still the chance that *Troilus and Cressida* yielded to a contemporary literary fashion as well as looked to the past. That the play's character becomes plain through its belonging to a new type of comedy is the thesis of Oscar J. Campbell's *Comicall Satyre and Shakespeare's "Troilus and Cressida"*.[1] When in 1599 a ban was put on satire and epigram, the satirical impulse was diverted to a new type of comedy professing to derive from the personal type, the Attic Old Comedy. Jonson began the mode with *Every Man out of his Humour* in the same year and continued it in *Cynthia's Revels* and *Poetaster*. Marston was the next practitioner in *Antonio and Mellida*, *Antonio's Revenge*, *Jack Drum's Entertainment*, and *What You Will*. All these plays leave the reader not serene but "in an aroused state of scorn at human folly and futility". Campbell holds that the difficulties of *Troilus and Cressida* vanish if it is read as a satirical comedy of this kind, if we expect it to leave us uneasy and apt to go on criticising the abuses we see about us. Shakespeare satirised not only Cressida but Troilus, not only Greeks but Trojans. Though not writing a pacifist tract he did attack undisciplined warfare where the generals quarrelled, which was only too common in some late Elizabethan expeditions.

As a whole the thesis cannot stand and it has been successfully challenged. I should myself question several

[1] San Marino, California, 1938.

of the premisses on which it rests. Far from lacking seren-
ity after *Every Man out of his Humour*, the reader identifies
himself with Jonson's steady belief in good sense and the
social norm and rejoices that the various satirised characters have been purged of their ridiculous or wicked
peculiarities. Indeed the conversion of Sordido is too in-
genuously simple and pious and melodramatic. The play is
anything but a problem play. Marston's Antonio plays
contain satirical elements, but they are nearer to the
revenge play of Kyd than to any conceivable satirical
comedy; certainly nearer to *Hamlet* than to *Troilus and
Cressida*. They lack indeed the Jonsonian repose, but their
unease is quite other than the difficult and complex unease
by which *Troilus and Cressida* is characterised. Campbell's
thesis fails when applied to this play partly because he
misses its complexity. The Trojans may have their faults
but they have them differently from the Greeks. Hector
may err but he is noble compared with Achilles. And to
turn Troilus into an adept in lechery is to wreck one of
Shakespeare's masterpieces of characterisation and to go
flat against what his poetry is telling us. It is not a mere
sensualist who, awaiting Cressida, says

> I stalk about her door
> Like a strange soul upon the Stygian banks
> Staying for waftage,

and

> My heart beats thicker than a feverous pulse,
> And all my powers do their bestowing lose
> Like vassalage at unawares encount'ring
> The eye of majesty.

The last words tell of a noble devotion, which we know to
be tragically misplaced. But the misplacement does not
alter the nobility.

Nevertheless Campbell's thesis is useful in making us

think of Jonson and Marston in relation to Shakespeare at this time. *Hamlet* somehow gathers body when read with the Antonio plays and the *Malcontent*. The satirical element in *Troilus and Cressida*, though deriving from the medieval treatment of the Troy story, is strengthened by the intellectual massiveness of Jonson and by his vast command of words. Jonson was a stiff pace-setter, and Shakespeare benefited by this stiffness. In particular Shakespeare would hardly have made Thersites what he is without Jonson's stimulus. In many ways Macilente in *Every Man out of his Humour* is unlike Thersites, notably when he begins to take an active part in the plot. But as the satirical commentator he resembles him. Carlo Buffone can do the same job. In this passage, for instance, he speaks very like Thersites:

> I never hungered so much for anything in my life as I do to know our gallants' success at court; now is that lean bald-rib Macilente, that salt villain, plotting some mischievous device and lies a-soaking in their frothy humours like a dry crust, till he has drunk 'em all up. Could the pummice but hold up his eyes at other men's happiness in any reasonable proportion, 'slid the slave were to be loved next heaven, above honour, wealth, rich fare, apparel, wenches, all the delights of the belly and the groin whatever.

Finally, Peter Alexander[1] had adduced a possible contemporary circumstance to explain some of the peculiarities of *Troilus and Cressida*. The cynicism, the scurrility, and the academic tone of some of the speeches could be accounted for, if Shakespeare were writing for the sophisticated audience of the Inns of Court.[1] It is an interesting and attractive theory that may facilitate the first stages of understanding, and it has proved widely acceptable. There is, however, one scene which does not fit. This is III. 2,

---

[1] *Shakespeare's Life and Art*, pp. 195-6.

where Pandarus, Troilus, and Cressida emerge from their own distinctive and dramatic characters and become types: Pandarus as the Bawd, Troilus as Fidelity in Love, Cressida as Falsehood in Love. It is also the one scene that confirms L. C. Knights's [1] notion that the play is partially akin to the Morality. The scene is quaint and primitive and alien to the sophisticated audience of the Inns of Court. Indeed it resembles in intention those crude informative passages in Elizabethan History Plays where the author seeks to satisfy the appetite for facts likely in a simple audience. It is as if Shakespeare was saying "I think you have a notion in your heads of Troilus, Cressida, and Pandarus as proverbial persons and you are curious to know how they have become such. Generally, I give you my own version of the story, but in this scene here they are, for your satisfaction, in the guise in which you have habitually pictured them." First, Troilus says that "as true as Troilus" will be the chief of all comparisons of constancy, then Cressida says much the same of "as false as Cressid", and then Pandarus sums up, including himself:

> Go to, a bargain made: seal it, seal it; I'll be the witness. Here I hold your hand, here my cousin's. If ever you prove false one to another, since I have taken such pains to bring you together, let all pitiful goers-between be called to the world's end after my name: call them all Pandars. Let all constant men be Troiluses, all false women Cressids, and all brokers-between Pandars. Say, amen!

Here Troilus has quite ceased to be Troy's second Hector, the furious fighter and fiery politician, and is simply the Constant Lover; Cressida has ceased to be the charming and witty, if wanton, Trojan society lady and is simply Female Fickleness; and Pandar is no longer Lord Pan-

---

[1] *Times Literary Supplement*, 2 June 1932, p. 408.

darus, the simpering courtier and kindly sympathiser with Troilus in the extremity of his romantic passion, and has turned into the eternal Common Bawd. To the Elizabethans such transformations would be perfectly natural. An eminent example occurs at the end of the tenth canto of Book Three of the *Fairy Queen*, where Malbecco, once a jealous old man with a recognisable character, is left Timon-like to live in a cave near the sea-shore till he ceases to be a man and becomes Jealousy.

> There dwells he ever, miserable swain,
> Hateful both to himself and every wight,
> Where he through privy grief and horror vain
> Is woxen so deform'd that he has quite
> Forgot he was a man and Jealousy is hight.

But Spenser and his methods, and the Morality tradition, though familiar enough at the Inns of Court of 1602, were not the latest, fashionable things; and Shakespeare's archaic scene comes queerly and yet with wonderful dramatic effect in the midst of matter so much more sophisticated.

I have dwelt so long [1] on the play's background, because for a play about which opinion is so divided no extrinsic help in interpretation can be spared. I will recapitulate some of the conditions that might have prompted Shakespeare to frame his play in this or that fashion. Most important of all he must have had a certain large conception of the Trojan War, acquired beyond doubt several years before and in all probability fixed deep and firm in his memory by youthful reading. According to it the war was one of the great examples of the ruin wrought by Time, a war fought for an unjust cause but marked by superlative displays of knightly prowess, displays now

---

[1] For another illustration of how Lydgate can explain a difficulty in *Troilus and Cressida* see Appendix C, p. 149.

belonging to an antique age. Next, Shakespeare's conception of a single episode of the war, the loves of Troilus and
Cressida, would be rather alien to his general conception
of the war and even inconsistent in its parts. The most
eminent version was comic, but other versions were satirical. Shakespeare's options here were wide. Thirdly, there
was a quite different version of the whole war that contradicted the version he and his contemporaries were used
to, that of Homer. It would have been possible, but daring
and heterodox, to have adopted it. More important, to do
so would have been to deny a firmly seated and perhaps
very dear portion of his mental stores. Anyhow, he was
aware of the version and took some details from it.
Fourthly, Shakespeare was exposed to the influence of a
biting type of comedy practised just then by his greatest
contemporary dramatist. This satirical type was nicely
fitted to reinforce the critical temper already strong in the
main inherited conception of the Trojan War. Finally,
Shakespeare may have had in mind an exceptionally
sophisticated audience to which to address his play.

The sum of all these circumstances should be such as to
prevent our being at all surprised at any of the ingredients
of *Troilus and Cressida*; it should, at this hour of day, have
quenched all moanings that Shakespeare was guilty of
degrading the high Homeric tradition. It should reassure
us that in substance Shakespeare was being decently conventional. But I cannot share the optimism of those critics
who have believed that this or that traditional strain or
nearer influence gives the entry into the play itself. Indeed,
in seeking extrinsic help in understanding *Troilus and
Cressida*, I have reached the same conclusion as in studying Shakespeare's History Plays, about which I wrote
"Shakespeare's Histories are more like his own Comedies
and Tragedies than like others' Histories". Some help we
may get from Lydgate and Jonson, but more still from

Shakespeare's other plays. And in the end the critic is forced to his basic task of interpreting the text: a task whose difficulties and dangers are obvious through a diversity of interpretation as great as of any play of Shakespeare.

Since the character of a play (if it has any consistent character at all) is determined by its opening scenes, I will begin by recording how these scenes in *Troilus and Cressida* strike me.

Everyone would agree that in *Troilus and Cressida* Shakespeare set himself a double theme, that of the Trojan War and that of the loves of the title characters. They would further agree that the two themes are approximated through having as motives a woman, each bad in her own way. It is especially important to remember that Lydgate is strong on the worthlessness of Helen. But more prominent, as the link between the themes, is Troilus himself, who is both lover in the one story and knight in the other. And again we must remember the surpassing prowess of Troilus in the Lydgate tradition: second only to Hector in the field and having the last word in the council chamber. Shakespeare therefore chose the most effective method of bringing in both themes jointly when he began with Troilus. But he also chose to complicate matters by showing him along with Pandarus, in a comic light inherited from Chaucer. It is unusual comedy, for in it verse and prose are mixed; and this mixture is in itself a pointer to the kind of play it is to be. Troilus speaks verse and Pandarus prose. Troilus is young, very much in love, changeable, taking himself with terrible seriousness. He is ridiculous, and yet he speaks such poetry that we have to take him seriously as well:

> Her bed is India; there she lies, a pearl:
> Between our Ilium and where she resides
> Let it be call'd the wild and wandering flood,

Ourself the merchant, and this sailing Pandar
Our doubtful hope, our convoy, and our bark.

This mixture of the ridiculous and the serious is not that proper to comedy. It is comic when the ridiculously romantic excesses of youth are tamed to the terms of good sense. But Pandarus does not stand for good sense and he does not inhabit the same world as Troilus. He is good-natured but he is coarse; and the kind of love that possesses Troilus is quite outside his experience or power of imagination. And so we have the rather bitterly ironical spectacle of two people, both apparently united in their end, yet at bottom conceiving that end in incompatible terms. There is thus much richness in the things presented and much zest in the spectacle. The effect of the alternating verse and prose is inflation and deflation. But what is deflated is in part good, and the deflation is but partly valid. Our responses are thus complicated; and not every spectator likes thus to be played on. Most prefer to know at once just how they stand. Those who enjoy such complication will find the scene a perfect opening: it is masterly done. When Pandarus goes out, Troilus hears the sounds of war and comments on them in words that both tell us the colour in which the Trojan War will appear and clinch the irony that has already been indicated:

Peace, you ungracious clamours, peace, rude sounds!
Fools on both sides! Helen must needs be fair,
When with your blood you daily paint her thus.
I cannot fight upon this argument;
It is too starv'd a subject for my sword.
But Pandarus—O gods, how do you plague me!
I cannot come to Cressid but by Pandar;
And he's as tetchy to be woo'd to woo
As she is stubborn-chaste against all suit.

Troilus speaks about Helen in a way that grossly contra-

53

dicts his words about her in the Trojan council scene (II. 2); and we can take our choice between saying that he is in a highly changeable mood and saying that he here speaks out of character because Shakespeare needs just here to tell us how he will picture the war, and Troilus is handy. Anyhow the two main themes are brought in by the simultaneous mention of the two motivating ladies: while Troilus's disillusion over Helen and his illusion over Cressida as "stubborn-chaste" are successfully ironical. Finally Aeneas enters, and Troilus shows his mutability by consenting to enter the battle in spite of having just said he "cannot fight upon this argument".

The second scene of the play, between Cressida and Pandarus, shows the two "arguments", of love and of war, and the passing of the main Trojan warriors, supporters of the second "argument". Pandarus and Cressida talk in prose together; they are of the same world. Pandarus, in his silly story about the hairs in Troilus's chin, lets us see the triviality of Helen and her courtiers; Cressida by her mechanically witty interruptions shows herself an efficient society woman without depth of feeling. It is directly after Pandarus's story, and with ironical intent, that the Greek warriors are made to pass by. The importance of Hector among them has been made clear during the whole scene. The tone of the scene is comic, with a strong mixture of satire. Deflation is the rule; and it prepares by contrast for the highly inflated scene that follows, the war council of the Greeks.

So far the intention of the play has been pretty plain; but what are we now to make of the ample rhetoric that flows from the mouths of Agamemnon, Nestor, and Ulysses for over two hundred lines from the beginning? Van Doren hates it so much that he calls the style of the whole play "loud, brassy, and abandoned". Ulysses's speech on *degree* is "merely as rant, tremendous". Others see in this same speech one of the high places in Shakespeare's most considered and serious writing, while the scene itself becomes a weighty and earnest piece of political theorising. I cannot accept either opinion. The style throughout is quite deliberate and not in the least "abandoned"; and yet Shakespeare was not writing in the full passion of earnestness, was not quite sunk in what he did, but (to alter the metaphor) had his tongue at least part way in his cheek. He does in fact continue his method of inflation and deflation; only here, in addition to the anticipatory deflation of the previous scene, the inflated style contains, through its excess, its own deflatory self-criticism. Shakespeare does in fact slightly parody himself, but he enjoys such writing and knows that it is grand stuff though somewhat burlesque: with the same implication (but without the depreciation and apology) as Eliot's comment in *East Coker* on his lapse into an earlier way of writing:

> That was a way of putting it—not very satisfactory:
> A periphrastic study in a worn-out poetical fashion.

Now the interesting thing (and Van Doren has noted it) is that the style from which the speeches in question take off is that of certain parts of *Henry V*. The speeches are rhetorical rather than conversational, containing long sentences, frequent synonyms or near-synonyms, and an unusually latinised vocabulary. Here are a few places in *Henry V* that come near to the rhetorical style of *Troilus and Cressida*:

> O pardon! since a crooked figure may
> Attest in little space a million;
> And let us, ciphers to this great accompt,
> On your imaginary forces work.
> Suppose within the girdle of these walls
> Are now confin'd two mighty monarchies,
> Whose high upreared and abutting fronts
> The perilous narrow ocean parts asunder.

And, to relief of lazars and weak age,
Of indigent faint souls past corporal toil . . .

And never noted in him any study,
Any retirement, any sequestration
From open haunts and popularity.

The severals and unhidden passages
Of his true titles to some certain dukedoms . . .

For government, though high and low and lower,
Put into parts doth keep in one consent,
Congreeing in a full and natural close
Like music. Therefore doth heaven divide
The state of man in divers functions,
Setting endeavour in continual motion;
To which is fixed as an aim or butt
Obedience.

Ulysses's speech on degree echoes in many ways the Archbishop's speech on the commonwealth of the bees, actually hinting at it in

When that the general is not like the hive
To whom the foragers shall all repair,
What honey is expected?

But of all the speeches in *Henry V* the nearest in style to *Triolus and Cressida* is Burgundy's in V. 2 on the plight of the land of France, which may suggest that the occurrence of the word *deracinate* here and in Ulysses's speech on degree, and nowhere else in Shakespeare, is more than an accident.

The resemblances between these speeches and parts of *Henry V* count the more, because there is nothing like them in *Julius Caesar*, the political play that comes between. Antony there may not be an amiable character, and Brutus may be a poor politician, but there is not the slightest suggestion that politicians are windbags. But in

Henry V the spirit of criticism plays on the minor characters who are politicians and may even extend to the man
of action in general, if only unconsciously. In *Troilus and
Cressida* this spirit comes right into the open and is
intensified.

But though the common tone of the Greeks' speeches is
inflated, there is scope for dramatic differentiation within
it. Agamemnon is slow-witted and genuinely pompous:
witness his lack of initiative as a commander throughout
the play and some of his later speeches. Not for nothing
does Patroclus, for Achilles's amusement, assume Agamemnon's "topless deputation . . . with terms unsquared,
which from the tongue of roaring Typhon dropp'd would
seem hyperboles". After Hector's challenge has been
delivered, later in this scene, Agamemnon can think of
nothing subtler than to tell Achilles of it; and it remains
for Ulysses to turn it to good account. For Agamemnon's
continued inflation take his few words at the beginning of
IV. 5, when Ajax stands ready for the duel:

> Here art thou in appointment fresh and fair,
> Anticipating time with starting courage.
> Give with thy trumpet a loud note to Troy,
> Thou dreadful Ajax, that the appalled air
> May pierce the head of the great combatant
> And hale him hither.

The inflation of Nestor's style is perhaps more on the side
of proverbial amplification and suggests the old man as
well as the pompous politician. Ulysses's is more complicated. He can be direct enough if he cares, as when he
describes Patroclus acting Nestor and the mirth of
Achilles, who cries

> O, enough, Patroclus,
> Or give me ribs of steel! I shall split all
> In pleasure of my spleen.

His is an assumed inflation, an example of a good politician's adaptability to his surroundings. And he knows exactly what he is doing. His speech on degree is a cunning piece of rhetorical generalisation in the current style initiated by Agamemnon and Nestor, splendid and beating them on their own ground, and leading on to something concrete, a reference to Achilles, the chief offender against discipline. Through this speech, so correct in sentiment yet so exciting to a later age as an epitome of contemporary commonplaces, so lacking in personal passion and yet so enchanting in its golden and leisured orotundity, Ulysses sets up (as he was to maintain and increase) his pre-eminence among the Greek leaders. When he speaks of the contempt of Achilles and others for staff work,

> So that the ram that batters down the wall,
> For the great swing and rudeness of his poise,
> They place before his hand that made the engine,
> Or those that with the fineness of their souls
> By reason guide his execution,

he knows that he is the one leader with an effective fineness of soul and that his mission is to get the most effective ram, Achilles, into action again.

As Ulysses finishes this criticism of the Greek officers on strike, the trumpet sounds for Aeneas's delivery of Hector's challenge. At first appearance Aeneas's words, so taut and sprightly, offer an utter contrast to the Greeks' sluggish and protracted oratory. The Trojans, he says, are

> Courtiers as free, as debonair, unarm'd,
> As bending angels; that's their fame in peace:
> But when they would seem soldiers, they have galls,
> Good arms, strong joints, true swords; and, Jove's accord,
> Nothing so full of heart.

That might be well enough by itself, but what of the challenge, itself?

> Hector, in view of Trojans and of Greeks,
> Shall make it good, or do his best to do it:
> He hath a lady, wiser, fairer, truer,
> Than ever Greek did compass in his arms;
> And will to-morrow with his trumpet call
> Midway between your tents and walls of Troy,
> To rouse a Grecian that is true in love.
> If any come, Hector shall honour him;
> If none, he'll say in Troy when he retires
> The Grecian dames are sunburnt and not worth
> The splinter of a lance.

Certainly the style here is fresher, quicker, more energetic than the Greek rhetoric, and intentionally so. But can we take it that Shakespeare is, as it were, quite on the Trojan side and that he sets up Trojan forthrightness against Greek pomposity and cunning? I fear not. Aeneas's energy, like the Greeks' magniloquence, carries within it its own agent of deflation. Although much of the Middle Ages survived into the Elizabethan age, although a traditional romantic episode like the wager can pass accepted and uncriticised in a romantic play like *Cymbeline*, this presentation of *amour courtois*, in a context such as Shakespeare has created, can only be slightly absurd, a piece of engaging if you will, but not serious antiquarianism. Puntarvolo and his surroundings in *Every Man out of his Humour* are a greatly exaggerated version of the same notion; and the Baron of Bradwardine in *Waverley* is very close to Shakespeare's Trojans. The Trojans have admirable qualities but they are antiquated in their ideas and they lack the realism of the Greeks who, though in their way inefficient, are at least modern and free from the antiquarian illusions of chivalry. The ineffectiveness of the Trojans' admirable qualities can, as the play proceeds, hover on the borders of the tragic and the ridiculous. If we need confirmation that Hector's challenge is not to be taken in full seriousness we can find it in the speeches of Agamemnon and Nestor. Agamemnon's

> And may that soldier a mere recreant prove
> That means not, hath not, or is not in love!
> If then one is, or hath, or means to be,
> That one meets Hector—

Or Nestor's

> tell him that my lady
> Was fairer than his grandam and as chaste—

are surely not to be taken in all seriousness.

The scene ends with Nestor and Ulysses remaining behind. Ulysses finds Nestor useful as a political ally and tells him his scheme to put Hector's challenge up to a lottery, which shall be rigged so as to fall to Ajax. Achilles, through jealousy, may thus be stirred to action. Ulysses thus emerges as the indubitable motive force of the Greek camp.

The next scene (II. 1), which the editors should never have separated from the last by an act division, introduces us to the factious Greek leader and to Thersites. It is pure comedy, embittered by Thersites's exuberantly foul vocabulary. To make Thersites into a chorus, the authentic commentator on the play's action, is ridiculous. His function is that of a Fool, to give a twist to every action and every motive. And this twist is always to the vile and the loathsome. Sometimes he hits the mark, at others he is wide of it. His exclamation at the end of V. 2, "Lechery, lechery; still wars and lechery; nothing else holds fashion", has been taken as a choric comment on the play as a whole. Actually, in its context, it refers to Diomed and Patroclus alone; but Troilus, Aeneas, and Ulysses have just gone out, and to the last two it applies not at all and to the first only in small part. Thersites is a consistently bitter element in the play, not a coloured glass through which we watch it. His genuine if diseased curiosity makes his ubiquity credible; and his ubiquity helps to join one part of the Greek camp with another. For instance in the present scene he shows his knowledge that Ulysses with Nestor is the true motive force among the Greeks and he tells Achilles and Ajax so:

> There's Ulysses and old Nestor . . . yoke you like draught-oxen
> and make you plough up the wars. . . . 'To, Achilles! To, Ajax!'

Achilles, the lolling bully for the moment, but with a keen practical eye to his self-interest, is brilliantly drawn. He defends Thersites against Ajax with hulking leisureliness, but speeds up at the end when he speaks of the challenge and his own possible part in it, his eyes narrowing in self-centred jealousy.

> *Achil.* Marry, this, sir, is proclaim'd through all our host:
> That Hector, by the fifth hour of the sun,
> Will with a trumpet 'twixt our tents and Troy
> To-morrow morning call some knights to arms
> That hath a stomach; and such a one that dare
> Maintain—I know not what: 'tis trash. Farewell.
> *Ajax.* Farewell. Who shall answer him?
> *Achil.* I know not: 'tis put to lottery; otherwise
> He knew his man.
> *Ajax.* Oh, meaning you. I will go learn more of it.

The next scene shows Priam and his sons in council. It is of almost the same length as the Greek council scene and is an obvious companion piece. But it is more difficult to interpret; and before attempting its difficulties I will note some of the undoubted or probable results of the comparison Shakespeare wants us to make.

First (and this is no more than a probability) Aeneas and Antenor are absent from the Trojan council, which consists only of Priam and his sons; it is thus antique and patriarchal in contrast to the more normal mixed council of the Greeks. Secondly, the Trojans, though beginning with a matter of concrete policy, whether to keep or to return Helen, go back to the great abstract moral questions, while the Greeks had never left practical politics. Even Ulysses's general doctrine of degree was never detached from its practical application. As well as being more moral the Trojans allow a larger scope to the emotions. Thirdly, as Ulysses emerged as the virtual leader of the Greeks, so Troilus emerges as the dynamic power of the Trojans. Hector rebukes Troilus and Paris for being young men in a hurry; yet it is Troilus's counsel that prevails, and (most important) he speaks incomparably the finest poetry. Hector, for all his talents and his magnanimity, does in effect match Achilles as the battering-ram rather than the hand directing it, only, as it were, one gifted with brains which it does not use. Troilus, like Ulysses, is the guiding hand. And Troilus and Ulysses remain the dominant characters throughout. To establish this important position I will anticipate and give two illustrations from later parts of the play. First, it is Ulysses, the wisest of the Greeks, that describes Troilus to Agamemnon. Now we know already that in the Trojan tradition used by Shakespeare Hector and Troilus were the two first Trojan commanders, with the others far behind them. Ulysses makes Troilus the more formidable and single-minded,

> a true knight,
> Not yet mature, yet matchless, firm of words,
> Speaking in deeds and deedless in his tongue,
> Not soon provok'd nor being provok'd soon calm'd:
> His heart and hand both open and both free,
> For what he has he gives, what thinks he shows;
> Yet gives he not till judgement guide his bounty

> Nor dignifies an impair thought with breath:
> Manly as Hector but more dangerous;
> For Hector in his blaze of wrath subscribes
> To tender objects, but he in heat of action
> Is more vindicative than jealous love.

Secondly, in one of the play's culminating places, if not the culminating place itself, the revelation of Cressida's infidelity, it is Ulysses who is Troilus's companion. Shakespeare wanted us to think of them together; and the things the two stand for must surely be an important part of the play's meaning.

But at this point the question cannot but intrude: what has become of the romantic lover of the play's first scene, the young man slightly comic though with the hint of profounder feelings? To claim a psychological consistency would be possible: young men very much in love are in fact able to conduct practical business efficiently. But to use such a possibility as an aesthetic justification would be to flout Aristotle's just preference for probable impossibilities over possible improbabilities. The change from the harassed and mercurial lover to the fiercely resolute and overmastering young commander is too violent to be swallowed without effort. It is very greatly mitigated in the acting, because sufficient has happened between Troilus's two appearances to induce a good measure of oblivion. But it cannot be taken with ultimate ease; and I fancy that one reason why the play fails to satisfy us completely is that Troilus as a character is made to bear too much, that his double part of romantic and unfortunate lover and of leading spirit among the Trojan commanders taxes the spectator's aesthetic credulity beyond its powers. Shakespeare here may have been tempted to try the impossible through loyalty to his originals, Chaucer and Lydgate, who give such different versions of Troilus.

I come now to the difficulties of the scene itself: the

interpretation of the Trojan debate. And first I had better summarise it. Priam announces the Greek offer to make peace, wiping out all old scores, if Helen is returned to them, and asks Hector's opinion. Hector says that though personally fearless of the Greeks, he is prone on grounds of general policy to consider the actual event. Helen in herself is not worth the results of her seizure. Therefore let her go back. Troilus breaks in violently to the effect that it is an insult to Priam's honour to reduce motives to a scale of reason. Helenus contradicts him; and Troilus scornfully proves how reason in Helenus teaches him to run away. Hector repeats that Helen is not worth the cost of holding her. Troilus retorts that worth is not in the object but in the minds of those considering the object. Hector passionately asserts the principle of self-value and that it is mad idolatry to make the service greater than the god. Troilus evades the argument and puts forward another: that it is dishonourable to go back on our commitments. The Trojans consented to Paris's expedition and they must back him up. Then he shifts his argument again: Helen is not worthless but a peerless beauty; she is self-valuable and those responsible for her other kind of value must not cheapen it by lowering their first esteem. Cassandra breaks in, foretells Troy's ruin if Helen stays, and goes out. Hector asks Troilus if fear of failure in a bad cause does not move him. Troilus replies that we must not think of the event. Moreover Cassandra is mad, and her madness must not compromise a course hallowed by the engagement of the honour of all. Paris then echoes Troilus's pleas, interrupted by Priam, who tells him he is an interested party. Hector compliments Paris and Troilus on their speeches but says they are nevertheless superficial, not grounded on ethical truth but the one on lust and the other on revenge. Ethically, there is a great overriding argument: the sanctity of marriage based on natural law and international consent. The plea that it is dishonourable to go back on a commitment is false, if that commitment was in itself wicked. To persist in it is but to augment the crime. The plain morality is that Helen should be returned; and yet, Hector says with a surprising turn, he agrees with Paris and Troilus in their resolution to keep her, for it is a matter affecting the honour of each of them. Troilus is delighted and, dropping any pretence at argument, enthusiastically proclaims the glory for which Helen is the pretext.

The scene advances the action not at all; its dramatic purpose is to depict the minds of the two principal Trojans, Hector and Troilus. And it does so through a contrast that would have been plain to any educated Elizabethan. The above summary should have shown that Troilus is not strong in argument: his understanding is ruled by his emotions. He finds plenty of reasons why Helen should be kept, but they are reasons hastily shuffled together to support a resolution already taken. He refuses to use his understanding on the fundamental ethics of the case. Thus, in Elizabethan terms, he is defective in wit but strong in will. Hector is just the opposite. He has a perfectly clear understanding and recognises unerringly the fundamental ethics of the case and the prejudiced understanding of his brothers. But there is a divorce between his wit, in which he is so strong, and his will, in which he is so defective. He is a plain case of "video meliora proboque, deteriora sequor". And as it is the will that directs action, Hector as a directing force of the Trojans must yield to Troilus.

Such an opinion of Hector will provoke opposition because there is so set a prejudice for the opinion of him as the soul of honour, the one really good man in the play, tragically murdered by Achilles. But I simply cannot see how we can gloze over the terrible rift in him between his understanding and his will, which Shakespeare shows us with an emphasis so strong as sometimes to stun rather than awaken the critics' perceptions. Nor is this picture of Hector's fatally divided mind, unmistakably evident, as I believe, from the present scene, unsupported. In IV. 5, when Ulysses and Hector talk, Hector in reply to Ulysses's assertion that Troy's towers will fall, says

> I must not believe you.
> There they stand yet, and modestly I think
> The fall of every Phrygian stone will cost
> A drop of Grecian blood. The end crowns all,
> And that old common arbitrator, Time,
> Will one day end it.

Hector does in fact believe it, and yet he says he must not. Then there is V. 3, where Hector leaves Troy for the last time. Cassandra in trying to keep him back uses exactly the same arguments Hector uses in the council scene for sending Helen back; and we are meant to think of both scenes together. Here Cassandra argues that his vow to fight has proved wrong and unreasonable in view of the adverse omens and that he ought to go back on it. Just as with his understanding he knew that for the general good Helen should be restored, so he must now know that it is for the general good that he should avoid fighting on this fatal day. Again his will follows not his understanding but the emotional direction of his sense of honour. In the same scene Hector shows his practical ineffectiveness when he treats Troilus as a boy when clearly he has ceased to be one. Troilus in his turn rebukes his vice of excessive generosity in the field, a vice that favours the enemy overmuch. Hector, for all his nobility, stands for a double ineffectiveness: personally for a mind divided between reasonable, realistically moral, action and unreasoning point of honour; symbolically, for the anachronistic continuance of the chivalric code into a world which has abandoned it.

My opinion of Hector gets some confirmation also from Shakespeare's originals, Lydgate and Caxton. There is a scene in Lydgate (II. 2063-3318) which is so close to the Trojan council in Shakespeare that he must have had some memory of it. The occasion is different from Shakespeare and is of the discussion Priam holds with his sons after he has got the sanction of his regular council to seek to avenge the abduction of Hesione; and it follows Lydgate's earnest reprimand of Priam for not being content with his present prosperity.[1] Priam begins with a passionate plea for vengeance and calls on Hector to back him up. Hector speaks in much the same way as in Shakespeare but with arguments in reverse order and with the opposite conclusion. He begins by professing warmly his belief in the obligation to promote chivalry and his desire for revenge. Nevertheless, he goes on, you must consider the event or end. The Greeks are actually stronger; and though we may begin well the end may be ill. Further, Hesione is not worth the risk of all their lives:

> And though also myn aunte Exioun
> Ageyn al right be holde of Thelamoun,
> It is not good for her redempcioun
> To putte us alle to destruccioun.
> I rede not to beyen hir half so dere.

Paris disagrees, and, having recounted his dream of the three goddesses, proposes stealing a Greek woman and exchanging her for Hesione. Deiphobus supports Paris. Helenus opposes Paris because he knows by his divination that Troy will be destroyed if Paris goes. At this speech all sit silent and troubled, till at last Troilus "young, fresh,

---

[1] The corresponding scene in Caxton is much shorter, less impressive, and less moralised.

and lusty" springs up and chides his family for being so
cast down. He furiously attacks Helenus for a coward and
scorns the truth of divination. Let Helenus allow "lusty
knights" to prove their valour in battle and to be avenged
on their enemies. The whole gathering praise Troilus's
high spirit, and not even Hector opens his mouth against
him. Later, when Cassandra hears of Paris's success and
Helen's arrival, she condemns the adultery in words that
were quoted early in this chapter. In this scene of Priam
discussing his proposed vengeance on the Greeks with his
sons, Hector shows the best understanding and foresight
but his will is quite borne down by Troilus. The position
therefore that Shakespeare's Hector was strong in wit but
not in will is confirmed by the corresponding scene in
Lydgate.

Hector's other vices, the covetousness that causes his
death and his disastrous excess of magnanimity in the
field, have been mentioned already. The first is not
stressed by Shakespeare, who merely makes Hector say,
when he sees one "enter in sumptuous armour", that he
has a liking for that armour. But when Troilus accuses
him of a dangerous and excessive magnanimity we tend
to justify the accusation, and with Lydgate in the background can be confirmed in so doing.

To return to the Trojan council scene as a whole, it
differs from the corresponding Greek scene in being
written in swifter and tauter verse and in touching on
matters which Shakespeare, having them more at heart,
treats with a nearer and more intimate fervour. The irony
of Troilus arguing that value rests in the valuer and not in
the thing valued is terrible when we apply his argument
to his own fate at the hands of Cressida, and looks forward
to the play's emotional climax. And the same question, in
the department of war, was obviously haunting Shakespeare through its occurrence so prominently in *Hamlet*;

for it is precisely this question that Hamlet discusses when on his way to embark for England he meets the forces of Fortinbras (IV. 4): first with Fortinbras's captain, and then with himself in his soliloquy beginning "How all occasions . . ." Each scene may grow clearer in the light of the other's treatment of this common subject; so I will make a comparison. The episode in *Hamlet* is of the hero's seeing Fortinbras and his soldiers pass by on their way to fight the Poles for the possession of a piece of land not worth five ducats' rent or even purchase. While talking to Fortinbras's captain, Hamlet is critical of the coming contest:

> This is the imposthume of much wealth and peace,
> That inward breaks and shows no cause without
> Why the man dies.

In other words the bloodshed has no higher function than to get rid of an excess of blood in the body politic, of population in the state. But this thought is not single; it is fiercely denied in the soliloquy that follows. For Hamlet proceeds to take sides against the ethics both of Lydgate's and of Shakespeare's Hector by condemning a precise thinking on the event. Fortinbras was right in cocking a snook at the invisible event and considering present glory. And he, Hamlet, is the more despicable in his shirking the glory of present action, for having a much more compelling cause. True greatness consists not in doing something for a trivial issue but in exalting that issue through turning it into a matter of honour. Helen in the Trojan council has exactly the same position as the barren piece of land in Hamlet's questionings: her final justification is that she is an argument of honour. The most interesting thing that emerges from the comparison is the contrasted positions of Hector and Hamlet. Hector is clear on the ethical side and in theory opposes the ethics of Hamlet's soliloquy; but in practice he follows Hamlet's advice. Hamlet is tortured on the ethical side and ends by opposing the theories of Hector. But in practice he follows Hector's theories with a pertinacity that argues some unconscious acceptance. Hamlet's conflict is deeper, nobler, more interesting than Hector's. With his conscious mind he flogs himself into the belief that action about a triviality is justified; with his deeper self he can consent to embrace only the worthiest of causes. The conflict is fierce, and Hamlet is a tragic figure. Hector reasons clearly and then weakly allows custom and convention to bear down his reasoning—which he has put up with a kind of frivolous academicism knowing that he will not follow it out. In the division of his mind he is no more than a pathetic figure: a great man of action without ultimate conviction about the grounds for that action; lacking at once the ruthless practical impulse of Troilus and the deep emotions of Hamlet.

But if Shakespeare is nearer emotionally to the problems that exercise the Trojan council, he treats the Trojans no less critically than he treated the Greeks. The Trojans have more capacious minds, deeper feelings, and a freer speech than the Greeks, yet they achieve less. Out of Greek pomposity and cunning a line of action has emerged; all the Trojans can do is to accept the news of a picturesque but pointless challenge and to decide to go on as before.

By the end of the scene just discussed, the temper of the play has been made clear; and from now on I can abbreviate. II. 3 takes us back to the Greeks, to the abuse of Thersites and to the leaders feeding the pride of Ajax to provoke Achilles. The tone is mainly comic; but Thersites's "all the argument is a whore and a cuckold" is a satirical comment on Troilus's description of Helen in the last scene as

a Grecian queen, whose youth and freshness
Wrinkles Apollo's and makes stale the morning.

In the next scene (III. 1), when Pandarus visits Helen
to ask her help in excusing Troilus's expected absence
from the royal supper table that evening, the Trojans get
their turn of satire and ridicule. Paris's servant is insolent
to Lord Pandarus—an upsetting of degree; Pandarus's
conversation with Helen and Paris degrades the "argument" of the war and those about her through satirising
contemporary affectations of speech in the most frivolous
section of high society. The scene leads on to a greater:
the coming together of Troilus and Cressida through the
offices of Pandarus, ending with the curious episode,
already mentioned, of the three characters ceasing to be
themselves and becoming types. Now that Troilus has
won Cressida, his love has shed its comic side and has
become wholly tragic—as befits the powerful character
revealed in the council scene. The only plane on which the
two can meet is the sensual; and for a first meeting this
can suffice them. But the lovely poetry Troilus speaks and
the speculations his passion prompts mark him off decis-
ively from the world of Cressida and Pandarus. Tragic
irony reaches its height when hearing of Cressida's
nervous and sensual flutter from Pandarus he says:

> Even such a passion doth embrace my bosom.
> My heart beats thicker than a feverous pulse,
> And all my powers do their bestowing lose
> Like vassalage at unawares encount'ring
> The eye of majesty.

He is doubly deceived: his own passion is not at all such
as Cressida's, and she is anything but the regal character
he makes her out. Anyhow, the fortunes and the mind
of Troilus have greatly advanced in prominence.

It is partly to match this prominence that the next scene

exists. It begins with a brief account of Calchas obtaining his request to have Cressida exchanged for Antenor,[1] but its larger substance is Ulysses's plea with Achilles to be active once more. And through it Ulysses's pre-eminence among the Greeks is increased and confirmed. He is in charge. He makes the other Greek leaders pass by Achilles's tent and greet him coldly, and himself remains behind to have his say. Here he is at the height of his powers. His policy is consummate. He introduces the desired topic, first by his device of reading something in a book. Then, instead of applying the moral to Achilles direct he cites Ajax as the spectacle of what chance can do to advance a mediocrity into momentary glory. Achilles, envious of Ajax, is likely to be thrown off his guard and to be the less prepared for Ulysses's application of the moral to himself. Ulysses's lie about the lottery, "an act that very chance doth throw upon him", when actually he had rigged it himself, is slipped in with the perfection of cool casualness. In his culminating speech on Time he clothes his worldly wisdom with a surpassing eloquence: an eloquence which, not to be degraded, demands as auditor an Achilles of superior mental capacity to the Achilles of the rest of the play; an Achilles whom Ulysses, even though partly in flattery, calls "thou great and complete man" and who, before seeing Ulysses, had spoken nobly and intelligently on the problem of reputation. In this the highest reach of Ulysses's eloquence we are surely meant to contrast his doctrine of honour with the corresponding doctrine of Troilus, his peer among the Trojans. For all his eloquence Ulysses's doctrine of honour is purely selfish and materialistic. The virtue that is bidden not to seek remuneration of the thing it was has nothing ethical about

---

[1] It is a good piece of craft that Diomed should have a double charge: to fetch Cressida and to make sure that Hector stands by his challenge. The two main themes are thus brought together.

it and is no more than the crude glory that feeds human pride. It is related to no abstract ideal. Troilus, though muddled in his notion of honour, is an idealist. Honour is related to a standard external to the individual. There cannot be too much of it, and even if it is in the eye of the beholder and not in the object, the eye is that of all beholders not just that of the one isolated self-centred person. Each type of honour shows up poorly when measured by the merits of the other.

The natures of the two sides in the war have now been fully developed in isolation; Cressida is due to be transferred from one side to another: so henceforth the two sides and the two themes will be mainly treated together. There is much business to be got through, and the play proceeds more hastily. In the next scene, IV. 1, Diomed on his mission to Troy to bring back Cressida talks with Aeneas and Paris. The quality and intention of these conversations are not very plain. Aeneas and Diomed mix fraternisation with defiance in a conventionally heroic way. Does Shakespeare intend any satire here? I think not; and when Paris says in comment

> This is the most despiteful gentle greeting,
> The noblest hateful love that e'er I heard of,

any satire is at the expense of Paris's affected language. If this conversation is not satirical, its point will be to prepare the spectator by its martial tone for the battle scenes at the end of the play. The bitter words of Diomed to Paris about Helen are not too easy to justify either. Helen has come in for plenty of criticism, and Diomed only reinforces a way of feeling we know already.

The next three scenes, IV. 2. 3, and 4, are all transacted in Pandarus's house and should be treated as one. They tell of the lovers after their night together, the fetching of Cressida, and of the lovers' farewell. They are part comic,

F

part pathetic: not tragic, because Troilus thinks he can trust Cressida and that he can visit her among the Greeks. They are scenes splendidly suited to the stage, very varied in passions, full of living characterisation. For instance when Cressida in her grief at parting calls herself "a woful Cressid 'mongst the merry Greeks", we feel that even then the thought flashes through her that the merry Greeks may compensate for what she is losing. Troilus behaves with dignity, already an older man than the youth of the play's opening scene: a clear analogy with Hamlet.

The next is a long scene, bringing first Cressida with Diomed and then Hector with his supporters to the Greek camp. It is nodal, uniting the play's several veins; and that it should be in the main comic or inflated is highly significant. Agamemnon's pompous opening has been quoted already. It is capped by Ajax:

> Thou, trumpet, there's my purse.
> Now crack thy lungs and split they brazen pipe.
> Blow, villain, till thy sphered bias cheek
> Outswell the colic of puff'd Aquilon.
> Come, stretch thy chest and let thy eyes spout blood:
> Thou blow'st for Hector.

It might almost be Ancient Pistol speaking. The episode of Cressida kissed by all the Greek leaders (except Ulysses) is broadly comic. The single fight between Hector and Ajax and most of the conversations between Greeks and Trojans after its tame conclusion are not exactly comic but stylised and a little quaint. Shakespeare is, as it were, writing between inverted commas, consciously giving his shorthand version of the antique matter of Troy. Hector maintains his character. He is nonchalant about the terms of the fight and warms up only when Achilles would bully him. Let those who question this deliberate antique quaintness compare Hector's speech to Ajax after the

fight (119-38) with any of Hector's previous speeches,
and they surely will find an altered style. Or can they take
this of Hector's as the full Shakespearean seriousness?

> Not Neoptolemus so mirable,
> On whose bright crest Fame with her loud'st Oyes
> Cries 'This is he' could promise to himself
> A thought of added honour torn from Hector.

But two characters are exempt from the inflation, the
comedy, and the antique quaintness alike. The first is
Troilus, whose dejected look causes Agamemnon to ask
who he is and Ulysses to testify so splendidly to his surpassing merit and courage. Till he is left alone with
Ulysses at the end of the scene, he speaks once only: to
tell Hector to fight more fiercely. His silence separates
him from the rest. The second is Ulysses, who towers
right above the other Greeks in good sense and acute or
sympathetic perception and he speaks in the full Shakespearean idiom. He sees through Cressida instantly, while
the other Greek leaders make fools of themselves. His brief
talk with Hector touches the issue of the whole war in contrast with the petty chivalric courtesies or pretences that
make up the other conversation. His brief talk with Troilus
at the end requires a longer note. Here are the lines.

> *Tro.* My Lord Ulysses, tell me, I beseech you,
> In what place of the field doth Calchas keep?
> *Ulyss.* At Menelaus' tent, most princely Troilus.
> There Diomed doth feast with him to-night;
> Who neither looks upon the heaven nor earth
> But gives all gaze and bent of amorous view
> On the fair Cressid.
> *Tro.* Shall I, sweet lord, be bound to you so much,
> After we part from Agamemnon's tent,
> To bring me thither?
> *Ulyss.*   You shall command me, sir.
> As gentle tell me, of what honour was

> This Cressida in Troy? Had she no lover there
> That wails her absence?
>
> *Tro.* O, sir, to such as boasting show their scars
> A mock is due. Will you walk on, my lord?
> She was belov'd, she lov'd; she is and doth:
> But still sweet love is food for fortune's tooth.

First, it is significant that the two characters who stood aloof from the rest should remain behind. Not only does their exchange of words at so prominent a place confirm their eminence over all the other characters, but its exquisite courtliness and simplicity show that these two arch-enemies, chief sources of strength on either side, are drawn to each other. Troilus instinctively chooses Ulysses as his confidant over Cressida; Ulysses has understood everything (and much more than Troilus yet knows) and in sympathy tries to show he knows and in so doing to enlighten. No passage in Shakespeare renders better a subtle and beautiful human relationship. It should among other things guard against the all too prevalent error that in this play Shakespeare abandoned his normal standards of sweetness and light for the bitter cynicism of Thersites. But I do not wish to sentimentalise either Troilus or Ulysses. Both are set with unbending resolution on their objects: Troilus on love and honour; Ulysses on practical politics. It is partly through admiration of the other's singleness of purpose that there is mutual attraction.

The next scene, V. 1 which in spite of the act-division follows without a pause, is deflatory. Thersites is at the top of his form. Achilles's bragging promise to meet Hector to-morrow in the field comes to nothing, because he has had a letter from Polyxena.

The next scene, V. 2, crowns the play. It happens at night and it shows Troilus and Ulysses watching the love-passage between Cressida and Diomed; both pairs being watched by Thersites. It includes not only Troilus's

terrible suffering and schizophrenia but his self-cure
through turning that portion of his mind which, against
the evidence of his senses, continues to love and idolise
Cressida into hatred for Diomed, a hatred which can find
vent in action. This mutation, often overlooked, is essential for understanding the play's true course.

In richness of content this scene far surpasses all others
in the play. In *Shakespeare's Last Plays* I wrote on the
different planes of reality in those plays, maintaining that
a sense of several possible planes was here a major theme,
though in a subordinate way Shakespeare had shown this
sense from the first. And I instanced among others the
present scene in *Troilus and Cressida*. Diomed and Cressida inhabit with obtuse and unreflecting singleness of
purpose the world of the senses. In that world each is
equally on the make for himself. Ulysses inhabits the
world of convention and practises the maximum of sympathy possible within that world. Samuel Butler would
have classed him with the Higher Ydgrunites. Troilus
inhabits a world largely emotional; and conflicting emotions threaten to destroy for him the mind's normal traffic.
He does in fact for a brief time inhabit two incompatible
worlds. But the self-control he maintained while the evidence for one of these incompatible worlds was accumulat-
ing enables him to subject the incompatibility to his will
and to transform one incompatible into something that
can fit into the rest of his experience. Thersites inhabits a
world uniformly sordid, in which all motives are monoton-
ously degraded; it contains no particle of pity, and he is as
brutal in his comment on Troilus's conflict ("Will he
swagger himself out on's own eyes?") as in any of his
ranker scurrilities concerning the Greeks.

This multiplication of planes of reality beyond anything
similar elsewhere in the play threatens to destroy the
play's internal harmony because it includes a type of feel-

ing not included elsewhere. I must speak about that feeling and explain why (like Shylock in the *Merchant of Venice*) it does not in fact fulfil its threat.

Charles Williams in his interesting but speculative treatment of *Troilus and Cressida* in his *English Poetic Mind*[1] speaks well of the type of experience Troilus undergoes in this scene, contrasting it with other types found in the play elsewhere:

> The crisis which Troilus endured is one common to all men; it is in a sense the only interior crisis worth talking about. It is that in which every nerve of the body, every consciousness of the mind, shrieks that something cannot be. Only it is. . . .
>
> There is a world where our mothers are unsoiled and Cressida is his; there is a world where our mothers are soiled and Cressida is given to Diomed. . . .
>
> Agamemnon and Nestor had made orations about the disappointments of life, the failure of 'the ample proposition that hope makes', and the need of courage and patience. Ulysses had answered by pointing out that degree and order were being lost, and had described what happens when degree is lost. It was all very wise, very noble, talk. But in Troilus the thing has happened: the plagues, portents, and mutinies have begun to 'divert and crack, rend and deracinate' his being.

Charles Williams is right in seeing this different order of emotion, vouched for, of course, by a more intense way of writing. In commenting on the Trojan council scene I said that Shakespeare was now writing on a subject of debate which he had more at heart and which he treated with a nearer and more intimate fervour. Nevertheless this fervour was largely intellectual, and he did not throw his whole emotional being into the matter. But here this is precisely what he does. The agonisings of Troilus are subtle and intellectualised and yet quite pervaded by the mind's full emotions:

[1] Oxford 1932. Pp. 59-61.

Within my soul there doth conduce a fight
Of this strange nature that a thing inseparate
Divides more wider than the sky and earth,
And yet the spacious breadth of this division
Admits no orifix for a point as subtle
As Ariachne's broken woof to enter.

In writing on *Hamlet* I pointed out that the speech from
which this comes tells us the kind of emotional crisis
Hamlet underwent when his mother re-married in haste.[1]
No one doubts the emotional intensity with which Shakespeare describes his disillusion. The same intensity will be
readily allowed in Shakespeare's treatment of Troilus.
How is it, then, that Troilus's agony, in itself the subject
of poetry dangerously intenser than poetry elsewhere in
the play, does not upset the total balance? First, because
unlike Hamlet Troilus quickly gains mastery over feelings
that threaten to break him. He ends his great speech by
saying that the bits and greasy relics of Cressida's o'er-
eaten faith are bound to Diomed. Ulysses interposes with

May worthy Troilus be half attach'd
With that which here his passion doth express?

This seems to mean "May Troilus even with half his self
be affected by the creature whose degradation he has just
described?" Troilus with an unexpected twist of thought
answers "yes", but means it in a way Ulysses had not
expected.

Ay, Greek; and that shall be divulged well
In characters as red as Mars his heart
Inflamed with Venus. Never did young man fancy
With so eternal and so fix'd a soul.
Hark, Greek: as much as I do Cressid love,
So much by weight hate I her Diomed.

Troilus is still the proverbial faithful lover, but that faith-

[1] For a second parallel, this time from *Henry V*, and for possible personal
applications of the kind of experience described, see Appendix D, p. 150.

ful love has been transmuted into a hatred of Diomed of
equal measure and durability. Such a transmutation is at
the other extreme from the protracted melancholy the
same shock creates in Hamlet. It also cuts short those
dangerous emotions, which, if allowed room, would have
wrecked the rest of the play. Secondly, Troilus is never
alone. Ulysses is there ready to prevent any violence
against Cressida or Diomed and to help Troilus contain
that storm of nerves which might have broken out if he
had been left to himself. Troilus protests his patience and
just succeeds in honouring his protest; and when Aeneas
enters he has regained his equipoise. "Have with you,
prince", he says to Aeneas; and to Ulysses, remembering
his good offices, "My courteous lord, adieu". This wonderful scene, then, is all gain. It is a thrilling and unexpectedly
rich culmination of one of the play's main themes and its
richness does not compromise the play's prevailing tenor.

The rest of the play deals with the matter of Troy, as
Shakespeare had committed himself to doing. It is not
especially interesting but will bear comparison with the
final battle scenes in *Macbeth*. I have already explained how
the Hector of V. 3, who insists on going to fight though
restrained by wife, father, and sister, confirms the Hector
of the Trojan council. The authenticity of the final scenes
from V. 4 has been questioned; and on very insufficient
grounds. Shakespeare was dealing with antique matter; he
had the difficult task of showing in outline a big mass of
sheer narrative. It is natural enough for him to be compressed and staccato or stylised. For instance, in describing how Achilles treacherously kills Hector Shakespeare
falls into his own early manner in *Henry VI*:

> Look, Hector, how the sun begins to set,
> How ugly night comes breathing at his heels.
> Even with the vail and darking of the sun,
> To close the day up, Hector's life is done.

Achilles's brutality reminds Shakespeare of the War of the Roses, where the decencies of chivalric warfare had been forgotten. If Shakespeare could archaise in the Hecuba passage in *Hamlet*, why not here? Further, Shakespeare maintains his characters throughout. It is the same Thersites. It is Ulysses and no one else who announces that the thing he had worked for all along has been achieved: the return of Achilles to battle. And it is his ally Nestor who adds just after, "So, so, we draw together." The difficulty of holding that a hack dramatist botching up the play could have made Nestor drop those words is in itself greater than all the difficulties that have been found in crediting these last scenes to Shakespeare.

The last two scenes need close reading. An innovation is that the gods come in very prominently: Agamemnon, speaking of Hector, ends scene nine with

> If in his death the gods have us befriended,
> Great Troy is ours, and our sharp wars are ended.

And we are meant to think of the "protractive trials of great Jove", the words applied by Agamemnon in the first council scene to the seven years of the war so far elapsed. Immediately after, in scene ten, Troilus takes up the theme of the gods. After telling of Achilles dragging Hector's body behind his chariot Troilus says,

> Frown on, you heavens, effect your rage with speed,
> Sit, gods, upon your thrones, and smite [1] at Troy!
> I say, at once let your brief plagues be mercy,
> And linger not our sure destructions on!

And when Aeneas chides him for alarming the army with these words, Troilus says Aeneas misinterprets. What Troilus must mean, therefore, is that he is ready for the worst that heaven can do, and if Troy is to fall let it be at

---

[1] I adopt the emendation of *smite* for *smile*. A scribe or compositor could easily have put *smile* in instinctive contrast with *frown* in the line before.

once. I do not think that Shakespeare here staged a last moment piece of piety to retrieve a play in which the gods figure hardly at all. His object is technical. Three years were to elapse before Troy was to fall, and Troilus (but only after prodigies of valour), Achilles, and Paris had to die first. Even Shakespeare could not crowd all this into a single play. So the issue is taken out of the hands of men and deposited conveniently in the laps of the gods. And with the change the play can more decently close. But not till Troilus confirms the fierce and resolute temper in which he left the scene of Cressida's infidelity and Pandarus has come on again, the Bawd not Lord Pandarus, to remind us of the other main theme.

W. W. Lawrence calls *Troilus and Cressida* "an experiment in the middle ground between comedy and tragedy in which experience often places us; nothing is settled clearly for good or ill"; and I should agree that like *Hamlet* it is a play of display rather than of ordering. It resembles both *Hamlet* and *Much Ado* in the way a main plan miscarries, the intended effect being reached by the agency of chance. Neither Hamlet's mouse-trap nor Claudius's despatch of Hamlet to England advances the contriver's plans; Beatrices's propulsion of Benedict to avenge Hero is superfluous through the accidental usefulness of Dogberry; Ulysses's masterly machinations for rousing Achilles are of no account, and what all this protraction of effort has failed to do the unexpected news of Patroclus's death achieves in a moment. The picture then is one in which human plans count for little and the sheer gestation of time and what it reveals count for much. On this topic I can quote from an excellent passage in an article on the play in the *Times Literary Supplement*.[1] The writer points out that Time here is not only a destroying or "calumniating" power but "a mysterious co-operator

[1] 19 May 1932.

with the individual in bringing events to pass whose 'thievish progress to eternity' must be stayed by seizing the value of the present moment". The writer goes on to speak of the play's characters as follows:

> They do not dominate Time, and, so to speak, force its pace. They rather combine with it and acquiesce in its movements. . . .
>
> > The end crowns all
> > And that same common arbitrator Time
> > Will one day end it.
>
> In the great tragedies Shakespeare had no use for a Time of that nature; in them man hurries events along on the swift tide of his will. But the pace of tragic Time is too swift and strong for men not of the highest temper.

This is said of *Troilus and Cressida* but it applies to *Hamlet* as well. Both are primarily dramas where the sheer wealth of the display counts for more than the lessons we learn from the way events are disposed. For such lessons we do indeed require characters who force the pace, who make time run; if display is required, no matter if designs cancel out or come to nothing and characters are either weak or stopped from doing. The Trojan council scene resulted in no action at all but was highly successful in revealing the cross-currents of human motives. Troilus's love could never have its proper fruition in a rich activity of mind and deed because its object was unworthy; yet the sheer display of its striving and of its betrayal is sufficiently exciting and instructive. Ulysses's politics turn out to be superfluous in practice, yet how fascinating in themselves.

Of course, *Troilus and Cressida* is inferior to *Hamlet*. The verse, though wonderfully varied and fresh, lacks the surpassing thrill. And there is no implication of life beyond what is explicitly presented: nothing to correspond to Marcellus's description of the preparations for war. Further, in spite of Troilus's passions and sufferings when he witnesses Cressida's infidelity, the general temper is cooler and more critical. Hamlet may fail to force Time but he agonises over his failure, and in so doing heightens the emotional temperature. In *Troilus and Cressida* the characters are not aware of their failure. Lastly, the religious temper of *Hamlet* makes it richer than the other play. In Ulysses's speech on Degree the angelic end of the chain of being is omitted; and this is typical of the whole of *Troilus and Cressida*. The human beings here provide their own background. In *Hamlet* the setting is nothing less than the whole universe. Nevertheless, though more restricted than *Hamlet*, *Troilus and Cressida* is a very fine drama of display and as such deserves a higher than its normal reputation.

Like *Hamlet* again *Troilus and Cressida* shows a powerful intellectual grasp in the way events are disposed and characters manipulated. The one weakness is, as explained above, a possible inconsistency in the hero's character. But there are features that correspond to the masterly pattern in *Hamlet*, where certain motives are set forth in the first act and worked out with precise correspondence in the third. First, there is the cunning union of the two great themes: the love of Troilus and the war for Troy. Secondly, there is the emergence of Troilus and Ulysses as the dominant characters and the consequent subordination of the others to them. This emergence is a gradual process and it serves to give the play something like a plot and something which counteracts the more critical theme of motives miscarrying or being found superfluous.

But there is more yet in the dominance and contrast of these two characters, for they are more than their sole selves, standing for certain sides of life. Troilus, crudely, stands for Honour, and Ulysses for Policy; and as such they represent Trojans and Greeks. Further, the Trojans are antique, the Greek modern. Such an interpretation is not at all surprising. Shakespeare, I believe, had a livelier sense of history than is usually allowed. He had hinted at the decay of chivalry in the second and third parts of *Henry VI*. In *Richard II* the antique world, so full of colour but so inefficient, goes down before the new efficiency. In *All's Well*, as I shall point out, an old world, better than the young, is dying. Something of these contrasts is found in Shakespeare's Trojans and Greeks. The Trojans are the older chivalric aristocrats and they lack cunning. The Greeks are the new men; and though they are not very efficient and quarrel, at least Ulysses and Achilles have an eye to the main chance. They are not shackled by chivalric scruples; and Time, to which they are better attuned, is on their side. Finally—and this is pure conjecture not to be taken too seriously—may not the very persistent references to merchandise amount to something? Does Shakespeare associate the lowered tone of the play with the spread of the new commercialism, seeing in the Greeks the new commercial classes, not so very efficient but more so than the waning aristocracy? This is the kind of conjecture that I dislike; and this very dislike may slightly validate a notion which insisted on forming itself while I was studying the play.

Finally, it cannot be asserted too strongly that Shakespeare in writing *Troilus and Cressida* did not alter his moral standards. The old interpretation of the play as an outburst of unrestrained bitterness against life, to be overcome later, is fantastically false. Hector is honourable and generous and he fails to apply his virtues to real life: but that does not mean that Shakespeare temporarily despised honour and generosity. Cressida is shallow, hard, and lascivious. Had Shakespeare been really bitter, he

SHAKESPEARE'S PROBLEM PLAYS

would have been glad to see her making Troilus suffer. But he is not in the least glad. The same ethical standards prevail as in the rest of Shakespeare; and far from imposing his opinions on us, Thersites has his own foul interpretation of others' cast back on himself. On the other hand Shakespeare did, in this play, choose to show things happening rather than men so making things happen as to imply a clear and powerful moral scheme. But things *can* happen in the way he presents them; here is an undoubted (though by no means the only) aspect of experience. To present such an aspect rather than to order experience does not show that a man denies all possibility of an order. When he wrote *Troilus and Cressida* Shakespeare was a popular dramatist with work to his credit already very well known. To isolate the play from Shakespeare's total moral context up to that date is to violate the conditions in which he wrote it.

Shakespeare's presentation of a certain side of experience has its own proper fascination. Exploiting a range of feelings more critical and sophisticated than elemental and unfeignedly passionate, he can play with language, spring surprises on us, mingle pathos and satire, play with the fire of tragedy without getting burnt and end by leaving us guessing. If we accept it that he meant to leave us guessing, and if we allow that the material and the tradition he inherited forced him to accept a slightly bigger burden than he could bear, we can make all necessary allowances and can end in finding in *Troilus and Cressida* a powerful if astringent delight.

Notes on *Troilus and Cressida*

I had thought that my segregation of Troilus and Ulysses as the two main characters and my depreciation of

86

Hector's chivalric nobility were new and hence the more likely to give offence. But I find that Dowden has anticipated this opinion in the preface to his third edition of *Shakespere his Mind and Art*. There he makes Troilus and Ulysses counterparts, recognises that Troilus is of tough fibre and emerges a man, calls Hector "heroic but too careless how and when he expands his heroic strength" and classes him with Ajax and Achilles as "of minor importance". I am glad to have such support in a contention which affects the whole lay-out of the play.

I have not referred to Heywood, *The Iron Age*, because I agree with those who date it after *Troilus and Cressida* (see especially E. K. Chambers, *William Shakespeare*, I, p. 449).

I am glad to have the support of W. B. D. Henderson in my opinion that Shakespeare owed a lot to Lydgate (Parrott Presentation Volume, Princeton 1935, p. 128).

I must repeat that I am indebted to what W. W. Lawrence and Oscar Campbell have written on the play. In Lawrence's article, *Troilus, Cressida and Thersites*, in *Modern Language Review*, 1942, pp. 422-37, there is an excellent passage (p. 427) about Shakespeare's "leaving his audience to draw their own conclusions, just as each man constructs his philosophy of life out of his own experience" and (p. 429) a cogent refutation of some of Oscar Campbell's contentions. I think Lawrence exaggerates the play's violences and broad coarse effects. I must record my debt to Wolfgang Keller's sane and considered but rather conventional account of the play in *Shakespearejahrbuch*, 1930, pp. 182-207; to Olwen W. Campbell's acute and lively article in *London Mercury*, 1921, pp. 48-59 (though I disagree with her about Hector); and to Theodore Spencer's passage on the play in *Shakespeare and the Nature of Man*, New York 1942, pp. 109-21.

Finally, there is Una Ellis-Fermor's interpretation of *Troilus and Cressida* in the *Frontiers of Drama* (London 1945), pp. 56-76. She asserts that Shakespeare did really express a conviction of chaos, but unconsciously countered by a sense of order implicit in the artistic form. This is an interesting psychological interpretation, but I find that it makes the play less consciously critical in tone and more abandoned in its passions than I am prepared to make it.

ALL'S WELL THAT ENDS WELL

IT is agreed that *All's Well* is in some sort a failure. But there are many kinds of failure, some dull some interesting, some tame some heroic, some simple some complicated. The failure of *All's Well* is not indeed heroic, like that of *Measure for Measure*, but it is interesting and it is complicated: well worth the attempt to define.

But perhaps it is premature to talk of failure. Fail the play does, when read: but who of its judges have seen it acted? Not I at any rate; and I suspect that it acts far better than it reads. For one thing it is very well plotted; and in the usual Shakespearean manner. The main outlines of the opening position are set forth quickly and emphatically in the first act. We learn what has just happened at Rossillion, the natures of the chief characters, and the mainspring of the whole action, Helena's passion for Bertram. That passion drives her to Paris to try her luck; and the second act mounts to a swift climax in the two long scenes where Helena first persuades the French King to try her remedy and then claims her reward in the hand of Bertram, only to gain the show and not the substance of her wishes. The middle of the play, as so often in Shakespeare, is filled with preparatory action rather than fruition, with the process of incubation not of birth. But this process proceeds with firm logic from the more crowded and open events of the first two acts. In Florence, in the fourth act, events again thicken and gather speed. They culminate in the long third scene, which takes place at night. Here Bertram is assailed by one surprise or excitement after another. He receives a very disturbing letter from his mother, he hears of the French King's strong resentment at some of his actions, he thinks that he has triumphed in his illicit courtship of Diana, only to have his relationship with her altered and endangered by the supposed news that his wife is dead, and he finds he has been deceived in his friend and adviser Parolles. But he does not know the full truth, namely that his wife is alive and had substituted herself for Diana that very night. The last act works out all the things that result from the full truth's being revealed.

This admirable construction, which I cannot remember to have seen sufficiently praised, might be more evident on the stage than in the study and might ensure for the play a position far higher than its present one, should it ever force its way into the repertory that enjoys regular presentation. But on the only available criterion, that of reading, it remains true that in its total effect *All's Well* fails and that the failure is caused most obviously by the comparative feebleness of execution. This is not to deny the skill in plotting, but the effect and the virtue of plotting vary according to the success of other parts of a composition. If I may quote something I wrote before:

> The virtue of the plot only begins when other qualities are already there. Many modern detective stories are ephemeral in spite of excellent plotting. . . . But that does not mean that plot is never important. Easy though it is for a cool self-possessed mind to plot ingeniously, it becomes a matter of greater difficulty and greater importance when the imagination grows hot. The cool brain has no temptations not to plot well, but without these temptations plotting well amounts to nothing.[1]

And the trouble with *All's Well* is that though Shakespeare's imagination does grow warm at times and at a few points genuinely incandescent, there is no steady

[1] E. M. W. Tillyard, *Poetry Direct and Oblique* (revised edition, London 1945) pp. 75-6.

90

warmth pervading the whole creation. And this lack of imaginative warmth shows in a defective poetical style. I will quote two examples of Shakespeare's imagination half-kindled but only half and hence not succeeding. The first is from the play's first scene and is spoken by Helena of Parolles, after she has soliloquised on her love for Bertram and when she sees Parolles approaching:

> Who comes here?
> One that goes with him. I love him for his sake,
> And yet I know him a notorious liar,
> Think him a great way fool, solely a coward.
> Yet these fixt evils sit so fit in him
> That they take place, when virtue's steely bones
> Look bleak i' th' cold wind. Withal full oft we see
> Cold wisdom waiting on superfluous folly.

These lines act on us as Chapman often does. They raise high expectations, creating a promising sense of afflatus, and yet fail to fulfil them. There is something very striking about virtue's steely bones looking bleak in the cold wind, but what strikes initially is an irrelevant image: bones or a skeleton in the open blown on by the winds of heaven:

> O'er his white banes, when they are bare,
> The wind sall blaw for evermair.

But Virtue is pictured as a person and not as a skeleton; so we have to correct and, when we do so, we do not get an immediate and undoubted image. We may first think of a thin haggard face with prominent cheek-bones and jaw; but such faces look bleak whether exposed to the cold air or not: there is little propriety in the thought. Finally, we may argue back from cold, that is naked, wisdom waiting on superfluous, that is overdressed, folly and conclude that Virtue is a naked wretch excluded from a firm place in society while Vices are received. But even so the picture hardly exists: the imagination is hardly stirred; and we must conclude that the author's imagination too was not properly kindled.

The second passage is spoken by Helena after Bertram, unknowing, has begotten his child on her:

> But O strange men,
> That can such sweet use make of what they hate,
> When saucy trusting of the cozen'd thoughts
> Defiles the pitchy night: so lust doth play
> With what it loathes for that which is away.
>
> (IV. 4. 21-5)

This, roughly, means: how strange men are in being able to get such pleasure from and give such pleasure to the person they hate, when a proneness, bred of wanton thoughts, to be deluded more than matches in its moral darkness the actual darkness of night. So it happens that lust enjoys the object of its hate in place of the absent object of its desire. The first line and a half are perfect, simple in expression yet striking in effect, conveying much in little. But the next line and a half are obscure and clotted, yielding their sense to the intellect rather than to the imagination, creating no lively image; they are strange, but barrenly so. The defects show up at once when set beside the lines of *Measure for Measure* which, dealing with the same subject, Claudio's intercourse with Juliet, and using the same words, *saucy* and *sweet*, cannot be independent of the present passage. Here Angelo, commenting on this intercourse, says:

> Ha, fie, these filthy vices! It were as good
> To pardon him that hath from nature stolen
> A man already made as to remit
> Their saucy sweetness that do coin heaven's image
> In stamps that are forbid.
>
> (II. 4. 42-6)

Here all is brilliantly clear and pointed, and the imagery

can be dwelt on with advantage. Murder is a theft from nature and is likened to the theft of gold: than such theft forging illicit coin is no better. But begetting an illegitimate child is just such forgery; hence no better than murder. Helena's words indeed "defile the pitchy night" in comparison with this clarity.

This failure of the poetic imagination in these two passages typifies a general failure throughout the play. The construction is, as already noted, masterly and so is the way the characters are outlined; and these ensure great interest for the play: but the execution, lacking the supreme imaginative warmth, fails to bring these great virtues to fruition. We shall never know the reason for this failure, which may well have been nothing more complicated than an attack of the toothache at the critical time of creation; but it may help a little to point out that Shakespeare had, in the plot he chose and in the treatment he proposed to give it, set himself a task of great difficulty.

One of Shakespeare's recurrent problems as a comedy writer was how to combine the romantic and improbable and fantastic plots he usually chose with a vitality and a realism of characterisation which his own inclinations insisted on. He had more than one solution. For instance, in *Much Ado* he puts his realism into the sub-plots: the persons in the so-called main plot, Claudio, Hero, Don John, are so little characterised that they pass well enough in their improbable setting. In the *Merchant of Venice* the most realistic and highly developed character is Shylock and he threatens through his overdevelopment to upset the fairy-tale world to which in his original capacity of Big Bad Man he was appropriate. Shakespeare maintains the harmony, or rather creates a richer one, by bringing out the Jewish character of the real world Shylock inhabits: for Jewish meant strange and alien; and this strangeness is the connecting link with the different strangeness of the world of the fairy-tale. In *All's Well*, as W. W. Lawrence has brought out so admirably, the main material is from folk-lore. It comprises two different but immemorial folk themes: the healing of a king leading to marriage and the fulfilment of certain seemingly impossible tasks. Shakespeare in choosing such material and then in making the main characters concerned, the French King, Bertram, and Helena, highly realistic set himself a problem of the first difficulty, far harder than those in the *Merchant of Venice* and *Much Ado*, only to be solved by the application of his highest powers. Consider these three characters for a moment. Of these the French King is the most sketchily drawn, yet set him beside some of the other royal persons in mature Shakespearean comedy and see the result. Orsino is lover rather than ruler and is hardly comparable. But take Don Pedro from *Much Ado* and the two Dukes in *As You Like It*, consider what flat figures these are, and then notice the relative realism of the French King, with his tiredness, his strong sense of duty, his warm-hearted loyalty to his newly dead friend, Bertram's father, his distrust of the steadiness of the younger generation, and his noble yet pathetic anxiety not to outlast his usefulness. "Would I were with him!" is his comment to Bertram on his dead father:

> Would I were with him! He would always say—
> Methinks I hear him now—his plausive words
> He scatter'd not in ears but grafted them
> To grow there and to bear: 'Let me not live'—
> This his good melancholy oft began
> On the catastrophe and heel of pastime
> When it was out—'Let me not live', quoth he,
> 'After my flame lacks oil, to be the snuff
> Of younger spirits, whose apprehensive senses
> All but new things disdain, whose judgments are

Mere fathers of their gaments, whose constancies
Expire before their fashions.' This he wish'd.
I, after him, do after him wish too,
Since I nor wax nor honey can bring home,
I quickly were dissolved from my hive
To give some labourers room.

(I. 2. 52-67)

There you have living characterisation, recalling the portrayal of Henry IV more than that of the comedy princes. Bertram, again, is a far more detailed study than the Claudios and Antonios and Orlandos of the genuine comedies; a character drawn from a close and not very friendly study of spoilt and unlicked aristocracy. Helena, too, is far closer to actual life than the heroine, psychologically untroubled, charming and witty, usual in the comedies, and reminds one rather of the troubled psyche of Euripides's Electra. Now Shakespeare was really interested in such characterisation when he wrote *All's Well*; and we know it because the play's freest poetry goes to establish it—witness the French King's speech just quoted. All the greater therefore was his difficulty in dealing with folk-lore material where psychological subtlety is least to the point.

It is interesting to compare Shakespeare with his original and to see how Boccaccio coped with his inherited fairy-tale material. Boccaccio's problem was similar: he had to tame the fabulous into the realistic and the sophisticated. But he set himself a less exacting standard of realism: all he aimed at was a diverting story that would not overtax the powers of a lively and critical audience to suspend willingly their disbelief. So he contented himself with keeping the characters simple, with inserting a few realistic touches like Helena's efficient management of Bertram's estate while he is in Italy, and with taking the fabulous lightly. Above all he has that supreme confidence

95

of the great artist really in control of his material enabling him to tell his story, fabulous though it may be, in a simple and compelling way that leaves the reader no option but unqualified acceptance. He allows his reader no more doubt than Dostoevski when he describes the monastery at the beginning of the *Brothers Karamazov*. All this is remote from Shakespeare both as regards the task set and the way it is carried out.

Such then are some of the ways in which Shakespeare failed as a whole and incidentally some of the ways in which he scored partial successes. Before passing to what Shakespeare did achieve I must speak of some of the subsidiary problems that confront any critic of the play.

Some of these problems have been thoroughly disposed of by W. W. Lawrence. For instance, he makes it clear that, by the rules of the game Shakespeare was playing, our sympathies are meant to be with Helena. Such a contention is important, and it warns us to be careful of sympathising overmuch with Bertram in what appears to a modern a wickedly cruel situation. By modern standards the King acts very hardly to Bertram in forcing Helena upon him. We are too apt to explain this hardness as something forced on the King by his oath. Doubtless some such motive is required but not to the extent usually thought necessary. For, by Elizabethan standards, the King is less hard than by ours. Bertram was his ward, and at his disposal. Helena was beautiful and intelligent, a fit bride for any young nobleman apart from her birth. And when the King says,

> 'Tis only title thou disdain'st in her, the which
> I can build up,

an Elizabethan audience would have accepted the plea and have considered Bertram to have had as fair a deal as the way of the world made usual.

Another problem that Lawrence seeks to settle is the modern resentment at the theme of the substitute bride, or the bed-trick, as it is sometimes called. He argues that this was a traditional motive, familiar to the audience, a piece of fairy-lore that could be accepted without question. Here, however, I doubt if the matter can be settled so simply. The popular opinion against the bed-trick here and in *Measure for Measure* has been too strong to be disregarded or explained away. It is a safe rule that you should always respect popular opinion or apparent prejudice and always suspect the reasons alleged for it. And, as a preliminary, it may be useful to ask why popular opinion has objected to the bed-trick and not objected to something in itself equally disgusting in *Twelfth Night*, namely Olivia's accepting Sebastian as a substitute lover for Cesario. The idea that Viola and Sebastian had interchangeable souls is a monstrous insult to human nature. Yet it is a convention which in the play popular opinion has had no difficulty in accepting. The conclusion seems to be that convention by itself is not enough to secure acceptance: the context has to be taken into account. Now in *Measure for Measure* the context is of that seriousness that the fairy-lore of the bed-trick is somehow shocking, and popular opinion has rightly been hostile. On the other hand this hostility has been wrongly extended to the same incident in *All's Well*. For all the realism of the characters, the moral earnestness of *All's Well* never approaches that of *Measure for Measure*. We remain in a moral climate where incidents may happen unquestioned and where convention can evade scrutiny. We are vaguely on Helena's side and we wish her well in her intrinsically dubious adventure.

Yet another problem concerns certain passages which some critics have found strange or unworthy of Shakespeare and which they have explained as being either not

SHAKESPEARE'S PROBLEM PLAYS

Shakespeare at all or relics of much earlier work.[1] There
are many such passages and I deal only with the longer.
The first is the talk between Helena and Parolles near the
opening of the play (I. 1. 117) on virginity. It is in part
both feeble and indecent, and critics have sought to relieve
Shakespeare of it and give it to a collaborator or inter-
polator. But is there any proof? The episode is not mere
accretion. Parolles is an important character, at once the
corrupter of Bertram and the excuse for his ill practices;
and we need to make his acquaintance early in the play.
Part of the feeble volubility of the wit may be dramatic:
Parolles must be voluble to live up to his name. And as
for the actual writing being unworthy of Shakespeare, he
had written this kind of rhetoric, for set rhetoric it is,
more than once before. Take first some of the sentences
on virginity:

> *Parolles.* There's little that can be said in't, 'tis against the rule
> of nature. To speak on the part of virginity is to accuse your
> mothers, which is most infallible disobedience. He that hangs
> himself is a virgin: virginity murders itself and should be buried
> in highways out of all sanctified limit, as a desperate offendress
> against nature. Virginity breeds mites, much like a cheese;
> consumes itself to the very paring and so dies with feeding his
> own stomach. Besides, virginity is peevish, proud, idle, made
> of self-love, which is the most inhibited sin in the canon. Keep.
> it not: you cannot choose but lose by it; out with it.

Parolles does not speak so well on virginity as Falstaff does
on honour, but their words belong to the same author. Or
take the following passage on conscience:

> I'll not meedle with it: it is a dangerous thing. It makes a man
> a coward: a man cannot steal but it accuseth him; he cannot
> swear but it checks him; he cannot lie with his neighbour's wife

---

[1] For more detailed treatment of supposed "stratification" in *All's Well*
see Appendix E, p. 151.

but it detects him. 'Tis a blushing shamefast spirit that mutinies in a man's bosom; it fills one full of obstacles: it made me once restore a purse of gold that I found; it beggars any man that keeps it. It is turned out of all towns and cities for a dangerous thing; and every man that means to live well endeavours to trust to himself and to live without it.

This is Clarence's Second Murderer in *Richard III* speaking and he treats conscience just as Parolles treats virginity, enumerating the different crimes the quality is guilty of and referring to scripture through the Ten Commandments where Parolles does so through parodying St. Paul on charity. Since Shakespeare had written already at least twice in this vein, why seek to deprive him of a third manifestation? And as to the ineptitude of Helena joining in the talk, that is prepared for by her comment on Parolles as he enters to the effect that she knows him to be a liar, a fool, and a coward but that she loves him because he is Bertram's companion. Parolles, speaking in the vicarious glamour of Bertram, can be tolerated, however nasty or windy his talk.

Then there are the couplets; and it is true that these are many and that some occur in places where they are least expected in Shakespeare's mature work. The most conspicuous places are in the second act. In II. 1. 133, when Helena makes her final and successful attempt to persuade the King to try her remedy, blank verse gives place to couplets; and in II. 3. 78 Helena, having spoken mature and lovely blank verse before making her actual choice of a husband, falls into the stiffness and ceremony of rhyme. This use of rhyme at the high moments of action is indeed extraordinary. But it is not unparalleled in Shakespeare, for exactly the same thing happens in the *First Part of Henry VI* where Talbot and his son perish in couplets. But though the parallel may argue for the authenticity of the couplets in *All's Well*, the question remains why he chose to use them in such places. In my answer to it the matter of "stratification" may come up at the same time, but it is in itself subsidiary; for if Shakespeare chose to use chunks of earlier work these must be considered no less organic to his scheme than the actual insects or postage stamps or leaves gummed on to the canvas of a surrealist picture.

In the conversation between Helena and the King it is the King who gives the cue with (line 133),

> Thou thought'st to help me; and such thanks I give
> As one near death to those that wish him live.

But Helena takes up the cue and has most of the talk to the end of the scene. What is most evident in her first speeches is their piety and their suggestion of a miracle:

> He that of greatest works is finisher
> Oft does them by the weakest minister.
> So holy writ in babes hath judgement shown,
> When judges have been babes; great floods have flown
> From simple sources and great seas have dried,
> When miracles have by the greatest been denied.

The "baby judges" could be Daniel judging Susanna, or the wise "babes and sucklings" of the Gospels. The "flood" is the water struck from the rock by Moses at Horeb and Kadesh; the sea is the Red Sea as described in *Exodus*. In her second speech Helena continues in the same strain in answer to the King's doubts:

> Inspired merit so by breath is barr'd.
> It is not so with Him that all things knows
> As 'tis with us that square our guess by shows.
> But most it is presumption in us when
> The help of heaven we count the act of men.
> Dear sir, to my endeavours give consent;
> Of heaven, not me, make an experiment.

Here again there is scriptural reference, in the first line; a general reference to Hebrew kings who denied the truth of the inspired prophets. This accumulation of scriptural reference, this calling in the help of God, and this confidence in a forthcoming miracle combine to give a special character to this portion of the scene. Shakespeare may have got his hint from his original, which runs "The King, hearing these words, said to himself: 'This woman peradventure is sent unto me of God'." But, whether or not, he surely must have used the pomp and stiffness of rhyme as appropriate to a solemn and hieratic content. The hieratic tone is continued in Helena's next speech, a speech habitually quoted as obviously early work and as strong evidence for stratification. To the King's question of how long the cure will take Helena replies:

> The great'st grace lending grace,
> Ere twice the horses of the sun shall bring
> Their fiery torcher his diurnal ring,
> Ere twice in murk and occidental damp
> Moist Hesperus hath quench'd his sleepy lamp,
> Or four and twenty times the pilot's glass
> Hath told the thievish minutes how they pass,
> What is infirm from your sound parts shall fly,
> Health shall live free and sickness freely die.

Now though it is very queer that Shakespeare should write so tall at so crucial a place in the play, it is pretty plain what he is doing. He is deliberately evading drama and substituting ritual and cloudy incantation. And it makes matters more rather than less queer to postulate just here a theft from an old play or the calling in of a bad poet to do an inferior job of work. The resemblance of these lines to the beginning of the *Murder of Gonzago* in *Hamlet* has sometimes been noticed; and to some this resemblance indicates a collaborator still more strongly. To me it suggests that Shakespeare had at his call a rather clumsy and heightened style in rhyme which he used from time to time to mark certain passages in his plays violently off from the rest. Some such style was plainly needed for a play within a play: the need for its use in the scene under discussion is far from obvious, but, that need granted, the style itself should not cause us undue surprise or necessitate unusual explanations.

I maintain therefore that you need not invoke stratification or collaborators to help explain the play: first because they cannot explain the really puzzling things and secondly because what they can explain admits of other explanations. It is, on the other hand, impossible to disprove stratification or collaboration; and if I now dismiss the notion of them it is for reasons of probability not of verifiable truth.

I revert now to what I have principally noted of the play: Shakespeare's failure to kindle his imagination at the high places of the action. I have pointed out the difficulty, exceptional in his comedies, in which he involved himself: that of fitting a highly realistic set of principal actors into a plot belonging to the fantastic world of fairy-lore. And it is quite possible that this difficulty explains the imaginative failure: that Shakespeare, knowing when he came to actual composition that he could not succeed, evaded the attempt and resorted, when the crises came, to the conventional, the sententious, or the hieratic, never taxing his full imaginative powers. The very consistency makes this apparent evasion the more likely. There is no weight of evidence that Shakespeare changed his mind during composition. There is indeed one place where action and high poetry are combined: Helena's soliloquy after she has heard Bertram's refusal to return to France while his wife is there. She blames herself for the dangers he now undergoes in the Florentine wars and resolves to quit the country so that he may return:

                            O you leaden messengers,
That ride upon the violent speed of fire,
Fly with false aim, move the still-piecing air,
That sings with piercing; do not touch my lord.
Whoever shoots at him, I set him there;
Whoever charges on his forward breast,
I am the caitiff that do hold him to't.
And though I kill him not I am the cause
His death was so effected. Better 'twere
I met the ravin lion when he roar'd
With sharp constraint of hunger; better 'twere
That all the miseries which nature owes
Were mine at once. No, come thou home, Rossillion,
Whence honour but of danger wins a scar
As oft it loses all. I will be gone:
My being here it is that holds thee hence.
Shall I stay here to do't? No, no, although
The air of paradise did fan the house
And angels offic'd all.

It is futile to ask why Shakespeare's imagination was here, uniquely, kindled. The present point is that such kindling is unique, that the high places of the action before and after fail to evoke high poetry, and that such failure remains the consistent rule. It looks as if Shakespeare, however ill-satisfied with what he was doing, at least knew it from the start and stuck to it.

Not that he stuck to the same method of writing below his stylistic height at the high places. As noted already, he makes Helena speak heavy and involved couplets when at the end of the play's first scene she makes her great resolve to try her fortune in Paris, he makes Helena and the King speak strange and hieratic couplets when she persuades him to try her cure, and he makes Helena drop into couplets when she chooses her husband. Between this last scene (II. 3) and the scene (IV. 3) containing many nocturnal happenings and critical for Bertram there is no long emphatic scene. The intervening happenings are parcelled out into short scenes; action is competently described in a middle style, mature but in point of poetry not distinguished though better than the sententious or hieratic couplets. But the effect is to dissipate, to make the temperature of action warm not hot. Such dissipation was wise, for the critical scene which crowns the action (IV. 3) is nearly all in prose. It is in itself admirable, but its prose provides yet one more example of the means of depressing high action. The unmasking of Parolles could, of course, in any kind of treatment be only in prose, but the preliminary moral comments of the two French Lords on Bertram and Bertram's own mental crises could have lent themselves to high poetical treatment. The last scene of the play, when the whole truth comes out, again offered excellent chances of poetry. Shakespeare refuses or evades them, not (on the whole) by sententious couplet writing, nor by using prose instead of verse, but by sheer ingenuity and complication of plot. In Shakespeare's original, Giletta, having fulfilled her tasks, confronts Beltramo, who has returned home, on a feast day and makes good her claims simply and directly. Shakespeare could have imitated this simplicity, but he vastly complicates the action by the business of the rings and by making Diana and her mother travel to France. There is so much business and so many surprises that there is little room for the deeper feelings and hence no call for high poetry.

So far I have spoken mainly of what the play fails in and of how possibly it comes to do so. I pass on now to some of its positive qualities.

Though we need not impute bitterness or cynicism to the general complexion of the play, we cannot but find it full of suffering. And the sense of suffering is heightened because there are hints of an earlier prosperity which the final reconciliation of Bertram and Helena does not promise to equal. The earlier prosperity is detected through the aged characters. The Countess resembles the old lady on whom William Empson wrote one of his best poems. She is "ripe", full of experience and with wide and generous sympathies; but she is also a "cooling planet" and the crops she reaps though in her sole control are scanty. Her husband had been a splendid person, and Rossillion in his day must have had other and gayer representatives than his "unbaked and doughy" son, his taut-nerved physician's daughter, and the "shrewd and unhappy fool" whom his widow keeps in her service out of kindness and respect for her husband's memory. The French King had evidently been all that a king should be, but now he "nor wax nor honey can bring home". And even after Helena has cured him he regains no joy in life. He conducts his examination of Bertram in the last act efficiently enough, but his chief vitality goes to fostering his (very natural) suspicions that Bertram has murdered Helena:

> My fore-past proofs, howe'er the matter fall,
> Shall tax my fears of little vanity,
> Having vainly fear'd too little. . . .
> I am wrapp'd in dismal thinkings.

And even in the efficient exercise of his duties is insinuated the fact of his age:

> Let's take the instant by the forward top;
> For we are old, and on our quick'st decrees
> The inaudible and noiseless foot of time
> Steals, ere we can effect them.

Lafeu indeed has plenty of vitality, as when he calls his desponding master "my royal fox" and asks him if he will eat no grapes and when he detects the fraud of Parolles. Yet we know all the time he is old:

> Iam senior, sed cruda *viro* viridisque senectus.

H

In front of these memories or relics of past happiness
and vigour are set the hungry and unsatisfied or dour
representatives of the present generation: the boorish and
unlicked aristocrat Bertram, the Clown who hates being
one, the two adventurers, one good the other contempt-
ible, Helena and Parolles, Diana, correct but uneasy
through poverty and a widowed mother, and the two
French Lords faintly drawn perhaps but correct rather
than gay, and severely orthodox and even theological in
their talk. The whole presentation is wonderfully interesting, and the closeness to actual life of some of the
characters is remarkable. Yet the world these characters
inhabit is cold and forbidding. We get no feeling, as we
do in *Hamlet*, of varied life being transacted along with
the happenings proper to the play itself. The sense of in-
completeness noticed in the poetry of two short passages
hangs over the whole play. The imagination has not done
its full work. The artistic process has somehow halted
before completion. Of all poets Shakespeare is least prone
to violate the drama by speaking in his own person. Yet
here there is the suspicion that his personal feelings, un-
objectified and untransmuted, have slipped illegitimately
into places which his poetic imagination, not fully kindled,
has not succeeded in reaching. The evident dislike of the
younger generation, for instance, has got a slight touch of
the personal in it, as if, at that time, Shakespeare did
actually compare it, to its disadvantage, with a more
settled and more gracious age, now expiring and ineffective.

For the pious and theological tone, the conversation
between the French King and Helena, when she persuades
him to try her cure, has already been cited. It is of heaven,
not of Helena, that the King makes experiment; and his
cure is miraculous, not only as proclaimed by Helena, but,
when effected, as reported by Lafeu:

They say miracles are past; and we have our philosophical persons, to make modern and familiar, things supernatural and causeless. Hence is it that we make trifles of terrors, ensconcing ourselves into seeming knowledge, when we should submit ourselves to an unknown fear. . . . A showing of a heavenly effect in an earthly actor. . . . The very hand of heaven.

Nor does the conception of Helena as a person specially favoured by heaven cease with her curing the King. The Countess, hearing Bertram has cast her away, says

> What angel shall
> Bless this unworthy husband? he cannot thrive,
> Unless her prayers, whom heaven delights to hear
> And loves to grant, reprieve him from the wrath
> Of greatest justice.

Nor does Shakespeare let the theme of Helena's divine agency drop. In IV. 4 she says to Diana's mother

> Doubt not but heaven
> Hath brought me up to be your daughter's dower,
> As it hath fated her to be my motive
> And helper to a husband.

But the most explicitly theological place in the play is the beginning of the culminating scene, IV. 3, where the two French Lords comment on Bertram's conduct. Not only the position but the speakers make this comment important. The two French Lords are the choric characters, the *punctum indifferens* of the play, and what they say gives a standard to which the play itself can be referred. After the First Lord has recounted, with strong disapproval, Bertram's seduction of Diana, these words follow: [1]

Second Lord. Now God lay our rebellion! As we are ourselves,
  what things are we.

---

[1] I adopt Dover Wilson's assignment of the speeches to the two Lords and his emendation of *lay* for *delay* at the beginning.

First Lord. Merely our own traitors. And as in the common course of all treasons, we still see them reveal themselves, till they attain to their abhorred ends; so he that in this action contrives against his own nobility in his proper stream o'erflows himself.

Second Lord. Is it not meant damnable in us to be trumpeters of our unlawful intents?

There are two doctrines here: first and most emphatic, the theological doctrine of man's depravity unaided by divine grace, second, the doctrine that great crime will out, and often by the criminal giving himself away, to his ultimate punishment. Bertram, in his acts, has shown himself to be man cut off from grace, and by his indiscreet confidences, his "o'erflowing himself", has prepared his own detection and punishment.

It looks, therefore, as if Shakespeare not only made Helena and Bertram highly realistic figures but made them represent heavenly grace and natural, unredeemed, man respectively. In fact, he had in his mind, possibly, the Spenserian practice of multiple meanings with so obvious an analogy as Britomart, who is at once a realistic character, a fiercely monogamous and jealous woman, and an allegorical representation of chastity; and, more likely, the Morality Play. And as in *Henry IV* there has been detected the Morality theme of man or the prince fought over by the virtues and vices (represented by Prince Hal, the Lord Chief Justice, and Falstaff); so here there are signs (not very emphatic) of the same theme. Bertram, as natural man, corresponds to Hal, the Prince; Helena corresponds to Honour and Justice as represented by the Lord Chief Justice; and Parolles, as often noted, corresponds to Falstaff. But I am far from wanting to press these correspondences; and it is nearer the truth to say that a second version of the Morality theme can be detected in *All's Well* than that Bertram copies Hal and

Parolles Falstaff. Alexander [1] has rightly warned us not to press Johnson's remark that "Parolles has many of the lineaments of Falstaff" too far, and rightly insists that "Falstaff for all his vices belongs to another order of character". Further, the Morality role of the tempter protrudes more obviously from the slight character of Parolles than from Falstaff's massiveness. In the same way Prince Hal, with his strong intellect, his wide knowledge of men, his irony, and his fundamental sense of duty, is remote from the unsophisticated and boorish Bertram. Moreover the relations between Prince Hal and Falstaff on the one hand and Bertram and Parolles on the other are totally different. Prince Hal knows what he is doing and has summed up Falstaff; it is Falstaff who is self-deceived about his influence on the Prince. Bertram is the simple dupe of Parolles's pretensions.

To detect the Morality motive in *All's Well* may be to add a new fact to the nature of the play; it does little to explain its character, for it is not strong enough to make itself powerfully felt. If Shakespeare had made the Morality motive very obvious and at the same time furnished it with his highly realistic characters, he might have done for Elizabethan drama what Euripides did for the Greek. This is not to say that Shakespeare copied the Morality perversely and without reason. In his last plays he was largely concerned with adjusting symbolism and real life; and only in the *Winter's Tale* and the *Tempest* did he succeed. It is perfectly natural that he should have made analogous experiments earlier in his career. Such an experiment I believe we have in *All's Well*.

I come now finally to the characters; and it is in the delineation of the main characters joined with the solid merit of the plot that the play's virtue most consists.

Of the three main characters—and they correspond to

[1] *Op. cit.*, pp. 192-3.

the Morality motive—least need be said about Parolles. Ever since Charles I substituted *Parolles* for *All's Well* as the play's title in his copy of the Second Folio, readers have recognised Parolles as a successful comic figure. He is a small impostor, but he puts up a tolerable show. His sermon on virginity to Helena is genuinely voluble; and he has a genuine if limited talent in imitating the language of his social superiors and claiming a knowledge of their manners. This talent comes out in the excellent comic passage (II. 1. 24-61) where Bertram laments to the two Lords and Parolles that he has been forbidden the wars:

> Noble heroes, my sword and yours are kin. Good sparks and lustrous, a word, good metals. You shall find in the regiment of the Spinii one Captain Spurio with his cicatrice, an emblem of war, here on his sinister cheek. It was this very sword entrenched it.

And when the Lords have gone and Bertram has been unable in the courtesy of farewell to squeeze out more than the ridiculous "I grow to you, and our parting is a tortured body", Parolles shows some talent in his confirming his hold on Bertram with

> Use a more spacious ceremony to the noble lords. You have restrained yourself within the list of too cold an adieu. Be more expressive to them; for they wear theemselves in the cap of the time, there do muster true gait, eat speak and move under the influence of the most received star: and, though the devil lead the measure, such are to be followed. After them, and take a more dilated farewell.

That is quite good imitation of the Rosencrantz and Guildenstern stuff; and it is not surprising that it needed the superior penetration of Lafeu to detect the fraud.

Critics have been too apt to exalt Helena at the expense

of the other characters. She is no more interesting or instructive than Bertram; and the measure of neither character can be taken apart from the other. Nor is Van Doren
right in saying that they both "thin into a mere figure of
fable as the plot wears on". We learn indeed little new
about Helena after she has put on her pilgrim's habit, but
the crises through which Bertram passes in the last half of
the play at once form the gist of the plot and reveal his
nature. But though I disagree with Van Doren in this and
in his centring all the "blazing brightness of the play" in
her, he has succeeded better than other critics in defining
her character. Here are some of his remarks:

> One of her favourite words is 'nature', and there is much of it
> in her. She has body as well as mind, and can jest grossly with
> Parolles.... There is nothing frail about Helena, whose passion
> is secret but unmeasured. And because her body is real her mind
> is gifted with a rank, a sometimes masculine fertility. It is easy
> for her to achieve the intellectual distinction of,
>
> 'In his bright radiance and collateral light'
>
> just as it is natural that she should dress her longing for Bertram
> in the tough language of physics and metaphysics.... She has
> in her own dark way the force of Imogen, though she inhabits
> an inferior play.[1]

Van Doren is right. There is a formidable tautness in
Helena's passion, which allies her with Spenser's Britomart, who, riding to rescue her lover Artegal from the
Amazon Radegund, looked right down to hide the fellness
of her heart, or to Susan, the fiercely monogamous woman
in Virginia's Woolf's *The Waves*, who says that her love
is fell. Rosalind and Viola are indeed in love but not with
the strained passion of Helena. They say nothing to
match, for instance, those lines she speaks, just before her

---

[1] *Op. cit.*, pp. 215-16.

open avowal of love, in answer to the Countess's protest "I say, I am your mother":

>   Pardon, madam;
> The Count Rossillion cannot be my brother.
> I am from humble, he from honour'd name;
> No note upon my parents, his all noble.
> My master, my dear lord he is; and I
> His servant live, and will his vassal die.
> He must not be my brother—

nor her words just before she chooses Bertram as her husband from the King's wards:

> The blushes in my cheeks thus whisper me,
> 'We blush that thou shouldst choose; but, be refused,
> Let the white death sit on thy cheek for ever;
> We'll ne'er come there again.'

Not that Shakespeare makes her a mere humour of predatory monogamy. Twice her nerve fails her momentarily: first, when, like Isabella pleading with Angelo, she accepts the French King's first rebuff and nearly gives up; and second, when, having chosen and finding Bertram unwilling, she begs the King not to force the wedding. Such touches make us remember the terrible ordeal Helena had set herself: not to have quailed would argue her less or more than human. A further natural touch is her self-knowledge. Her strong intelligence does not spare her own self; as when she admits to the Countess that her resolve to cure the French King was not disinterested and that she would not have thought of it but for Bertram's journey to Paris. Nor has she the least illusion about Bertram's disposition.

The irony and the truth of Helena's situation are that with so much intelligence and so firm a mind she can be possessed by so enslaving a passion for an unformed, rather stupid, morally timid, and very self-centred youth:

for by the standards of real life there is nothing surprising in Helena's having fallen for Bertram's handsome outside, his high rank, and her unconscious knowledge that she could dominate him and give him moral backbone, granted the chance. What is surprising is to see such truth of actual motivation, and one so little related to conventional motivation, figuring in an Elizabethan play.

For Bertram himself we must remember that the fight was not between himself and Helena. Helena had powerful allies, while he had only Parolles. The play's action is largely the story of how he yields to the pressure of numbers. But before pointing to that story, which as far as I know has not been clearly detected, I must substantiate some of the qualities I have given his character and indicate others.

In that list of qualities I did not include "vicious"; and it is a triumph of art that Bertram can do so many selfish or mean things without incurring that epithet. Though never more than natural man, he is never, we feel, beyond the reach of grace. And that Shakespeare just then appeared to rate natural man decidedly low does not alter the fact. He keeps Bertram from positive viciousness by asserting from the first, and then reiterating, his crude immaturity. His mother, taking leave of Bertram in the first scene, hopes he will "succeed his father in manners as in shape", and then adds "'Tis an unseason'd courtier" —which suggests that her hope is far from certainty. The French King, on first seeing Bertram, echoes the Countess's parting words

> Youth, thou bear'st thy father's face;
> Frank nature, rather curious than in haste,
> Hath well compos'd thee. Thy father's moral parts
> Mayst thou inherit too!

and goes on to praise Bertram's father in detail and to

dispraise the present generation of young men. Bertram's father "looked into the service of the time", that is had keen insight into military affairs, and "was discipled of the bravest", in other words was glad to learn from his betters. Knowing that Bertram was under the discipline of Parolles, we can infer his shortcomings easily enough and the lubberly sense of guilt he must have felt when compared with his elders and betters. Thereafter (quite apart from the scanty and abrupt and sometimes boorish tone of Bertram's speeches) the theme of his immaturity is maintained, for instance through Lafeu's remark just before Helena chooses him for husband, "There's one grape yet, I am sure thy father drank wine: but if thou be'st not an ass, I am a youth of fourteen; I have known thee already", and through his later remark (beginning of IV. 5) including Bertram among the "unbaked and doughy youth of a nation". There is something pathetic as well as disagreeable in Bertram's gruff and inhibited bearing. Hardly ever has he the confidence to speak freely. He does so once when, in unguarded fury at the proposed marriage, he disputes the King's command:

> *King.* Thou know'st she has rais'd me from my sickly bed.
> *Ber.* But follows it, my lord, to bring me down
> Must answer for your raising? I know her well:
> She had her breeding at my father's charge.
> A poor physician's daughter my wife! Disdain
> Rather corrupt me ever.

That is emphatically spoken indeed; and we can see how on the field of battle, where the moral issues were elementary, Bertram would have shone. But his resistance is a mere unguarded flare-up, and he soon collapses.

This moral cowardice joined to physical courage most characterises Bertram and explains his actions, making him not only mean and repellent but pathetic and to be pitied. It is in the last two acts that Shakespeare develops and illustrates this defect of Bertram, just as he had done Helena's qualities in the earlier part of the play. Here he gives us, with brilliant insight into human nature, the processes by which Bertram quite gives way in the matters where he had most resisted. Part of that process takes place in IV. 3, the night-scene into which so much of the play's action is crowded, and part in the last scene of all. At the beginning of IV. 3 Bertram has achieved the utmost self-assertion of which he was capable. He has defied his mother (and public opinion generally) in refusing to acknowledge his wife, he has defied the French King in stealing away from Paris to the wars, he has defied conventional morality by succeeding, as he thinks, in seducing Diana. Further he has risked being proved wrong by allowing Parolles to be tested, and he has violated his own sense of family loyalty by surrendering his ancestral ring to Diana. The scene itself, though largely occupied with the comic business of Parolles's unmasking, mainly recounts the heavy series of blows to Bertram's confidence in the various acts of defiance he has committed. First there is his mother's letter: "there is something in't that stings his nature; for on his reading it he changed almost into another man". And it is not for nothing that these words come just before the pious words, quoted above, about the depravity of natural man. Bertram, though depraved, has still got a sensitive conscience. Next we hear of the French King's high displeasure. Then we hear of Helena's supposed death through grief ("the tenderness of her nature became as a prey to her grief; in fine, made a groan of her last breath and now she sings in heaven"); and in view of the effect the Countess's letter had on Bertram we are expected to assume some remorse for this death. But this death has another consequence: his seduction of Diana has become serious, for he could now marry her. It has been a heavy series of blows, but for the moment he keeps control of himself and bluffs it all out with a brutal callousness and a bravado which we know conceal an inner qualm:

> I have to-night dispatched sixteen businesses, a month's length a-piece, by an abstract of success. I have congied with the duke, done my adieu with his nearest; buried a wife, mourned for her; writ to my lady mother I am returning; entertained my convoy: and between these main parcels of dispatch effected many nicer needs. The last was the greatest, but that I have not ended yet. . . . The business is not ended, as fearing to hear of it hereafter.

This last business was the supposed seduction of Diana; and his fear on that score is both the index of his habit of mind and the connecting link with the last scene of the play. There follows the unmasking of Parolles, which Bertram watches in sullen anger—not, like the others, with fun. As Parolles grows more explicit and imaginative in his lies, one of the French Lords says "He hath out-villained villany so far, that the rarity redeems him". To which Bertram replies angrily "A pox on him, he's a cat still". The events of the night leave Bertram thoroughly shaken.

Sir Arthur Quiller-Couch, in his introduction to the New Cambridge edition of the play, sought to mitigate the unpleasantness of Bertram's character, but could not extend the mitigation to his behaviour in the last scene. I do not think there is any discrepancy. Bertram's nerve had been thoroughly undermined by the events just related; he was frightened of Diana. When confronted with her, his nerve gives way still more and he resorts in panic to any lie that will serve his turn. This exhibition of human nature is ignoble and unpleasant to witness, but it is perfectly true to the facts. Then, when the whole truth is out and Helena reappears, Bertram gives in completely. His former pursuer is now his saviour from a conspiracy of people and events which has overwhelmed him. And when to Helena's lovely complaint that she is but the shadow of a wife, the name but not the thing, he replies "Both, both, O, pardon!", there is not the least cause for doubting his sincerity. However true it may be that the Elizabethans would expect and accept such a revulsion of feeling, there is no need to invoke such expectations to justify a situation assumed to be incredible to a modern. Psychological truth and the conventions of the fairy-tale are here at one. And when Bertram goes on to say that he will love Helena "dearly, ever dearly", we should believe him implicitly. Helena has got her man; and he needs her moral support with such pathetic obviousness that she never need fear his escape.

Notes on *All's Well That Ends Well*

Helpful criticism of this play is scarce. The relevant sections of Van Doren's and Alexander's books have helped me most. I have mentioned Sir Arthur Quiller-Couch's good and sympathetic account of Bertram, but on many points I disagree with him completely. For instance (p. xxv), he considered Parolles an accretion:

> Apart from the business of the drum and his exposure as a poltroon, all Parolles does is to engage Helena early in chat which he intends to be bawdy.

Parolles, though a light-weight as a character, is Bertram's evil genius and essential to the balance of the play. E. E. Stoll has an interesting chapter (xiii) on *All's Well* and *Measure for Measure* in his *From Shakespeare to Joyce* (New York 1944). I go a good way with him, but disagree too on many points.

MEASURE FOR MEASURE

MEASURE FOR MEASURE has been singularly apt to provoke its critics to excess; and in the most different manners. Earlier critics vented their excesses on two of the main characters, Isabella and the Duke. Later critics have, in reaction to the earlier, gone to two different extremes. Some, in righteous and justified defence of the play's heroine, have refused to see any fault in the play at all; others, rightly recognising a strong religious tone, have sought to give the whole play an allegorical and religious explanation. This is not to say that the above critics have not written well of the play. Many of them have; but nearly all have yoked their truths to strong and palpable errors. If I now proceed to enumerate some of the errors, it does not mean that I fail to recognise and pay tribute to the truths.

I begin with an earlier type of criticism. To an age whose typical mistake in criticism was to judge the persons of Elizabethan plays by the standards of actual life it is very natural that the Duke should be offensive. He is an eavesdropper; he chose as his deputy a man whom he knew to have behaved shabbily to his betrothed lady; and he displayed the utmost cruelty in concealing from Isabella for longer than was strictly necessary the news that her brother still lived. Certainly, as a real person, he is a most unsympathetic character; and though we may feel wiser than the Victorians and find no difficulty in the Duke as an allegorical figure or as a convenient stage machine, we can understand Victorian resentment. With Isabella the case is different. Here is a character who, in those parts of the play where she really counts, will stand up to the test of the most rigid realism; and yet how they hated her!—this hard, smug, self-righteous virgin, preferring her own precious chastity to the actual life of a far more sympathetic person, her brother, and then, having got the utmost kick out of her militant virginity, having it both ways by consenting to marry the Duke at the end of the play. This actual error of interpretation no longer requires refutation. There is a fine defence of Isabella in R. W. Chambers's British Academy Shakespeare Lecture for 1937, the *Jacobean Shakespeare and "Measure for Measure"*, while trouble, not long before that date, over the royal succession had revealed latent in the British public at large superstitious feelings on the virtue of chastity that had their bearing on the way Shakespeare's audience would have taken Isabella's problem. Not that these happenings were necessary to point to the truth; for the definitive interpretation of Isabella's action was given by Walter Scott when he prefixed quotations from *Measure for Measure* to some of his culminating chapters in the *Heart of Midlothian*. Before the twentieth chapter, when Effie Deans in prison pleads with her sister Jeanie to save her life by swearing to something which she cannot know to be true, Scott set these lines:

> Sweet sister, let me live;
> What sin you do to save a brother's life,
> Nature dispenses with the deed so far,
> That it becomes a virtue.

Isabella and Jeanie Deans are, as characters, very different women; yet Scott knew that he was here competing with Shakespeare and that Jeanie's problem was Isabella's problem. Jeanie's regard for truth was, like Isabella's for chastity, a matter of fundamental principle, a condition of life's validity. And both regards were equally redeemed from hypocrisy through their holders being less reluctant to sacrifice their own lives than to contribute by their ineluctable inaction to the required sacrifice of the lives of their kin. Let anyone who doubts how Shakespeare meant the principal episodes in *Measure for Measure* (and none of these occurs after the first scene of Act Three) to be taken read or re-read these culminating episodes of the *Heart of Midlothian*, including Jeanie's resolution to go to London to obtain a royal pardon for her sister. Not only will he learn how to take the first half of *Measure for Measure* but he should note that in the play there is nothing to correspond to Jeanie Deans's journey to London in the novel.

So much generally for Isabella's nature and motives. Why was it that many readers mistook them? Partly, I think, because of an unfortunate habit of treating Shakespeare's heroines as a repertory of ideal brides, quite detached, poor things, from their native dramatic settings. If *you* were a young man, free to choose a bride, would it be Miranda or Beatrice? Wasn't Beatrice something of a risk? And wouldn't you really be safer with Portia? Yes, perhaps, if your tastes were high-brow enough. And so on, and so on. You will find that a proportion of writing on Shakespeare's heroines was conducted on those lines. Now Isabella comes off very ill on such a criterion. The husbands of such female saints or martyrs as were married have, as far as I know, never been the object of much envy; the role of martyr-consort is a hard one. And such would have been that of Isabella's husband. And so the day-dreaming bride-pickers very naturally found her distasteful and turned and rent her. And yet, in defending her, we must not forget that in the play Isabella marries and in so doing makes herself the more open to irrelevant comparisons. Her enemies have at least that excuse for their attacks; and her friends, like R. W. Chambers, however well justified in defending her behaviour towards her brother, have erred in justifying the sum total of her conduct.

This brings me to the other type of error, which is roughly that of seeing nothing wrong with the play. There are several ways of establishing it. One (and I here think mainly of R. W. Chambers) is to begin by making hay of the mythical sorrows of Shakespeare and of the mythical hypocrisy of Isabella and to go on to prove that the high ethical standards set in the first half are maintained and carried through in the second. And the proof can be fascinating. Nothing could be more ingenious and plausible than Chambers's notion of Shakespeare's keeping Isabella ignorant of her brother's survival and filled with justified fury at Angelo's having done him to death, in order that her powers of forgiveness might be tested to the uttermost when she brings herself to join Mariana in pleading for Angelo's life. And how much more creditable to Shakespeare and pleasanter to most of us, to whom his credit is very dear, if he did in fact keep Isabella in the dark for so high and moral a motive and not merely to pander to that appetite for ingenious plot-complications and improbable and strained moments of suspense which was one of the regrettable qualities of an Elizabethan audience. Nothing, too, could help to colour the last part of the play more happily than a truly heartfelt and impressive repentance on the part of Angelo. And, relying on the undoubted truth that Angelo does profess himself very repentant, Chambers does duly find Angelo's repentance very impressive. The other way to find the play faultless is to cut out all the Bradleian character-stuff from the start and to go straight to ideas or allegory or symbols. There is much thought and much orthodox piety in *Measure for Measure*, and during the time when Shakespeare was writing the Problem Plays he had the Morality form rather prominently in his mind. That in some sort the relation of justice and mercy is treated, that Angelo may stand at one time for the letter of the law or for the old law before Christian liberty and at another for a Morality figure of False Seeming, that the Duke contains hints of heavenly Grace and that he embodies a higher justice than mere legality, that Isabella is Mercy as well as Chastity—all these matters may very likely be concluded from the text and they may help us to understand the play. But they are conclusions which are ineffective in just the same way in which Chambers's theories on Isabella's ignorance and Angelo's repentance are ineffective: they have little to do with the total play, however justifiable they may appear by these and those words or passages in abstraction. Now the doctrinal or allegorical significance of *Measure for Measure* culminates in the last long scene. And this scene does not succeed whether witnessed or read. Its main effect is that of labour. Shakespeare took trouble; he complicated enormously; he brought a vast amount of dramatic matter together. The actors know it is a big scene and they try to make it go. Perhaps their efforts just succeed; but then the success will be a tribute more to their efforts than to the scene itself. In the strain the supposed subtle reason for Isabella's ignorance or Claudio's survival goes unnoticed, while Angelo's repentance is a perfunctory affair amidst all the other crowded doings. Similarly, fresh from reading or seeing the play, how little aware we are of any allegorical motive. Even if the Duke stands for Providence, he does not begin to interpose till after the first and incomparably the better half of the play. Claudio and Juliet may have been designed by their author to represent unregenerate mankind; yet Claudio at his first appearance is in a highly chastened and penitent frame of mind, well on the road to salvation: as when he says,

> The words of heaven: on whom it will, it will;
> On whom it will not, so. Yet still 'tis just.

Claudio is paraphrasing scripture, namely St. Paul's words in *Romans* ix: "Therefore hath he mercy on whom he will have mercy, and whom he will he hardeneth". But though he may class himself among the hardened sinners on account of his misdeed, there is no hardness left in him now. And quite apart from whether Claudio can, from his words, represent the unregenerate *homo* of the Moralities, he does in fact show himself to us first and foremost as a most unfortunate young man, deeply to be pitied.

The simple and ineluctable fact is that the tone in the first half of the play is frankly, acutely human and quite hostile to the tone of allegory or symbol. And, however much the tone changes in the second half, nothing in the world can make an allegorical interpretation poetically valid throughout.

Recent critics, in their anxiety to correct old errors, have in fact gone too far in the other direction and ignored one of the prime facts from which those old errors had their origin: namely that the play is not of a piece but changes its nature half-way through. It was partly through their correct perception of something being wrong that some earlier critics felt justified in making the Isabella of the first half of the play the scapegoat of the play's imperfections.

The above inconsistency has long been noted, but since of late it has been so strongly denied, I had better assert it once more, and if possible not quite in the old terms. Briefly, the inconsistency is the most serious and complete possible, being one of literary style. Up to III. 1. 151, when the Duke enters to interrupt the passionate conversation between Claudio and Isabella on the conflicting claims of his life and her chastity, the play is predominantly poetical, the poetry being, it is true, set off by passages of animated prose. And the poetry is of that kind of which Shakespeare is the great master, the kind

that seems extremely close to the business of living, to the
problem of how to function as a human being. One character after another is pictured in a difficult, a critical,
position, and yet one which all of us can imagine ourselves
to share; and the poetry answers magnificently to this
penetrating sense of human intimacy. Up to the above
point the Duke, far from being guide and controller, has
been a mere conventional piece of dramatic convenience
for creating the setting for the human conflicts. Beyond
that he is just an onlooker. And, as pointed out above, any
symbolic potentialities the characters may possess are
obscured by the tumult of passions their minds present
to us. From the Duke's entry at III. 1. 151 to the end of
the play there is little poetry of any kind and scarcely any
of the kind described above. There is a passage of beautiful
verse spoken by the Provost, Claudio, and the Duke in
the prison, IV. 2. 66 ff. Take these lines from it:

> *Prov.* It is a bitter deputy.
> *Duke.* Not so, not so: his life is parallel'd
> Even with the stroke and line of his great justice.
> He doth with holy abstinence subdue
> That in himself which he spurs on his power
> To qualify in others. Were he meal'd with that
> Which he corrects, then were he tyrannous;
> But this being so, he's just.

In their way these lines cannot be bettered but they do not
touch the great things in the early part of the play; their
accent is altogether more subdued. Again, the episode of
Mariana and Isabella pleading to the Duke for Angelo's
life, in the last scene of all, does rise somewhat as poetry.
But this exceptional passage counts for little in the prevailing tone of lowered poetical tension. Where in the first
half the most intense writing was poetical, in the second
half it is comic or at least prosaic. While the elaborate last

scene, as I have already pointed out, for all its poetical
pretensions is either a dramatic failure or at best a Pyrrhic
victory, it is the comedy of Lucio and the Duke, of Pompey
learning the mystery of the executioner from Abhorson,
of Barnardine (for Shakespeare somehow contrives to keep
his gruesomeness this side the comic) that makes the
second half of the play possible to present on the stage
with any success at all. And the vehicle of this comedy is
prose, which, excellent though it is, cannot be held consistent with the high poetry of the first half. Another
evident sign of tension relaxed in the second half of the
play is the increased use of rhyme. Not that it occurs in
such long stretches as in *All's Well*; but there are many
short passages, like this soliloquy of the Duke after hearing Lucio's scandalous remarks on his character in III. 2:

> No might nor greatness in mortality
> Can censure 'scape; back-wounding calumny
> The whitest virtue strikes. What king so strong
> Can tie the gall up in the sland'rous tongue?

or the couplet containing the title of the play:

> Haste still pays haste, and leisure answers leisure;
> Like doth quit like, and Measure still for Measure.

Here an antique quaintness excuses the lack of poetic intensity. Most characteristic of this quality in the last half
of the play are the Duke's octosyllabic couplets at the end
of III. 2:

> He who the sword of heaven will bear
> Should be as holy as severe:
> Pattern in himself to know,
> Grace to stand, and virtue go;
> More nor less to others paying
> Than by self-offences weighing—

and the rest. Far from being spurious, the Duke's couplets

in their antique stiffness and formality agree with the whole trend of the play's second half in relaxing the poetical tension and preparing for a more abstract form of drama.

A similar inconsistency extends to some of the characters. From being a minor character in the first half, with no influence on the way human motives are presented, the Duke becomes the dominant character in the second half and the one through whose mind human motives are judged. In the first half of the play we are in the very thick of action, where different human beings have their own special and different problems and are concerned with how to settle them. Mistress Overdone's problem of what's to be done now all the houses of resort in the suburbs are to be pulled down stands on its own feet quite separate from Claudio's problem of what's to be done now he has been arrested. We are in fact too close to them both to be able to distance them into a single perspective or a common unifying colour. Reality is too urgent to allow of reflection. In the second half the Duke is in charge. He has his plans, and, knowing they will come to fruition, we can watch their workings. Reflection has encroached on reality. W.W. Lawrence wrote a fine chapter on *Measure for Measure*, in which he points to the Duke's multifarious functions. The Duke's part derives both from the old folk-motive of the sovereign in disguise mixing with his people and from the conventional stage-character of the plot-promoting priest. He combines the functions of church and state. In his disguise he "represents the wisdom and adroitness of the Church in directing courses of action and advising stratagems so that good may come out of evil". He is also the supreme ruler of Vienna who at the end "straightens out the tangles of the action and dispenses justice to all". He is also a stage figure, highly important for manipulating the action and contrasted strikingly with the realistic characters. Admitting most truly that "Shakespeare's art oscillates between extreme psychological subtlety and an equally extreme disregard of psychological truth, in the acceptance of stock narrative conventions", Lawrence may imply that the Duke does succeed in uniting these extremes. If so, I can only disagree, because Lawrence's description of the Duke applies only faintly to the first half of the play.

Nowhere does the change in the Duke's position show so strikingly as in Isabella. There is no more independent character in Shakespeare than the Isabella of the first half of the play: and independent in two senses. The essence of her disposition is decision and the acute sense of her own independent and inviolate personality; while her own particular problem of how to act is presented with all that differentiation which I attributed to the problems of Claudio and Mistress Overdone. At the beginning of the third act, when she has learnt Angelo's full villainy, her nature is working at the very height of its accustomed freedom. She enters almost choked with bitter fury at Angelo, in the mood for martyrdom and feeling that Claudio's mere life is a trifle before the mighty issues of right and wrong. Her scorn of Claudio's weakness is dramatically definitive and perfect. To his pathetic pleas, "Sweet sister, let me live" etc., the lines Scott prefixed to the twentieth chapter of the *Heart of Midlothian*, comes, as it must, her own, spontaneous retort from the depth of her being,

> O you beast,
> O faithless coward, O dishonest wretch!
> Wilt thou be made a man out of my vice?
> Is't not a kind of incest to take life
> From thine own sister's shame? What should I think?
> Heaven shield my mother play'd my father fair,
> For such a warped slip of wilderness
> Ne'er issued from his blood. Take my defiance,

> Die, perish! Might but my bending down
> Reprieve thee from thy fate, it should proceed.
> I'll pray a thousand prayers for thy death,
> No word to save thee.

That is the true Isabella, and whether or not we like that kind of woman is beside the point. But immediately after her speech, at line 152, the Duke takes charge and she proceeds to exchange her native ferocity for the hushed and submissive tones of a well-trained confidential secretary. To the Duke's inquiry of how she will content Angelo and save her brother she replies in coolly rhetorical prose:

> I am now going to resolve him: I had rather my brother die by the law than my son should be unlawfully born. But, O, how much is the good duke deceived in Angelo! If ever he return and I can speak to him, I will open my lips in vain or discover his government.

But such coolness is warm compared with her tame acquiescence in the Duke's plan for her to pretend to yield to Angelo and then to substitute Mariana:

> The image of it gives me content already, and I trust it will grow to a most prosperous perfection.

To argue, as has been argued, that the plan, by Elizabethan standards, was very honourable and sensible and that of course Isabella would have accepted it gladly is to substitute the criterion of ordinary practical common sense for that of the drama. You could just as well seek to compromise the fictional validity of Jeanie Deans's journey to London by proving that the initial practical difficulties of such a journey at such a date rendered the undertaking highly improbable. In Scott's novel Jeanie Deans does travel to London, and, though Scott had better have shorn her journey of many of its improbable and romantic complications, it is a consistent Jeanie Deans who takes the journey, and her action in taking the journey and in pleading with the Queen is significant. Isabella, on the contrary, has been bereft of significant action, she has nothing to do corresponding to Jeanie's journey, and she has turned into a mere tool of the Duke. In the last scene she does indeed bear some part in the action; but her freedom of utterance is so hampered by misunderstanding and mystification that she never speaks with her full voice: she is not, dramatically, the same Isabella. That the Duke is in his way impressive, that he creates a certain moral atmosphere, serious and yet tolerant, in the second half of the play need not be denied; yet that atmosphere can ill bear comparison with that of the early part of the play. To this fact Lucio is the chief witness. He is now the livest figure and the one who does most to keep the play from quite falling apart, and he almost eludes the Duke's control. He is as it were a minor Saturnian deity who has somehow survived into the iron age of Jupiter; and a constant reminder that the Saturnian age was the better of the two.

The fact of the play's inconsistency, then, seems to me undoubted: the reason for it must be conjectural, yet conjectural within not excessive bounds of probability. I believe it may be found through considering Shakespeare's originals.

The plot of *Measure for Measure* goes back to one or both versions of a similar story by George Whetstone. The earlier is a play in two parts called *Promos and Cassandra* and published in 1578, the later a short narrative called the *Rare History of Promos and Cassandra* and included in his story-collection called the *Heptameron of Civil Discourses*, 1582. Behind both versions is a story of Cinthio. I think Shakespeare was indebted to both versions. He certainly must have known the play, for this contains, as the narrative does not, scenes of low life that correspond to similar scenes in *Measure for Measure*. There is also the incident (*Promos and Cassandra*, Part 2, V. 5) when Polina (=Juliet), though wronged by Promos (=Angelo) through the death of her plighted lover Andrugio (=Claudio), joins Cassandra (=Isabella, but in this version of the story married ultimately to Promos) in praying God to relieve Promos. It is not found in the narrative and it seems to be behind the incident in *Measure for Measure* of Isabella joining Mariana to plead for Angelo although he has done her brother Claudio to death. But the way Shakespeare deals with the theme of the principles of justice is nearer the narrative. There is a lot about justice in Whetstone's play, including disquisitions on the true meaning of what Shakespeare called measure for measure. But there is more about the wickedness of bribery in the government and the need for the magistrate to be a pattern of virtue. It is in the narrative that the theme of what true justice is predominates. That Shakespeare was drawn to that theme, and possibly in the first stages of roughing out his plot, may be conjectured.

But there were things in Whetstone's play that kindled his imagination more warmly than the theory of justice, whether derived from narrative or drama. Whetstone's best scene (and even so it is a very poor affair) is Part 1, III. 4 where Cassandra debates with her brother Andrugio and with herself whether she will let him die or whether she will yield her honour to Promos. Like Isabella she would gladly die in place of her brother and she thinks death in itself a lesser evil than loss of honour. But Andrugio points out that Promos might after all end by marrying her and then all might be well. And Cassandra is so impressed by this argument that she decides to save her brother. However feeble the scene, it does present to the reader or the re-caster certain simple and basic human

passions and conflicts: Promos's dilemma between justice
and lust; Andrugio's instinct to save his life at almost any
cost; Cassandra's dilemma between the desires to save her
brother's life and to save her honour. The human interest
and the dramatic possibilities of these passions and conflicts kindled Shakespeare's imagination and he proceeded
in the first half of *Measure for Measure* to give his version
of them.

But in so doing he altered Whetstone in one very important matter: he made his heroine resist the appeal of
her brother to save his life. In accordance with this change
he turns his heroine into a much more decided and un-
compromising person. In Whetstone the chief dramatic
interest is the heroine's divided mind, her struggle with
herself: Shakespeare's heroine has a whole mind and has
no struggle with herself: all her struggles are outside,
with her brother and her would-be seducer. It looks as if
Shakespeare had been carried away by his conception of
Isabella without realising the dramatic difficulties it involved. Whetstone's Cassandra, however inferior in execution to Shakespeare's Isabella, was through her very
weakness a more flexible dramatic character. Her mind,
divided once, can be divided again and provide interesting
dramatic situations. After Promos has enjoyed her, he
decides nevertheless to have Andrugio killed, because to
spare him would be to show partiality in the eyes of the
world. Actually Andrugio is spared and set free by his
jailors, but neither Promos nor Cassandra knows this.
Hearing of Andrugio's supposed death, Cassandra would
like to take her own life. But, then, she reflects, Andrugio
will lack an avenger; and her mind is divided between the
desires for death and for revenge. The first part of the
play ends with Cassandra's resolve to take her life only
after having appealed to the King for vengeance. Yet a
third struggle occurs when the King, hearing of Promos's

crimes, has him married to Cassandra, and then orders his death. As Andrugio predicted, marriage puts everything right between Promos and Cassandra; and Cassandra is now divided between loyalty to a dead brother and loyalty to a new, living, husband. The second loyalty prevails. Little as Whetstone made of the play's dramatic possibilities, he did at least allow those possibilities to permeate the whole story consistently. Shakespeare by altering the plot and by re-creating his heroine, however superb the immediate result, could only ruin the play as a whole. Not having been violated, Isabella has no call to meditate suicide. Not having become Angelo's wife, she has no reason to recommend him to mercy as well as to justice. Her one possible line of action was to appeal outright to the Duke; and that would be to sabotage most of the substance of the last half of the play. With significant action denied to Isabella, Shakespeare must have seen that to carry the play through in the spirit in which he began it was impossible; and after III. 1. 151 he threw in his hand.

Whether in the second half Shakespeare reverted to an original plan from which he had played truant, or whether he began to improvise when he found himself stuck, we shall never know. But conjecture may be easier when we recognise the large differences in the material from which he derived the two portions of his play. That we can do so is largely due to W. W. Lawrence. Lawrence distinguishes two kinds of material in *Measure for Measure*. The central episode of a sister having to decide whether to save her brother's life at the expense of her honour may go back to a historical incident and anyhow is related to real life and not to folk-lore. Similarly the setting in the low life of a city, not found before Whetstone, is realistic and not traditional or magical. But Shakespeare grafted onto the realistic material of Whetstone two themes that belong to the world of the fairy-tale: first, the disguised king mingling with and observing his own people, and second the secret substitution of the real bride in the husband's bed. At first sight the case seems to be much that of *All's Well*. There we have a highly realistic setting and array of characters, to which are attached the folk-themes of the person who by healing a king obtains a boon, of the setting of certain seemingly impossible tasks, and of the substitute bride. But actually the cases are very different and suggest that the plays were differently put together. In *All's Well* realism and folk-lore are blended from beginning to end; in *Measure for Measure* realism admits no folk-lore for half of the play, while all the folk-lore occurs in the second half. The same is true of allegory. The notions of Helena standing in some way for an emissary of heaven and of Bertram as a Morality figure drawn on one side by his mother and bride to good and on the other by Parolles to evil, faint in themselves, are yet spread throughout the play. Corresponding notions of the Duke as Heavenly Justice, or Isabella as Mercy, and so forth, though in themselves more evident and stronger than their parallels in *All's Well*, are quite absent from the first part of the play and appear quite suddenly in the second. It looks therefore as if *All's Well*, however deficient in execution, was conceived and executed consistently and with no change of mind, but as if the two types of material from which *Measure for Measure* was drawn betoken two different types of execution, and an abrupt change from one to the other. Exactly what happened in Shakespeare's mind we shall never know. He may or may not have meant initially to write a play on the great themes of justice, mercy, and forgiveness. If he did, he seems to have changed his mind and sought above all to give his own version of the human potentialities of Whetstone's theme. Self-defeated half-way, through the turn he gave that theme, he may have reverted to his original, more abstract intentions, to help him out. More likely, to my thinking, he sought help from the methods and the incidents of the play, written shortly before and still in temper akin to his present self, *All's Well that Ends Well*.

It is, incidentally, because the folk-material is so differently spaced and blended in the two plays that the theme of the substitute bride is quite seemly in *All's Well* and is somehow rather shocking in *Measure for Measure*. In *All's Well* we have been habituated to the improbable, the conventional, and the antique: in *Measure for Measure* the change to these from the more lifelike human passions is too violent; and it is here a case not of a modern prudery unaware of Elizabethan preconceptions but of an artistic breach of internal harmony.

But I am loth to end on matters mainly conjectural, and I will revert to the first half of *Measure for Measure* and pay my tribute to a quality in it that has not quite had its due. Full justice can never be done to what Shakespeare really achieved here, on account of the imperfections of our only text, that of the First Folio. For instance, scene II. 4, when Angelo tempts Isabella to buy Claudio's life by her virtue, is terribly obscure in places and simply cannot be read with unimpeded pleasure. But in spite of textual impediments it has been recognised that the prevailing style matches that of *Hamlet* and possibly of *Othello*. This comment of Claudio on Angelo and his new official zeal has surely the accent of *Hamlet*:

> And the new deputy now for the Duke—
> Whether it be the fault and glimpse of newness,
> Or whether that the body public be
> A horse whereon the governor doth ride,
> Who, newly in the seat, that it may know
> He can command, lets it straight feel the spur;

Whether the tyranny be in his place
Or in his eminence that fills it up,
I stagger in—but this new governor
Awakes me all the enrolled penalties
Which have like unscour'd armour hung by the wall
So long that nineteen zodiacs have gone round
And none of them been worn; and, for a name,
Now puts the drowsy and neglected act
Freshly on me.

(I. 2. 161-75)

The power of the verse in the early part of *Measure for Measure* has indeed been allowed. Less notice has been taken of the extreme subtlety of characterisation. I will illustrate this from scene II. 2, where Isabella, seconded by Lucio, first pleads with Angelo for her brother's life. It is a scene whose power is obvious and has been generally admitted. Close reading is necessary to bring out the accompanying subtlety with which all the movements of Isabella's mind are presented. At first Shakespeare risks failure by asserting psychological truth almost at the expense of dramatic probability. Isabella begins her attack on Angelo with a crudity and a lack of strategy which on a first impact are staggering:

There is a vice that most I do abhor
And most desire should meet the blow of justice;
For which I would not plead but that I must;
For which I must not plead but that I am
At war 'twixt will and will not.

Yet this crudity is absolutely natural. Claudio's arrest could not, from Isabella's point of view, have been timed worse. Young, ardent, neophytic, she has bent all her strength to embrace an other-worldly ideal. And in the very act of embracement she is called on to plead in mitigation of that which is most abhorrent to her. Her crude

135

self-explanation is psychologically inevitable. And what is so brilliant in the rest of the scene is the way in which she gradually discards the drawing-in of herself into cloistral concentration and reaches out again to a worldly observation she has newly renounced. And that observation includes a bitter anger that this mere man, this Angelo, this precisian, should be able to decide her brother's fate.

At first she is helpless and is for giving over at the first rebuff:

> O just but severe law!
> I had a brother then. Heaven keep your honour!

But Lucio intervenes and urges her to a fresh attack. The best she can do now is to recall and utter some current commonplaces about mercy and about the judge being no better than the accused. But her accent is, surely, still formal and cool:

> Well, believe this,
> No ceremony that to great ones 'longs,
> Not the king's crown, nor the deputed sword,
> The marshal's truncheon, nor the judge's robe,
> Become them with one half so good a grace
> As mercy does.

But something, whether an unconscious clash of wills or a secret sense of Angelo's being stirred by her own self, prompts Isabella to be personal and she goes on:

> If he had been as you and you as he
> You would have slipt like him; but he like you
> Would not have been so stern.

And when Angelo tells her to be gone, at once her personal opposition stiffens, and, no longer the awesome wielder of the law and God's deputy, he becomes in her eyes mere man and as deeply in need of God's mercy as any sinner. Her renewed plea for mercy is now impassioned, and

when he tells her that Claudio must die to-morrow he
arouses the whole stretch of her mind. Her concern for
Claudio is cruelly sharpened and prompts her to the kind
of humour that lies next to the tragic:

> He's not prepared for death. Even for our kitchens
> We kill the fowl of season. Shall we serve heaven
> With less respect than we do minister
> To our gross selves?

Angelo still resists but feels called on to defend his action
at greater length. His cold pompousness infuriates her
and calls forth her culminating and classic denunciation
of human pride. But first by her bitter emphasis on the
personal pronouns she makes it plain that her attack on
pride is far from being on an abstract and impersonal sin:

> So *you* must be the first that gives this sentence,
> And *he*, that suffers.

And we do Shakespeare's art less than justice if, absorbed
in the detachable splendour of the lines that follow, we
forget the personal application.

> O, it is excellent
> To have a giant's strength; but it is tyrannous
> To use it like a giant. Could great men thunder
> As Jove himself does, Jove would ne'er be quiet;
> For every pelting, petty officer
> Would use his heaven for thunder, nothing but thunder.
> Merciful heaven,
> Thou rather with thy sharp and sulphurous bolt
> Splits the unwedgeable and gnarled oak
> Than the soft myrtle. But man, proud man,
> Drest in a little brief authority,
> Most ignorant of what he's most assur'd,
> His glassy essence, like an angry ape
> Plays such fantastic tricks before high heaven
> As make the angels weep; who, with our spleens
> Would all themselves laugh mortal.

Such eloquence cannot lack effect. Lucio (and we may assume Isabella too) sees that some change is taking place in Angelo. There is one kind of irony in Isabella's and a very different kind in Lucio's, who must have prided himself on his connoisseurship of the tokens of lust, being quite deceived as to the nature of that change. Isabella, now confident of victory, speaks less vehemently, and Lucio, anxious lest too much of the same thing may spoil the victory, signals for them to go at once, when Angelo says he will see Isabella again to-morrow.

The whole scene, and especially Isabella's speech on pride, illustrates the truth that in the drama the most powerful general effect comes by way of absorption into the immediate dramatic business, just as writers in general are most likely to speak to all ages when most sensitive to the spiritual climate of their own. Here, at any rate, problem play or no problem play, Shakespeare is at the height of his strength.

Notes on *Measure For Measure*

There is a useful account of recent criticism of the play in Roy W. Battenhouse's *"Measure for Measure" and Christian Doctrine* in *Publications of the Modern Language Association of America*, 1946, pp. 1029-59. But Battenhouse's theory that the play is an allegory of the Atonement I find over-ingenious and unconvincing. For the Morality theme in *Measure for Measure* see Muriel C. Bradbrook in *Review of English Studies*, 1941, pp. 385 ff.

EPILOGUE

In my introduction I pointed to certain resemblances within the Problem Plays. It remains to ask in what ways these plays look forward or take their place in Shakespeare's general progress as a dramatist.

I made out *Hamlet* to be a tragedy only in a limited sense. Its success in that sense may have prompted Shakespeare to attempt something further: a less restricted form of tragedy. I have not noticed in *Troilus and Cressida* anything that looks forward. It has analogies with contemporary Elizabethan drama, and in a certain point of style it looks back to *Henry V*. But it is not seminal. The truly seminal plays are *All's Well* and *Measure for Measure*: and it remains to say how these lead on to a further Shakespearean efflorescence.

Those who think these plays essentially bitter and satirical will have no use for what follows, which rests on the belief that, however much incidental gloom or bitterness may be there, the themes of mercy and forgiveness are sincerely and not ironically presented. Bertram is made out a very unpleasant young man, but we are not meant to take his forgiveness by the French King and by his wife to be a cynical comment on how in this world the wicked prosper. We must accept Isabella quite simply for what she is and refuse to consider her as a vicious comment on how inhumanly a self-centred and pious prude can behave. Through Angelo Shakespeare certainly does convey the dreadful limitation and inequity of mere legality. But the portrait is not primarily satirical and takes its place in a context of sincere tolerance and forgiveness. In both plays Shakespeare is more positive than negative, more *for* certain things than *against* certain other things. The themes therefore of mercy and forgiveness are genuine as well as prominent, and they unite *All's Well* and *Measure for Measure* with *Cymbeline*, the *Winter's Tale*, and the *Tempest*. But the ethically genuine and the dramatically successful are not the same. No one of course claims high success for *All's Well*, yet *Measure for Measure* has been put, as a drama of forgiveness, on a level with the *Winter's Tale*. This, I believe, is to confuse the above two qualities and to fail really to read *Measure for Measure*. On the other hand it is plain that long before Shakespeare wrote his last plays he wanted to treat the theme of forgiveness; and his early artistic failures can hardly not be related to his later successes. It remains to trace this relation.

In both the earlier plays there is one main object of forgiveness, Bertram in one and Angelo in the other. Secondary to Bertram is Parolles, and to Angelo a number of people. The technique of both plays is to accumulate through their course matters standing in need of forgiveness; and to postpone the time of reckoning to a long and elaborate last scene. Such scenes, where large numbers of characters are gathered together, where sections of these characters are ignorant of facts known to other sections while the audience knows everything, must have tickled the Elizabethan taste. They have not stood the test of time and emerge as melodramatic rather than dramatic, giving the serious the taint of frivolity. Treated thus, the theme of forgiveness could never succeed. Apart from this staking so much on a grand finale, there is the problem, recurrent in Shakespeare, of how to avoid bathos between a climax occurring about the middle of the play and the renewed elevation of the ending. In both plays Shakespeare fills in with comic business between characters already introduced. In *All's Well*, where the poetical level has never been high, this succeeds perfectly well within the limits of the play's possible success; in *Measure for Measure*, however good in itself, it cannot counterpoise the immensely powerful poetical effect achieved in the first half of the play.

Shakespeare's next play on the theme of forgiveness is *Cymbeline*, and it is closely allied to the earlier pair by repeating and even exaggerating the technique of the grand finale. Another resemblance is the way it mingles the material of real life and of folk-lore. But there are new elements derived from a related play but one in which the theme of forgiveness is not very prominent, *Pericles*. These elements are the finding of something lost and the incubation of something new in the thing lost. Cymbeline's two sons were lost in infancy and they appear later in the play leading a kind of existence new to anything hitherto revealed. The grand finale fails just as surely as in *All's Well* and *Measure for Measure*, though there is less mystification. But the scenes in Wales where Cymbeline's two sons figure do help to fill the awkward gap between the middle climax and the finale. The innovation is, technically, quite effective. But the play contains too much matter, and though it can pass, through the excellence of some of its verse, the splendour of some of the separate scenes, and a kind of pantomimic variety that helps it along when staged, it fails to make the theme of forgiveness significant.

At last, in the *Winter's Tale*, things come right. First, Shakespeare dropped the disastrous practice of the grand finale. He settled much of the necessary plotting and explanation through prose narrative and left only the minimum of recognition to be accomplished in the final scene of Hermione's statue. Here at last the theme of forgiveness has a worthy setting. Then he followed and improved on his success in *Cymbeline* in introducing new elements in that part of the play where bathos is most likely. If Guiderius and Arviragus in Wales help *Cymbeline* along, the lovely pastoral in Bohemia, the loves of Florizel and Perdita, and the splendour of Perdita herself, not only triumph technically in filling a dangerous gap, but create that new life without which the mere forgiveness of old crimes is apt to be hollow. True forgiveness is not the cancellation of old debts, but the reduction to health of a life process that has been impeded and can now proceed once more.

But this is not the place to praise the *Winter's Tale*. Rather I must point out how much it has in common with *Measure for Measure*. First, it falls definitely into two halves, the division marked by a long lapse of time and a chorus. Secondly, there is an abrupt contrast between the tones of the two halves. The first half deals with violent human passions: jealousy, cruelty, persecution, and grief. The tone of the second, though intense and powerful in its way, is predominantly idyllic. Only in *Measure for Measure* of Shakespeare's other plays is there so sharp a cleavage in the middle and so sharp a change of tone from one section to the other. There is also the common theme of the supposed victim of the tyrant's cruelty being secretly kept alive. I believe Shakespeare had *Measure for Measure* in mind when he wrote the *Winter's Tale*; and I suspect that he was resolved to redeem that splendid failure.

It is natural that one play of Shakespeare should contain elements that are absorbed into another. Artists answer differently to the flux that life presents. We cannot suppose that the Athenians of the fifth century were less aware of that flux than the Elizabethans, yet their artists delighted in giving their art the greatest apparent fixity, in, as it were, crystallising all possible elements of the flux into great static creations. Such must have been the nature of Phidias's Zeus at Olympia and his Virgin Athena at

Athens. Shakespeare prefers a method closer to life's actual workings. He can indeed be monumental in certain scenes, but he is most himself when boundaries are not too glaring, when one part slides into another, when through a series of plays a notion is born, flowers, and is fulfilled. The three plays I have mainly dealt with are not any of them supreme in Shakespeare's canon but they are true to his typical kaleidoscopic genius. Of that canon they are a deeply interesting and a worthy part.

APPENDICES

Appendix A

Hamlet's Defiance of Augury (V. 2. 203-35)

The interpretation of this passage is crucial to the way the play as a whole is taken. I will discuss it here in more detail than would fit the text itself. Osric has just gone out, bearing with him to the King Hamlet's acceptance of the fencing-match. After a few words between Hamlet and Horatio a Lord enters and asks Hamlet if he is still agreeable to beginning the match at once. Hamlet answers,

> I am constant to my purposes; they follow the King's pleasure; if his fitness speaks, mine is ready; now or whensoever, provided I be so able as now.

The Lord then says that the King and Queen will arrive shortly, and, adding that the Queen wishes Hamlet to be courteous to Laertes, goes out. Horatio and Hamlet then speak as follows:

Hor. You will lose this wager, my lord.
Ham. I do not think so. Since he went into France, I have been in continual practice; I shall win at the odds. But thou wouldst not think how ill all's here about my heart; but it is no matter.
Hor. Nay, good my lord—
Ham. It is but foolery; but it is such a kind of gain-giving as would perhaps trouble a woman.
Hor. If your mind dislike anything, obey it; I will forestall their repair hither and say you are not fit.

Ham. Not a whit, we defy augury; there's a special providence in the fall of a sparrow. If it be now, 'tis not to come; if it be not to come, it will be now; if it be not now, yet it will come; the readiness is all: since no man has aught of what he leaves, what is't to leave betimes? Let be.

If only one knew just what this passage implies, what a help in understanding the rest of *Hamlet*. But it is fatally easy to advance plausible and incompatible interpretations. I will put forward two, roughly to suit the two opposed notions of change or lack of change in Hamlet's mind.

1. Hamlet's answer to the Lord bears two meanings. As well as saying that Hamlet is still ready to fence at short notice, it means as follows: *I am constant to my purposes*, that is to kill Claudius; *they follow the King's pleasure*, my purposes seek out the occasion of "the incestuous pleasure of his bed" or of some other pleasure "that has no relish of salvation in't"; *if his fitness speaks, mine is ready*, if I find him in a case where death will be followed by the deepest damnation, I am ready to act; *now or whensoever, provided I be so able as now*, now or at any time, provided my present new mood of resolution holds. Hamlet, therefore, has thrown off his irresolution, he has made up his mind, and he proceeds to kill Claudius as the opportunity offers. Not only is he resolved to do his duty, but in his conversation with Horatio he shows that he has ceased to brood on the after-life and has put his trust in God. He will face death whenever it comes. Hamlet is thus doubly regenerate.

2. It is possible to take the passage at a much lower pitch of seriousness. Hamlet's reply to the Lord will bear no more than its surface meaning that he sticks to his willingness to fence, and that he will play the match at any time, provided he is in as good practice as he now is. His conversation with Horatio is not to be pressed too hard. He *does* feel a premonition, which serves a useful dramatic purpose in pointing forward to the end of the play.

When he makes light of the premonition he does so rather in the easy fatalistic mood of the soldier who repeats the stock phrase of every bullet's having its billet. The lightness of the final "let be" is a true pointer to the spirit of the passage.

From the run of the prose I have no doubt myself that the second interpretation is correct and that the implications set forth in the first interpretation are fortuitous and not intentional. A. C. Bradley (*Shakespearean Tragedy*, pp. 144-6), though thinking Hamlet in some ways changed on his return to Denmark, thinks him unchanged in the main matter of his melancholy. He feels himself more than before in the hand of God, but the passages showing this do not show "any material change in his general condition, or the formation of any effective resolution to fulfil his appointed duty". He falls indeed into a kind of fatalism. I think Bradley right.

I suspect that "the interim is mine", the crucial phrase in the verse preceding the prose from which the extract discussed above was taken, is ironic; for soon after the words he falls into the trap of the duel. The interim is, in fact, not his at all.

Appendix B

Why did Hamlet spare Claudius at his prayers?

In assessing Hamlet's motives for sparing Claudius at his prayers recent opinion has been over-suspicious of the psychological interpreters, who detect the presence of unacknowledged motives, and over-credulous of the "tough" interpreters, who can take at its face value Hamlet's resolve to inflict nothing but the deepest damnation. However wrong the nineteenth century may have been in making the play only a psychological study, it is no better trying to rationalise it and reduce its motives to those of expediency and common sense. The world of

Hamlet is one in which unexpressed motives are likely to count. There is no need to decide whether Hamlet would have killed Claudius had he found him less piously employed, for that has nothing to do with the play, but the tenor and tone of Hamlet's speech shows him glad to have an excuse not to kill him, an excuse which to Shakespeare's audience was quite colourable, and which we can believe or disbelieve to have been so to Hamlet himself, according to our tastes. That Hamlet is here taking cover behind an excuse is made the more likely because on the Ghost's reappearance he makes a frantic effort to transfer the burden of inaction from himself to his instigator, when he cries out,

> Do not look upon me
> Lest with this piteous action you convert
> My stern effects: then what I have to do
> Will want true colour; tears perchance for blood.

Hamlet knows that once already what he has to do has wanted true colour. As to the motives of Hamlet's gladness to have an excuse, we may conjecture to our hearts' content. It may be no more than that he was so absorbed in his resentment against his mother that the revenge of his father's death—an irreversible event—was a mere irrelevance, a matter of minor importance, to which his mind was never truly directed. No amount of vengeance on Claudius would alter the fact of his mother's defilement. And his mother must be dealt with directly. Hamlet with his clear intellect minded about the relevance of things. He was pleased enough to let Rosencrantz and Guildenstern die, for their crime had nothing to do with any overriding motive and its punishment he found to be apt. But I must mention Peter Alexander's sensitive and penetrating notion. This, occurring as it does in a book which, though admirable in content, makes the strategic error of uniting in one treatment the most severely factual with the delicately critical, is only too likely to be passed over. Alexander's treatment is too long to quote entire; and the following sentences must suffice:

> Hamlet's purpose has been blunted by nothing more than the natural reluctance in a man of proved nerve, courage, and resolution, to stab a defenceless man. For this is his only resource. He cannot challenge the king; if the deed is to be done, it must be done in cold blood, in circumstances such as the prayer-scene does no more than set out in extreme form. And the more helpless the murderer the more reluctant the avenger. Hamlet's adversary must strike the first blow. Not that Hamlet can admit to himself, even for a moment, that this is what holds his hand. So unconscious is he of any virtue in this noble compunction that he cannot find words shameful enough to characterize it or blasphemous enough to excuse it.

Finally, it must be remembered that the notion of Hamlet's withholding his true motives for sparing Claudius had nothing originally to do with the new psychology but was formulated in the eighteenth century. Here is William Richardson's version of it from *Essays on Shakespeare's Dramatic Characters* (1784), p. 159. Speaking of Hamlet's expressed motives for sparing Claudius he says:

> These are not his real sentiments. There is nothing in the whole character of Hamlet that justifies such savage enormity. . . . I would ask, then, whether, on many occasions, we do not alledge those considerations as the motives of our conduct, which really are not our motives? Nay, is not this sometimes done almost without our knowledge? Is it not done when we have no intention to deceive others; but when, by the influences of some present passion, we deceive ourselves? . . . Sense of supposed duty, and a regard to character, prompt Hamlet to slay his uncle; and he is with-held at that particular moment, by the ascendant of a gentle disposition; by the scruples, and perhaps weakness, of extreme sensibility. But how can he answer to the world, and to his sense of duty, for missing this opportunity? The real motive cannot be urged. Instead of excusing, it would expose him, he thinks, to censure; perhaps to contempt. He casts about for a

motive; and one better suited to the opinions of the multitude, and better calculated to lull resentment is immediately suggested. He indulges and shelters himself under the subterfuge. He alledges, as direct causes of his delay, motives that could never influence his conduct.

Appendix C

" This dull and long-continued truce "

Close study would reveal many ways in which Lydgate could explain difficulties of detail in *Troilus and Cressida*. Here is an example.

When in the play's third scene Aeneas arrives in the Greek council to bring the challenge he says that Hector complains of "growing rusty in this dull and long-continued truce". This flagrantly contradicts the previous scene, whose date in the play appears to be just before the council scene, where Pandarus hears the retreat sounded and comments on the Trojan leaders as they return from battle. Hector is among them, and Pandarus points out the hacks on his helmet. Now when Shakespeare mentioned the truce he was remembering Lydgate or Caxton and forgetting his own previous scene. There are several long truces in Lydgate. The first, of eight weeks, comes after the first general battle which ended with Hector's mistaken magnanimity in calling off the battle at Ajax's request. During this truce there is a Greek council, and Palamedes undermines Agamemnon's authority by complaining that his election as commander-in-chief was irregular. And he says he will not obey him. Now Shakespeare's council of Greeks, although Palamedes is not of it, concerns the questions of discipline and obedience like Lydgate's, and Shakespeare, thinking of their common theme, thinks also of the truce during which Lydgate's council occurs.

Appendix D

"*This is, and is not, Cressid*"

Observation of the kind of spiritual crisis noted in my text (p. 79) as common to Hamlet and Troilus will be but too apt to confirm the opinions of those who see in the two plays a reflection of Shakespeare's own experience at this time. Gertrude let Hamlet down, Cressida Troilus: therefore in these years someone let down Shakespeare. Although in these plays I cannot see any lack of dramatic aptness that might make us suspect a personal, non-dramatic, extrinsic emotion, I must note that this is precisely what I did find [1] in a different and unexpected context, the scene of *Henry V* where Henry confronts the conspirators. In Henry's words to Lord Scroop I found the same type of feeling, the bewilderment and incredulity of a trusting man who finds that he has been let down, expressed with an emotional sincerity not found elsewhere in the play and not at all apt to the character of the speaker. Here are the lines from the speech closest to the words of Troilus:

> Thou that didst bear the key of all my counsels,
> That knew'st the very bottom of my soul,
> That almost might'st have coin'd me into gold
> Wouldst thou have practis'd on me for thy use,
> May it be possible that foreign hire
> Could out of these extract one spark of evil
> That might annoy my finger? 'tis so strange
> That, though the truth of it stands off as gross
> As black and white, my eye will scarcely see it.

The idea is the same: this is and is not Scroop. Those who want to draw biographical conclusions from the idea will thus have to go back to *Henry V* at least, and will find that

---

[1] In my *Shakespeare's History Plays* (London 1945, New York 1946) p. 308.

play a more likely field for conjecture than *Troilus and Cressida.*

Appendix E

Stratification in All's Well

A problem that must be posed, though it cannot be solved, is that of stratification. Are there or are there not relics of an earlier play incorporated in our text? That the text is bad, that there are gaps, and that, as Dover Wilson holds, there is evidence of a hasty copyist may be true; but these facts do not in themselves prove either different Shakespearean strata or the work of a collaborator. The hasty copyist could have worked on a number of scrappy sheets of Shakespeare's writing, all contemporary. Again the stage direction at II. 3. 190 "Parolles and Lafeu stay behind commenting on this wedding" does indeed look like an intrusion; and may well be a memorandum on the original manuscript referring to the actual composition of the play and wrongly perpetuated into a stage direction. But there is no need to think with Dover Wilson that it is Shakespeare's direction to his collaborator. Anyone who has written books will know the habit of jotting down in the manuscript itself a memorandum of what is to follow, lest interruption should produce oblivion and spoil the scheme. The stage direction may well be Shakespeare's memorandum at the end of a day's work, or at some other interruption, of how he intended to continue. Other explanations can be manufactured; and the plain truth is that there is no certainty.

I have dealt in the text with the authenticity of Parolles's conversation with Helena on virginity (I. 1. 117) and with the two long stretches of rhyme (II. 1. 133 and II. 3. 78). Other pieces of rhyming are less surprising and can be largely explained as an exaggeration of common practice; yet this exaggeration in conjunction with the more surprising uses must make us think. Here are the

151

main instances. At the end of I. 1, when Parolles has left, Helena soliloquises for fourteen lines, a large measure of couplets to give the common indication of finality. More-over these couplets are like those in Act Two in that they promote action: in fact it is here that Helena first discloses her resolve to cure the King—

> The King's disease—my project may deceive me;
> But my intents are fixt and will not leave me.

In I. 3. 134, where the Folio gives Helena's entrance in response to the Countess's summons, the Countess solilo-quises on Helena's love-sick air in rhyme:

> Even so it was with me when I was young.
>   If ever we are nature's, these are ours: this thorn
> Doth to our rose of youth rightly belong;
>   Our blood to us, this to our blood is born.
> It is the show and seal of nature's truth,
> Where love's strong passion is impress'd in youth.

Such rhyming may recall *Love's Labour's Lost*; but the Countess here indulges in personal reminiscence, and it is quite appropriate if she marks off the past by a formal and stylised kind of utterances. In II. 3, where Helena makes her choice in rhyme, the King, after chiding Bertram in blank verse, suddenly falls into couplets for a homily on honour depending on native virtue and not on titles, and then, after a few lines of blank verse, speaks five lines con-taining two internal rhymes (160-4):

>   . . . that canst not *dream*
> We, poising us in her defective scale,
> Shall weigh thee to the *beam*; that wilt not *know*
> It is in us to plant thine honour where
> We please to have it *grow*.

Here the strata-hunters find powerful evidence. In the actual couplets, they think, Shakespeare borrowed from

an old play and when he began again turning couplets into
blank verse he gave himself away by admitting two rhymes
which originally ended a pair of couplets. But, when
examined, the evidence is not conclusive. The surprising
thing is that Shakespeare used couplets at this place at all;
and you in no wise explain this surprise by asserting that
his couplets were borrowed. And granted that Shakespeare wanted couplets just there, there is not the slightest
reason why he should not have written them then and
there without recourse to an old play. And as for the internal rhyme, a cursory inspection of the first act of *Hamlet*
has revealed three places where it occurs, one of them
about the length of the passage in *All's Well* and containing one pair and one trio of internal rhymes:

> . . . whose common theme
> Is death of fathers, and who still hath *cried,*
> From the first corse till he that *died* to-day,
> 'This must be *so*'. We pray you *throw* to earth
> This unprevailing *woe.*

To find in all the internal rhymes of Shakespeare evidence
of "fossil" couplets is patently absurd. And if this is a
general rule, what justification is there for breaking it at
convenience? Again, I am not saying that the notion that
Shakespeare was using an old play can be disproved: I
merely maintain that the notion is not necessary.

In III. 4 Helena's letter to the Countess, beginning "I
am St. Jaques' pilgrim" is in rhyming quatrains. But a
pilgrim has forsaken the norm of life and may fitly use an
abnormal way of expression. Finally there are a few couplets in the last scene of the play. First, the King (V. 3. 61)
speaks three rather flat couplets on Helena's supposed
death; but he adds his own explanation of them by calling
them "Sweet Helen's knell", and they are not out of
keeping with the other couplets of the play. Later Diana,
speaking in riddles, just before the whole truth comes out,
uses a few couplets; and riddles should of course be in

rhyme. And Helena, after a few words of moving blank verse—

> No, my good lord,
> 'Tis but the shadow of a wife you see;
> The name and not the thing—

joins with Bertram to speak a few conventional couplets in final reconciliation. They are not in themselves surprising.

Shakespeare's use of the couplet, then, should make us think. But our thoughts need not demand as explanation the intrusion of earlier verse. Some of these couplets are doing much what his couplets usually do, others in their strangeness point to an unusual mood in him when he wrote the play.

INDEX

Quiller-Couch, A. T., 116-17

Richardson, William, 148-9

Schücking, L. L., 31
Scott, 59, 119-20, 127-9
Shakespeare, *As You Like It*, 94;
Cymbeline, 9, 59, 140-2; *Henry
IV*, 9, 74, 95, 98, 108-9;
Henry V, 6, 55-7, 74, 150;
Henry VI, 5, 80, 85, 99; *Julius
Caesar*, 6, 56; *King Lear*, 15,
28; *Love's Labour's Lost*, 152;
Lucrece, 35-7; *Macbeth*, 14,
30-1, 80; *Merchant of Venice*,
78, 93-4, 120; *Much Ado*, 8,
120; *Othello*, 6, 14, 28;
Pericles, 41, 141; *Richard II*,
9, 85; *Richard III*, 13, 99;
Tempest, 9, 29, 109, 120, 140;

Twelfth Night, 97; *Winter's
Tale*, 5, 109, 140-2
Sisson, C. J., 2
Smart, J. S., 12
Sophocles, 15
Spencer, Theodore, 17, 87
Spenser, 50, 111
Stoll, E. E., 117

Van Doren, Mark, v, 54-5, 111,
117

Waldock, A. J. A., 19, 32
Webbe, 40
Webster, *Duchess of Malfi*, 12
Whetstone, George, 129-32
Williams, Charles, 78
Wilson, J. Dover, 31, 41, 107, 151
Woolf, Virginia, 111